D-BLK ST

*Antislavery, Abolition, and the Atlantic World*
R. J. M. Blackett and James Brewer Stewart, Editors

# The River Flows On

## Black Resistance, Culture, and Identity Formation in Early America

Walter C. Rucker

Louisiana State University Press

Baton Rouge

Copyright © 2006 by Louisiana State University Press
Manufactured in the United States of America
FIRST PRINTING

*Designer:* Barbara Neely Bourgoyne
*Typeface:* Quadraat
*Printer and binder:* Edwards Brothers, Inc.

Library of Congress Cataloging-in-Publication Data

Rucker, Walter C., 1970–
   The river flows on : Black resistance, culture, and identity formation in early America /
Walter C. Rucker.
      p. cm. — (Antislavery, abolition, and the Atlantic world)
   Includes bibliographical references and index.
   ISBN 0-8071-3109-1  (cloth : alk. paper)
   1. Slave insurrections—United States.  2. Government, Resistance to—United States—
History.  3. Slaves—United States—Social conditions.  4. African Americans—History—
To 1863.  5. African Americans—Social life and customs.  6. African Americans—Ethnic
identity.  7. African Americans—Rites and ceremonies.  8. Folklore—Political aspects—
United States—History.  9. United States—History—Colonial period, ca. 1600–1775.
10. United States—Race relations.  I. Title.  II. Series.
E447.R83 2005
306.3′62′0973—dc22

                                                                2005010249

For my mother,
Njeri Kamaria & Na'eem Hezekiah

# Contents

Tables

## Acknowledgments

Along the winding path I took in writing this manuscript, a number of individuals proved quite helpful. I owe my largest debt to Sterling Stuckey, who served as my dissertation advisor. Despite his initial misgivings about the project, I vividly remember Sterling informing me that I "was on to something" after reading the first chapter. Since that time he has been the ever mindful mentor and though I have not always followed his sage advice—which has created some tensions—this project owes a great deal to the scholarly example he has set. I should add that all the interpretive or structural shortcomings of this work are my own.

Many others have provided invaluable assistance and encouragement along the way, whether through private conversations, questions raised at conference panel sessions, or careful readings of chapters or the entire manuscript. They include Ray Kea, Sharon Salinger, John Wunder, Herbert Aptheker, John Thornton, Margaret Washington, Jim Rawley, and Linda Heywood. In some significant way, all of their input was useful. Michael Gomez provided the most insightful critiques of the full manuscript, and I will be forever indebted for his guidance and support.

I have also received support from my former colleagues at San Bernardino Valley College, the State University of West Georgia, and the University of Nebraska–Lincoln. In particular, Colleen Calderon read and commented on my work during the very early phases of my research. Also, Leon Caldwell allowed me to accompany a group of his students on a three-week study-abroad program in Ghana. The insights I gained by visiting the Elmina and Cape Coast slave "dungeons," learning rudimentary Twi, and informally interviewing Akan-speaking spiritualists greatly enriched my discussions of slavery, culture, and Akan spirituality in the chapters on Gold Coast African imports into colonial New York. In addition, I am indebted to the following people—friends and colleagues alike—for their support of my work over the years: Jermaine Archer, Leslie Alexander, Hasan Jeffries, Akinyele Umoja, Marcellus Barskdale, Alton Hornsby, Zawadi Barskile, Augustine Konneh, Cita Cook, Cecil Blake, Pete Maslowski, Jason Young, Keith Parker, Ahati Toure, Kwakiutl Dreher, Wendy Smooth, Eloy Zarate, D'andra Orey, Tim Mahoney, Ben Rader, James Garza, Carole Levin, Marcela Raffaelli, Jim Le Sueur, Daniel Walker, Venetria Patton, Tom Calhoun, and Ken Winkle.

My thanks also to the University of Nebraska–Lincoln for funding I received to support this research. Financial support from the Research Council and the Layman Trust made possible my extended stays at archives and research libraries in South Carolina, Virginia, New York, Louisiana, California, and Legon, Ghana. A National Endowment for the Humanities Summer Stipend proved quite useful in this regard as well. A number of research facilities were quite gracious during my visits. The staffs of the following libraries and archives were particularly helpful: the New-York Historical Society Library, the New York Public Library, the New York City Municipal Archives and Records Center, the Virginia Historical Society Library, the Virginia State Library, the Huntington Library, the South Caroliniana Library, the South Carolina Historical Society Collection, and the South Carolina Department of Archives and History. The Interlibrary Loan staff at the University of California Riverside provided me with tireless and invaluable service from the very beginning of this project.

Finally, to my mother Sarah, my daughter Njeri, and my son Na'eem, who provided the best encouragement and incentive during this long journey —I dedicate this manuscript to them.

Chapter 5 appeared previously in slightly different form as "'I Will Gather All Nations': Resistance, Culture, and Pan-African Collaboration in Denmark Vesey's South Carolina," *Journal of Negro History* 86 (Spring 2001): 132–47. Chapters 1, 5, and 6 appeared previously as "Conjure, Magic, and Power: The Influence of Afro-Atlantic Religious Practices on Slave Resistance and Rebellion," *Journal of Black Studies* 32, no. 1 (September 2001): 84–103. Used by permission.

The River Flows On

# Introduction

In the 1968 introduction to his novel *Black Thunder*, Harlem Renaissance writer Arna Bontemps claimed he had chosen Gabriel Prosser as the subject for his fictional account because Gabriel "had not depended on trance-like mumbo jumbo." A devout Seventh Day Adventist, Bontemps felt that Nat Turner, "with his visions and dreams," and Denmark Vesey were influenced by disturbingly esoteric religious influences that significantly detracted from their overall image. He saw Gabriel's 1800 conspiracy in sharp contrast as devoid of these factors.[1] Anticipating arguments made later by Michael Mullin, Bontemps assumes that the context that shaped Gabriel's life was one which allowed his insurrection to be motivated by primarily secular and, to a lesser degree, orthodox Christian impulses. Not surprisingly, Michael Mullin refers to Bontemps's assumptions in *Africa in America*, noting how "Gabriel ignore[d] an old conjurer woman's warning that the rebels were inviting disaster by not seeking religious guidance."[2] Of course this guidance in the fictional account was more about wearing charms and using protective "hands" than seeking inspiration from the Bible.

The "trance-like mumbo jumbo" that Bontemps sought to avoid in *Black Thunder* was so ubiquitous in colonial and antebellum America that even the fictionalized Gabriel Prosser could not fully escape its influences. Noting that enslaved African Americans "remembered Africa in 1800," Bontemps ultimately concludes that Gabriel's lack of veneration for African folk culture was part of his undoing. Though he was seemingly disdainful of conjure in the introduction to *Black Thunder*, the events of the novel imply that Gabriel's failure to rely on charms and interpret signs resulted in the plot not coming to fruition. His fatal flaw was that, unlike most others depicted by Bontemps, Gabriel had no memory of Africa. Unlike the revolutionaries of Haiti, Gabriel did not seek to kill a hog and drink its blood to ensure success. Because their leader had little cultural connection to Africa, Gabriel's followers lacked complete confidence in his leadership, which undermined the ability of the conspirators to commit fully to the rebellion. Bontemps's conclusion can only be due to the overwhelming number of references to African folk culture he saw as he read through the large collection of slave narratives at Fisk University's library in preparation for writing the novel. As will become obvious, Gabriel was likely influenced by an African cultural context that represented a larger and pervasive phenomenon in the Atlantic World.[3]

The historiography of slave resistance begins in the most paradoxical space. In *American Negro Slavery*, the very same work in which he mentioned that Africans were "inertly obeying minds and muscles," Ulrich B. Phillips includes an entire chapter entitled "Slave Crime," which details a number of resistance movements in the United States.[4] Despite the polemical and racist nature of this work, even Phillips could not ignore the real and imagined fears of white planters. A large portion of his thesis rests on the claim that plantation paternalism made slavery a relatively benign institution, but this claim could not fully explain away the ubiquitous danger of servile resistance. While the image of "Sambo" may have been promoted during the antebellum era, planters knew that childlike and simple-minded slaves could not help reap the enormous profits they sought from cash-crop cultivation. Nor would southern whites lose sleep at night in fear that their "loyal" slaves would cut their throats, burn their houses, poison their food, or smother their children if paternal relations had been genuine or the Sambo personality type real.

At question in the mind of Phillips, and many southern historians during the early decades of the twentieth century, was the very humanity of enslaved African Americans. Phillips's stereotypical and otherwise questionable views of African Americans were not limited solely to slaves. In describing race relations at an army camp in pre–World War I Georgia, Phillips notes "the Negroes themselves show the same easy-going, amiable, seriocomic obedience and the same personal attachments to white men, as well as the same sturdy light-heartedness and the same love of laughter and of rhythm which distinguished their forbears."[5] Phillips saw docility and obedience as engrained racial characteristics of Africans and their descendants; thus, any disruptive actions engaged in by slaves on antebellum plantations must have been crimes rather than legitimate resistance. His fascination with the murder of white men and rape of white women during the antebellum era was an articulation of issues of power and white supremacy which dominated antebellum and post-Reconstruction southern society. Phillips even pardons lynching as a justifiable corrective for enslaved black men who raped white women—an attitude fully reflective of the South he was both a part of and an apologist for during the early twentieth century.

The pioneering work of Herbert Aptheker created a substantial shift in scholarly interpretations of slave resistance. Despite considerable opposition to both his political affiliations and theoretical approach, he was able to create a foundation for future studies of slave resistance. Writing in the 1940s, Aptheker built on the work of notable black scholars including Carter G. Woodson, W. E. B. Du Bois, and John Cromwell by contending that Africans and African Americans never accepted slavery and frequently expressed their opposition in the form of rebellion and other acts of resistance. He points to over 250 alleged plots and insurrections as evidence of the widespread nature of discontent.[6] To Aptheker, the root cause of slave revolts was slavery—a conclusion that undermines any romantic perceptions of plantation life. Taking full aim at U. B. Phillips, Francis Gaines, James Schouler, John Fiske and others who viewed enslaved African Americans as "child-like, easily intimidated, incapable of deep plots," Aptheker effectively demonstrates the ubiquity of resistive behavior on southern plantations.[7]

Aptheker also viewed slave resistance as a necessary and natural phenomenon; in essence, it was a human response to inhumane conditions and circumstances. In his assessment, "The fundamental factor provoking rebellion against slavery was that social system itself, the degradation, exploitation, oppression, and brutality which it created, and with which, indeed, it was synonymous."[8] Slavery, in this view, produced its own enemies and its own internal disorder. The utter brutality and inhumanity evident in this system did not have the power to transform enslaved Africans and African Americans into a race of Sambos, as Stanley Elkins would conclude more than a decade later in *Slavery: A Problem in American Institutional and Intellectual Life.* In the preface to his 1969 edition of *American Negro Slave Revolts,* Aptheker claims that "Humans, no matter of what color, beings human (sic) have rebelled when their treatment was bestial and when opportunity and capacity for rebellion was present."[9] Aptheker's effort to humanize slaves was followed by Kenneth Stampp's sustained rebuttal of Phillips, *The Peculiar Institution*, in which he states: "I have assumed that the slaves were merely ordinary human beings, that innately Negroes *are*, after all, only white men with black skins, nothing more, nothing less."[10]

Both Aptheker and Stampp sought to make their subjects human beings with the same range of emotions and motivations as any other group. These efforts, while well intentioned and historiographically significant, sometimes obscure as much as they reveal. Resistance is indeed a human reaction to oppressive circumstances, but this conclusion does not fully reflect the nuances and multifaceted realities evident in the slave-era Atlantic world. Slaves were humans, but they were also Africans from specific cultural and sociopolitical contexts. The types of resistive behavior Africans and African Americans engaged in were largely shaped by their African past.

One set of interpretations that deal with the influences of African culture on slave resistance can be found in Michael Mullin's *Flight and Rebellion* and his more recent *Africa in America*. In *Flight and Rebellion* he contends that African-born slaves in North American "inwardly" resisted slavery. These "outlandish" slaves had a tendency to engage in self-defeating and self-destructive modes of resistance that often lacked sufficient planning. Actions by newly arrived enslaved Africans were characteristically short-ranged, sporadic, desperate, and punitive. According to Mullin, new arrivals rarely planned mass rebellions and only through acculturation to Euro-American ways could they gain the capacity to develop any form of organized resistance that threatened slavery as an institution.[11] In *Africa in America*, Mullin again proposes a dichotomy between the "unseasoned" new arrivals and the "assimilated" American-born creoles which had direct implications for the nature of slave resistance. Africans were predisposed to "sudden, violently destructive," acts of resistance that were "charged with African ritual." Enslaved Africans somehow lacked the ingenuity and resourcefulness of the "creoles" and, thus, were unable to create and sustain real revolutionary movements.[12] Mullin's conclusion is quite clear that the maintenance of cultural links to Africa prevented modes of resistance that threatened slavery. For Mullin, adoption and assimilation of Euro-American culture was the only viable means the enslaved had to combat effectively the system that continuously oppressed them.

Taking a different approach, Eugene Genovese contends that "newly arrived Africans mounted the most dramatic insurrectionary thrusts." He argues that creoles throughout the Americas tended to side with their masters against African rebels. This would change however by the late eighteenth and early nineteenth centuries when creoles such as Gabriel Prosser, Denmark Vesey, and Nat Turner led insurrectionary, if not very popular, movements. Genovese basically forwards the notion that early revolts had an "unmistakable African base," but the increasing proportion of creoles to African-born slaves led them to make practical considerations and to accept a "defensive strategy of survival" over suicidal rebellions. In this view, black Christianity was the principal mediating force. It allowed slaves to accommodate the planter aristocracy while acting as a form of "resistance to dehumanization and enslavement."[13] While this argument seems sound, Genovese may be guilty of underestimating the perseverance of African culture even among second, third, and fourth generation creoles. As much as Gabriel Prosser "took heart from the American conflict with France," or Denmark Vesey "seized upon the implications of the Missouri debate," or Nat Turner "moved in an atmosphere charged . . . with rumors . . . of renewed war with Britain," each was influenced by African concepts, values, and cultural metaphors.[14]

While Genovese has acknowledged the early importance of African culture in slave rebellions, a number of scholars have argued that African culture actually impeded resistance. Both Stanley Elkins and Richard Dunn, for example, have argued that African "tribalism" contributed heavily to the undermining of slave collaboration and resistance. Elkins notes that "it was the very distance between tribes, the helpless diversity of languages, and the Negroes' inability to communicate with one another, that was counted on to minimize the danger of insurrections on shipboard." Richard Dunn states that both linguistic barriers and tribal rivalries "hindered these blacks, once enslaved, from combining against their masters."[15] In both cases the nature of African cultures, their assumed unbridgeable diversity, becomes an obstacle to organized resistance.

Though ship captains and plantation owners may have fully intended to promote diversity in order to avoid collective resistance, this goal was far from accomplished. Instead, what emerged on slave ships and on plantations in the Americas were what Michael Gomez in *Exchanging Our Country Marks* refers to as "ethnic enclaves." Obvious examples in the Western Hemisphere include the Angolan-Yoruba enclaves in Brazil and Cuba, the BaKongo-Fon-Dahomean enclaves in Haiti, and the Igbo-Akan enclaves in

Jamaica, Barbados, and Antigua. North America was no exception to this pattern, and similar African ethnic groupings and concentrations were present there as well. Relying on the work of Philip Curtin, James Rawley, and John Thornton, Gomez demonstrates the presence of a Biafran (Igbo) enclave in the Chesapeake and a West-central African enclave in South Carolina and Georgia.[16]

The Du Bois Institute database bears out the conclusion that significant ethnic enclaves developed throughout the Americas. Representing roughly two-thirds of all slave voyages, this important project significantly modified the findings of Philip Curtin and provides a more accurate picture of the patterns and shape of the Atlantic slave trade. The Du Bois database, for example, demonstrates that of 101,925 enslaved Africans from identifiable locations sent to Virginia, 45 percent came from the Bight of Biafra. In comparison, enslaved Africans sent from the Bight of Biafra accounted for just 10 percent of all Africans disembarked from ships in South Carolina; in the U.S. as a whole, Bight of Biafra exports were 19 percent of the 317,748 enslaved Africans recorded in the Du Bois database.[17] So it is possible to discuss a Bight of Biafra (Igbo) enclave in Virginia as a phenomenon unique in North America, a conclusion supported recently by Lorena Walsh.[18] The Du Bois database and other relevant sources also show that particular ethnic enclaves in New York, Virginia, and South Carolina produced unique and possibly representative modes of resistance in those areas before the 1830s. Hence, African culture, instead of serving as a barrier or hindrance to resistive behavior, may have been one of many shaping principals in several examples of North American slave resistance during the colonial and antebellum eras.

In recognition that Africans in North America did not experience a "spiritual holocaust" or become *tabula rasas*, Gomez asserts that "in order to understand the process by which African American identity formed, and to flesh out the means by which relations within the African American community developed, it is essential to recover the African cultural, political, and social background, recognizing that Africans came to the New World with certain coherent perspectives and beliefs about the universe and their place in it."[19] In analyzing resistance movements, the current study tracks the various steps Africans made in the process of becoming "African American" in culture, orientation, and identity. Resistance then became a crucible in which African people actively created a collective identity centered on unifying principles. In many ways this approach is similar to Frederick Jackson Turner's frontier thesis. Instead of focusing on "place as process," as Turner does in his discussion of the transformation of Europeans into Americans along the advancing frontier line, this study details "actions as process."

Through their actions rebels, conspirators, runaways, and maroons facilitated the creation of new historical realities and identities. The principal outcome of their resistance activities was a unique ethnogenesis out of which African American consciousness and culture emerged. While its foundations were the myriad of African "nations" and ethnic groups that comprised the enslaved population in North America, African American cultural identity was the product of a transformation that took centuries. The mechanisms facilitating the creation of this ethos were many. Sterling Stuckey effectively evokes the ring shout as one mechanism that preserved core elements of African religion and, thus, became a unifying cultural principle among African Americans.[20] The current study expands on this important conclusion by looking at resistance as a liminal realm encompassing cultural bridges—conjure, animal tricksters, martial dances, burial customs, and beliefs associated with ironworking—that promoted collective action and collaboration between African ethnic groups.

African and African American slaves displayed a unique type of group consciousness during the course of key resistance movements. At first glance, the world created by enslaved Africans and African Americans in the Western Hemisphere was alien and, for some scholars, completely undecipherable. The things that gave slaves inspiration, the spiritual forces that inhabited and shared their space, and the multifaceted characters in their folkloric traditions all shaped this array of cultural values. Paying serious heed, therefore, to the African background can help scholars unravel and better grasp the convoluted complexities of slave life.

Definable African ethnolinguistic groupings—the Akan, the Mande, the Igbo—rather than some essentialized "African" culture contributed distinctly to the resistance movements in question. Even within these groups, however, there were complex webs of fractures and interconnections, divisions and unions, ambiguities, and boundaries. In the case of the Yoruba and the Igbo, for example, Gomez and David Northup demonstrate that these ethnic and national terms were not applicable in precolonial Atlantic Africa. Yoruba, for example, was a term of possible Hausa origin and referred to the people living in the town of Oyo Ile. As Gomez contends, "The Yoruba emerged as a 'nation' not only in North America but also in the West Indies and Brazil." While the Yoruba were a very real group in the Americas, this ethnolinguistic identity emerged only recently in Africa and as a direct result of British colonial administration in Nigeria.[21]

Likewise, the Igbo did not exist as a distinct ethnicity in Atlantic Africa until they were "created" by British officials in the twentieth century. According to Northrup, "Twentieth-century colonial forces and post-colonial politics fostered solidarity among the millions of Yoruba- and Igbo-speaking peoples that had no pre-colonial counterpart." Like a number of ethnonyms used by Europeans during the slave trade era, Calabar, Moko, and Igbo were imprecise and, at times, overlapped identities that Africans in this region did not create or embrace. As Northrup shows, however, "*Igbo* was a name Igbo-speaking people seem to have readily accepted abroad."[22] What was true for the Yoruba and the Igbo was probably true for other Atlantic African "nations" and "ethnic" groups. Although the effort to complicate ethnicity is a significant trend in the recent historiography of Atlantic World culture, enslaved Africans adopted these seemingly false ethnonyms and actively referred to themselves as "Coromantee," "Amina," "Eboe," "Chamba," "Canga," or "Lucumí," suggesting that tangible and identifiable ethnolinguistic groupings were present in the Americas. In order to deal with this problem, Douglas Chambers contends that "we must, as David Geggus some time ago suggested, 'decipher rather than dismiss' this lexicon of historical diasporic ethnicity."[23] Completely dismissing these identities, no matter how problematic they may be, would be another step toward the denial of African or African American agency. Perhaps those who embraced these ethnic terms did so for very real reasons and we should investigate those reasons.

In addressing the false monolith of "African culture," Sidney Mintz and Richard Price state that "enslaved Africans . . . were drawn from different parts of the African continent, from numerous ethnic and linguistic groups, and from different societies in any region." Though Mintz and Price tend to exaggerate the actual amount of diversity in Atlantic Africa, they raise issues that have forced some reassessment of Africanisms in North America.[24] In his recent analysis of African cultural survivals, John Thornton asserts that "African slaves arriving in Atlantic colonies did not face as many barriers to cultural transmission as scholars such as Mintz and Price have maintained.

However, they probably also did not simply recommence an African culture in the New World."[25] To be sure, slavery was not the best medium for the transmission of African cultures. Enslaved Africans demonstrated an incredible resourcefulness as they adapted to a new and hostile environment while simultaneously forging a shared culture and consciousness. The dynamism of this adaptive process cannot be limited to a simplistic Hegelian dialectic, to strict and static categories, or to fixed concepts of culture and ethnicity. African American culture and consciousness emerged from a series of cultural "negotiations" between African ethnic enclaves. In this process, common values and customs were maintained, elaborated (or simplified), and expanded (or contracted) while others were discarded. African American culture, therefore, is less a combination of "African" and "European" cultures than a synthetic spectrum of "Igbo," "Akan," "Mande," "Edo," "Fon," "Bakongo," and "Yoruba" forms, values, and customs.

Slave resistance in three regions—New York, South Carolina, and Virginia—forms the principal focus of this book. From colonial-era revolts to Nat Turner's 1831 insurrection, this resistance demonstrated the continuity of African influences on resistive behavior engaged in by African- and American-born slaves. As Michael Gomez contends, the 1830s represent an important historical watershed: "The relative numbers of American-born slaves far outnumber those of the native African, and the general patterns of the emerging African American identity are discernible."[26] With the emergence of an African American culture and identity, the "African sociocultural matrix" envisioned by Gomez was effectively replaced. By the time of Nat Turner's rebellion, an important cultural transition had already taken place. Nat was American-born, literate, and Christian. Most importantly, his insurrection lacked the directly African influences evident in other conspiracies and rebellions. A generation after the federally mandated end of the slave trade to the United States, particular African cultural impulses were less obvious and more difficult to discern.

Focusing on major conspiracies and rebellions necessitates a close inspection of trial records, which obviously can be unreliable sources. Trial testimony was often coerced and fears of imminent torture or death may have motivated those accused to alter their testimony or lie to court officials. Because of these problems some scholars have cast doubts on the existence of some of the more significant examples of slave collaboration and resistance —the New York City plot of 1741 and the 1822 Denmark Vesey conspiracy being the notable examples. By carefully corroborating willing testimony with coerced confessions, comparing statements made by multiple defendants or witnesses, and using evidence available outside the context of the court room I have tried to provide some certainty for particular facts and conclusions.

Other sources for these rebellions and their contexts include folktales, published narratives and interviews, runaway advertisements, travel accounts, diary entries and personal correspondence, government documents, and newspaper accounts. Supplementing these more traditional sources are elements of material culture that further illuminate African influences on slave resistance—graveyard sites, coffin decorations and carvings, conjuring implements, and examples of African American metalwork. Primary and secondary sources come from both sides of the Atlantic in order to draw connections between cultural and sociopolitical phenomena in Africa and North America.

Where possible, I have been careful to use eighteenth-century data to analyze eighteenth-century phenomena, and I have resisted the urge to either "upstream" or "downstream" the evidence. In certain cases, I have been more than tempted to compare cultural phenomena in the twentieth century to very similar phenomena in the eighteenth or nineteenth centuries. Despite the striking nature of some of these links, they have been relegated to footnotes or replaced by contemporaneous evidence. In the absence of any other source of evidence, I have used twentieth century ethnographic observations to draw specific connections. This type of caution can be quite confining at times, but it is necessary in order to avoid some of the many pitfalls that abound in any study of culture. This sustained effort to complicate culture (and therefore ethnographic materials) is part of a recent historiographical trend. I owe this approach to the thoughtful advice of two Africanists—Ray Kea and John Thornton.

Another convention followed closely in this work is naming slaves according to the surname of their "owners" on first mention and by the slave's first name thereafter. Thus, "Prosser's Gabriel" is rendered as "Gabriel Prosser" and then simply "Gabriel." The reasons for this are stylistic and sensitivity to the subject matter. By referring to slaves and their relationship to their owners in the possessive, the notion that they indeed were things to be bartered, traded, and owned would be improperly emphasized. Slaves, of course, occupied a nebulous social space. They controlled many aspects of their own lives, but their status as human property meant that they faced insurmountable barriers to being completely autonomous agents and actors in plantation society. They were, by this measure, in both object and subject position. This book is a story of how slaves actively challenged the notion of human bondage. They proved, through a variety of actions that they were agents, not merely passive nonentities; subjects of historical processes, not simply objects acted upon; indeed, at times, slaves were their own masters.

The issue of slave names is not one merely of semantics. The use of surnames should not imply or reinforce notions of subordinate social relations and object positioning. The intention is to avoid confusion, since a number of slaves giving testimony or facing charges connected to slave revolts and plots had the same first name. Surnames, therefore, function as identifying markers. The subsequent use of first names is due to a more complex array of reasons. Identifying Nat Turner as "Turner" instead of "Nat" becomes extremely problematic when one considers what he was and what he hoped to do in order to become free. Slaves often did not identify themselves through use of a white owner's surname, especially in the case of a rebel. Some slaves fully accepted surnames of white owners, however, because the names were handed down by their parents or grandparents. This seems to be the case with a majority of African Americans after emancipation. Arguably, a slave's first name took on added significance since, with some exception, it may have been the only name truly given or chosen by loved ones. Lastly, because dozens of slaves from particular plantations were sometimes involved in rebellions and conspiracies, first names are the only accurate and logical way to denote particular people from a group that would have shared the same surname.

One stylistic convention not closely adhered to is the relatively new trend of referring to "enslaved Africans" instead of "slaves." Given the full recognition of agency and subject position given to Africans and their descendants in this work, the use of "enslaved African" over "slave" becomes an issue of semantics. At times I alternate between the two terms, but this is a decision based on which term better fits the historical context or the particular sentence. Thus my reasoning for continuing the use of the word "slave" throughout the present work is not the result of politically-inspired debates or philosophical orientations. Very simply, second, third, and fourth generation African Americans cannot accurately be referred to as "African," whether enslaved or free. To do so would undermine the broader attempt to outline the transition from a series of African identities to an African American one. Likewise, the terms "enslaved African Americans" and "enslaved blacks" become too unwieldy to use on a frequent basis.

Historians' terms and their usage are situated in specific historical contexts and exemplify historiographical trends, methodological approaches, and innovations in the use of sources. In the 1940s, for example, it would be perfectly acceptable to refer to African Americans as "Negroes," to look at plantation records as a method of revealing the inner workings of the slave community, to place free and enslaved blacks in an object position, and to use consensus history as a lens to view the plantation South. By the 1970s, "black" was beginning to replace "Negro," slave narratives and interviews were being widely used to understand slave consciousness, free and enslaved blacks were being viewed as agents of historical change, and both conflict historiography and revisionism made their way into historical discourse as legitimate approaches. Perhaps a new generation of historians and Africana studies scholars will develop appropriate vocabularies and theoretical approaches to deal adequately with the history of Western Hemisphere slavery. The present work however does not claim to perform that monumental feat and can be seen as evolutionary, rather than revolutionary, in terms of its contributions to the discourse.

The book follows a more or less chronological order. The first part examines colonial era revolts and conspiracies in the middle colonies and lower South. Chapters 1 and 2 focus on resistance in New York City between 1712 and 1741. African conjurers facilitated resistive behavior in eighteenth-century Manhattan Island. Particularly, Akan-speaking Africans from the Gold Coast who concentrated in the colony brought their understandings of spirituality, transmigration, conjure, and death, which directly influenced their interactions with the world around them. The historical events of eighteenth-century New York City are also placed in context with events in other eighteenth-century regions with Akan-speaking concentrations as well as events in the Gold Coast. This Atlantic World context provides the best interpretive window in analyzing the actions of enslaved Africans in the early history of New York.

Chapter 3 analyzes the role West-central Africans played in eighteenth-century South Carolina. Again, an Atlantic World approach is used as an insightful interpretive tool. The actions of West-central Africans in South Carolina are seen in the context of the actions of their counterparts in both Brazil and Africa. The military cultures that developed in West-central Africa contributed to a unique system of martial arts in Brazil known as *capoeira*. In both 1730 and 1739, there was an association between dance and resistance among enslaved Africans in South Carolina which was similar to the martial practices found among captives from West-central African polities and the American regions where they were dispersed and concentrated.

The second part emphasizes antebellum-era resistance movements and the formation of an emergent African American cultural identity, especially the three most notable nineteenth-century examples of resistance—Gabriel's 1800 plot, Denmark's 1822 conspiracy, and Nat's 1831 revolt. The conclusion analyzes slave folklore and the process by which African American culture was born. At some indeterminable point after 1619, Africans in North America literally became African American in culture, orientation, and consciousness. As patterns of African ethnic distribution and concentration became less relevant and less meaningful in the post-slave-trade era, African- and American-born slaves discovered methods of adjusting to a new set of circumstances. Atlantic Africans had already found certain cultural bridges and shared cultural spaces in the Americas, which allowed for a common understanding of the world around them. Additional means of strengthening the connections between slaves developed and fostered a sense of cultural and political solidarity. What resulted was the creation of a relatively unitary ethos with broad, and at times fluid, parameters but one whose roots were firmly planted in African soil.

Slave folklore is the best way to develop an understanding of the internal workings of the slave psyche and the dynamics that produced a unique African American cultural and sociopolitical identity. Sterling Stuckey has contended that an understanding and analysis of folklore—and especially animal trickster tales—allows one to trace the outlines of the slave ethos.[27] Indeed, folklore was both a central aspect of slave culture and one of the mechanisms that facilitated the creation of an African American consciousness. It was among the tools that combined disparate elements from a number of African ethnolinguistic groups present in North America and allowed for the formation of a relatively unitary outlook. Analyzing animal trickster tales and the complex stories of power relations, community building, and resistance to oppression demonstrates that the concerns of African peasants and American slaves were remarkably similar. Moreover, animal tricksters, African divine priests, slave conjurers, and rebel leaders were all fundamental in inspiring resistance, empowering a people perceived to be powerless, and formulating a new collective identity. In essence, resistance in its multitude of forms helped create African American people.

## PART ONE

African Resistance in Colonial America

# CHAPTER 1

# Fires of Discontent, Echoes of Africa
## The 1712 New York City Revolt

*From Dutch New Netherland to British New York*

The history of forced labor in New Netherland began in 1625 when a Dutch warship unloaded a cargo of Africans plundered from a Portuguese vessel on the Atlantic. Similar circumstances just six years earlier had brought the first Africans to British North America. In 1619, another Dutch warship captured the *São João Batista*, a Portuguese vessel heading to Vera Cruz, and its cargo of about twenty Africans. This group of West-central Africans were disembarked, in exchange for food and supplies, to become the first African laborers to arrive in Jamestown, Virginia. The status of the first Africans brought to both Dutch and British North America was not clearly defined initially, and for at least a few decades there existed a number of avenues forced laborers could use to obtain freedom. The idea of permanent and racialized slavery did not develop in either region until the mid-1660s. These Africans inhabited a nebulous social space between indentured servitude and slavery. Initially it seemed that they would have the same opportunities as European servants and would, perhaps, share the fruits and rewards the New World offered. To borrow the words of Peter Wood, the "terrible transformation" that led to the eventual development and proliferation of race-defined slavery during the second half of the seventeenth century helped determine the poisonous race relations that have manifested throughout much of North American history.[1]

New Netherland was established primarily as a fur trading post by the Dutch West India Company, and the colony and its Dutch settlers struggled during the early-seventeenth century to find sufficient sources of revenue and labor. Concentrating most of their efforts on major territorial claims in West Africa and the Caribbean—Gorée and Curaçao respectively—the company's directors had little interest in investing the significant amount of capital necessary to make New Netherland a successful settler colony. As a result, the Dutch West India Company proposed two separate plans to solve the economic problems faced by their North American colony. The first solution was the establishment of patroonships, or landed estates granted to the wealthy. Patroonships, much like the headrights the Virginia Company bestowed in the Chesapeake, were incentives meant to encourage immigration to America. Wealthy Dutch settlers receiving landed estates under this system had the responsibility of attracting and paying the necessary transportation costs for up to fifty new settlers each. Only one patroonship was established during the entire period of Dutch rule in New Netherland. The company's second, and most successful, plan was the importation of Africans to be used primarily as agricultural laborers and as workers in the construction of public buildings and military fortifications.[2]

The names of some of the first Africans imported into New Netherland— Paul d'Angola, Simon Congo, and Anthony Portuguese—clearly denote their origin in West-central Africa. In the early 1570s, Portugal conquered Angola and established peaceful commercial relations with the nearby Kongo kingdom. West-central Africa would be an early source of labor for the Portuguese colony of Brazil and, due to the actions of Dutch warships and privateers on the Atlantic, both British Virginia and Dutch New Netherland would import a number of Africans from this region as well. When the Dutch West India Company was first chartered in 1621, it began an aggressive campaign against Portuguese claims in Atlantic Africa and the Americas in an attempt to undermine the Portuguese trade monopoly and to acquire Africans by more direct means. The company captured portions of Brazil by 1637 and moved to wrest control of a number possessions in Africa away from its Portuguese rivals.[3]

In an attempt to fulfill their public promise to "use their endeavors to supply the colonists with as many Blacks as they conveniently can," the company sought to become the primary conduit for Africans entering Dutch American colonies.[4] Between 1637 and 1647 alone, the Dutch West India Company claimed the Portuguese possessions of El Mina, Príncipe, Angola, and São Tomé through military conquest. Even though the Dutch could only manage to control Angola from 1641 to 1648, they had effectively replaced the Portuguese as the dominant European power in Atlantic Africa by the mid-1640s. This complex web of interconnections within the Atlantic

World, fostered by trade, international rivalry, and war, became an essential component in the development of a number of Euro-American societies.[5]

By 1627, a total of fourteen Africans had arrived in Dutch New Netherland, but this initially slow trickle became a torrent over the course of the next half century. The absence of cash crops such as sugar, tobacco, or rice did not slow the need for African labor in Dutch North America. The Dutch West India Company helped fuel further demand, noting in a 1629 report to the States-General of the United Netherlands that the colonists "being unaccustomed to so hot a climate can with great difficulty betake themselves to agriculture," a feat made even more arduous by the fact that they were "unprovided with slaves and not used to the employment of them . . ."[6] This situation would soon change, and the importation of Africans became the company's principal focus with the arrival of the first slave ship in 1635.

In 1644, the Dutch Board of Accounts advised that for the purposes of cultivating land and growing wheat on Manhattan Island, "it would not be unwise to allow, at the request of the Patroons, Colonists and other farmers the introduction from Brazil, there, of as many Negroes as they would be disposed to pay for at a fair price."[7] This request was followed by the arrival, two years later, of the second recorded slave ship in New Netherland, the *Amandare*. Because it directly controlled large portions of Brazil between 1637 and 1654, the company was able to create a unique trade relationship between New Netherland and Brazil. In a trade arrangement drafted in 1648, the colonists in New Netherland agreed to ship fish, flour and produce to Brazil in exchange for as many African laborers as they required. Within four years of the establishment of the Brazil–New Netherland commercial agreement, direct trade with West Africa for slaves was opened and a slight reorientation of the slave trade began. In prior decades, the Dutch were satisfied with plundering Portuguese slave ships or procuring African laborers from Brazil or Spanish America. As a result, the majority of Africans entering New Netherland were from Loango and other West-central African regions.[8] One contemporary source notes that Africans entering New Amsterdam in the decade after 1625 were "Angola slaves, thievish, lazy, and useless trash."[9] Despite this negative characterization, enslaved "Angolans" or West-central Africans would prove essential to the economic viability of the colony during its early years.

By allowing Africans to be directly imported into North America via Dutch West India Company–owned or commissioned ships, New Netherland soon began to receive a number of Gold Coast Akan-speakers exported from Dutch-controlled trading factories in West Africa to supplement the West-central African imports. After capturing El Mina Castle from the Portuguese in August 1637, the Dutch controlled the most important slave trading factory along the Gold Coast until its transfer to the British in 1872 (see fig. 1.1). The immediate result of the capture of El Mina was the importation of Gold Coast Africans into Dutch American colonies. The 1659 charter for the ship *Eyckenboom* allowed the captain of this vessel to trade at El Mina Castle and "from thence proceed further to the islands of Curaçao, Bonaire, and Aruba . . . and also to New Netherland."[10] This new source of African laborers became even more important after 1648 when the Portuguese managed to recapture their Angolan possessions from the Dutch, which effectively cut off a major source of West-central African imports. Also, with the Portuguese recapture of Brazil, the unique commercial arrangement between New Netherland and Brazil was brought to an abrupt halt.[11] In New Amsterdam, and later New York City, this reorientation of the slave trade and the importation of Akan-speakers from the Gold Coast would have profound implications for the history of slavery and the development of African American culture in the region.[12]

FIGURE 1.1. El Mina Castle, ca. 2002. *Photo by Walter Rucker.*

The dominant position the Dutch enjoyed in Africa and the Americas came to an end in 1664. The Second Anglo-Dutch War of 1664–1667 helped create a major power shift throughout the Atlantic World. During the war, the English seized most of the Dutch claims along the Gold Coast, with the notable exception of El Mina Castle. The English also managed to capture New Netherland. Angered over repeated violations of the Navigation Acts of 1651 and 1660, the English crown decided that New Netherland was a significant obstacle to its economic interests in the Americas. By claiming the region, the English grabbed control of the contiguous territory from the Chesapeake to the New England colonies. Having already proven the military vulnerabilities of Dutch colonies during the First Anglo-Dutch War of 1652–1654, the English were able to peacefully capture New Netherland after a brief naval blockade. Peter Stuyvesant—director general of the Dutch West India Company and governor of New Netherland—capitulated on September 8, 1664, effectively ending four decades of control by the company over what would soon become New York.[13]

When the English appropriated this region under King Charles II, it was already one of the most culturally and ethnically diverse regions in seventeenth-century North America. When James, the Duke of York, assumed control of New Netherland and renamed the area New York, sizable populations of Dutch, English, French, Germans, Scandinavians, and at least 375 Africans from varying ethnic groups already lived on Manhattan Island. The Dutch West India Company's incessant, and at times desperate, need for European settlers or African laborers had helped create a diverse and cosmopolitan society. The colony had been forced to accept settlers of various European nationalities out of sheer expediency; the comparatively high living standard in the Netherlands during the seventeenth century compelled the Dutch to stay in Europe. The failure of the Dutch West India Company to attract sufficient settlers led to its eventual bankruptcy and British control over its North American colonial possessions.[14]

The system the company established simply did not provide a strong enough incentive to lure the Dutch to North America in sufficient numbers and, according to historian Edgar McManus, "The prospect of living as feudal dependents of a great landlord had almost no appeal to the ruggedly independent Dutch."[15] The dearth of colonists during the early years of Dutch settlement in North America provided an obvious impetus for the continued importation of African labor. This reliance on Africans was epitomized by the arrival of the last Dutch West India Company commissioned ship—the *Gideon*—in New Amsterdam in the summer of 1664. The *Gideon* carried a cargo of 300 from Loango in West-central Africa, representing 80 percent of the African population residing in New Amsterdam, 6 percent of Manhattan's total population, and 3 percent of the entire population of New Netherland. The *Gideon* was also the ship that loaded the remaining Dutch soldiers from Fort Amsterdam after the company capitulated to English rule in September 1664.[16]

Almost instantly, the English recognized slavery as a legal institution. The "Duke's Laws," passed a year after British rule was established, included provisions that allowed the practice of service for life. While the Dutch had never codified slavery, the experiences of the Dutch West India Company in Atlantic Africa and Brazil gave its proprietors a keen understanding of the concept, and some Africans were already serving lifelong labor contracts before 1664. According to Joyce Goodfriend, with English control came "a constellation of laws governing the lives of slaves" which "substantially restrict[ed] the latitude of black people in New York City." The end of Dutch rule in Manhattan made slavery a very real and lasting concept for its African inhabitants. The opportunity for Africans to obtain their freedom, own land, or even have their own pool of dependent European or African laborers would be completely shut off by the eighteenth century.[17]

Africans made up roughly 20 percent of New York City's population at the time of the British conquest (see table 1.1). The steady influx of labor from the Caribbean and Africa, initiated by the Dutch West India Company, would persist under British rule, especially after the Royal African Company was chartered in 1672. Though the Royal African Company concentrated primarily on the trade from West Africa to the Caribbean, they actively encouraged the reshipment trade in which private traders sold Caribbean slaves to New York and other North American colonies.[18] In 1676, Sir John Werden noted that once the Royal African Company traded enslaved Africans from West Africa and "when they are once sold in Barbados, Jamaica, etc. by them or their factors, they care not whither they are transported from thence . . . and therefore you need not suspect the Company will oppose the introducing of black Slaves into New Yorke from any place (except from Guiny) if they were first sold in that place by the Royall Company or their agents."[19] In this manner, New Yorkers could guarantee as many enslaved Africans as

TABLE 1.1. New York City Population

| Year | Africans | Europeans | Total Population | Percentage African |
|------|----------|-----------|------------------|--------------------|
| 1664 | 375 | 1,500 | 1,875 | 20.0% |
| 1698 | 700 | 4,237 | 4,937 | 14.1 |
| 1703 | 630 | 3,732 | 4,332 | 14.5 |
| 1712 | 1,100 | 4,846 | 5,946 | 18.5 |
| 1723 | 1,362 | 5,886 | 7,248 | 18.8 |
| 1731 | 1,577 | 7,045 | 8,622 | 18.3 |
| 1737 | 1,719 | 8,945 | 10,664 | 16.1 |

Sources: Greene and Harrington, *American Population before the Federal Census of 1790*, 92–101; Morgan, *Slavery in New York*, 28–29.

they needed, and the population continued to swell unabated. By the 1730s, New York City had the largest African population of any colonial city north of Baltimore. In fact, it was second only to Charleston, South Carolina, as the city with the highest concentration of Africans in North America.

### Restrictive Eighteenth-Century Slave Laws
With the arrival of British rule in New Netherland in 1664 came a series of laws that helped define the parameters of slavery in what later became New York. The first British mainland colony to legalize slavery was Massachusetts, which did so in 1641. Slavery would eventually be legalized in all thirteen North American colonies. Because slavery existed in some form on Manhattan Island before the arrival of the British, the slave laws the new government created were merely reflections of an ongoing reality. The Duke's Laws stipulated that "No Christian shall be kept in Bond-Slavery, except such who shall be judged thereto by Authority, or such as willingly have sold or shall sell themselves." Consciously modeled after a comparable law in New England by a group of Puritan settlers residing in Long Island, the Duke's Laws exempted any African professing Christianity. This loophole would soon be corrected. In 1674, the law would be amended to read "This law shall not set at liberty any Negro or Indian Slave, who shall have turned Christian after they had been bought by any person." This new provision helped solidify the notion of perpetual racialized slavery in New York until the time of the American Revolution.[20]

The Act of 1706 further defined enslaved Africans and Native Americans in New York as inferior in status to English settlers. This act went against English Common Law, which stipulated that children would adopt the status of their fathers. Instead, the Act of 1706 mandated that "all and every Negro, Indian, Mulatto or Mustee shall follow the state and condition of the Mother and be esteemed and reputed, taken and adjudged to be a Slave or Slaves to all intents and purposes whatsoever." The enslavement of the womb of African and Native American women was the most effective step in the creation of a permanent and racialized caste for non-Europeans in New York. As the rights of the enslaved dwindled and their opportunities to become free gradually disappeared, a climate conducive for rebelliousness was fostered. Residents on Manhattan Island would very soon understand the difficulties in using laws and force to make slaves more compliant to the new hegemonic order.[21]

Between 1684 and 1708, a series of laws were enacted in New York to limit the "freedoms" of the enslaved population and to prevent the possibility of collaborative resistance efforts. On March 15, 1684, the Corporation of New York passed an ordinance that stipulated "No Negro or Indian Slaves, above the number of four, shall meet together on the Lord's day, or at any other time, at any place, from their master's service." Fearing servile insurrection, the creators of this ordinance also mandated that slaves were forbidden from possessing "guns, swords, clubs, staves, or any other kind of weapon" under penalty of ten lashes.[22] These types of restrictive provisions were not aimed solely at the behavior of enslaved Africans. Laws that sought to prevent slave insurrection in colonial and antebellum North America came in two basic varieties—repressionist and reformist. Repressionist laws, like the Ordinance of 1684, sought to limit and control the actions of slaves through the creation of an elaborate system of discipline and punishment.

Reformist laws sought to control the behavior of whites—masters and overseers alike—whose abusive behavior could possibly encourage slaves to rebel.[23] This is the case with the formulation of the Law for the Restraining of Inhuman Severitys found in the instructions given to Thomas Dongan, governor of New York from 1686 to 1692, by the Board of Trade in England. In their instructions, the board suggested on May 29, 1686, that Governor Dongan should "pass a Law for the Restraining of Inhuman Severitys which by all master or overseers may bee used towards their Christian servants or slaves wherein provision is to be made that yᵉ wilful killing of Indians & Negroes may bee punished with death, And that a fit penalty bee imposed for the maiming of them."[24] On the surface, these instructions seemed to be attempts to protect the "rights" of Christian slaves, but they actually attempted to prevent overly abusive whites from inspiring slaves to rebel and possibly destroy the colony as a result. This effort was followed in 1709 when Robert Hunter, governor of New York from 1710 to 1719, received instruction from England to insure that private slave punishment was not inhumane and overly brutal and that the material needs of slaves were not ignored by their owners.[25]

The Act for Regulateing of Slaves passed on November 27, 1702, became the first attempt at a comprehensive slave code in New York. This act further reduced the number of slaves allowed to publicly assemble to no more than three on penalty of up to forty lashes. It also made it unlawful for any free person to harbor, conceal, or entertain male slaves without the consent of their masters. This particular aspect of the act was in part aimed at ship captains who may have consciously aided slaves in their attempts to find employment on board their vessels and therefore escape from bondage.[26]

The 1702 act did not stop at limiting the assembly and mobility of enslaved men and women. Another provision called for slave owners to handle the responsibility of punishing their slaves with the approval of the Crown.[27] It specifically decreed that "here after it shall and may be lawful for any master or mistress . . . to punish their slaves for their crimes and offences at discretion." This was stipulated because "the Number of slaves in the Citty of New York and Albany . . . doth daily increase, and that they have been found oftentimes guilty of Confederating together in running away, or other ill practices."[28] The provincial courts could not adequately punish all rebellious and runaway slaves in the province; thus the onus was placed on slave owners to discipline their "property." This was unprecedented in the history of the region. By granting slave owners seemingly unlimited powers over their slaves, this act found what was thought to be an effective means to impair the ability of slaves to resist white control.

Once slaves became the full purview of their owners, and not the responsibility of the courts of New York, it followed that they would, in effect, become nonentities in other judicial matters. Thus, the 1702 act mandated that slaves would no longer be allowed to give testimony in court in cases involving free persons. This ended a policy created under Dutch rule which allowed slaves to testify in any court case: "And it is further Enacted by the authority aforesaid, that hereafter no slaves shall be allowed good evidence in any matter, cause or thing whatsoever, excepting in cases of Plotting or confederacy amongst themselves, either to run away, kill, or destroy their Master or Mistress, or burning of houses, or of their Master's or Mistress's Cattle and that against one another in w'ch case the Evidence of one slave shall be good against another slave."[29] In his report to the Lords of Trade, Lord Cornbury, governor of New York from 1702 to 1708, applauded the Act of 1702, saying it was "absolutely necessary through the great insolency that sort of people are grown to." Fearing the possibilities of servile insubordination or revolt, the Lords of Trade renewed the act for seven more years on August 4, 1705.[30]

The Lords of Trade would receive another communiqué from Lord Cornbury on February 10, 1708 regarding an actual act of "insolency" among the enslaved population of Newton, Long Island, in what appears to be the first slave revolt in the history of British New York: "a most barbarous murder has been committed upon the Family of one Hallet by an Indian man Slave, and a Negro Woman, who have murder'd their Master, Mistress, and five Children; The slaves were taken and I immediately issued a special commission for the Tryal of them which was done, and the man sentenced to be hanged and the Woman burnt: and they have been executed. They Discovered two other Negroes their accomplices who have been tryed, condemned & Executed."[31] Under the Act of 1702, masters and mistresses were responsible for punishing their slaves. In this particular incident, however, both the master and mistress died forcing the governor to commission a special court session to try the case and punish the offenders. Due to these circumstances, an act for "preventing the Conspiracy of Slaves" was created which allowed the courts to sentence slave rebels to be executed in any way they saw fit.[32] In cases in which slaves were alleged to have killed or attempted to kill "their Master or Mistriss or any of Her Majesty's leige People (not being Negroes, Malotta's, or Slaves)," a court of oyer and terminer or three justices of the peace would try the case and condemn the guilty to death. The act also stipulated that owners would be paid £25 for each executed slave as compensation from the colonial government.[33] Although there would be a number of regulatory slave acts created in New York between 1684 and 1708 to prohibit particular types of behaviors and activities, no set of laws could effectively destroy the spirit of insurrection among the enslaved.

### The 1712 New York City Revolt

After midnight on April 6, 1712, a group of African slaves and some "Spanish Indians" set fire to an outhouse on Maiden Lane owned by Peter Van Tilburgh—slave owner and resident of the East Ward. When unsuspecting whites arrived at the scene to stop the blaze from spreading, the group of about thirty armed with guns, knives, clubs, axes, and hatchets, attacked them. Nine whites were killed and seven others injured before a militia unit stationed at the nearby garrison was notified. Governor Robert Hunter ordered a cannon to be fired from Fort George to warn others in the area about the revolt. The militia eventually dispersed the rebels, who escaped to the northern forest of Manhattan Island. Of the twenty-eight individuals captured and facing charges ranging from murder to conspiracy, Governor Hunter writes, "Twenty seven [were] condemned whereof twenty one were executed . . . some were burnt others hanged, one broke on the wheele, and one hung alive in chains in town, so that there has been the most exemplary punishment inflicted that could be possibly thought of."[34] Six of the slaves killed themselves rather than be captured. On a practical level, suicide provided an escape from torture and public execution, though there were possibly spiritual reasons, tied to particular West African concepts, for this action. Seven slaves charged in this case were reprieved and never tried. The master of each slave executed received fifty ounces of "Pillar Plate" silver as compensation from the provincial treasury.[35]

Three of the existing contemporary accounts of the New York City rebellion of 1712 reveal sparse but insightful details regarding this uprising.[36] The April 7–14, 1712 edition of the *Boston News-Letter*, which at the time was the only newspaper operating in British North America, reported:

> Some *Cormentine* Negroes to the number of 25 or 30 and 2 or 3 Spanish Indians having conspired to murder all the Christians here, and by that means thinking to obtain their Freedom, about two a clock this morning put their bloody design in Execution, and setting fire to a House, they stood prepar'd with Arms to kill every body that approach'd to put it out, and accordingly barbarously murdered [persons] that were running to the fire . . . Upon

which the Town was soon Alarm'd, which occasion'd the Murderers flying into the Woods, where several parties are set after them, and have taken some (who are committed) and hope to take the rest before night. This has put us into no small Consternation the whole Town being under Arms.[37]

The following week the *Boston News-Letter* informed its readers of the fate of the rebels: "We have about 70 Negro's in Custody, and tis fear'd that most of the Negro's here (who are very numerous) knew of the Late Conspiracy to Murder the Christians; six of them have been their own Executioners by Shooting and cutting their own Throats; Three have been Executed according to Law; one burnt, a second broken upon the wheel, and a third hung up alive, and nine more of the Murdering Negro's are to be Executed to morrow."[38]

In a letter dated June 23, 1712, Reverend John Sharpe—chaplain of the English garrison in New York—provides a detailed account of the events for David Humphreys, the secretary of the Society for the Propagation of the Gospel in Foreign Parts:

> Some Negro Slaves here of y$^e$ Nations of *Caramantee* & Pappa plotted to destroy all the White[s] in order to obtain their freedom and kept their Conspiracy [so] Secret that there was not the least Suspicion of it (as formerly there had often been) till it come to the Execution. It was agreed to on New Years Day *the Conspirators tying themselves to Secrecy by Sucking y$^e$ blood of each Others hands, and to make them invulnerable as they believed a free negroe who pretends Sorcery gave them a powder to rub on their Cloths* which made them so confident that on Sunday night Apr. 7 ab$^t$ 2 a Clock about the going down of the Moon they Set fire to a house which allarming the town they stood in the Streets and Shot down and Stabbed as many as they could, till a great Gun from the fort called up the Inhabitants in arms who soon Scatter'd them they murdered about 8 and wounded 12 more who are since recovered some of them in their flight shot themselves, one shot first his wife and then himself and some who hid themselves in Town when they went to Apprehend them Cut their own throats many were Convicted and ab$^t$ 18 have Suffer'd death.[39]

Rev. Sharpe visited and interviewed the condemned in prison and on the way to the gallows. He spoke in particular to Robin Hooghlandt, the slave of a prominent merchant named Hendrich Hooghlandt. After being convicted of murder in the stabbing death of his master, Robin was sentenced to "be hung up in Chains alive and so to Continue without any sustenance until he be dead" on April 11. Rev. Sharpe, certain of Robin's involvement in the revolt, visited him after the third day of his sentence in order to obtain a confession of guilt. During this session, Sharpe notes that Robin was "often delirious by long continuance in that posture, thro hunger, thirst and pain but he then answered directly to what I enquired . . . so that I might conclude he had some intervals of the exercise of reason." Though he divulged heretofore unrevealed and uninvestigated aspects of the conspiracy and subsequent revolt, Robin claimed that "he knew of yᵉ Conspiracy but was not guilty of any bloodshed in the tumult." Since Sharpe's letter is the only account of the revolt referring to a blood oath of loyalty and the anonymous conjurer, this additional evidence likely came from Robin, a slave who had first-hand knowledge of the plot.[40]

Governor Hunter offers the third account in a dispatch to the Lords of Trade dated June 23, 1712: "I must now give your Lordships an account of the bloody conspiracy of some of the slaves of this place, to destroy as many of the Inhabitants as they could, It was put in execution in this manner, when they had resolved to revenge themselves . . . they agreed to meet in the orchard of Mr. Crook the middle of the Town, some provided with fire arms, some with swords and others with knives and hatchets . . . when about three an twenty of them were got togeather, one [C]*offee* and negroe slave to one Vantilburgh set fire to an out house of his Masters . . . the people began to flock to it upon the approach of severall the slaves fired and killed them."[41] Together, these sparsely detailed contemporary accounts reveal information about the ethnic origins, the specific spiritual beliefs, and the possible motivations of the enslaved Africans who were involved in the 1712 revolt.

## Gold Coast Origins of the Insurgents

The terms "Caramantee" and "Cormentine" referred to in two accounts of the revolt point to an important English trading post located on the Gold Coast of West Africa during the seventeenth and eighteenth centuries.[42] Kromantine was both a key commercial village controlled by the Fante Kingdom of Efutu and a major trading fort established by the Dutch in 1598. Fort Kromantine, located near the modern-day village of Abanze, was destroyed in 1645 and rebuilt later by the English (fig. 1.2). It was to become the first English trading post along the coast of the Gulf of Guinea. From Fort Kromantine and other coastal factories like it, the English exported Africans principally to their Caribbean possessions throughout the seventeenth and eighteenth centuries. During the second Anglo-Dutch War, the Dutch West Indies Company seized Fort Kromantine and renamed it Fort New Amsterdam—

FIGURE 1.2. Fort New Amsterdam, ca. 2002. *Photo by Walter Rucker*

perhaps in direct response to the seizure of its namesake in North America by British forces.[43] As a result of the combined Fante, English, and Dutch trading activities at Kromantine, slaves exported from this region of the Gold Coast were lumped together and referred to incorrectly as "Kromantine" by European slave traders, factors, and ship captains during the seventeenth and eighteenth centuries. While this ethnic term has its ambiguities, "Kromantine" does refer to mostly Akan-speakers from the Gold Coast who were transported to the Americas.[44]

According to the Du Bois Institute slave trade database, British, Dutch, and Danish colonies in the Caribbean and mainland North and South America received a disproportionately high number of Gold Coast Africans during the long course of the Atlantic slave trade. In the period between 1601 and 1800, roughly 80 to 85 percent of all Gold Coast Africans involved in the slave trade were embarked on ships destined for British, Dutch, and Danish colonies (see table 1.2). This emphasis reflects the dominating positions all three European powers had over the forts and castles along the Gold Coast.[45] As Orlando Patterson notes, of the twenty-four European forts present in the Gold Coast during the early eighteenth century, "eight were English; twelve were Dutch; two belonged to the Brandenburgers; and two to the Danes."[46] As a direct consequence of these trade patterns, "nations," ethnic enclaves, cultural groupings, or "ethnies" of enslaved Akan-speakers —principally the Coromantee, the Mina, the Amina, and the Delmina—

TABLE 1.2. Gold Coast Africans Disembarked

| American Destination | 1601–1700 | % of Total | 1701–1800 | % of Total |
|---|---|---|---|---|
| Jamaica | 4,449 | 17.1% | 162,550 | 42.2% |
| Barbados | 13,645 | 52.5 | 33,832 | 8.7 |
| Guianas | 806 | 3.1 | 45,162 | 11.7 |
| Virgin Islands | 1,390 | 5.4 | 14,363 | 3.7 |
| Antigua | 468 | 1.8 | 11,753 | 3.1 |
| Dutch Caribbean | 1,053 | 4.1 | 8,829 | 2.3 |
| St. Vincent | — | — | 9,170 | 2.4 |
| St. Kitts | — | — | 5,678 | 1.5 |
| British North America | 511 | 2.0 | 18,663 | 4.8 |
| Unspecified Destination | 3,405 | — | 49,338 | — |

Source: Eltis, Behrendt, Richardson, and Klein, *The Trans-Atlantic Slave Trade.* Percentages are total number of Africans disembarked at specific destinations.

Note: In the 1601–1700 sample, British North America only includes Virginia; in the 1701–1800 sample, British North America includes the Carolinas, Virginia, Georgia, Maryland, Rhode Island, Florida, New York, Pennsylvania, Delaware, and New Jersey.

formed in the British, Dutch, and Danish Americas which had their cultural and sociopolitical origins in the Gold Coast.[47]

Again, the marked concentration of Akan-speakers in the late-seventeenth- and early-eighteenth-century English slave trade was due to English control over key commercial entrepôts in the Gold Coast. In 1664, the Royal African Company claimed and greatly expanded Cape Coast Castle, a vital military and trade fort geographically situated between Accra and Sekondi. By 1674, the company possessed smaller Gold Coast forts and factories at Accra, Kommenda, Anashan, Egya (Aga), Anamabo, and Winnebah. This significant foothold in the Gold Coast explains why the English managed to export approximately 320 slaves per month from the Gold Coast between 1690 and 1730. It also explains the enormous quantity of trade goods sent to the region by the Royal African Company. Between 1690 and 1704 the Royal African Company exported an estimated £27,000 per year in trade goods to the Gold Coast, an amount that exceeds any two combined West African coastal regions during that period (see table 1.3).[48] The Gold Coast would be the principal concern of English trading interests in West Africa for close to two centuries.

TABLE 1.3. Distribution of Trade Goods in Pounds Sterling

| African Region | 1690–91 | 1692–93 | 1694–95 | 1696–97 | 1698 | 1701–2 | 1703–4 |
|---|---|---|---|---|---|---|---|
| Gambia/Sierra Leone | 8,746 | 16,943 | 13,322 | 2,130 | 8,567 | 14,607 | 10,582 |
| Windward Coast | 2,340 | 11,404 | 5,553 | 2,558 | 1,174 | 1,859 | 772 |
| Gold Coast | 25,566 | 32,330 | 20,542 | 19,428 | 22,145 | 24,195 | 64,875 |
| Bight of Benin | 1,516 | 1,943 | 1,075 | — | — | 3,558 | — |
| Bight of Biafra | 3,550 | 15,354 | 6,167 | 7,105 | 5,231 | 15,712 | 13,448 |
| Angola Coast | 2,522 | 7,714 | — | 1,820 | — | 5,913 | — |
| Unnamed Destination | 1,573 | 1,588 | — | — | 4,840 | 3,258 | — |

Source: Davies, *Royal African Company*, 233. Emphasis added.

According to the Du Bois Institute database, the British Caribbean colony of Jamaica imported more Gold Coast Africans in the eighteenth century than any six colonies combined in the Western Hemisphere (see table 1.2). Due to the marked concentration of Gold Coast Africans in the British slave trade to Jamaica, this island colony witnessed the formation of a number of "Coromantee" or Akan-speaking communities, providing insight into trading linkages and parallel cultural developments in early-eighteenth-century New York.

As the most lucrative colony in the British Americas, Jamaica had an enormous demand for African imports. It was the destination of roughly 37 percent of all slave ships entering colonies in the British Americas during the eighteenth century; as a direct result, Jamaica became the center of an important reexport trade. The most significant destinations in this reexport trade were the Spanish colonies in the Caribbean and mainland South and North America. Beginning in the seventeenth century, between 15 and 20 percent of all enslaved Africans were redirected from Jamaica to Spanish colonies via the much coveted and extremely lucrative *asiento*, or slave-trading license. This trade relationship peaked after 1700 and went through a protracted period of decline between 1748 and 1783.[49]

In addition to providing Spanish colonies with enslaved Africans, Jamaica was the center of a transshipment trade network that connected to a number of British mainland possessions. During the eighteenth century, mainland colonies like South Carolina, Rhode Island, Virginia, Maryland, and New York received cargoes from Jamaica, though this facet of the intra-American slave trade was much smaller relative to the *asiento* traffic. David

Eltis estimates that this trade brought no more than 400,000 Africans from the Caribbean into what became the United States. Based on what is known about the African ethnic groups imported into the British Caribbean, we can deduce the ethnic composition of some of the cargoes intended for British North America though the transshipment network. Four regions supplied about 90 percent of the enslaved Africans entering Jamaica during the course of the eighteenth century. Africans from the Bight of Biafra, likely Igbos and others, represented 34.5 percent of all Africans from identifiable regions and embarked on ships headed to Jamaica. Africans from the Gold Coast (28.9 percent), West-central Africa (14.5 percent), and the Bight of Benin (11.2 percent) made up the remainder. The presence of a heterogeneous slave population seemingly supports the claims made by Sidney Mintz and Richard Price who contend that traders and planters engaged in the purposeful randomization of African imports. However, Jamaican planters chose which enslaved Africans to keep and which ones to ship elsewhere, resulting in a disproportionately high number of Akan-speakers remaining on the island.[50]

Though they largely agree with the randomization thesis, Trevor Burnard and Kenneth Morgan observe that "Anecdotal evidence abounds that Jamaican slave buyers were both aware of supposed strengths and deficiencies of particular African ethnicities and carried those prejudices into their slave-buying calculations."[51] If prejudices or preferences factored into slave purchasing, then it is likely that slave selling was influenced by similar forces. The *asiento* trade provides the best evidence for this point, as a disproportionate number of Africans from the Bight of Biafra and West-central Africa were reexported to Spanish colonies. Jamaican planters held on to as many Gold Coast imports as possible. Also, between 1701 and 1725, fully 45.7 percent of all Jamaican imports were from the Gold Coast, prompting David Eltis to note "three quarters of all slaves retained in Jamaica before 1725 probably were from the adjacent Gold Coast and Slave Coast."[52]

The structure of the reexport trade implies that Jamaica shipped Africans from the Bight of Biafra, West-central Africa, the Bight of Benin, and, to a lesser degree, the Gold Coast to New York during the eighteenth century. The British Caribbean in general was responsible for the bulk of enslaved Africans imported into the colony. During the first half of the eighteenth century, the top four sources for slave imports into New York were Jamaica (29.9 percent), Africa (25.6 percent), Barbados (15.3 percent), and Antigua

(8.6 percent). Barbados and Antigua had significant populations of Gold Coast Africans. Given the earlier Dutch emphasis on Gold Coast imports, it seems likely that Gold Coast Africans were active elements in the slave population of colonial New York.[53]

Eighteenth-century New York slave owners had a strong preference for slaves directly from Africa, as opposed to slaves imported from the British Caribbean, though this preference is not readily traced in the available import records. The partiality for direct African imports was ingrained in a series of import duties. In 1702, for example, New York began to tax imported slaves, a policy that would continue until the American Revolution. Slaves imported from Africa were taxed fifteen shillings while slaves from other American lo-cales, including the British Caribbean, were taxed at a rate of thirty shillings and above. By the 1720s, this rate of taxation had increased dramatically. Slaves imported from Africa were taxed £2 while others were taxed at dou-ble that amount.[54]

One reason for the different import duty schedules was the notion that Africans shipped from other colonies had undesirable characteristics such as physical weakness or rebellious temperaments. This assumption was epitomized in the 1718 African Duty Act passed by the New York City legis-lature. In addressing Governor Hunter, the legislature hoped that this duty would not be viewed as inconsistent with British interests because of the difference "betwixt the Duty of Negroes, brought directly from Africa and those brought from the Plantations; because it will encourage a direct im-portation from Africa, and discourage an Importation from the Plantations, by whom we are supplied with the Refuse of their Negroes and such Male-factors, as would have suffered Death in the Places from whence they came, had not the Avarice of their Owners, saved them from the publick justice by an early Transportation into these parts, where they not often fail of repeat-ing their Crimes."[55] In particular, Akan-speakers from the Gold Coast were perceived to be the most recalcitrant group in the British Caribbean and were likely a sizable portion of the "Refuse" and "Malefactors" sold to New York on the eve of the 1712 revolt.

The perception of Akan rebelliousness was ubiquitous in eighteenth-century commentary. As Daniel Littlefield notes, the English generally viewed the Gold Coast Africans as "especially hardy, ferocious if angered, unmind-ful of danger, unwilling to forgive a wrong, but loyal if their devotion could be captured."[56] In a 1727 report written by William Snelgrave—an English ship captain working with the Royal African Company in the Gold Coast—the Akan were viewed as prone to shipboard revolts: "I have been several Voyages, when there has been no Attempt made by our Negroes to mutiny; which, I believe, was owing chiefly, to their being kindly used, and to my Officers Care in keeping a good Watch. But sometimes we meet with stout stubborn People amongst them, who are never to be made easy; and these are generally some of the Cormantines, a Nation of the Gold Coast . . . We were obliged to secure them very well in Irons, and watch them narrowly: Yet they nevertheless mutinied, tho' they had little prospect of succeeding."[57]

Another contemporary source in full agreement with the notion of Akan recalcitrance was Edward Long, an eighteenth-century Jamaican planter and historian. In his discussion of the Jamaican Maroons, Long states that a "committee of the assembly, appointed to enquire into the rise and progress of this rebellion some time afterwards, reported, That it had originated (like most or all others that had occurred in the island) with the Coromantins; whose turbulent, savage, and martial temper was well known."[58] As a result of this association between Akan-speakers and slave revolts, lawmakers in Jamaica proposed a bill "for laying an additional higher duty upon all Fantin [Fante], Akim, and Ashantee [Asante] Negroes, and all others commonly called Coromantins, that should after a certain time, be imported, and sold in the island."[59]

### Akan Cultural Connections in the 1712 Revolt

In his description of the uprising, Rev. Sharpe noted that an anonymous free African conjurer rubbed powder into the clothing of slaves "to make them invulnerable."[60] This act may reveal where in Africa this conjurer originated and why the slaves involved in the uprising felt that his actions gave them a real advantage over their oppressors. Sharpe's account indicates that this African conjurer was not a slave.[61] Of the forty-seven Africans and Native Americans either giving testimony or facing criminal charges in the subsequent court trial, only one was free—Peter the Doctor. Described in the trial record as a free African laborer, Peter was the last person allegedly involved with the revolt to be tried. On May 30, 1712, he was accused of stabbing Joris Marschalck with a dagger but was not formally tried until June 3. After spending the entire summer in jail he finally went before the Supreme Court of Judicature on October 14. The trial lasted four days and, strangely enough, he was acquitted and discharged. He was apparently spared because the climate of the case had shifted dramatically by mid-June, owing to the actions of Attorney General May Bickley, who repeatedly prosecuted a slave named Mars belonging to a rival attorney—Jacob Regnier. After a third prosecution and acquittal, it became obvious to Governor Hunter and others that the attorney general had begun to use the trials to carry out personal quarrels.[62] By June 12, Governor Hunter reprieved six of the seven slaves still awaiting trial, claiming in a letter to the Lords of Trade on June 23 that "more have suffered than we can find were active in this bloody affair."[63] In another letter dated September 10, 1712, Governor Hunter further stated, "There has been much blood shed already on that account, I'm afraid too much, and the people are now easy."[64]

Though Peter was to remain in jail through the entire summer, New Yorkers had grown weary of the trials and were perhaps apt to acquit him after the various abuses of authority Bickley had committed. During the trial no testimony was presented regarding Peter's role as a sorcerer, to which Rev. Sharpe had alluded likely based on Robin Hooghlandt's confession. The reasons for this are unclear but may be due to some of the problems the Anglican Society for the Propagation of the Gospel in Foreign Parts and Trinity Church faced in the revolt's aftermath. A great deal of scrutiny was placed on the society's activities and on Elias Neau, a Huguenot Catechist of Trinity Church who operated a school for the Christian instruction of Africans and Native Americans. Neau's catechetical school, which operated from 1705 to 1723, instructed as many as one hundred slaves at the height of its influence. However, the 1712 revolt would decidedly change popular sentiments regarding the religious instruction of slaves in New York City.[65]

According to David Humphreys, secretary of the society, the revolt "opened the Mouths of many, to speak against giving the *Negroes* Instruction. Mr. *Neau* durst hardly appear abroad for some Days, his School was blamed as the main Occasion of this barbarous Plot." After further investigation, New Yorkers discovered that "but two, of all his School, so much as charged with the Plot; and only one was a baptized Man . . . Upon full Trial, the guilty *Negroes* were found to be such as never came to Mr. *Neau's* School." Despite this evidence, Humphreys concludes that "a great Jealousy was now raised and the common Cry was very loud, against instructing the

Negroes."[66] Rev. Sharpe adds that "Upon the Whole as y^e Christian Religion had been much Blasphemed, and the Society's pious design has been much obstructed, by the bloody Attempt of y^e Negroes." He would later claim that "The school was charged as the cause of the mischief, the place of conspiracy and that instruction had made them cunning and insolent. The Catechism and all that were known to favour the design were reproached, and the flagitious villany was imputed to the Catechumens."[67]

In this volatile environment, Rev. Sharpe perhaps wanted to keep his distance from court officials, especially since the confession he obtained would only further implicate Robin—one of the two slaves instructed at Neau's School—in the planning of the rebellion. This could only create more scrutiny on the society's activities and the proselytizing efforts of Elias Neau. It is quite likely, then, that Peter was spared because of Rev. Sharpe's concerns regarding the society's support of Neau's catechetical school. The 1712 trial would not be the last time Peter the Doctor appeared in the records of colonial New York City. Three years later, on February 1, 1714, he was brought before the Court of General Sessions on the charge that he was illegally entertaining slaves in his East Ward home. After being found guilty of entertaining one Sarah Walton without her master's permission, "Doctor Peter" was fined £10.[68]

The role Peter likely played in the New York City revolt becomes clearer when seen alongside similar evidence from other Atlantic world locales. During a rebellion in Jamaica in 1760, a slave named Tacky, who was claimed to be "Kormantin," led a rebellion with the aid of a number of Obeah doctors.[69] A spiritual practice similar in form and function to Haitian Vodun or Cuban Santeria, Obeah became a very troublesome phenomenon for British, Dutch, and Danish slaveholders throughout the Americas. In the early phase of the rebellion, one of the Tacky's doctors was captured. Edward Long, the Jamaican planter and chronicler of Tacky's Revolt, described the man as "an old Coromantin, who, with others of his profession, had been a chief in counseling and instigating the credulous herd, to whom these priests *administered a powder, which, being rubbed on their bodies, was to make them invulnerable:* they persuaded them into a belief that Tacky . . . could not possibly be hurt by the white men, for that he caught all the bullets fired at him in his hand, and hurled them back with destruction to his foes. This old impostor was caught whilst he was tricked up with all his feathers, teeth, and other implements of magic . . . he was so easily put to death, notwithstanding all the boasted feats of his powder and incantations."[70] Like this Obeah man, the sorcerer in Sharpe's account rubbed powder onto the New York slaves to create the same desired effect. This connection suggests that Peter the Doctor was possibly an Akan-speaking Obeah doctor.[71]

A specific Akan presence can be found in the contemporary accounts of the 1712 New York City revolt and the subsequent trial records. Of the twenty-eight Africans facing criminal charges in connection with the uprising, nine had Akan day-names. In Governor Hunter's report to the Lords of Trade on June 23, 1712, he mentions that a slave named "Coffee" was responsible for setting fire to an outhouse at the beginning of the revolt.[72] "Coffee" was a popular anglicized version of the Akan day-name for a male born on a Friday—Cuffee. In total two Cuffee's, four Quacko's, a Quashi, a Quasi, and a female named Amba were among the slaves accused of involvement in the rebellion. Seven of the nine slaves with Akan-day names were found to have played some role in the revolt, and four were executed.[73] In addition, a slave named Jack may have also been Akan. The names "Jack" and "Joe" were often English variants of the Akan names "Quack" and "Cudjo."[74] With few exceptions, Akan children receive a first name determined by the actual day of their birth (see table 1.4). On reaching adulthood, the original day-name is typically used in conjunction with familial names, and its continued use creates a sense of camaraderie, which often transcends gender lines, among those born on the same day.[75]

Many of the slaves charged in connection with the revolt could not speak English. A young male slave by the name of Dick Burger served as a court interpreter. Dick had been charged in the coroner's inquest with the murder of William Asht on April 9, but he and Cuffee Vantilborough received immunity in return for services rendered to the Crown. The court drew on Dick's skills on several dates, including April 11, 12, 14, 16, and 17; May 7, 20, and 27. Significantly, Dick interpreted for the majority of cases involving enslaved Africans with Akan day-names. These were, in all likelihood, people born in the Gold Coast who had just recently arrived in the Americas.[76] Based on Dick's participation in the proceedings, a reasonable conclusion would be that at least eleven or twelve of the twenty-eight slaves facing charges, not including the six unnamed slaves who committed suicide before capture, spoke and understood a variant of Akan.

TABLE 1.4. Akan Day-Names

| | GOLD COAST | | AMERICAS | |
| Day of the Week | Male | Female | Male | Female |
| --- | --- | --- | --- | --- |
| Sunday | Kwasi, Kwesi | Akosua | Quash, Quashy, Quashie | Quasheba |
| Monday | Kwadwo, Kojo | Adwoa | Cudjo (Joe) | Juba, Addie |
| Tuesday | Kwabena | Abenaa, Abenaba | Cubena | Benni, Beneba |
| Wednesday | Kweku, Kwaku | Ekuwa, Akua | Quacko, Quack (Jack) | Cubba |
| Thursday | Kwaa, Yaw | Aba, Yaa | Quao, Quaw | Abba, Auba |
| Friday | Kwefi, Kofi | Efiwa, Afua | Cuffy, Cuffee, Coffee | Pheba |
| Saturday | Kwame, Kwamena | Amba, Amma | Quamina, Quamino | Amba, Mimbah |

Sources: Pitman, "Slavery on British West India Plantations," 641; Dolphyne, A Comprehensive Course in Twi, 14; Camp, "African Day-Names in Jamaica," 139; Handler and Jacoby, "Slave Names and Naming in Barbados," 699.

## Obeah and Resistance in the Caribbean

In addition to the likelihood that Peter the Doctor was an Akan-speaker, he was possibly an Obeah doctor. As Monica Schuler asserts, the Akan in the Americas "were particularly distinguished, especially in the records of slave trials, by their belief in obeah—a supernatural force given to man to protect and heal him (the term also refers to the charms which derive their power from this force), and by their Akan day-names."[77] As a spiritual system with significant and direct links to Gold Coast Africans, Obeah was a familiar term and practice in regions that imported large numbers of Akan-speakers. The word "Obeah" possibly derives from the Akan word "Obayifo," which denotes witchcraft and sorcery in the Akan spiritual universe.[78] The "fo" suffix is added to all proper names in the Akan family of languages.[79] By dropping the suffix, the resulting word is "Obayi," which was linguistically and phonetically transformed into "Obeah," "Obia," and "Obi" throughout the Americas.[80] Another possibility is that "Obeah" derives from the Twi word "Obeye," which refers to a spiritual being inhabiting a diviner. As a major subset of the Akan family of languages, Twi was perhaps the most widely spoken language in the Gold Coast and includes both Fante and Asante as its most prevalent variations. Either etymology would place the linguistic origins of the word in the Gold Coast.[81]

Another plausible origin of the word is discussed in separate works by historian Douglas Chambers and anthropologists Jerome Handler and Kenneth Bilby. These scholars contend that the correct etymology for the term, and the true origin of the spiritual practice, can be found among the Igbo of the Bight of Biafra. They assert that the Igbo term *dibia*, meaning healer or divine priest, was transformed into "obia," "Obeah," and other phonetic variations in the Anglophone Americas.[82] Chambers states ,"As in Igboland, therefore, obeah men (and sometimes women) in the Caribbean were diviners, doctors, and petitioners who specialized in finding out why things happened in daily life."[83] This contention regarding the links between this practice and Igbo culture is given support by the Du Bois Institute database, which shows that both Jamaica and Barbados—regions in which Obeah flourished—imported a large number of Africans from the Bight of Biafra. Given the presence of Obeah in regions that did not import a large percentage of Africans from the Bight of Biafra (e.g., the Dutch Caribbean, the Guianas, and Antigua) or evidence of Obeah doctors with obvious Akan day-names, Handler and Bilby are probably correct when they write that the spiritual beliefs and practices associated with this concept "have multiple origins in African ethnic groups." While considerable debate exists regarding the cultural origins of Obeah, there is no doubt that Akan-speakers throughout the Americas embraced this practice and utilized it to their collective advantage.[84]

Obeah often served as an important impetus to, and shaping influence for, Akan slave revolts in the Americas. One example would be the 1685 Jamaica revolt. During the initial stages of this revolt, the Akan-speaking insurgents attacked the Widow Guy's estate but were forced to retreat, "having lost one of their conjurors, on whom they chiefly depended."[85] The Leeward Maroons of Jamaica, a community established after 1690, were led by an Akan-speaker named Cudjoe who often relied on the advice of an Obeah man. A contemporary witness who visited the Leeward Maroons during the 1730s noted, "They were very superstitious having during their State of Actual Rebellion, a Person whom they called *Obea Man* who they greatly revered, his Words Carried the Force of an Oracle with them, being Consulted on every Occasion."[86]

In 1728, a figure named Queen Nanny emerged as the military and spiritual leader of the Windward Maroons in Jamaica. Her name was likely derived from a combination of two Akan words: *nana*, a term used to denote a respected chief or elder; and *ni*, which translates as "first mother."[87] Her role was a very familiar one for Akan-speakers; Queen Nanny not only led the independent Akan polity in eastern Jamaica known as Nanny Town, she was also described in contemporary accounts as an "Obea woman." Queen Nanny's involvement in the First Maroon War, 1724–39, was facilitated by her alleged abilities to catch bullets with her hands or between her thighs (or *Nantu-compong*), to heal injured warriors, and to produce magical charms that rendered her soldiers invulnerable.[88]

In Antigua, at least three separate Obeah men—Caesar Matthew, John Obia, and Quawcoo Hunt—were instrumental in a 1736 conspiracy. Both John and Quawcoo administered Akan oaths of loyalty involving drinking a concoction made from a mixture of blood, graveyard dirt, and rum. Quawcoo was known in contemporary documents to be "a Negroe Obiaman, or Wizard, who acted his Part before a great number of Slaves . . . and assured them of Success." He was so frightening a figure that Quamina—a slave who turned King's evidence and betrayed the plot—confessed to court officials: "By God if you had not Catched me I would not have told you now. I am afraid of this Obey Man now, he is a Bloody fellow, I knew him in Cormantee Country."[89]

Obeah also played a role in Jamaica following the Second Maroon War, 1795–96. In 1798, a group of Akan-speakers led by a man named Cuffee conspired to kill their masters and establish their own independent community. In planning the revolt, Cuffee consulted on at least one occasion with Old Quaco—an Obeah doctor who reportedly used a magic anklet to determine the movements of the colonial militia.[90]

Edward Long related the following account regarding the influence of Obeah doctors in eighteenth-century Jamaica:

> The most sensible among them fear the supernatural powers of African *obeah-men*, or pretended conjurers; often ascribing those mortal effects to magic, which are only the natural operation of some poisonous juice, or preparation, dexterously administered by these villains . . . Not long since, some of these execrable wretches in Jamaica introduced what they called the *myal dance*, and established a kind of society, into which they invited all they could. The lure hung out was, that every Negroe, initiated into the myal society, would be invulnerable by the white men; and, although they might in appearance be slain, the obeah-man could, at his pleasure, restore the body to life . . . Not long ago, one of these myal men, being desirous of seducing a friend of his to be of their party, gave him a wonderful account

of the powerful effects produced by the myal infusion, and particularly that it rendered the body impenetrable to bullets; so that the Whites would be perfectly unable to make the least impression upon them, although they were to shoot at them a thousand times.[91]

In this case, the belief that Obeah could render individuals invulnerable had tragic results. After the man who joined this group received his protective preparations, "he stood up to receive the shot." His friend fired a pistol and "killed him dead."[92] This story illustrates that the belief in the power of Obeah doctors was so complete that slaves were often willing to accept risks they would not ordinarily take. This is one of the reasons that regions in the Americas with the presence of both Obeah and Akan-speaking slaves witnessed so many conspiracies and rebellions during the eighteenth century.

The central importance and influence of Obeah doctors in slave rebellions throughout the Western Hemisphere has an important analogue in eighteenth- and nineteenth-century Gold Coast militaries. According to Monica Schuler, Obeah doctors and Akan divine priests performed essentially the same functions:

> The role of the obeah man in the Akan slave rebellions, for instance, is very like the role of priests and magicians in Ashanti military campaigns. Before a military campaign the principal commanders of the Ashanti army met with the priests at night and participated in a ceremony designed to weaken the enemy each time it was repeated. Priests also recommended propitious days for advancing and attacking, usually consulting oracles. Individual soldiers and companies also had recourse to magic. Each company had a shrine and a priest of its own. The priests (*esamankwafo*) also accompanied the soldiers on their campaigns and provided them with protective charms and amulets, some of which were believed to make their wearers invulnerable to bullets.[93]

Because priests often accompanied armies in the Gold Coast, some of them were likely captured and sold to European merchants as slaves. The priest's role in Akan militaries is confirmed by the account of an eighteenth-century eyewitness. Willem Bosman, who served as a Dutch factor on the Gold Coast in the early 1700s, observed what he considered an undue influence priests had over Akan military affairs. Without the aide of these divine priests, the Akan were "not easily induced to attempt a Battle; they advice them against it, under pretence that their Gods have not yet declared in favour of them;

and if they will attempt it notwithstanding, they threaten an ill Issue . . . In short, let the Event prove how it will the Priest is infallibly Innocent, and his Character always maintains its own Reputation."[94]

Like their Gold Coast counterparts, Obeah doctors in the Americas used spiritual forces to bring about desired effects and actions. The effect could be either positive or negative depending on the specific scenario in which an Obeah man or woman was employed. Similarly, Akan priests in the Gold Coast often employed *aduru*—medicine in the form of liquid or powder—as well as magical amulets (*suman*) in their incantations. *Aduru* can be categorized as benevolent medicine (*aduru pa*), malevolent medicine (*adubone*), or poison (*aduto*).[95] The powders used by Peter the Doctor in New York City and the Jamaican Obeah doctors would most likely be categorized as benevolent *aduru pa* because they sought to provide protection from evil agents and to increase the likelihood of success in these revolts. Powders and other forms of benevolent *aduru* function because of the spiritual power they naturally contain. The plants, herbs, human blood, graveyard dirt, and other substances that might comprise the powders, amulets, and other spiritual or magical implements all contain a certain amount of spiritual power—or *sunsum*—which, under the proper preparations, could prove quite powerful in the hands of Obeah doctors.[96]

By rubbing powder onto the clothing or bodies of slaves, the Obeah doctors sought the positive end of using spiritual forces to protect slave insurgents from physical harm. For this to work, slaves had to believe in the doctors' power to alter the outcome of events that humans normally could not determine. Objective observers may call into question the actual effectiveness of Obeah charms and spells. Whether or not Obeah doctors really wielded spiritual forces is not the heart of the issue. If enslaved Akan-speakers believed in the power of Obeah doctors, that belief alone would boost morale and give them a psychological edge in their endeavor to secure their freedom. In the hands of relatively powerless slaves, Obeah became an important weapon in their struggles throughout the Americas.

### *Blood and Graveyard Dirt: The Akan Loyalty Oath*

Participants in the 1712 revolt joined in an oath ceremony that involved, according to Rev. Sharpe, "the Conspirators tying themselves to Secrecy by Sucking y$^e$ blood of each Others hands."[97] Analogous activities are cited in a number of Akan rebellions in the Americas. In the months preceding the

1736 Antigua conspiracy, for example, slave rebels took an oath of loyalty administered by an Obeah man "by drinking a health of liquor with grave-dirt and sometimes cock's blood infused, and sometimes the person swearing laid his hand on a live cock."[98] Presumably, this ritual helped maintain silence and unity as the rebels made their destructive plans. On another occasion in the planning of the 1736 Antigua revolt, two slaves, Johnno and Secundo, "went Down to a Silk Cotton Tree to the Grave of Secundo's Sister Cicile and talked at the Grave . . . [T]hey returned to Secundo's house, Secundo bringing up some grave Dirt in his hands; he put some of it in a Glass, and then poured Rum on it out of a Bottle and Drank the Damnation oath to Johnno."[99] Secundo reportedly "Spoke to him in *Cormantee; Drank* to him and Said, Here Country Man (Chawa Worra Terry) i.e. Cutt your Masters head off."[100]

One of the slaves involved in the Antigua revolt was banished to St. Croix, where he helped plan another rebellion in 1759. The rebel named Qwau—who had turned king's evidence and testified against his own father in the trials following the Antigua revolt—joined with and led a number of other Akan-speaking insurgents in the formation of the St. Croix plot. Once again, the ubiquitous loyalty oath was a central aspect of the rebellion. According to court records, an insurgent named Prince Qwakoe confessed that two slaves "cut themselves in the finger . . . mixed the blood with earth and water, and drank it with the assurance that they would not confess to the conspiracy no matter what pain they were subjected to." Another captured rebel revealed that "the most binding oath that a Negro could take, was when he took earth from a dead Negro's grave, mixed it with water, and drank it."[101] In this case, however, the loyalty oaths did not prevent disclosure of the plot by the conspirators. After the governor of St. Croix ordered an investigation, two slaves with Akan day-names—Kwame and Kwadwo—were among a group of three conspirators who revealed key aspects of the plot, including a list of names.[102]

The Akan loyalty oath can be found in the 1760 Jamaica rebellion. The Obeah doctors who helped organize this rebellion administered an oath that included "a quantity of rum, with which some gun-powder and dirt taken from a grave had been mingled, blood was put, drawn in succession from the arm of each confederate . . . this cup was drunk from each person, and then came the council."[103] After this revolt failed, the oath of loyalty taken by the conspirators prevented betrayal by those who were captured and executed. One of the slave rebels named Cardiff reportedly warned, while being burned alive, that the "multitudes . . . took Swear, who now lay Still, that if they failed of Success in this Rebellion to rise again the same day two years."[104] There were disturbances in the region in 1761 and again in 1765. According to one contemporary source, the 1765 revolt involved many of these same oath-takers, who met in July of that year to form a new rebellious plot.[105]

Writing in 1774, Edward Long described the Akan loyalty oathing ceremonies performed by eighteenth-century Jamaican Maroons:

> Their priests, or *obeiah-men*, are their chief oracles in all weighty affairs, whether of peace, war, or the pursuit of revenge. When assembled for the purposes of conspiracy, the obeiah-man, after various ceremonies, draws a little blood from every one present; this is mixed in a bowl with gunpowder and grave dirt; the fetishe or oath administered, by which they solemnly pledge themselves to inviolable secrecy, fidelity to their chiefs, and to wage perpetual war against their enemies; as a ratification of their sincerity, each person takes a cup of the mixture, and this finishes the solemn rite. Few or none of them have ever been known to violate this oath, or to desist from the full execution of it, even although several years may intervene.[106]

Long was among a number of planters seeking to prohibit the continued importation of Akan-speakers into Jamaica because of the power of this type of oath and the constant threat of resistance.

Oaths were an important aspect of Akan societies in the eighteenth-century Gold Coast. Bosman spends considerable time discussing Akan oaths in his firsthand account of the cultural practices of Gold Coast inhabitants. According to him, "When they drink the Oath-Draught, 'tis usually accompanied with an Imprecation, that the Festiche may kill them if they do not perform the Contents of their Obligation. Every Person entring into any Obligation is obliged to drink this Swearing Liquor."[107] Known in the Akan family of languages as the *Ntam*, the oaths used by the eighteenth-century Asante were meaningful political tools that, in the words of J. K. Fynn, helped "to remind the people of the inseparable link between them and their dead ancestors who protected them."[108] According to James Patrick Hubbard, the *Ntam* was typically administered by divine priests at the beginning of a military campaign and was a virtually unbreakable pact: "Ashanti commanders in chief swore, as the original Osei Tutu had done, to pursue the war vigorously, not retreat, and to return the state sword encrusted with

the blood of the enemy. The force of the oath was such that, rather than return to Kumasi a failure, defeated commanders might blow up themselves
and their regalia with a barrel of powder."[109]

Blood and graveyard dirt therefore had obvious implications for Akan
rebels in the Americas. Blood represented the forged bond between the living, while the graveyard dirt bound the living to the ancestral spirits. Michael Mullin claims that the use of blood in oathing ceremonies is mirrored
in practices among Akan-speaking societies in the Gold Coast. For the
Akan, blood "signifies nationality: it is public, it fixes one's legal and political existence, and it is used in oath rites to bind groups. No matter how
widely scattered, rite participants remained brothers—'all of one blood.'"[110]
As David Barry Gaspar concludes, "For the Coromantees, taking the oath
with grave dirt signified that the world of the living was intertwined with
that of the dead, that they were united with the ancestors, by whom they
swore to be true to their obligations or incur dreadful sanctions."[111] Combined, blood and graveyard dirt helped forge virtually unbreakable bonds
among Akan-speaking slaves in the Americas and greatly facilitated resistance efforts.

With the power of the ancestors, rebels believed they could achieve any
manner of extraordinary feats. Graveyard dirt linked the conspirators to
ancestral spirits, creating an inviolable oath. Severe sanctions followed a
broken oath. One contemporary witness in Jamaica, Charles Leslie, noted
in 1740 that Akan Maroons would "range themselves in that Spot of Ground
which is appropriate for the Negroes' Burying-place, and one of them opens
a Grave. He who acts the Priest takes a little of the Earth, and puts [it] into
every one of their Mouths; they tell, that if any has been guilty [of violating
the oath], the Belly swells and occasions their Death."[112] In a similar vain,
Bosman reports that early-eighteenth-century Gold Coast Akan held the belief that anyone guilty of violating an oath "shall be swelled by that [Oath]
Liquor 'till he bursts; or if that doth not happen, that he shall shortly die
of a languishing Sickness."[113] Thus, for those who adhered to this matrix of
spiritual beliefs, painful deaths were the ultimate penalty for conspirators
guilty of being disloyal to the ancestral spirits.

Though the records for the 1712 New York City revolt do not reveal the
particular elements of Peter the Doctor's spiritual arsenal, it is likely that
he was familiar with the uses and meaning of graveyard dirt. Graveyard dirt
was so commonly used by Jamaican Obeah doctors that the colonial legis-

lature, in direct response to the 1760 rebellion, passed a law that banned the use of "any materials relative to the Practice of Obeah or Witchcraft," including grave dirt, blood, feathers, rum, eggshells, and teeth from various animals.[114] This law was renewed in 1784 and 1788, stipulating "any Negro or other slave who shall pretend to any supernatural power, and be detected in making use of any blood, feathers, parrots-beaks, dogs-teeth, alligators-teeth, broken bottles, grave-dirt, rum, eggshells, or any other materials relative to the practice of Obeah or witchcraft, in order to delude and impose on the minds of others, shall . . . suffer death or transportation."[115] Other elements of the Obeah doctor's arsenal were revealed with the death of the notorious Jamaican Obeah bandit Three-finger Jack, who was slain by a Maroon in 1780. An inspection of his personal effects revealed "a goat's horn, filled with a compound of grave dirt, ashes, blood of a black cat, and human fat, all mixed into a kind of paste."[116]

### Akan Burial Customs, Spiritual Transmigration, and Suicide

It is unknown what items Peter the Doctor used in his protective powders or oathing ingredients; regardless, his actions can be linked to Obeah and Akan spirituality. The presence of this system of spiritual beliefs in colonial North America runs counter to the notion that Africans experienced a "spiritual holocaust" between 1680 and 1760. This view, as voiced by Jon Butler, contends that one of the most profound religious transformations before the American Revolution was "an African spiritual holocaust that forever destroyed traditional African religious systems as *systems* in North America and that left slaves remarkably bereft of traditional collective religious practice before 1760." The destruction of traditional beliefs facilitated the acceptance of Christianity by enslaved Africans and African Americans, which "more closely resembled European expressions of Christianity than might ever be the case again." Peter the Doctor and his belief system, however defined, represents at least one exception among many to Butler's conclusions.[117]

By examining the actions of the New York rebels in an Atlantic World context, it becomes quite obvious that they were linked to specific spiritual beliefs and systems. Although Butler might define Obeah as a "particular or discrete religious practice," and not a full-fledged religious system, the ubiquity, longevity, and sheer complexity of this practice clearly elevates Obeah above the level of a fragment surviving from a system that "collapsed in the shattering cultural destructiveness of British slaveholding."[118] The belief that African conjurers had the real power to interpret the unknown and avenge wrong meant that African slave rebels, whether Akan or not, brought their spiritual worldviews across the Atlantic; any discussion pertaining to an African spiritual holocaust may not reflect the endurance of this or any other African religious system.

The recently rediscovered African Burial Ground in New York City—the oldest and largest colonial-era African/African American graveyard in the United States—demonstrates, in tangible terms, that African religious beliefs did not simply dissipate upon reaching North American shores. Apparently dating back to the late 1630s, the first known statute for the creation of the African Burial Ground did not appear until October 23, 1684. This separate space for the burial of Africans was made even more necessary beginning in 1697, when Trinity Church prohibited the continued interment of Africans in its cemetery. In active use from the 1600s until 1796, the African Burial Ground was likely a central focus of African cultural activities in New York City.[119] In the aftermath of the 1712 revolt, Rev. John Sharpe reported that both free and enslaved Africans "are buried in the Common by those of their country and complexion without the office [Christian funeral service], on the contrary the Heathenish rites are performed at the grave by their countrymen."[120] As a portion of the Municipal Commons, the African Burial Ground was the main site for the executions of rebel slaves following both the 1712 uprising and the 1741 conspiracy.

In the 1850s David Valentine, writing about slaves buried there, noted that "Many of them were native Africans, imported hither in slaveships, and retaining their native superstitions and burial customs, among which was that of burying by night, with various mummeries and outcries."[121] African conjurers and priests, relying on religious and spiritual principles originating in their homeland, were among the individuals presiding over the ceremonies taking place at the graveyard and performed the various "heathenish rites," as well as the other "mummeries and outcries" mentioned by Sharpe and Valentine. The burial ground served as a shared cultural space, allowing Africans from a variety of ethnic backgrounds to engage in collaborative efforts ranging from spiritual ceremonies and rituals to acts of resistance. The "spiritual holocaust" discussed by Butler cannot fully explain these religious activities.

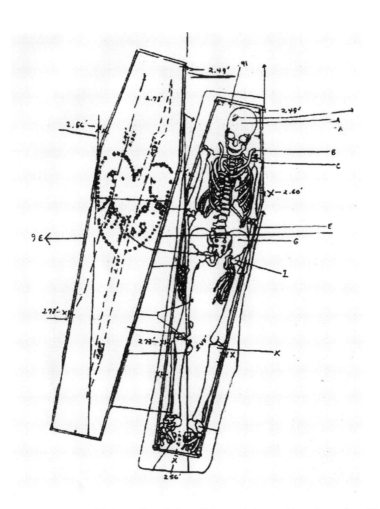

FIGURE 1.3. Possible heart-shaped Akan *Adinkra* symbol created by tacks on the coffin lid of Burial #101. *Photo furnished by the U.S. General Services Administration.*

Though only 427 of approximately 20,000 graves were excavated by November 1993, it is clear from this small sampling of remains that certain African cultural practices were frequently carried out at the burial ground. Of particular note is the coffin lid on "Burial #101" excavated in New York City on December 15, 1991 (see fig. 1.3). The lid has ninety-two metal tacks arranged in a heart-shaped pattern, which, according to Kwaku Ofori-Ansa—a Ghanaian historian of African art—is a representation of the Akan

*Adinkra* known as *Sankofa*. The *Sankofa* symbol would be quite appropriate on a coffin or grave-marker because, as Ofori-Ansa claims, "The symbol expresses the Akan social thought that espouses the essence of tying the past with the present in order to prepare for the future." *Sankofa* symbolizes the concept of spiritual transmigration among Akan-speakers. It requires one to look to the past in order to understand the present—a notion fully intertwined with the belief that every human being has lived many past lives.[122] Joyce Hansen and Gary McGowan, however, contend that the symbol found on Burial #101 is a different heart-shaped Akan *Adinkra* known as *Akoma*. *Akoma* means patience and is typically a symbol of endurance and perseverance. This interpretation of the symbol would also be fitting since patience and endurance were attributes that were highly valued by those forced to live in such debased and constrained conditions.[123]

There is, however, a great deal of uncertainty regarding the historical origins of Akan *Adinkra* symbols. The exact genesis of the *Adinkra* symbols is unknown, but a number of accounts point to an early nineteenth-century conflict between two Akan states: Asante and Gyaman. According to legend, the king of Gyaman, Kwadwo Adinkra, created a copy of the famous Asante Golden Stool for his own uses. This act incensed the Asante king (or *Asantehene*), Osei Bonsu, who sent an army to defeat Gyaman and capture Adinkra. After Adinkra was beheaded, his Golden Stool was stripped of its precious metal, revealing dozens of symbols that have since been known as *Adinkras*. The war between Gyaman and Asante occurred in 1818–19, so if the legend is true, it would be highly unlikely that the symbol found on the coffin of Burial #101 has any link to the Akan *Adinkra*. In the historical account of the conflict between Asante and Gyaman, no mention is made of a false Golden Stool or the discovery of the symbols. As a result, there is no method of accurately dating the origins of these symbols.[124]

More plausible connections to Africa were found in other graves at the African Burial Ground. Researchers have discovered as many as ten different filing patterns on the front teeth of a number of the skeletal remains found at this site which were consistent with Gold Coast and West-central African styles. Burial #340, which contained a clay pipe and 111 beads of various types, also points to a strong connection to African cultural vectors. Michael Blakey, anthropologist and scientific director of the African Burial Ground Project, surmises, "The string of 111 glass beads and cowrie shells around the waist of one woman's burial . . . suggest that she belonged to an Akan-speaking society in which such beads are buried with their owner. A quartz crystal and examples of shells buried with human remains point to a variety of African society's burial customs."[125]

Interment with personal items is a custom that has been long traced to several West and West-central African cultures. Confirmation of this practice in the eighteenth-century Gold Coast can be found in Willem Bosman's 1705 description of Akan religious beliefs. In describing Akan funerary customs, he notes that people were often interred with "fine Cloaths, Gold *Fetiches*, high-prized Corals, *Conte di Terra*, and several other valuable Things."[126] Large amounts of broken pottery were also found at the African Burial Ground. According to Robert Farris Thompson, this practice has a definite African origin: "The deliberate decoration of graves in the African manner with surface deposits of broken earthenware and possessions [can be found] in many parts of the Deep South." Thompson links this practice to the Akan of the Gold Coast, as well as to other West African groups.[127]

In addition to being a space for African spirituality and ritual, the African Burial Ground was also a space for slave resistance on a number of levels. As mentioned previously, it was the principal location for the executions of slaves involved in the 1712 and 1741 disturbances. Furthermore, Burial #25 excavated on October 16, 1991, provides some insight into the end result of rebellious activities in eighteenth-century New York City. The twenty-two-year-old woman interred in this grave was found with a musket ball in her rib cage, significant blunt force trauma to her lower skull and a diagonal fracture along her right forearm. Based on a forensic examination of her skeletal remains, it appears that she was shot in the back, severely beaten, and then restrained by someone who twisted her arm—thus causing the fracture. Since the fractures on her lower skull and arm had not healed, she likely suffered these injuries in the last hours or minutes of her life. Whether she was one of the slaves killed during the 1712 revolt will probably never be known. It is plausible, however, that she died during some act of resistance to white authority. Physical anthropologists studying the remains at the site have found distinct signs indicating that in at least two cases individuals were burned to death—a capital punishment associated with enslaved Africans found guilty of arson, rebellion, or murder.[128]

To prevent slave collaboration, colonial officials in 1722 and 1731 prohibited the slave customs of burying the dead at night and covering coffins with funeral palls. Such customs were not necessarily of African origin.

Nighttime funerals were necessary because slaves worked long hours during the day. The use of coffins was definitely derived from European practice. However, using cloth to cover the body of the deceased was a custom associated with Gold Coast Africans. Covering the coffin in cloth is an intriguing intersection of Akan and European funerary customs. After this practice was outlawed, slaves simply wrapped the dead in funeral shrouds and nailed the coffins shut. Evidence of the ubiquity of this adaptation can be seen in the five hundred shroud pins found at the African Burial Ground.[129]

With the new laws, funeral services had to be observed during daytime hours. Passed on October 6, 1722, the first "Law for Regulating the Burial of Slaves" was a direct response to the legitimate fears New Yorkers had of slave rebellion.[130] In a subsequent elaboration and extension of this law, the Corporation of New York stipulated in 1731 that no more than twelve slaves were allowed to gather at the burial site during a funeral on penalty of public whipping. The revision also prohibited the use of funeral palls since it was thought that slaves could conceal weapons in the cloth placed over coffins. New Yorkers' fears were made explicit in this law, its writers feeling that at funerals slaves "have great Opportunity of Plotting and Confederating together to do Mischief, as well as Neglecting their Masters service."[131] In 1748 and 1763, the "Law for Regulating the Burial of Slaves" would be reissued in order to quell additional concerns regarding slave collaboration.[132]

While certain funerary customs in New York's African Burial Ground may have had links to various African ethnic groups, suicide is another distinct practice that has connections to Akan culture. According to contemporary accounts, as many as six slaves involved in the 1712 uprising committed suicide before being captured by the militia. John Sharpe notes in his description of the revolt that "some of them in their flight shot themselves . . . some who had hid themselves in Town when they went to Apprehend them Cut their own throats." In one case, an anonymous slave rebel shot his wife and then himself.[133] On the one hand, these men may have taken their own lives to avoid being tortured, burned alive, or broken on the wheel—fates suffered by many of those who were captured and convicted. On the other hand, the act of suicide fully resonates with the actions of Akan rebels throughout the Atlantic World and, given the Akan belief in transmigration, suicide can also be viewed as a form of spiritual resistance.

Suicide as an ethnic or cultural "trait" is usually associated with Bight of Biafra imports, especially Igbos, in the Americas. As Daniel Littlefield contends, the principle reason why they were among the least desirable of African slave imports was due to the perception among American planters that Igbo or Calabar slaves had "a deplorable penchant for committing suicide."[134] More recently, Michael Gomez has summarized the historical and contemporary view of Igbos, noting that "the sources are therefore unanimous in ascribing to the Igbo greater self-destructive tendencies."[135] These perceptions had some basis in reality and will be discussed more fully in the coda. Suicide was never directly associated with Akan-speakers as a particular behavioral trait. The historical record aptly demonstrates, however, that self-destruction was a frequent response by enslaved Akan rebels involved in failed resistance movements or Akan soldiers and military leaders involved in failed campaigns in the Gold Coast. Their belief in spiritual transmigration prefigured these self-destructive modes of action.

Writing during the early eighteenth century in Jamaica, Charles Leslie notes that Akan-speaking slaves "look on death as a blessing . . . are quite transported to think their slavery is near an end, and that they shall revisit . . . their old Friends and Acquaintances."[136] As Ray Kea reports, a seventeenth-century governor of the Danish West Indies claimed that the Aminas (Elminas) or Akan-speaking slaves were "the worst runaways of all Blacks [and] they believe that at their death they return to their fatherland, or as they express it: 'mij dodte mij loppe in myn lande.'" Translated from Dutch Creole, this statement is rendered as "when I die, I shall return to my own land."[137] Kea's research is the most direct evidence that Akan-speakers in the Americas continued to believe in transmigration and used this concept as a means to facilitate resistance efforts. As a result of the failed slave rebellion in the Danish West Indies, thirty-six Akan rebels committed suicide between May 4 and May 15, 1734, after Danish rule was reestablished on St. John's Island. Suicide represented the ultimate contingency plan for Akan-speaking slave rebels. As Kea notes, "Death signified the end of the Amina slaves' absence from their homeland." If they could not enjoy physical freedom on this plane of existence, suicide allowed them to be reborn in Africa as free people.[138] Obviously, such a belief could inspire slaves engaged in otherwise hopeless resistance movements.

These actions and beliefs have parallels in a number of abortive Akan revolts in the Americas. In assessing eighteenth-century Akan rebellions in Jamaica, Edward Long discusses the use of firearms, Obeah doctors, oathing ceremonies, and "if at length their secret designs are brought to

light, and that hypocrisy can no longer serve their turn, they either lay violent hands on themselves, or resist till they are disabled."[139] As Orlando Patterson notes, one eighteenth-century planter in Jamaica would display the
corpses of dead Akan slaves as proof to others that they did not return to
Africa upon death. He did this in the hopes that it would discourage Akan-
speaking slaves from rebellion and suicide.[140] Yet despite their wariness of
Akan beliefs and conspiracies, European planters grudgingly admired one
Akan trait: their heroic courage. Bryan Edwards, an eighteenth-century Jamaican planter, noted that the Akan were known to have "a ferociousness
of disposition; but withal, activity, courage, and a stubbornness . . . which
prompts them to enterprizes of difficulty and danger; and enables them to
meet death, in its most horrible shape with fortitude or indifference."[141]

This courage and "ferociousness of disposition" was tied into Akan spiritual beliefs and ensured persistent rebellion. For example, a large group of
Gold Coast slaves rebelled on Easter Sunday 1760 in a number of parishes
throughout Jamaica. When the Akan-speaking slaves in Westmoreland parish faced the combined forces of the 49th British Regiment and a contingent of Maroon mercenaries, a number of the rebels committed suicide to
avoid defeat and capture. During the campaign against the St. Mary's parish
Akan revolt, once again Maroon mercenaries were employed by the British
to infiltrate the ranks of the rebels and disrupt the uprising. Maroons managed to kill two of the principal rebel leaders, Tacky and Jamaica, prompting
the seemingly disheartened survivors to retreat to a cave and commit mass
suicide. During the final stages of the 1760 slave revolt, the militia reported
that seven or eight additional rebels were discovered hanging dead from
trees, having apparently killed themselves.[142]

According to Monica Schuler, this pattern had its origins among Akan
military commanders in the Gold Coast. Suicide was considered an hon-
orable fate and much preferred to capture. As a result, a pact to commit
suicide was often a feature of state oaths given by military commanders.
Willem Bosman observed that Akan oaths were "usually accompanied with
an Imprecation, *that the Fetiche may kill them if they do not perform the Contents
of their Obligation* . . .When a Nation is hired to the Assistance of another all
the Chief ones are obliged to drink this Liquor, with an Imprecation, that
their *Fetiche* may punish them with Death, if they do not assist them with the
upmost Vigour to extirpate their Enemy." Anyone violating the terms of an

oath was doomed to "be Swelled by that Liquor 'till he bursts; or if that doth not happen, that he shall shortly die of a languishing Sickness."[143] Again, suicide must have seemed an attractive alternative when failing to live up to the terms of an oath invited shame and a painful death brought on by powerful spiritual forces.

### African Sociopolitical Currents in the 1712 Revolt

The firearm, a weapon used by the participants in the 1712 revolt, provides another direct link to West Africa. Gold Coast Africans were very familiar with the use of guns in the late seventeenth and early eighteenth centuries. Europeans introduced firearms to West Africa as early as the 1590s when the Dutch sold limited amounts of muskets, gunpowder, and musket balls at the coastal trading ports they frequented. By the mid-seventeenth century, the English began to sell large quantities of muskets and gunpowder in Gold Coast regions including Takoradi, Little Komenda, Kromantine, Winneba, and Accra. By the 1660s, firearms were increasingly integral components of Gold Coast military arsenals. This military revolution meant that, by the end of the seventeenth century, entire Gold Coast armies were armed with muskets.[144]

During the late seventeenth and early eighteenth centuries, Lower Guinea witnessed a vast expansion of slave exports in the transatlantic trade. According to Willem Bosman, the early eighteenth century was when the Dutch sold "incredible quantities" of firearms, which had become "the chief vendible Merchandise" in the Gold Coast trade.[145] The Dutch sold these arms to expansionist Akan states such as Akwamu, Denkyira, and Asante. The armies of these states engaged in military campaigns that stretched hundreds of square miles.[146] This extended battlefield led to the rise of mass armies of commoners instead of smaller armies composed of professional soldiers. Battles often involved tens of thousands of soldiers, and each side captured numerous prisoners of war.[147] Many of the Akan war captives, soldiers with knowledge of the use of firearms, were among those ensnared in the net of the transatlantic slave trade during this period.

In the contemporary accounts of the 1712 incident, specific mention is made of the rebels having "stood in the Streets and Shot down and Stabbed as many as they could."[148] Likewise, Governor Robert Hunter in his account of the 1712 revolt claims that slaves were "provided with firearms" and "upon the approach of severall [whites] the slaves fired and killed them."[149] New York did not allow the enlistment of enslaved Africans in the colonial militia, but if some of the enslaved Africans in New York were formerly soldiers who had received military training in Gold Coast armies, then their ability to use firearms makes sense.[150]

West African sociopolitical undercurrents, as well as the more obvious cultural vectors, prefigured events in colonial New York City. Ray Kea has discussed the possible presence of Gold Coast military commanders and soldiers in American slave revolts. In his analysis of the 1733–34 Danish West Indies rebellion, Kea is able to identify the presence of specific military leaders from a defeated Akan state—Akwamu—who helped spearhead this revolt.[151] Likewise, according to John Thornton, "Another instance where African military experience probably played a role in American revolts comes from Jamaica in the late seventeenth and early eighteenth centuries. Here a series of powerful revolts led by 'Coromantees' . . . threatened the island on a number of occasions. Indeed Coromantee revolts would trouble Jamaica, and occasionally the other islands and the mainland (where they revolted in New York in 1712), throughout the eighteenth century. In 1675, upon hearing of an alleged conspiracy in Barbados, Governor Adkins advised that the Coromantees were a great threat to the island, as they were warlike and robust."[152]

Former soldiers obviously had the skills and training necessary to foment rebellion, which explains, in part, why African polities were so eager to sell them to European merchants. Those trained in the martial arts represent destabilizing elements when captured and forced into slavery, which was one of the best reasons for selling them to foreign traders. Clearly, some of the enslaved Africans imported into Euro-American colonies would be predisposed to rebel. Many North American slave owners faced a similar problem. Being forced to rely on the Caribbean for the bulk of their slaves, they knowingly imported the most rebellious and intractable of the enslaved population. As a result, the transshipment trade from Jamaica and other British Caribbean possessions may have funneled a high percentage of former soldiers to North American colonies.

The possible presence of African soldiers in colonial New York City can be found in a contemporary description of a Pinkster festival appearing in a 1737 edition of the *New-York Weekly Journal*. The anonymous "Spy" who wrote the serialized account reports "the Negroes divided into Companies,

I suppose according to their different Nations . . . The Warriors were not idle, for I saw several Companies of the Blacks, some exercising the Cudgel, and some of them small Sticks in imitation of the short Pike."[153] Pinkster, the Dutch celebration of the Pentecost or Whit-Sunday, included a three- or four-day holiday, which allowed the enslaved population in New Netherland additional freedoms and time away from work. Though New York's Pinkster festival had distinctly Dutch origins, it was a biracial celebration during its beginnings in seventeenth-century North America. It would eventually be entirely appropriated by enslaved Africans in the eighteenth and nineteenth centuries, when Pinkster was celebrated in New York City, Albany, Kingston, Poughkeepsie, and elsewhere in the region. According to the 1737 account, Africans divided themselves according to their nations at the outset of the festivities and seemingly performed military drills. The lack of other contemporary accounts prevents much speculation about how representative the 1737 festival was. By the late eighteenth to early nineteenth centuries, one of the central elements of Pinkster was the coronation of an African "king" who presided over the various activities.[154]

It is plausible that the Pinkster kings were former military, political, or spiritual leaders originally from West-central African or Gold Coast states.[155] Were enslaved Africans in New York attempting to create symbolic replicas of their native polities? The actions of Akan-speaking Africans in other regions of the Americas suggest that this may have been the case. Maroon communities with Akan majorities in Jamaica and Surinam created independent states through resistant actions, appointed their own royalty and government officials, and relied heavily on spiritual understandings of the world that were uniquely Akan in nature.[156] Unable to establish and sustain their own independent states, the Akan of eighteenth-century New York might have sought to create a symbolic polity complete with soldiers, nobility, and divine priests.

The Akan-speakers forming the various real and symbolic polities in the Americas may have formerly been enemies from warring states in the Gold Coast. In creating a common condition and enemy, slavery helped forge a collective identity among Akan-speakers by eliminating previous rivalries and conflicts among Gold Coast Africans. This common "Akan" identity was not present in the Gold Coast and was unique to the Americas. A similar process occurred among other African "nations" and ethnic groups.[157] In New York City, the revolt of 1712, the activities at the African Burial Ground, and the festivities associated with Pinkster may have been elements of the contours of this new collective cultural and sociopolitical identity developing among the Akan in eighteenth-century North America. This was the first step of many in creating a collective "African," and later "African American," identity.

# CHAPTER 2

# "Only Draw in Your Countrymen"
## The 1741 New York City Conspiracy Revisited

*Demographic and Social Factors in New York, 1712–1741*

The fear of slave rebellion had no discernible impact on the slave trade or on the demand for enslaved Africans in New York after 1712. Slaves from the Caribbean and Atlantic Africa accounted for 35 percent of all immigrants entering the port of New York between 1732 and 1754. While the vast majority of these slaves entered by way of the British Caribbean, an increasing number of Africans were shipped to the colony directly from West Africa. Between 1715 and 1764, roughly 25 percent of all slaves entering New York had an African point of origin, and most of these were children under the age of thirteen. Whether Africans came directly from West Africa or the Caribbean, New York was to continue to have a discernable concentration of Akan-speakers from the Gold Coast in its enslaved population well into the eighteenth century.[1]

Enslaved Africans were unknown variables for the most part, but they came to New York without many of the dangerous characteristics said to be found among Caribbean slaves. One reason was that so many of the African imports were children, who, for obvious reasons, were seen as more tractable and less likely to initiate organized revolts. Contemporary observers believed that particular African ethnic groups were more prone to rebellion, but slaves transported from the Caribbean were almost certainly sold as a result of either bad health or as a result of some act of violent resistance. Hence, directly importing slaves from Africa seemed the safest and most logical way to increase the enslaved population in New York. Proposals were made to reduce or completely eliminate the restrictive duties that slowed the number of direct imports from Africa. Despite these efforts, however, New Yorkers continued to buy enslaved Africans primarily from the Caribbean.[2]

On December 20, 1726, New York governor William Burnet notified the Lords of Trade that import duties were not being collected for slaves entering the colony directly from Africa. In his estimate, this was the fault of the Royal African Company because "no Agent of that Company has been of late appointed to demand their dues."[3] These duties were initially instituted to protect company interests while simultaneously generating revenue for the colonial government. Though tariffs were imposed on all imported slaves, those imported directly from Africa were taxed at half the rate of slaves imported from the Caribbean during the eighteenth century. Since the company held a virtual monopoly on the African trade to British America, the prejudicial tariffs benefited its financial interests by making it more difficult for shippers not commissioned by the company to dominate the slave import market in New York.[4] Of course, not collecting duties would benefit those seeking to purchase slaves in New York. Because of its monopoly, the Royal African Company could guarantee a more profitable voyage for ships sailing from West Africa to New York if duties were not imposed on its cargoes. Private importers seeking to circumvent the company's monopoly would generate more revenue if they could avoid paying duties as well. Likewise, buyers of slaves would be able to purchase them at a cheaper price. However, the collection of import duties generated sizable government revenues for the colony, which explains Governor Burnet's concerns.

One Rip van Dam, acting governor of New York from 1731 to 1732, specified a method of circumventing the duty imposed on slave imports in a message to the Lords of Trade on November 2, 1731: "A Ship Belonging to this Colony with a considerable number of Negroes on Board her, in her voyage from Africa, touched at Antegua to purchase some provisions and Refreshments but landed none of her Slaves there, and then came to the Province of New Jersey, where there is no duty paid for any Slaves imported, but the owner of the vessel being desirious to import the greatest part of them into this province, if he might be allowed to pay only the duty of five ounces of plate for every head."[5] Since New Jersey did not impose duties on imported slaves from 1721 until 1767, shippers were often encouraged to land their slave cargoes there and transport them overland to New York. In this way, unscrupulous importers could successfully avoid paying New York's duties on slave imports. In the case van Dam describes, however, the ship's owner disembarked slaves in New Jersey but wished to pay the necessary import duties to have them sold in New York. Governor van Dam amended an existing law and allowed the owner of the ship to pay a much reduced import duty because it "would have been a considerable loss to the Revenue and might have encouraged the bringing them in clandestinely."[6]

Again, while it may have been mutually beneficial for both company and noncompany importers and New York slave buyers to avoid the collection of duties, government officials in the colony would not generate as much revenue if traders could successfully smuggle Africans into the colony. One anonymous ship managed to smuggle as many as 150 Africans into New York in 1726. This case may have been representative of a more pervasive phenomenon and demonstrates a source of direct African imports not officially counted in the Du Bois Institute dataset.[7]

Governor van Dam's successor, Colonel William Cosby, was appointed governor of New York in 1732 and given explicit instructions from the Lords of Trade to prohibit the imposition of duties on British imports in order to encourage more slave imports into the colony. Ignoring this dictate, Governor Cosby helped draft a new duty act in 1734 which continued the long-standing policy of taxing Caribbean slaves at twice the rate of those imported directly from Africa. The duty allowed the governor to continue generating revenue for colonial administration while filtering out the rebellious slaves likely to enter New York from the Caribbean; however, it was not very popular back in England. Merchants in Bristol petitioned for the repeal of Governor Cosby's import duty act, and on November 1, 1734, a committee of the Privy Council at Westminster submitted the petition to the Lords of Trade. The Lords of Trade regarded Governor Cosby's import duties as "greatly prejudicial to the Trade and Navigation of Great Britain" and a violation of their own explicit instructions. Eventually, the Lords of Trade ordered a repeal of the duty act and instructed Cosby to abide by a mandate that "no Duty be laid on any Slaves Imported payable by the Importer." As a direct consequence, the colony of New York would begin to force slave buyers to pay duties, effectively shifting this responsibility away from importers.[8]

The effort to increase the importation of slaves was successful. According to Mary Booth, by 1741 "New York was literally swarming with negroes, and presented all the features of a future Southern city, with its calaboose on the Commons and its marketplace at the foot of Wall street." With Africans and African Americans representing roughly 18 percent of its population in 1731, New York City continued to have the largest slave population of any city north of Baltimore. By 1746, slaves represented 21 percent of the total population in the city. The only factor preventing a more sizable increase in the slave population was that New York was not quite suitable for cash crops and, therefore, did not have the same enormous demand for enslaved Africans that was present in sugar-, rice-, or tobacco-producing regions in the British Americas. Nevertheless, slave imports and slavery were lucrative enough to continue in New York through the American Revolution.[9]

While slaves may have indeed "swarmed" the streets of New York, their numbers were not due to natural increases in the slave population. Men outnumbered women as much as two to one, and finding mates was a difficult prospect for many male slaves. In addition, the slave population was widely distributed. Slave-owning whites—accounting for 30 to 40 percent of all white households—typically owned between one or two slaves per household in early-eighteenth-century New York. With the severe legal restrictions on their mobility, it was difficult for young slaves to find mates. The growth in the slave population was principally due to the continued reliance on the slave trade.[10]

While the slave population was ever increasing, the number of free blacks in New York began to dwindle over the course of the eighteenth century. Joyce Goodfriend estimates that "not more than a dozen slaves were freed, either in wills or through instruments of manumission" between 1664 and 1712.[11] Despite the efforts of Governor Robert Hunter and the Lords of Trade to the contrary, manumissions became much more rare in the aftermath of the 1712 revolt. Instead, there was an increasing trend toward bequeathing slaves to relatives or selling them outright to other slave owners in wills. As Graham Russell Hodges notes, "Of 115 wills between 1712 and 1741, the largest number of bequests (forty-five) were to sons, with widows second (thirty-eight), daughters third (twenty-two), and nine instances of slaves ordered sold."[12] Thus the free black population in the city and throughout the colony would continue to be dwarfed by the numbers of enslaved Africans and African Americans.

One natural outcome of the increasing limitations on manumission was the effort by slaves to emancipate themselves. During the Dutch era, enslaved Africans routinely absconded to the northern forest of Manhattan Island and to Canada. The nations of the Iroquois Confederacy were well known for harboring escaped slaves. Governor Cosby even petitioned the Iroquois Sachems on September 8, 1723, for the return of runaways. In addition to the Iroquois Confederacy, the Minisinks of eastern Long Island gave

safe haven to slaves and even allowed them to become members of their societies. Government officials in the colony tried to induce Native American
nations to return fugitive slaves through treaties and the offer of monetary
rewards, but very few, if any, were ever returned to their owners. Colonial
leaders also created laws to severely punish runaway slaves. The New York
Assembly passed a law in 1705 that allowed capital punishment for any slave
captured more than forty miles north of Albany. There was little decline in
runaway attempts, and this law was reenacted in 1725.[13]

Some 776 slaves appear in runaway advertisements between 1711 and
1780. Those who fled New York City could not only flee overland to Iroquoia
or to Canada were they could seek asylum with the French, but they could
also escape by seeking refuge on ships. Merchant ship captains were frequently known to employ fugitive slaves on their vessels. This became such
a problem that colonial legislatures passed a number of acts between 1712
and 1730 imposing sizable fines on ship captains who willingly harbored
and employed fugitive slaves. This fact was not lost on slave owners. By the
1730s, runaway advertisements offered explicit reminders of these laws and
the penalties for those found in violation of them.[14]

Many slaves escaping from rural New York saw New York City as either
a temporary or permanent haven. New York City represented the possibility
of escaping by sea and the chance to simply "disappear" or pretend to be
free amid the teeming masses. Runaways were generally male slaves with a
median age of twenty-one. According to one study, as many as 80 percent
of all fugitives appearing in colonial New York runaway advertisements fit
this description. Fugitive slaves therefore formed a relatively homogeneous
group, which may explain the presence of a number of criminal street gangs
in colonial New York City composed primarily of fugitive slave men. Notable
among these were the Geneva Club (the Black Free Masons), the Smith's Fly
Boys, and the Long Bridge Boys—all of which reportedly played some role
in the 1741 conspiracy.[15]

The Geneva Club was the most notorious of these gangs; its history began with an infamous burglary in either 1735 or 1736. After robbing a tavern
keeper named Baker of a large amount of Geneva gin, a number of slaves
were captured and publicly whipped. From that time forward, they became
known as the Geneva Club. This gang was well organized, with its own
officers and code of conduct; it also had white fences who were more than
willing to purchase goods stolen by club members. Members also sought to

emulate or mock the style and form of European fraternal organizations—even referring to themselves on occasion as the Free Masons.[16]

While these gangs were not known to attack whites, colonial authorities nonetheless considered these cabals a serious threat to public order. The presence of black street gangs prompted legislators in the colony to take action.[17] The Common Council of New York City erected a series of codes in 1731 to regulate urban slaves and prevent the growth of criminal gangs. Of these codes was "A Law for Regulating Negroes and Slaves in the Night Time," which prohibited free blacks and slaves from being in "the Streets of this City, or in any Other place on the south-side of the fresh-water in the Night time above an hour after sun-set, without A Lanthorn and lighted Candle in it," as well as the permission of a "responsible" white male.[18] Those found in violation were jailed and received up to forty lashes at the public whipping post. The Code of 1731 also sought to ban gambling since it was seen to encourage theft and other criminal activities. The Common Council prohibited the assembly of more than three on Sundays, the disorderly riding of horses through the streets, and the carrying or ownership of firearms by slaves and free blacks.[19] Attempts to undermine criminal gangs through legislation were unsuccessful. These gangs would continue to be a public nuisance into the 1740s, with one major change. By the early 1740s, these street gangs became politicized and effectively transformed from criminal cabals into a revolutionary vanguard that may have sought to overthrow the colonial regime of New York.

*Details of the 1741 Plot*

The events surrounding the discovery of the 1741 slave plot apparently began on Saturday, February 28, with a burglary at the shop of a merchant named Robert Hogg. Items stolen from Hogg's shop on Broad Street included Spanish silver coins, linens, and other goods valued at about £60. After the theft, Robert Hogg's wife, Rebecca, recalled an encounter with eighteen-year-old Christopher Wilson three days prior. Wilson, a free black mate on board the medical warship *Flamborough*, frequently visited Hogg's shop on the pretense of meeting with two white servants working for people who rented rooms from the Hoggs. On this particular occasion, Wilson, accompanied by one of his shipmates, came to the shop to purchase linen and paid for the items with a Spanish nine-penny silver piece. Mrs. Hogg recalled that she had pulled out a money drawer full of "milled Spanish pieces of eight" in full view of Wilson. After she realized the wrong she committed in "exposing her money to an idle boy . . . who came so frequently to her house," Mrs. Hogg immediately closed the drawer.[20]

According to later court testimony, Wilson informed three disreputable slave men—Caesar Vaarck, Prince Auboyneau, and Cuffee Philipse—of the Spanish silver he had seen at Hogg's shop. All three men were leaders of the Geneva Club. Court testimony also reveals that Wilson "told them the situation of the house and shop; that the front was towards Broad-street, and there was a side door out of the shop into an alley, commonly called Jews-Alley . . . they might get an opportunity to shove back the bolt of the door facing the alley, for there was no lock on it." Though it appears that Wilson was not part of the criminal scheme himself, he consciously divulged sensitive information regarding Hogg's shop and its vulnerabilities to men he knew would likely do something about it.[21]

On Sunday, February 29, Mrs. Hogg questioned Wilson regarding the burglary. In her sworn deposition, Mrs. Hogg noted that Wilson claimed to have seen silver coins similar to the ones stolen being exchanged at a tavern owned by John Hughson near the North River: "At the house of one Hughson . . . he saw one John Gwin whom he saw pull out his pocket, a worsted cap full of coined silver; and that Philipse's Cuffee came into Hughson's . . . and seeing John Gwin have this money, he asked him to give him some, and he counted him out half-a-crown in pennies." She immediately informed authorities, prompting an inspection of Hughson's tavern and a search for the British soldier named John Gwin who allegedly played some role in the theft. However, no soldier named Gwin could be found, and nothing of consequence was discovered at Hughson's tavern. As it later turned out, "John Gwin" was actually an alias of Caesar Vaarck—one of the leaders of the Geneva Club. When authorities returned without any evidence, Mrs. Hogg questioned Wilson once again to obtain any additional details regarding the theft. It was at this point that Wilson implicated the slave Caesar Vaarck by name, whereupon an order for his arrest was issued and carried out by local constables.[22]

Caesar was jailed on Sunday, March 1, and examined by justices the next day. Since he had been arrested previously in connection to this robbery and released due to a lack of evidence, there is no reason to believe that Caesar felt he was in any more danger this time around. No material evidence could be found and, to this point, only the testimony of Wilson stood against him.

As Thomas J. Davis contends, "[Caesar] knew the constables had found nothing on him, and he was sure there were no witnesses to the burglary. He trusted Prince, as he trusted himself, to say nothing . . . and he expected Hughson also to keep quiet, because under New York law the knowing receiver of stolen goods was as liable as the thief: The ultimate punishment was the same—death."[23]

When Caesar denied involvement in the theft, authorities then detained Prince, John Hughson, and his wife, Sarah, for questioning. Still no satisfactory evidence was found or presented. This would all change on March 3, when Mary Burton—Hughson's sixteen-year-old indentured servant—admitted knowledge of the theft to Anne Kannady, the wife of a constable investigating the case. According to Anne Kannady's deposition, Burton claimed that Constable James Kannady "was not cute enough," for he had not found the stolen goods at Hughson's tavern even though he had "trod upon them." Mrs. Kannady informed undersheriff James Mills who visited Hughson's house to interrogate Burton further. The servant presented silver coins to the investigators which proved to be some of the stolen coins. According to Burton, Hughson had been employed as a fence for goods stolen by this criminal gang and other black street associations in New York City. The Hughsons would be formally charged with receiving stolen property—a crime punishable by death.[24]

Once Burton began to reveal further details regarding the theft at Hogg's shop and other criminal acts, a number of suspects were arrested. In the midst of the continued investigation into the theft ring and the subsequent arrests, several mysterious fires destroyed both private homes and public buildings throughout New York City. Ten fires between March and April 1741 consumed some rather strategic locations including, among others, the governor's house, the King's Chapel, and the soldiers' barracks. The first fire was the worst of all; it began March 18 at noon on the roof of the governor's house, and within two hours it had consumed much of Fort George, the headquarters of royal government in the province. High winds spread the fire to other buildings. Only a timely rainfall the next day saved the city from further destruction. Since New York City at the time of these blazes was an urban strip about one mile long and one-half mile wide with heavily concentrated clusters of wooden buildings, fire could potentially destroy everything built on the settled portion of Manhattan Island. Arson could be an extremely effective tool for insurrection.[25]

Two events put increasing suspicion on the enslaved population in the city. The first took place on the morning of Sunday, April 5, when Abigail Earle overheard a conversation among three slaves walking up Broadway toward Trinity Church. One of the slaves, Quaco Walter, allegedly stated to his companions "Fire! fire! Scorch! scorch! A LITTLE damn it BY AND BY!" after which he threw his hands in the air and laughed.[26] The next day there were four fires reported in the city. Within hours of hearing Quaco's words, Abigail Earle reported them to an alderman. When called before court officials on April 6, Quaco admitted to making the statement but denied that it meant he was involved in a conspiracy to burn the city. Giving what the judges considered a "cunning excuse," he claimed that he and his companions were talking about British Admiral Edward Vernon's taking of Porto Bello, Jamaica, from the Spanish. Quaco "thought that was but a small feat to what this brave officer would do by-and-by, to annoy the Spaniards," and even brought his two companions to court to attest to this interpretation. The court was "apt to put a different construction" on Quaco's statement, interpreting his words to mean "that the fires which we had already seen, were nothing to what we should have by-and-by for that then we should have all the city in flames, and he would rejoice at it." Seven fires erupted between April 4 and April 6, making Quaco's words seem even more alarming and pushing Lieutenant Governor George Clark to order a full military watch for the next few months.[27]

The second precipitating event involved a slave named Cuffee Philipse—one of the Geneva Club's triumvirate of leaders. He was seen acting in a very suspicious manner during a fire that threatened to destroy a building owned by his master. On Monday, April 6, Colonel Adolph Philipse's storehouse was set on fire at about four o'clock. Though the fire was soon extinguished, one man on the scene, Jacobus Stoudenburgh, witnessed Cuffee leap from the window of the building shortly after most of the people who helped put out the fire left to attend to another blaze several blocks away. Because the slave left the scene with "great haste" and "very good speed," Stoudenburgh cried out "*a negro; a negro . . . that the negroes were rising.*" Once the identity of the slave was known, the cry changed to "*Cuff Philipse, Cuff Philipse*" and a crowd of whites dragged the suspect from Philipse's house to a nearby jail the same day.[28]

On May 29, one of the men who helped extinguish the fire at Philipse's storehouse, Isaac Gardner, testified that Cuffee was the same individual who had tried to prevent the crowd from putting out the fire. When buckets of water were handed to Cuffee, Gardner claimed that "instead of handing them along to the next man, he put them upon the ground and overset them, by which means the ground was at first dry and hard, became so wet that the witness who stood next to him, was almost up to the ankles in mud." In addition, Gardner testified that Cuffee "huzza'd, danced, whistled and sung" in a most inappropriate manner considering the emergency at hand. These actions, plus his flight after the blaze was extinguished, made a number of people conclude that he was responsible for the arson.[29] Both of these precipitating incidents involved slaves with Akan day-names—Quaco and Cuffee—which could have been cause for further fear, especially with memories of the Akan presence in the 1712 revolt lingering in the city.

On April 11, the Common Council proposed rewards for the capture of arsonists and their accomplices. By April 21, Supreme Court hearings of a number of suspected conspirators began with Frederick Philipse and Daniel Horsmanden presiding. Mary Burton, the indentured servant who played a role in unraveling the earlier theft ring, was offered £100 and her freedom when she began to implicate various people in a massive plot to destroy the city by fire. According to trial testimony and court depositions, the planning of the revolt began to accelerate at the time of the disclosure of the burglary at Robert Hogg's shop. Two of the principal ringleaders—Caesar Vaarck and Prince Auboyneau—plotted to burn and loot the entire city, with the ultimate goal of establishing a black or biracial regime in New York. While it was clearly established in evidence and testimony presented to court officials that there were indeed biracial links in the theft ring and other criminal activities, there was also sufficient proof of the existence of a biracial scheme to destroy the city, kill most of its inhabitants, and end slavery.[30]

The conspirators would frequently gather at Hughson's tavern in open violation of laws prohibiting such nocturnal meetings. Hughson was not the only person guilty of entertaining slaves; during the trials, no fewer than ten keepers of public houses in New York City were charged with entertaining slaves after curfew and serving them liquor. This sort of freedom of movement and assembly greatly facilitated slaves and other conspirators in their elaborate schemes. They even employed the services of a slave conjurer named Doctor Harry who created an incendiary substance used to set fire to buildings throughout the city. On certain occasions, arson was used as a cover for burglary; in other instances the fires seem to have been purely strategic. The conspirators reportedly planned on "burning the king's house at [Fort George], and this whole town, and . . . murdering the inhabitants as they should come to extinguish the flames."[31]

According to the testimony of various informants, as many as twenty to thirty conspirators would typically meet at Hughson's tavern to discuss the plans. The plot was formed sometime after Christmas 1741 and involved as many as fifty individuals including slaves, white indentured servants, and other lower-class whites. Under the leadership of Cuffee, Caesar, and Prince, the rebels had reportedly accumulated seven or eight guns, several bags of shot, a keg of powder, swords, and a large quantity of knives "sharp enough to cut [off] a white man's head." Hughson had reportedly used the silver coins stolen from Hogg's shop to purchase some of these weapons. A drummer named Tom Rowe was appointed to signal the beginning of the revolt, which was to start on St. Patrick's Day. The rebellion would commence with the destruction of Fort George by fire. The reason for this particular action was purely tactical. In his confession, Dundee Todd noted that "there were too many guns in the fort, so they were to burn that first." Bastian Vaarck testified that "Hughson proposed burning the fort before any thing else; because at a former rising [likely the 1712 revolt], the white people ran into the fort; he said if that was set on fire it would blow up the powder, etc." In this manner then, it was hoped that as many whites as possible would die inside the fort after it was set on fire. Once the entire city was ablaze and the inhabitants subdued or killed, Caesar would be appointed as governor and Hughson king of New York.[32]

In addition to killing most of the white population, the conspirators pledged "to kill such of the negroes as would not assist them." Though a number of the rebels later testified that they would kill both their masters and mistresses, there was also explicit mention in court testimony of slave men "killing the gentlemen and taking their wives to themselves."[33] Whether this claim was a reflection of the irrational fears of white authorities or a practical reaction by black men to the shortage of black women in the colony will never be known. We do know that fears of the existence of interracial sexual relationships and either criminal or politically inspired biracial collaborations were voiced by a number of contemporary whites during the course of the trials.

Juror William Smith's summation of evidence presented at the trials exemplifies white elite concerns regarding biracial collaborations in New

York: "Gentlemen, no scheme more monstrous could have been invented; nor can any thing be thought of more foolish, than the motives that induced these wretches to enter into it! What more ridiculous than that Hughson . . . should become *King*! Caesar, now in gibbets, a *Governor*! That the white men should be all killed, and the women become prey to the rapacious lust of these villains! That these slaves should thereby establish themselves in peace and freedom in the plundered wealth of their slaughtered masters!"[34]

The concepts of social leveling and racial equality were considered vile enough, but for black men to dare think about taking white women as wives was to be prevented and discouraged at all costs. Court records reveal that Margaret Sorubiero was "a person of infamous character" not because she had conspired to kill fellow whites but because she was a "notorious prostitute, and also of the worst sort, a prostitute to negroes." Sorubiero was reportedly impregnated in the fall of 1740 by Caesar, one of the leaders of the theft ring, and this fact was supposedly proven because her child was "largely partaking of a dark complexion." Though Mary Burton would tell Anne Kannady that Sorubiero's baby was "as white as any of [Kannady's] children, or any other child" and that Caesar was not the father, Caesar did acknowledge later to court officials "his sleeping with [Sorubiero]." Although she turned king's witness, the court later decided to convict and execute Sorubiero, the so-called "Irish beauty."[35]

The conspirators developed a number of contingency plans in case the plot was betrayed or otherwise foiled. Doctor Harry, a conjurer from Long Island, had produced poison to be taken by captured conspirators so that they could avoid painful tortures and executions. Another contingency plan reportedly created by a white shoemaker named John Romme went as follows: "If the fire did not succeed, and they could not compass their ends that way; then he proposed to the negroes present, that they should steal all that they could from their masters; then he would carry them to a strange country, and give them their liberty, and set them free." Likewise, Jack Murray confessed to court officials that Hughson expected aid from French and Spanish forces and after the city had been burned and plundered, he promised to "carry them off into another country."[36]

While there was no proof that France or Spain had actually committed to direct involvement in this revolt, slaves who confessed to their role in the conspiracy consistently made such a claim. Court officials found this notion easy to believe because England was at war with both Spain and France in the late 1730s and early 1740s. The events of the War of Jenkins' Ear (1739–41), the War of Austrian Session (1740–48), and King George's War (1741–48) were well known to the inhabitants of New York City.[37] In addition, General James Oglethorpe of Georgia presented a letter to Lieutenant Governor Clarke dated May 16, 1741, which was used as proof of Spanish collusion in the New York conspiracy. After interrogating a captured Spanish soldier from St. Augustine, Florida, Oglethorpe claimed there was indeed sufficient evidence of Spanish involvement in the 1741 conspiracy: "Some intelligence I had of a villainous design of a very extraordinary nature, and if true, very important, viz. that the Spaniards had employed emissaries to burn all the magazines and considerable towns in the English North-America, thereby to prevent the subsisting of the great expedition and fleet in the West Indies. And for this purpose, many priests were employed who pretended to be physicians, dancing masters, and other such kinds of occupations, and under that pretence to get admittance and confidence in families."[38] As a result of this evidence, a number of Catholics and suspected papists were arrested in connection to the New York conspiracy, including several Irish soldiers.

The "country" Romme and Hughson promised to carry slaves to could have easily been French Canada or Spanish Florida. Canada was the likely destination of a number of individuals escaping New York once the conspiracy was betrayed. As many as five people connected to the plot somehow managed to escape the dragnet, including a slave named Cuff Jamison, a free black butcher named Frans, and three white men—an unnamed soldier, Robert Saunders, and John Earl—were implicated but never found or arrested for their alleged roles in the conspiracy. John Romme reportedly said that if the revolt failed, he would "make his escape, and go to North Carolina, Cape Fear, or somewhere thereabouts; or into the Mohawk's country, where he had lived before."[39]

The amount of biracial collaboration in this conspiracy was unprecedented in the history of North American slave resistance. The trial testimony hints at one of the forces that allowed this cooperation. In his deposition on May 29, 1741, Fortune, a slave owned by John Wilkins, noted that "Cuffee used to say, that a great many people had too much, and others too little; that his old master had a great deal of money, but that in a short time, his master would have less and himself have more." For certain conspirators, this plot had dual goals—the abolition of slavery and social leveling. The black criminal gangs had used these disparate goals to provide a political framework for their activities. This notion is exemplified in evidence used against whites connected to the plot. According to the testimony of Margaret Sorubiero, John Romme, a white man intimately involved in this conspiracy, observed in front of a group of slaves "how well the rich people at this place lived, and said, if they . . . would be advised by him, they . . . should have the money." Romme's intentions may not have been altruistic; like Hughson, he had probably been a fence for stolen goods procured by black street gangs. He in fact suggested that "he . . . should captain over them . . . till they could get all their money, and then he (Romme) would be governor." Though the slave conspirators appeared to agree with most of Romme's propositions, they found this last to be untenable. To the suggestion that Romme would become their "captain" and "governor," Cuffee responded that the slave conspirators "could not do it."[40]

Because of the sheer complexity of the conspiracy, contemporary observers assumed that whites like Hughson and Romme had to be central figures in its formation. They believed that the Africans and African Americans lacked the necessary intelligence and creativity. Daniel Horsmanden, third judge of the Supreme Court of Judicature and recorder of the trials, assumed that "white people were confederated with them, and most probably were the first movers and seducers of the slaves; from the nature of such a conjunction, there was reason to apprehend there was a conspiracy of deeper design and more dangerous contrivance than the slaves themselves were capable of." His doubts were due to the "great secrecy" and the "utmost diligence" required to create and maintain such an elaborate plot. The circle of suspicion therefore expanded beyond just young black men and began to include all "alien" (e.g., non-Protestant or non-English) elements present in New York City. Thus colonial authorities assumed that a "Popish" priest, an Irish prostitute, five Spanish-speaking slaves, several Irish soldiers, and other professors of the "murderous" and "bloody" religion of the Catholics were part of this larger conspiracy against Protestant English rule in North America.[41]

On June 10 the attorney general claimed that the planned slave insurrection "may justly by called *Hughson's Plot*" because Hughson was the "chief contriver" and "director" of the plan.[42] The attorney general went on to detail, on June 13, the principal reasons why whites had to be the leaders of the revolt:

*Gentlemen*, I shall shew you by the witnesses for the king upon the trial of these five negroes, that they, with many others, frequently met at Hughson's house, where they entered into a confederacy with and were sworn by him, to carry on this most wicked and villainous plot . . . to bring all their booty to him, to enrich him and make him great. Thus were these stupid wretches seduced by the instigation of the devil, and Hughson his agent, to undertake so senseless as well as wicked enterprize . . . Gentlemen, it cannot be imagined that these silly unthinking creatures (Hughson's black guard) could of themselves have contrived and carried on so deep, so direful and destructive a scheme, as that we had prepared for us, without the advice and assistance of such abandoned wretches as Hughson was.[43]

It was this sort of underestimation of black intelligence that lulled New Yorkers and other North American slaveholders into a false sense of security regarding their chattel property.

In the madness that consumed New Yorkers for two summer months, 150 slaves and twenty-five whites, including seventeen soldiers, were arrested. It is highly unlikely that the theft ring and slave conspiracy involved any more than fifty people. Moreover, the existence of a papal conspiracy led by the suspected Catholic priest, John Ury, is quite doubtful. However, a massive panic, similar in magnitude to the one that plagued Salem in the early 1690s, ultimately led to the deaths of many innocent slaves and whites. After a lengthy and emotional trial, four whites were executed, including Hughson and his wife Sarah, Margaret Sorubiero, and John Ury. Of the 150 slaves incarcerated, thirteen were burned alive, sixteen were hanged, two were starved in chains, and seventy were banished from the province. Not surprisingly, the first two slaves condemned to death on May 30, 1741 had Akan day-names—Quack and Cuffee.[44]

### Historical Perspectives on the 1741 Plot

Unlike the 1712 revolt, the 1741 conspiracy generated substantial commentary from contemporary participants and witnesses.[45] The best and most detailed primary source is Daniel Horsmanden's *Journal of the Proceedings in the Detection of the Conspiracy Formed by Some White People, in Conjunction with Negro and Other Slaves, for Burning the City of New York in America, and Murdering the Inhabitants,* published in 1744 and reissued as *The New York Conspiracy* in 1810 and again in 1971. At the time of the alleged conspiracy, Horsmanden was recorder of the City of New York, third judge of the Supreme Court of Judicature, and judge of the Admiralty Court. His role in the court proceedings for the 1741 conspiracy was significant, and his *Journal* serves as both a detailed record of the investigation and trials and as an account of his own personal, and therefore subjective, assessment of the events.[46]

Thomas J. Davis, editor of the 1971 version of *The New York Conspiracy*, estimates that less than 15 percent of the Horsmanden's *Journal* is personal commentary. The subjective element of this valuable work is therefore quite limited and does not overly distort the evidence revealed in the court proceedings and confessions. Davis adds, "The prejudice he demonstrated during the proceedings and his reputation as a career partisan in New York politics leave no question about his objectivity. On that basis alone many scholars have immediately dismissed the *Journal*."[47] Horsmanden's subjectivity does not change the fact that the work is one of the few that records the collective voices of the slaves involved in the plot, but historians have raised legitimate questions about the reliability of the *Journal* and the veracity of much of the evidence presented in court.

Acting out of fear and anxiety, whites overreacted and exaggerated the extent of the plot, leading many modern historians to conclude that, in fact, no conspiracy existed. A close read of Horsmanden's *Journal* demonstrates, however, that much of the evidence presented at the trial can be corroborated by testimonies and confessions slaves and whites provided. Admittedly, some of the trial testimony was given under duress, but some was given freely and willingly—a fact ignored by a number of the conspiracy's detractors. By itself, Horsmanden's *Journal* may not be enough to prove the existence of this plot. Examined within the context of the 1712 uprising and the various accounts of British Caribbean Akan revolts, the evidence revealed in the *Journal* becomes more useful and meaningful.

Historians have long questioned both the existence of an organized rebellious plot and the usefulness of Horsmanden's *Journal*. One of the first black historians of note, George Washington Williams, was the first to doubt the plot when in 1883 he compared the 1741 trials to the alleged 1679 Popish plot in England led by Titus Oates. In both cases, "the evidence that convicted and condemned innocent men and women was wrung from lying lips of doubtful characters by an overwrought zeal on the part of legal authorities." Because the one "historian" of the 1741 affair was also a trial judge, Williams warns his readers to take Horsmanden's account *cum grano salis*. He points to the various flaws in Mary Burton's testimony, the incentives given to the condemned to lie and make false testimony, the court's reliance on individuals of unscrupulous character and motive, and the significant use of unreliable or circumstantial evidence in the proceedings.[48]

The first twentieth-century analysis of the conspiracy appeared in the June 28–August 23, 1902, edition of the *New Haven Saturday Chronicle*. The piece, written by Walter Franklin Prince, begins by comparing the alleged conspiracy to the Salem witchcraft trials. Noting that even the length of the trials—eleven months—was the same in both cases, Prince adds that "the trials of 1741 in the City of Manhattan Island exceed in frenzy, cruelty, and horror, those of Massachusetts in 1692 . . . they even constitute the crowning perversion of criminal justice in the annals of American history."[49] The first part of this statement is quite true. Of the twenty individuals tried and executed in Salem for the crime of witchcraft, nineteen were hanged while one was pressed to death with heavy stones; on the other hand, fourteen slaves accused of taking part in the 1741 plot were burned alive—a punishment suffered only by blacks according to laws throughout the British colonies.[50] More specifically, Prince accuses Horsmanden of excluding any exculpatory testimony from his *Journal* in a conscious attempt to hide evidence of judiciary misconduct and prejudice. The *Journal*, according to Prince, "only needs a detailed examination of that which [Horsmanden] selected to show how flimsy and unsound were the conclusions reached." Much of the evidence presented is deemed "worthless," "stupefying," "fragmentary," and "darkly tragic."[51]

Among the many others who followed in the footsteps of Williams and Prince were scholars like Roi Ottley who claimed "Conspiracy! Actually there was none."[52] T. Wood Clarke notes in a 1944 assessment of the conspiracy that once Mary Burton was offered her freedom from servitude and £100 in exchange for testimony, "her tongue and her imagination were loosened." Like the bewitched young women of Salem fifty years earlier, Burton had the uncanny ability of "concocting" fantastic stories that were fully believed by court magistrates. According to Clarke, the judges in their rush to find the parties responsible for the theft ring and the numerous arsons, overlooked obvious incongruent elements in Burton's account. She claimed, for example, that "the whole plot was to be carried out under cover of darkness," but most of the fires had started during the daytime. Margaret Sorubiero, in an obvious effort to receive a pardon, falsely implicated seven black men whom she accused of being part of an oath-bound cabal. Burton however denied that these men were involved; as a result, Clarke claims that a "rivalry" arose between the two women.[53]

Clarke's picture of the alleged conspiracy also closely matches the Salem witchcraft trials. All the necessary ingredients were present for this parallel: young, lower-class white women seeking social acceptance, a besieged populace willing to accept any sort of explanation for the troubles threatening their community, a court that exonerated liars who "confessed" while executing innocent people, and a large amount of dubious testimony—spectral evidence in Salem and "Negro" evidence in New York City—used to condemn the accused to death sentences. Clarke points out that the madness only stopped when Burton began to accuse people of high standing. He shows that "judges and the city magistrates became frightened . . . with lightning striking so near their own homes."[54]

Edgar McManus continued this trend of scholarly inquiry in 1966 when he argued it was Burton's "sensational accusations," her "lurid testimony," and her "confused tale" that led to the trial and execution of numerous innocent people. Resisting the impulse to place the 1741 plot in the context of the Salem witchcraft hysteria, McManus instead claimed that the 1712 revolt was the event that "set the stage for a bloody panic a generation later." Like Clarke, McManus doubts much of Burton's testimony. He also notes that the accused had less than adequate legal protection since practically every lawyer in New York refused to help with the defense. Hence, "this boycott not only crippled the defense but encouraged the prosecutor . . . to use tactics which the mere presence of a defense counsel would surely have prevented." One such tactic was the use of a convicted thief—Arthur Price—to spy on people accused of involvement in the arsonist plot still awaiting trial. Price did indeed testify against Quack and Cuffee, and his evidence ultimately led to their executions. McManus also points out the numerous examples of hearsay evidence and the testimonies of slaves against whites used in the trials. Even the most inept defense attorney would have objected to the use of such evidence since both forms would have been inadmissible under normal circumstances.[55]

Citing the large number of scholars that doubted the existence of the 1741 plot—including Joseph C. Carroll, Cleveland Rodgers, R. B. Ranken, E. Franklin Frazier, M. W. Goodwin, and Walter Franklin Price—Ferenc M. Szasz insists that "there existed no Negro conspiracy in 1741 to take over

New York." Instead, a number of smaller plots in some connection with each other sought to "rob the richer citizens of New York City." Szasz estimates that the various theft rings involved no more than five whites and three slaves total and contends that Horsmanden's *Journal* is "unquestionably false." The testimony provided by Burton was "preposterous" and "absurd," and he even questions whether slaves could successfully maintain a secret conspiracy without being detected by whites. Szasz concludes that the hysteria surrounding the conspiracy was likely provoked by an unusually harsh winter, coupled with an inadequate supply of food and constant military threats from Spain, France, and the Iroquois Confederacy. The trials and executions served a cathartic function for white New Yorkers, a conclusion Szasz arrives at despite his claim that "a psychological study of New York's *année terrible*" was "beyond [his] training and the materials available."[56]

Leopold Launitz-Schurer Jr. also references the "hard winter" of 1740–41 and fears of a Spanish invasion as precursors to the 1741 panic. His argument follows very closely the earlier assessment by Szasz. Launitz-Schurer suggests that the plot really amounted to an expansive criminal conspiracy with Hughson and the Geneva Club at the center. He focuses less on Burton's reportedly false testimony than on Horsmanden's very conscious attempt in his *Journal* to bend the evidence to his interpretation of the events. Ultimately, court magistrates were primarily responsible for elevating a theft ring to the level of a biracial conspiracy to overthrow the city's social, political, and religious order. This was due to the "fear and revulsion which the majority of white New Yorkers felt for whites who associated with blacks," such as John and Sarah Hughson, Margaret Sorubiero, and John Romme. Though Launitz-Schurer sees the trial of reported papist John Ury as a "farce" and based on the testimony of witnesses of "dubious reputation and character," he argues that Mary Burton may have been truthful in her descriptions of a black theft ring with Hughson and Romme serving as fences.[57]

There also has been a lengthy line of scholarship questioning the usefulness of Horsmanden's *Journal* altogether. Some have expressed doubts about whether slaves had the wherewithal to plan and execute such an elaborate plot. Others have focused on judicial misconduct and the false testimony given by individuals seeking to obtain their freedom or avoid punishment. And there are those who believe a criminal ring indeed existed, but that it was expanded by court officials into a full-fledged slave conspiracy due to

irrational fears. This lack of clarity and consensus among scholars studying the plot prompted a rebuttal from Herbert Aptheker: "The hysteria of
1741 in the City of New York has been treated by some historians as aris-
ing from a complete hoax, or an unaccountable mob delusion, while others
have dealt with it as resulting from a real and considerable slave conspiracy.
It seems fairly certain that neither of these views altogether coincides with
the facts."[58]

Perhaps Aptheker's assessment more closely approximates the truth.
While it is likely that Horsmanden exaggerated aspects of the trial testimony to protect himself from charges of judicial incompetence, there are
too many elements in the trial record that are congruent and corroborated
by people who had no prior knowledge of each other. It is quite clear that
certain people did lie in their testimony and that the court allowed questionable evidence and gave prosecutors excessive latitude in their cases against
the alleged conspirators. Court officials likely exaggerated the scope of the
plot, and memories of the 1712 revolt or the more recent uprising in Stono,
South Carolina, impelled leaders to quash any form of slave recalcitrance.

So the 1741 incident was neither a "mob delusion" nor a "considerable
slave conspiracy" but something in between. Burton may have had some real
reason to lie, or significantly embellish the truth, but not everything she told
the court was perjured testimony. Thomas J. Davis argues that, aside from
the trial of John Ury, "none of the other conspiracy trials had such obvious
flaws . . . In other trials the prosecution had at least circumstantial evidence,
corroborated testimony, or subsequent confessions. They had the facts of
arson, and theft, and illicit meetings."[59] Too many people testified and
confessed to the same essential facts, even without the threat of imprisonment, torture, or death, and relatively reliable sources corroborated much
of the testimony. While the conspiracy may not have been as expansive
as white authorities feared, it was much larger than the theft ring that set
everything else in motion.

Davis offers the most likely set of circumstances for the conspiracy. He
claims:

> The broadcast of discontent carried enough rebellious seeds for conspir-
> acy to grow in the hothouse climate and liquor at Hughson's, but ripen-
> ing revolution was a bogus crop. Horsmanden and his cohort falsely ad-
> vertised a wholesale harvest of a scorched city with slaughtered white men
> and ravished white women. The actual forecast at Hughson's called for

nothing so improbable . . . the sober reality centered on much more limited goals and specific targets. Strategic points such as Fort George and the Fly Market, warehouses like Philipse's and Van Zant's, and residences . . . were the places fixed for burning—not the whole city. Particular whites were marked for murder, not the whole population. And the issue was not so much blacks against whites, as haves against havenots—a fact made plain by whites at Hughson's joining in with blacks. The [conspirators'] common motivation seemed simply a desire to kick back at the society's oppression and get something more than they had for themselves.[60]

This more plausible scenario still misses some important elements. It is very likely that the original theft ring organized by black street gangs developed more politically motivated interests and biracial connections. However, such a synopsis does not fully explain the Akan cultural dimensions that shaped aspects of the conspiracy.

If the conspiracy could be viewed as a series of concentric circles, the outer ring—encompassing the largest number of people—would include slaves and whites seeking some semblance of social leveling; the next largest ring would include the black street gangs and their white fences interested in theft and willing to use arson as a cover; the innermost ring would include a smaller number of slaves, most of whom had significant links to Akan culture, seeking to gain their freedom through the use of arson and rebellion. This last group may have been seeking to establish their own polity and likely wanted to destroy most of New York City as one of their principal goals. The definite presence of this cultural enclave and distinct cultural practices associated with Akan-speakers throughout the Americas lends credibility to the claim that a very real plot to destroy the city existed in 1741.

### Akan Cultural Factors in the 1741 Plot

As in the case of the 1712 revolt, Akan cultural factors played a role in 1741. One of the most evident of these factors was the role of Doctor Harry. Living in Nassau, Long Island, as a slave of the Mizreal family, Harry was well known to the magistrates of New York City. Described by Horsmanden as a "smooth soft spoken fellow . . . [with] the air of sincerity and innocence," Harry had been forbidden from returning to New York City upon penalty of a severe whipping due to his involvement in a malpractice suit several years earlier. Doctor Harry had been employed to cure a mysterious ailment contracted by a Mrs. Riggs, daughter of a prominent merchant named John Watts. Harry had given the young woman medicine to cure her condition, but she died, and Harry was brought before the magistrates to answer to charges of malpractice. Though he claimed that his prescription had been altered by one of Mrs. Riggs' servants, Harry was found guilty and ordered to stay away from Manhattan.[61]

Harry's function was two-fold in the planning of the 1741 conspiracy. He first provided the insurgents with what was called "black stuff," an unknown incendiary substance that, according to the William Kane's confession, was used to "set fire to the roofs of houses in dry weather."[62] Bastian, a French-speaking slave held by Mr. Fauconnier, claimed, "We had combustibles prepared by doctor Harry, made up into balls, which we were to set fire to and throw them upon the roof of the church, which sticking fast would set fire to the shingles."[63]

Doctor Harry also provided the plotters with poison to use if they were captured. Again, William Kane revealed that Harry gave a certain amount to the ringleaders of the conspiracy and also some to a man named Quack. The conspirators assumed that since Quack would not be suspected in the plot if their plans were somehow betrayed, and thus not in jail with the others, "he might go to the prison to carry victuals, and so could give the poison to those that were condemned, to prevent their execution."[64] In that way, they would not have to suffer the torture of being burned alive or broken on the wheel. Quack may have indeed been successful in delivering poison to the condemned. Many people speculated that Doctor Harry's poison caused the "miraculous" and "surprising" way that the bodies of Caesar Vaarck and John Hughson changed colors upon death. As detailed in Horsmanden's *Journal*, Caesar's body had turned "white" while Hughson's corpse was strangely blackened. In addition, Horsmanden gives the following description:

> Hughson's body dripped and distilled very much . . . from the great fermentation an abundance of matter within him . . . At length, about ten days or a fortnight after Hughson's mate, York, was hung by him, Hughson's corpse, unable longer to contain its load, burst and discharged pail fulls of blood and corruption . . . It has been related already that Hughson when he was brought out of jail to be carried to his execution, had a red spot in each cheek . . . which at that time was by some thought very remarkable, because he was always pale of visage . . . Upon the supposition that Hughson

had taken poison, it has been made a question whether that might not have occasioned the swelling of his corpse to so amazing a bulk? Nay, his arms legs and thighs, were enlarged in proportion to the body; this is submitted to the consideration of the curious and connoisseur in physic.[65]

Horsmanden speculates that if Hughson had taken some of Harry's poison, he did not take enough to cause a quick and easy death. This was because "his thoughts might have been confused, and nature prevailed; as long as there is life, there is hopes, and his deliverance might be uppermost in his mind." While it did not cause an easier death, Horsmanden and others assumed that the poison did cause Hughson to turn "black as the devil" in death as a sign of his guilt.[66]

More about Doctor Harry's poison is revealed in the deposition of Elias Rice, a ship's captain who transported seventeen of the slaves allegedly involved with the plot to Hispaniola. The statement he gave details an incident on the passage to the island in which the slaves on board suspected the cook—a slave named Dick Eyck—of putting poison in their food.[67] "The negroes suspected [Dick] had a design of poisoning them, and saw him busy with yellow stuff in shells in a bag; which upon examination the negroes looked upon to be poison, which he had from doctor Harry, the negro. Some of the negroes knew it to be poison, *the same sort they saw in Guinea.*"[68] Rice's statement is the only piece of evidence linking Harry's esoteric knowledge of poisons directly to Africa. Not only would his knowledge and practice have African origins, but the slaves that could identify the particular poison that Doctor Harry and Dick were attempting to use quite possibly originated from the same region of Africa.

Throughout the Americas, Obeah practitioners have been associated with the use of various toxic substances. Obeah doctors and other West African spiritualists had broad knowledge of roots, bark, leaves, and herbs used for both medicinal and destructive purposes. Harry's knowledge of poison and his connection to a man with an Akan day-name in conveying the toxic substance to captured rebels implies a strong link to Obeah practice and possible Gold Coast origins. New Yorkers were quite frightened by this type of knowledge in the hands of slaves, especially since just a year earlier a number of slaves had been suspected of trying to poison the city's water supply. This fear had caused some of the city's residents to purchase water from reputable vendors for several months after the alleged poisoning conspiracy had been uncovered.[69] Doctor Harry's toxins, instead of being tools for insurrection, were meant only to ease the deaths of conspirators seeking to commit suicide.

Harry's story remains incomplete however. He was apprehended on July 6, 1741, and his Supreme Court hearing began the next day. Despite the fact that two slaves testified against him, Doctor Harry maintained his innocence. On July 10, 1741, he pled not guilty to the charges of conspiring to commit arson and to murder the whites in the city. A week later, Harry was found guilty and sentenced to burn to death. Even while he was being secured to the stake, he remained resolute and stated in his "confession" that he still knew nothing of the plot and would not implicate any co-conspirators. His statement, taken by John Splat, ends: "being asked about the combustible stuff for burning houses, and about the poison for negroes, he said he knew nothing of it, and that it signified nothing to confess."[70] Doctor Harry went to his grave with all of his secrets.

A number of significant links to Akan culture can be found in the trial testimony. Two Cajoes (a variation of Cudjo), three Cuffees, three Quacks, a Quamino, a Quash, and a Cuba were among the slaves with Akan day-names implicated in the 1741 conspiracy.[71] Two additional slaves involved in this plot were claimed to be "Caromantee" in the court records: an elderly woman named Jenny owned by Gerardus Comfort and Caesar owned by Benjamin Peck.[72] With the inclusion of Doctor Harry, fourteen slaves involved in this conspiracy had strong links to Akan culture. A number of other slaves may have had similar cultural ties. The seventeen slaves being sent to Hispañiola on board Captain Elias Rice's ship reported that Dick Eyck had in his possession some of the poison prepared by Doctor Harry. They recognized the yellow substance as a type of poison used in "Guinea."[73] None of the seventeen slaves on that ship had Akan day-names, but some of them likely had connections to the Gold Coast which allowed them to identify the poison of a possible Obeah doctor.[74]

Another individual who had very strong and plausible links to Akan culture was a slave named Will owned by Anthony Ward. He had been sent to New York from Antigua in the aftermath of the 1736 "Coromantee"- and creole-led conspiracy which seriously threatened the island. Will was to be hanged for his role in the Antigua plot, but having turned king's evidence, his life was spared by the court. In his 1741 confession to John Williams, Will claimed, "I could not stay there on account of the other negroes, being apprehensive of their intending to kill me."[75] Of the slave witnesses giving testimony to the Antigua courts, was one "Billy" owned by a Mr. Langford. Billy, along with twelve other slave witnesses were transported to North American colonies between March and April, 1737.[76] Will, who was occasionally referred to as "Bill" in Horsmanden's *Journal*, may have regretted betraying the slave rebels in Antigua and perhaps this explains why he involved himself in the New York City conspiracy. He was one of the very few slave conspirators who willingly pled guilty to the charges during his initial indictment on June 25. According to other testimony presented during the 1741 trial, Will was also involved in another earlier rebellion on St. John in the Danish Virgin Islands in 1733. Again, during the course of this rebellion, Akan-speaking slaves identified as "Aminas" sought to create an Akan polity and came close to succeeding in that endeavor.[77] As a result of Will's guilty plea and direct involvement in two previous acts of slave resistance, he was burned at the stake on 4 July 1741.[78] Having been involved in two previous revolts involving Akan-speakers on Caribbean islands links Will to a possible Gold Coast origin.

In addition to the presence of slaves with Akan day-names and at least one conjurer, other elements of the 1741 plot made it quite similar to the various examples of Akan rebelliousness in the Americas. Typically one set of actions appeared in Akan-inspired resistance movements which bore a definite Akan cultural stamp: oathing ceremonies. On several occasions during the planning of the 1741 plot, the conspirators took oaths of loyalty to bind themselves to secrecy. At a meeting held in the house of Gerardus Comfort—a next door neighbor to the Hughson's—slaves committed themselves to the conspiracy by swearing "to be true to one another, on the oath, *that God Almighty would strike them dead with the first thunder.*" Present at this particular oathing ceremony were a number of "Caromantees" including Cuffee Philipse, Jenny Comfort, and Quack Roosevelt.[79]

Another oathing ceremony occurred at Hughson's tavern during the early stages of the conspiracy. According to the June 11, 1741, testimony of a slave named Bastian, Hughson initiated the oath by reading a passage from the Bible and stating "that the first thunder might strike them dead that discovered, or did not stand to their words to perform what they had engaged to do." While this oath was administered by someone who was not an Akan-speaker and used the Christian Bible and the wrath of the Christian God to solidify the bond, certain elements of this ceremony would have resonated with Akan-speaking slaves. After the conspirators swore to burn New York City and kill its inhabitants, Hughson and the slaves partook of an oath drink or "punch" composed primarily of rum. After the conspirators drank some of the punch, Bastian notes that "all the negroes agreed to what was proposed as before." Again, it is important to note that a number of slaves with Akan day-names and others claimed to be "Caromantee" were present at this particular oath as well, including Cuffee Philipse, Quack Roosevelt, Cuffee Gomez, Cajoe Gomez, Caesar Peck, Will Ward and Quash Rutger. Though the form of these oathing ceremonies was certainly alien from the cultural standpoint of the Akan-speakers in attendance, the meaning and significance were definitely not lost to them.[80]

The fact that many of the conspirators had ethnic links to each other was something Hughson was keenly aware. In the confession of Cato Shurmur, Hughson reportedly told the conspirators present at this oathing ceremony "that they must not attempt to draw in any one that was not their country-man; that if they met with any countrymen, they must tell them so; and if they found they were likely to come in, then they might tell them of the plot." This, Hughson implored, after the conspirators agreed that Quack Roosevelt would set fire to Fort George. Clearly, both the slaves and whites involved in aspects of this plan were conscious of a common ethnic link, with significant and identifiable Akan cultural parameters, between certain conspirators.[81] In the context of the loyalty oath, this Akan presence in eighteenth-century New York has connections to similar phenomena throughout the Atlantic world as mentioned in the previous chapter.

One likely demonstration of a distinctly Akan cultural element in the efforts to administer loyalty oaths during the 1741 conspiracy can be found in the trial testimony of Fortune Wilkins. About a week before Fort George was burned, Fortune was urged by Quack Roosevelt to accompany him to the Common for reasons he would not immediately explain. Once they arrived, Quack left for a while "and went down into the swamp, near the powder-house, where he gathered something, and returned to him again." Upon his return, Fortune asked Quack what he had gathered from the swamp but his companion refused to answer. Quack then asked Fortune to "go down with him to the fort, and said he would give him some punch." Once they arrived at Fort George, Quack took Fortune to the kitchen and asked him to drink a dram of punch. Fortune refused the offer and both men left the Fort and parted ways. Two days before the Fort was burned the two met again, whereupon Quack said to his companion "that in a few days there would be great alterations in the fort." When Fortune questioned him about what was meant by "alterations," Quack said "that the fort would be burnt."[82]

On the surface, this story seems quite perplexing. However, some knowledge of the physical layout of New York City at the time of the 1741 conspiracy greatly clarifies both the story and the intentions of Quack Roosevelt. When the two men met in the Common and Quack went into the swamp near the powder house, he would have been at the northern edge of the African Burial Ground, southwest of Collect Pond. Clearly he was seeking to recruit Fortune into the conspiracy and to find an effective way to force his comrade to remain loyal and silent about the plan. By going against Hughson's suggestion to only tell his countrymen about the plot, Quack seriously compromised the conspiracy and his own life. However, the grave-yard had a substance with a great deal of significance and spiritual meaning to Akan-speakers. The material that Quack gathered was probably grave-yard dirt which would fully explain why he took his companion north of the Common—and thus within a brief walk of the African Burial Ground—and why he later offered a dram of "punch" for Fortune to consume.

As mentioned in the previous chapter, drinking oath drinks containing grave dirt creates a virtually unbreakable bond between the ancestral spirits and the living according to Akan beliefs; it also solidifies any oath among Akan-speakers, essentially forging an inviolable contract. Quack likely gathered some graveyard dirt to place into an oath drink and offer it to Fortune in the form of "punch." Fortune clearly was not an Akan-speaker, but Quack sought to allay his own fears in recruiting someone he did not know well and who was not a fellow countryman. After his unsuccessful attempt to recruit Fortune, Quack also tried to recruit Sandy Niblet to help set fire to Fort George who "answered no, he would not run the risk of being hanged." In response, a dejected Quack replied "he would do it himself." Ultimately, Quack would get help from a fellow Akan-speaker, Cuffee Gomez. The fact that a slave with an Akan day-name possibly attempted to perform an Akan loyalty oath with grave dirt demonstrates one of the ways that Akan culture shaped an important element of this conspiracy.[83]

Though the 1741 conspiracy was not a classic example of an "Akan" revolt, it did have a number of Akan elements which further supports the claim that a real plot or series of plots existed. Because of what we know about other slave rebellions in which Akan-speakers participated elsewhere in the eighteenth-century Americas, an outline of a typical Akan revolt or conspiracy can be created. The most obvious element of an Akan-inspired revolt would be the appearance of a number of slaves with Akan day-names as leaders and participants. Because of some of their prior experiences as soldiers in Gold Coast armies, firearms would be the likely tool of destruction. An oathing ceremony of some form would help forge solidarity between those involved in the planning of the revolt. Importantly, the rebellion or conspiracy would not be devoid of spiritual components; conjure would likely be present and the ability to produce poisons, charms or protective powders by an Obeah doctor would bolster the confidence of the slave rebels. If all else fails, their particular understanding of the after-life and the transmigration process would make them prone to suicide before or after capture. In their worldview suicide would become the only means to effectively resist if the revolt failed. It allowed the rebels to "re-shuffle the deck," so to speak, by facilitating the transmigration process—in this way, they would be reborn in freedom back in their African homelands.

With all of these elements present in New York in 1741—Akan day-names, knowledge of firearms, oathing ceremonies, conjure and suicide—the likelihood that a real conspiracy existed increases exponentially. Coincidence or even fabricated trial testimony alone cannot account for the striking parallels that exist between the examples of Akan slave resistance in New York City in 1741 and the many examples in the British, Danish, and Dutch Caribbean during the eighteenth century. Unless Mary Burton and the officials presiding over the 1741 trials had a keen awareness of these elements of Akan rebelliousness in the Americas, the likelihood that they could concoct such a plausible story with so many historically accurate and culturally viable components is quite small. Again, the remarkable amount of ethnographic information found in the trial record defies any attempt to completely dismiss the 1741 conspiracy as a figment of the collective imagination of white New Yorkers. To do so would effectively deny the agency of those who sought to break the bonds of slavery and establish their own polity or regime.

Will, the slave of Anthony Ward, may hold the key to the true intentions of the Akan-speaking contingent involved in the 1741 New York conspiracy. Again, based on court testimony, Will had been "concerned in two conspiracies in the West Indies, the first at St. John's, the last at Antigua, in the year

1736."[84] As Ray Kea notes, the 1733–34 St. John uprising sought to create an "Amina" or Akan-speaking polity "where the Aminas themselves would exercise an uncontested political suzerainty and social mastery over the island of St. John as a new planter class."[85] Strengthened by a collective belief in transmigration, the Akan rebels burned about eighty-five plantations and a number of sugar production facilities. They also killed about forty whites before being defeated by a military coalition which included French, Swiss and Danish forces. After this military defeat, as many as thirty-six of the Amina rebels—including practically all of the leaders—committed suicide. This revolt apparently combined the paradoxical goals of ending Danish planter rule while, at the same time, establishing a new slaveocracy in which the Amina political elite would control sugar production and other important affairs on the island.[86] Given this paradox, what the Aminas sought to accomplish was to replace or replicate a polity which was once a source of their social, political and cultural identities.

Among the survivors of the failed revolt, Will was then transported to Antigua on the eve of yet another Akan conspiracy. This time, Will was an active participant in a large-scale plot involving both creole and "Coromantee" leadership. These groups represented vastly different social and cultural realities and had differing objectives. The Coromantees, led by the charismatic Court Kerby, sought to use binding loyalty oaths and the spiritual power of three Obeah doctors—Caesar Matthew, John Obia, and Quawcoo Hunt—as inspiration in an attempt to construct an Akan polity. Court, who was revered as much as a king among the Coromantee, went as far as to stage an ikem, or military dance, on October 3, 1736, to recruit additional followers. Owing to their relatively small numbers however, the Akan-speakers could not carry out the rebellion without the aid of the creoles. Despite the active role played by creoles, the Coromantees fully expected them to abide by loyalty oaths, to fear the power of the three Obeah-men and to view Court as the Coromantee king.[87]

According to Gaspar, this uneasy alliance between the creoles and Coromantees fell apart after "some of the rebels became overconfident and loosely talked of the whites' fate, while the behavior of others in defiance of authority also aroused suspicion."[88] Though a willing participant in the plot, Will betrayed his countrymen and turned King's witness only after the conspiracy failed. As reward for his testimony, he was banished to New York

City in the early months of 1737. In an unfamiliar environment, he would soon take comfort in the fact that the enslaved population of Manhattan Island had not forgotten Africa. Within a month of Will's arrival in New York City, Africans divided into their different "nations," danced "to the hollow Sound of a Drum" and played music during the course of a Pinkster celebration. As one contemporary witness states, this March 1737 festival was also characterized by the formation of black military companies which danced, marched and engaged in martial drills in which they used "cudgels" and small sticks. To a recently arrived Akan rebel, this raucous assembly, the election of a Pinkster "king," the various competitive dances, the "horrid Oaths" and the military drills would bear strongly resemblance to an ikem dance.[89] As described by slave informants in the aftermath of the 1736 Antigua conspiracy, the ikem was performed "when a [C]oromantee king has resolved on war . . . The king appears at the place appointed under a canopy with his officers of state, guards and music, the people forming a semicircle about him. The king then begins the dance, carrying an ikem or shield of wicker and a lance: when fatigued, he delivers the ikem to the next dancer. When several have danced, the king dances again with his general and swears an oath to behave as a brave prince should or forfeit his life. If he is answered by three huzzas from those present it signifies a belief that the king will observe his oath and an engagement to join him in the war."[90] This was the very context Will came from, and, indeed, the meaning of the ikem dance or other Akan cultural icons were not simply forgotten once he disembarked in New York City.

Another Akan cultural concept Will would not have forgotten was the ubiquitous loyalty oath. Though he had previously violated the terms of one such oath, it still had real meaning for Will, even after his arrival in New York. In a confession Will reportedly made to John Williams, he admitted to participation in a loyalty oath during the planning of the New York conspiracy: "Williams asked [Will Ward], what would become of him in case the plot had gone on, whether he had greater antipathy against him than any other? he said, No; but he would have fared as the rest; he should have killed all that came in his way; for he had taken the oath of the priest; and that there was a matter of twenty or thirty of them in all, that were sworn together by a priest, a little man, with a long gown on; but he did not know him, or ever had seen him before as he know of."[91] Though this priest was likely not an Akan-speaker, the oath he administered resonated strongly with Will. Though he did turn king's evidence during the trials, Will also willingly pled guilty to the charge of conspiring to kill whites, knowing the penalty for this admission was death. While his two betrayals may signal Will's lack of belief in the Akan loyalty oath, in both cases he gave confessions only after the conspiracies were foiled and after he was already condemned to death.

In both the Antigua and New York trials, Will pled guilty to the charges, apparently prepared for his imminent execution. The judges in Antigua, in fact, explicitly stated that his execution was stayed "because wee think if he behaves ingenuously to Represent him as fit to be banished, tho, wee have promised nothing to him, but have made use of him already as an Evidence."[92] So Will did not give evidence under the belief that his life would be spared. In neither the Antigua nor the New York conspiracy trials did he offer exculpatory evidence in order to save himself. Perhaps then, instead of viewing his trial testimony as a betrayal of an Akan oath, it may be that Will, like his Amina comrades in St. John, fully believed in transmigration and committed the judicial equivalent of suicide as a result.[93]

Mary Burton's lies, Daniel Horsmandens' judicial incompetence, or the irrational fears of biracial collaboration voiced by a number of contemporary observers do not, in any way, alter what we know about Will's past. He was willingly involved in one revolt and two conspiracies between 1733 and 1741. During his experiences in St. John and Antigua, he participated in loyalty oaths, believed in the divine power of Obeah doctors and even witnessed an *ikem* dance. Will had personal associations with men in New York City with Akan day-names including Quack Walter, Quack Goelet, Quack Roosevelt, Quash Rutger, Cuffee Philipse, and Cuffee Fortune. He was reportedly present for two separate oathing ceremonies during the planning of the New York conspiracy and heard Hughson's appeal that the rebels only mention the plot to fellow countrymen.[94] Will, therefore, made conscious decisions to surround himself with familiar cultural elements. Though their experiences in the Gold Coast were distant memories by 1741, Will Ward, Quack Roosevelt, Doctor Harry, and Cuffe Philipse were prepared to use arson, poison and loyalty oaths to create a new political order on Manhattan Island. The alliances the Akan formed with poor whites, Irish soldiers, social-levelers, black street gangs, creoles, and others—what the court deemed to be "the outcasts of the nations of the earth"—demonstrates practical considerations as well as an emerging political and social consciousness that was increasingly "African-American" in nature.[95] The underpinnings of their particular cultural identities, however, would continue to be Akan throughout much of the colonial era in New York.

# CHAPTER 3

# Dance, Conjure, and Flight
*Culture and Resistance in Colonial South Carolina*

## Colonial Beginnings in South Carolina

According to available documentary sources, African slaves first arrived in South Carolina as early as 1526. They accompanied a large Spanish expedition from Hispaniola that was seeking to establish a permanent settlement near Cape Fear. After a discouraging and unsuccessful initial attempt, this group of about six hundred Spaniards, Native Americans, and Africans moved toward the southwest to find a more hospitable locale. By the fall of 1526, they had founded the settlement of San Miguel de Guadalupe in what would later be South Carolina. A series of misfortunes befell the settlement in October—disease, starvation, inclement weather, and internal conflict, which placed the inhabitants in an extremely precarious position. After the expedition's leader, Lucas Vásquez de Ayllón, died on October 18, dissension over who would lead the colony culminated in the first slave rebellion in North American history. Some of the African slaves set fire to the new expedition leader's hut then left the colony and reportedly joined with local Native Americans. In the words of Herbert Aptheker, these Spanish-speaking Africans became "the first permanent inhabitants, other than the Indians, in what was to be the United States."[1] This development prefigured the rise of maroon or biracial African–Native American societies later in North American history.

The Spanish, and later the French, made several more unsuccessful attempts at colonizing the area, but English efforts to settle the region that became Carolina after 1663 were much more successful. Named after Charles II—the king who helped restore the monarchy following the fall of Puritan rule in England—Carolina was initially a colony of a colony. Many of its early settlers were originally from Barbados—a thriving sugar island in the British Caribbean. Some of the initial proprietors in Carolina, like Sir John Yeamans and Sir John Colleton, had been sugar or tobacco planters with significant landholdings in Barbados. Others, as Robert Weir notes, were "pushed aside by the consolidation of the sugar estates," which caused overcrowding on the small island and left its inhabitants starved for land. In stark contrast to the development of the labor system in the Chesapeake then, South Carolina's British settlers relied on African slaves very early on in the colony's history. British Caribbean planters brought with them concrete ideas about labor utilization from a firmly established plantation society; thus, there was no major transition from white indentured servants to African slaves, as was the case on tobacco plantations in Virginia and Maryland. Facing an increasing difficulty in obtaining land for crop production in Barbados, Sir John Colleton led a group of seven influential business and political figures to petition Charles II for proprietorship over this new territory. What followed was a sizable influx of English planters from Barbados and other British Caribbean islands along with a number of African slaves.[2]

With primarily commercial interests in mind, the proprietors struggled to find a viable means to make profits in the subtropical climate of Carolina. Expecting a quick and easy revenue stream, the proprietors probably imagined that readily exploitable commodities were to be found in the new territory. To their collective chagrin, Carolina proved to be much less profitable than Spanish Mexico, Portuguese Brazil, or even the British Caribbean. The English had not effectively determined the region's economic potential prior to their arrival and, like their efforts to establish settlements in other portions of North America, they were not well prepared to deal with this new and hostile environment. The Spanish, however, had accurately gauged Carolina's resources almost a century before the first English settlers arrived. During a 1566 military expedition, the Spanish sent Pedro Menéndez de Aviles to drive the French away from the area that would later become South Carolina. While there, de Aviles wrote detailed reports about Chicora (the Spanish designation for the region), which included his thoughts about which crops or livestock would thrive in its subtropical climate. He listed a number of these in his report, including wine grapes, sugar, rice, silk, tar, timber, and cattle. If the English had had access to de Aviles' survey, they would have had a more effective economic blueprint. Some of the commodities de Aviles suggested would eventually become linchpins in South

Carolina's colonial economy. For the first three decades of English settlement, however, the colony suffered severe economic distresses.[3]

Because they were planters from the British Caribbean, the colony sought to make profits from cash crop cultivation. The proprietors suggested cotton, olives, grapes, indigo, and ginger. Two years after the first settlers arrived in the colony, Joseph Dalton reported that tobacco, hemp, flax, and silk would possibly thrive in South Carolina as well. In varying degrees, these crops failed to become viable and lucrative exports; they either refused to grow in the climate or simply were not practical as cash crops. It became obvious that a simple replication of the Barbados plantation model would not work. Other crops the settlers attempted during these initial years included sugar, rice, and tobacco. Sugar failed to grow in South Carolina's soil, and rice was grown only in experimental quantities. Ironically, the colonists and proprietors deemed rice cultivation a failure. Tobacco was grown throughout the colony, but competition with more established regions made the crop an unlikely option. Fur, wood products, and livestock would be relatively stable sources of revenue, but all paled in comparison to the profits that could be generated by a viable cash crop.[4]

The meager revenues meant that the proprietors were not receiving much return on their significant investments in Carolina. As Converse Clowser notes, "The proprietors, who had held high hopes for immediate retirement of the debts, first showed patient through petulant forbearance, then irritation, and finally anger toward the ungrateful wretches living on their bounty." Failure to make sufficient profits compelled the early settlers to delay the start of debt repayments and to ask the proprietors for additional financial support. Between 1670 and 1675, the proprietors had to deal with an increasing number of requests of this sort and, due to the significant investments they had already made in the establishment of the colony, they were grudgingly forced to comply. In a May 6, 1674, decision, for example, they voted to "invest" £700 annually for the next seven years to avoid losing everything if the settlement was abandoned.[5] This economic uncertainty would last until the colonists—with the aid of African slaves—discovered the considerable profitability of rice cultivation.

*African Geographic Origins, Ethnic Stereotypes, and Preferences*
While rice would not become a profitable staple crop until the 1720s, the early English settlers in South Carolina still required a great deal of labor. Most

Africans in the colony were employed as domestic servants or in the cattle-raising and naval supply industries. Though the transition to rice cultivation as the colony's primary economic enterprise was gradual, the African slave population began to increase rapidly by the beginning of the eighteenth century. By 1720, South Carolina's black population was approximately 12,000 with about 2,500 new slave imports brought into the colony annually in the 1730s. Successful rice and indigo cultivation during the early decades of the eighteenth century created tremendous demands for additional forced labor.[6]

In South Carolina, the flow of slave imports had a peculiar pattern. Like their counterparts in colonial New York, South Carolinians had a strong preference for slaves imported directly from Africa. This preference was reflected in duty legislation passed throughout the eighteenth century. The statute of 1703, for example, taxed "seasoned" slaves imported from the West Indies at twice the rate of those originating from continental Africa. Another act, passed in 1721, taxed slaves originating from other American ports at £30 per slave, fully three times the rate of tariffs enforced on slaves from Africa. As a result of these duties, between 1733 and 1785 roughly 3 percent of the 65,466 slaves imported had an American origin.[7] Darold Wax concludes that "the rationale supporting discriminatory legislation in South Carolina was the same as elsewhere—a deep-seated fear that slaves shipped from New World ports would not meet the standards desired by prospective purchasers and might even be capable of criminal activities."[8]

This prejudice against Caribbean imports was voiced by a number of South Carolina slave traders and planters during the eighteenth century. For example, Henry Laurens—one of South Carolina's most important slave dealers—held a great deal of contempt for Caribbean slaves. In a letter to one of his customers, Laurens commented that "Several small parcels of Negroes have been imported here from the West Indies Islands and the best of them have sold pretty well but there is generally a mixture of refuse negroes amongst such." In 1736, another Carolinian observed that "no Negroes are brought directly from Guinea to North Carolina, the Planters are obliged to go into Virginia and South Carolina to purchase them where they pay a duty on each Negro or buy the refuse distempered or refractory Negroes brought into the Country from New England and the Islands which are sold at excessive rates." In a 1752 letter Charles Town slave merchant John Guerard congratulated John Nickelson for his "successful Voyage to

Guinea and great Market Your Negroes . . . came to I had a Parcell then in Port from Barbadoes but Yours Coming so quick on the back of them so farr interferd tht they did not etch so much as I might otherwise have gott because Yours coming directly from the Coast."[9]

South Carolina planters seemingly preferred slaves from West-central Africa—an area which encompasses the coastal regions of the modern nations of Zaire, Congo-Brazzaville, Gabon, and Angola. Africans from this region represented the largest segment of the export population from Atlantic Africa to South Carolina during the eighteenth century. Michael Gomez estimates that "during the 1730s, the figure was more than 50 percent, with 'Angolans' arriving in large shipments averaging 260 persons per cargo." Between 1735 and 1740, thirty-one of sixty-six ships brought slave cargoes from West-central Africa to South Carolina. Indeed, in that same half decade, fully 70 percent of all slaves imported into the colony were West-central Africans, many of whom were likely from the kingdom of Kongo. According to the Du Bois Institute slave trade database, West-central Africans represented 63 percent of all slaves identifiable by origin and exported to South Carolina between 1726 and 1750 (see table 3.1).[10]

TABLE 3.1.  Enslaved Africans Imported into South Carolina and British North America

|  | 1701–1800 | | 1726–50 | |
| --- | --- | --- | --- | --- |
| Coastal Region of Origin | South Carolina | British North America | South Carolina | British North America |
| Senegambia | 24.9% | 24.4% | 15.2% | 21.3% |
| Sierra Leone | 12.1 | 9.6 | 0.0 | 0.1 |
| Windward Coast | 9.2 | 7.7 | 1.1 | 1.3 |
| Gold Coast | 13.3 | 11.7 | 2.9 | 3.8 |
| Bight of Benin | 2.3 | 3.1 | 0.0 | 1.2 |
| Bight of Biafra | 11.3 | 20.9 | 17.8 | 34.7 |
| West-central Africa | 26.4 | 21.4 | 63.0 | 37.6 |
| Southeast Africa | 0.3 | 1.1 | 0.0 | 0.0 |
| Unknown | 21.3 | 30.3 | 38.6 | 46.8 |

Source: Eltis, Behrendt, Richardson, and Klein, The Trans-Atlantic Slave Trade.
Note: Percentages do not include unspecified destinations.

In the eighteenth century there was relatively easy access to slaves from West-central Africa, as well as difficulties in procuring the more highly coveted Akan and other groups. As early as the 1670s, the English had established slave-trading interests on the Loango Coast which would last until the end of the British slave trade. This trade was greatly augmented in the early eighteenth century by the ability of the British to mass produce "Angola guns." These cheap flintlock muskets became a coveted item for African polities near Loango. By the 1700s, British traders were exchanging two guns per slave exported, resulting in a sizable number of West-central African captives arriving in Jamaica, South Carolina, and Georgia.[11] This concentration of West-central Africans would have serious implications for the development of both slave culture and resistance in colonial South Carolina.

Although relatively fewer Africans from the Upper Guinea region (Senegambia and Sierra Leone) were imported into South Carolina before 1740, planters attached a high value to these slaves. Africans from the region were the first to introduce the English to African techniques of rice cultivation and livestock raising.[12] But rice cultivators from Upper Guinea comprised only a combined 15 percent of Africans from identifiable regions exported to South Carolina between 1726 and 1750. Following the Stono rebellion of 1739 white Carolinians imported fewer West-central Africans because they viewed the revolt as an "Angolan" uprising. Their interests began to shift to supposedly less recalcitrant, but decidedly more profitable, rice producers from Senegambia and Sierra Leone. More than likely, this shift was primarily facilitated by the profitability of rice cultivation in the low country.[13]

Carolina planters actively despised Igbos and other Africans from the Bight of Biafra. Daniel Littlefield notes that "Calabar or Ibo slaves" had traits that planters in South Carolina had strong aversions to—Igbos were "small, slender, weak, and tended towards a yellowish color." They also had a propensity for suicide. Igbos and other Biafrans represented only 11 percent of the regionally identifiable slave exports to South Carolina during the eighteenth century, whereas they comprised 21 percent of all Africans exported to British North America (see table 3.1). Even in the Jamaican reexport trade, which witnessed the transshipment of Igbos and other Biafrans to British North America and Spanish South America, South Carolinians managed to avoid purchasing these most unfavored Africans. While these numbers reflect the South Carolina planters' prejudices, they may also reflect the fact that Igbos and others from the Bight of Biafra lacked the skills that rice planters required. Rice cultivation was a known practice in Senegambia, Sierra Leone, and even Madagascar, but there is no record of it appearing in the Niger River Delta, where tuber crops like yams predominated during the seventeenth and eighteenth centuries.[14]

Several stereotypes were associated with the enslaved West-central Africans, who formed the largest segment of South Carolina's African population by 1740. One general view among contemporary observers, echoed in an analysis by Littlefield, claims that Kongo and "Angolan" Africans were "docile, comely, not especially strong, possessed of a peculiar predisposition towards the mechanical arts, but inclined to run away."[15] John Barbot, an agent of the French Royal Company of Africa, described West-central Africans as "the meanest of all; because, being used to live idly, when they are brought to labour they quickly die." Yet another eighteenth-century commentator wrote: "Negroes from Angola, Calabar, and other Parts of Africa, who live idle in their own Country, and are in general of a lazy Disposition, and tender Constitution; so that there is generally a Difference of about 10 or 20 [pounds] per Head between these and those of the Gold Coast and Whydah."[16] Not all Europeans shared these negative views however. West-central Africans were highly esteemed by Portuguese sugar planters in the seventeenth century.[17] Malachy Postlethwayt observed that the effectiveness of the trade network connecting Angola to Portuguese, Dutch, French, and English colonies was due to the fact that Angolan slaves were "more capable to undergo the labour and fatigue of cultivating and manufacturing sugar, tobacco, indigo, and the other hard work which these poor wretches are commonly put."[18]

According to W. Robert Higgins, West-central Africans were the third most sought-after African group among eighteenth-century South Carolina rice planters, following Gambians and the Gold Coast Akan.[19] This "preference" for Angolan slaves was really a rationalization for what the market offered in both South Carolina and Brazil. Limited access to other African groups shaped stereotypical perceptions of certain African ethnicities and preferences for others. Whatever the cause for the concentration of West-central Africans in South Carolina and Brazil, both colonies would bear witness to similar cultural developments and forms of slave resistance as a result.

*Slave Resistance in Colonial South Carolina, 1720–1740*
In an anonymous letter written to a Mr. Boone in London and dated June 24, 1720, explicit mention is made of what may have been the most significant act of slave resistance to that point in British South Carolina:

> I am now to acquaint you that very lately we have had a very wicked and bar-
> barous plott of the designe of the negroes rising with a designe to destroy
> all the white people in the country and then take the town in full body but it
> pleased God it was discovered and many of them taken prisoners and some
> burnt some hang'd and some banish'd.
>
> I think it propper for you to tell Mr. Percivall at home that his slaves was
> the principal rogues and 'tis my opinion his only way will be to sell them out
> singly or else I am doubtful his interest in slaves will come to little for want
> of strict management. Work does not agree with them 14 of them are now
> at the Savanna towne and sent for by white and Indians and will be executed
> as soon as they come down they thought to gett to Augustine and would
> have gott a Creeke fellow to have been their pylott but the Savanna garrison
> took the negroes up half starved and the Creeke Indians would not joine
> them or be their pylots.[20]

Though no other mention of this rebellion can be found in the records of colonial South Carolina, it is possible that the plot mentioned in this letter was the same one described in a handful of secondary sources. In 1860, Joshua Coffin reported "On the 6th of May, 1720, the negroes in South Caro-lina murdered Mr. Benjamin Cattle, a white woman, and a negro boy. Forces were immediately raised, and sent after them twenty-three of whom were taken, six convicted, three executed, and three escaped." While extant con-temporary sources fail to corroborate the existence of this plot, it could very likely be the case that both the anonymous letter and Coffin's report refer to the same revolt.[21]

Other examples of slave resistance in colonial South Carolina had forms that hint strongly to specific African cultural origins. On August 15, 1730, Charles Town was seriously threatened by an alleged slave conspiracy.[22] The only extant contemporary account is an anonymous letter written in Charles Town on August 20, 1730:

> I shall give an Account of a bloody Tragedy which was to have been executed
> here last Saturday Night . . . by the Negroes, who had conspired to Rise and
> destroy us, and had almost bro't it to pass: but it pleased God to appear

for us, and confound their Councils. For some of them propos'd that the Negroes of every Plantation should destroy their own Masters; but others were for Rising in a Body, and giving the blow at once on surprise; and thus they differ'd. They soon made a great Body at the back of the Town, and had a *great Dance*, and expected the Country Negroes to come & join them; and had not an overruling Providence discovered their Intrigues, we had been all in blood. For take the whole Province, we have about 18 thousand Negroes, to 3 thousand Whites. The Chief of them, with some others, is apprehended and in Irons, in order to a Tryal; and we are in Hopes to find out the whole Affair.[23]

Additional information pertaining to this conspiracy is found in Edward Clifford Holland's description of the plot. In his 1822 work entitled *A Refutation of the Calumnies Circulated against the Southern & Western States Respecting the Institution and Existence of Slavery among Them*, Holland wrote: "They resolved to adopt the other proposition, which was that they should assemble in the neighborhood of the town, under the pretence of a 'Dancing- Bout,' and, when proper preparations were made, to rush into the heart of the city, take possession of all the arms and ammunition they could find, and murder all the white men, and then turn their forces to the different plantations. Such was the secrecy with which this conspiracy was conducted, that it was discovered only a short time previous to its projected explosion, and many of the negroes had actually assembled."[24] After the plot was revealed, Holland claimed that the ringleaders were executed and the rest of the slaves were returned to their holders.[25] Herbert Aptheker asserts that Holland likely was able to use materials destroyed during the Civil War, which could explain why he refers to details relating to the revolt that are not found in the 1730 letter or corroborated by any extant contemporary source.[26] The fact that dancing was mentioned in both the primary and secondary accounts of this planned revolt points strongly to cultural origins in West-central Africa and links this conspiracy to other examples of resistive behavior enslaved West-central Africans engaged in throughout the Atlantic World.

The period between 1736 and 1740 was an especially troubling time for South Carolina's planters. No fewer than six revolts or conspiracies occurred over those four years. The first plot was uncovered in August 1736. According to a diary entry written by Captain Johann Hinrichs—a Hessian officer living in Charleston in the 1780s—the plotters, which included "the entire Negro population," intended to kill every white male, beginning with slave owners. As Hinrichs stated, "Two days before the intended uprising a large group had gathered two and one-half miles from Charleston . . . They were to attack the city, seize the magazines, and massacre the inhabitants." Ultimately, this conspiracy was foiled and the slaves were overpowered. "Within a few hours," Hinrichs reported, "the news spread through the province, and all leaders were tortured to death, while many others were subjected to severe bodily punishments."[27]

While little independent confirmation of the 1736 conspiracy exists, incidents in 1738 and 1739 are much better documented. In November 1738, a sizable group of slaves from St. Paul's Parish en route to freedom in St. Augustine, Florida, killed several whites in Georgia. According to an anonymous report from February 1739, "the Negroes in Carolina, [sought] to rise and forcibly make their Way out of the Province, to put themselves under the Protection of the Spaniards." After the rebellion was discovered and put down, the Council and Assembly of Georgia sought restitution from the governor of Spanish Florida for "all those Negroes who had lately fled to that Place." An October 4, 1733, royal edict delivered by the Spanish crown had made Florida a haven for fugitive slaves, and St. Augustine was the destination of many escaping from plantations in British North America. In exchange for four years of royal service, slaves escaping British colonies were promised freedom—under the guise of religious sanctuary—and even established their own independent towns. This inducement explains the slave uprising in November 1738 and the subsequent actions taken by legislatures in South Carolina. In 1740, for example, lawmakers in the colony issued monetary rewards for the scalp of any slave found on the south side of St. John's River attempting to escape to St. Augustine.[28]

The most disturbing colonial-era revolt in North America occurred in 1739 near Stono, South Carolina—some twenty miles southwest of Charles Town. On September 9, 1739, about twenty slaves killed two white storeowners, Robert Bathurst and Tom Gibbs, at a warehouse and took guns and ammunition. Led by a slave named Jemmy, the rebels then entered the house of a Mr. Godfrey, killing his entire family. They spared the life of an innkeeper named Wallace because he had been fair and kind to slaves. Wallace's neighbors were not so fortunate. The slaves killed a Mr. Lemy and his entire family and Colonel Hext's wife and overseer, and they attacked all other whites they encountered. According to a letter written on October 5, 1739, by Lieutenant-Governor William Bull, the combatants marched "in a warlike manner out of the Province" leaving six or seven burned houses and some thirty dead whites in their wake.[29] Because the Stono rebels were heading southwest toward Georgia, many of the contemporary commentators assumed that they were trying to escape to St. Augustine.[30]

Lieutenant-Governor Bull, returning from Charles Town on horseback, narrowly escaped death upon meeting Jemmy's forces on the road through the Pon Pon District, ten miles south of Stono. Bull alerted the local militia and other whites who took up arms to put an end to the uprising. A brief skirmish left about fourteen slaves dead or wounded and the rest in full retreat. It would take the militia another week before they were able to defeat the main body of the slave rebels some thirty miles further south. Contemporary records are unclear, but as many as fifty slaves were executed for their roles or alleged roles in the revolt. Slaves were tortured, shot, hanged, and gibbeted alive.[31] A ranger working for General Oglethorpe in 1739 reported "about fifty of these [slaves] attempted to go home but were taken by their Planters who Cutt off their heads and set them up at every Mile Post they came to."[32] The severity of the punishments was meant to generate fear among other slaves in an effort to dissuade them from rebelling or running away.

After the revolt there was a sharp decrease in whites' interest in slaves from West-central Africa. On the eve of the Stono rebellion, in 1737, a Swiss newcomer to the colony had noted that the colony was "more like a negro country than like a country settled by white people."[33] This demographic reality caused much anxiety among whites, especially where there were heavy concentrations of "Angolans" and other West-central Africans. In a runaway advertisement in the *South Carolina Gazette* of August 6, 1737, Isaac Porcher, owner of a plantation near Wassamsaw, sought the capture of "a new Angola Negro Man, named Clawss." Porcher feared that Clawss was being harbored by other Angolan slaves since "there is abundance of Negroes in this Province of that Nation."[34]

White Carolinians suggested that it was the concentration of West-central African slaves that made rebellion possible in 1739 and that further acts of resistance were possible if more were allowed into South Carolina. The group they identified as "Angolans" had already proven a most troublesome property to planters because of their propensity to take flight. Once they became associated with violent resistance, the once highly prized slaves from West-central Africa would no longer be coveted or desired by white Carolinians until the end of the eighteenth century. In the words of Michael

Gomez, it was the "fear, anxiety, and insecurity" caused by the Stono rebellion that fundamentally changed how whites perceived West-central Africans. As a result, the colonial legislature imposed a prohibitive duty that sought not only to balance the slave and white populations but also to limit the number of enslaved West-central Africans entering the colony. Thus between 1740 and 1800, Senegambians largely replaced the earlier stream of West-central Africans imported into the region.[35]

Despite the tremendous panic caused by the Stono uprising, it did not generate a great deal of contemporary commentary. There exists only one extant eyewitness account and several second-hand reports but no trial records or confessions. Despite the paucity of available sources, remarkable details about this rebellion can still be found. For example, an anonymous letter written by the eyewitness to the Stono incident makes specific mention of the slave rebels' ethnicity. The writer noted that the majority of the Africans in the colony at the time of the revolt were "brought from the Kingdom of Angola in Africa" and that it was "some Angola Negroes [that] assembled" at Stono to start the rebellion.[36] The letter also describes how the slaves, "calling out liberty . . . marched on with Colours displayed, and two Drums beating pursuing all the white people they met with . . . They increased every minute by new Negroes coming to them, so that they were above Sixty, some say a hundred, on which they halted in a field, and set to dancing, Singing and beating Drums to draw more Negroes to them."[37] In the minds of South Carolina's planters, dancing slaves began to be directly associated with rebelling slaves, and dancing became a characteristic element of resistance movements involving West-central Africans in other regions of the Americas.

In the immediate aftermath of the Stono revolt, two more slave conspiracies were discovered in South Carolina in 1739. The first, which occurred in November 1739 near St. John's Parish in Berkeley County, was mentioned in a letter to Andrew Pringle dated December 27, 1739. In the letter Captains Bishop and Snelling note that "we have been fatigued for this Week past keeping Guard in Town, on account of a Conspiracy that has been detected to have been covered before it came to any Maturity. We shall Live very Uneasie with our Negroes while the Spaniards continue to keep possession of St. Augustine & it is pity our Government at home did not encourage the dislodging of them from thence." According to an entry in the Commons House of Assembly Journal on January 30, 1740, sixty-seven slaves allegedly involved in the plot were captured and charged with conspiracy. Constables David Davis and Sam Edgar were paid a combined £123 for administering punishments to slaves convicted of involvement in the conspiracy. Five were hanged, twenty-one had their ears cropped, thirty-one were branded, and forty-six were whipped.[38]

The second conspiracy appears as a passing reference in a report drafted by the colonial legislature to the king. The report informed the king about the Stono revolt, adding "no sooner [was it] quelled than another projected in Charles Town, and a third lately in the very heart of the settlements, but happily discovered time enough to be prevented."[39] No other mention of this conspiracy exists in the records, but the very tense climate in South Carolina in the wake of Stono makes the existence of the plot more than plausible. As late as January 1742, slaves allegedly involved in the Stono uprising were still being captured.[40]

Two additional resistance movements were discovered in 1740 causing additional concerns for white Carolinians. The first was planned for early June of that year. Led by a slave named Cato, between 150 and 200 slaves conspired to attack Charles Town and kill its white residents. On the day planned for the revolt, city officials reported that a large body of slaves did "get together in Defiance: But as they were unprovided with Arms, and there was no Corn on the Ground ripe, for their Subsistence" the rebels lost most of their incentive to fight. In addition, two days before the planned uprising, a slave named Peter Cords alerted white authorities to the plot and, in turn, the city was well prepared to repulse the rebellion. As a reward for dutiful service, Peter was given new clothes and £20 by the Common House of Assembly. In the same entry, the assembly also ordered that another slave owned by a Mr. Spry be paid £10 for apprehending one of the Stono rebels who had managed to elude capture for more than ten months.[41]

In the midst of all of the rebellious activity between 1739 and 1740, the Commons House passed the most comprehensive slave code in South Carolina history. On September 21, 1739, the Upper House of Assembly drafted the "Bill for the Better Ordering and Governing of Negroes and Other Slaves," which included the following clauses: "1. A Clause to prevent more than 5 Negroes from travelling together in any public Road, without a white Man being in Company with them. 2. A Clause to regulate the Manner of Negroes working on the high Roads . . . 3. A Clause to appoint and regulate the Time when Slaves shall be kept to work . . . and 4. A Clause to prohibit the teaching of Slaves to write, which has been experienced to be of ill Consequence, as they have wrote Tickets for other Slaves in the names of their Masters without the Consent of Privity of such Masters."[42] The final version of this act, passed on May 10, 1740, allowed for the legal killing of any slave who assaulted a white person; ordered the execution of any slave guilty of plotting insurrection, committing arson, or creating poisons; strictly limited the mobility of slaves; mandated that the quarters of slaves could be searched at any time; prohibited slaves from owning weapons, boats, or livestock; and imposed a heavy import tariff of £100 for Africans and £150 for slaves from other colonies.[43] As a result of the high duty placed on all slave imports, South Carolina imported none between 1740 and 1744. The tariffs were reduced only after slave traders in Bristol, England, lodged complaints to the crown explaining the deleterious effects of the new duties on their lucrative business.[44]

### Dance and Drums: West-central African Military Culture in Colonial South Carolina

In both the 1730 Charles Town plot and the 1739 Stono revolt the act of dancing was specifically intertwined with slave rebellion. Even as late as 1772, the South Carolina Gazette reported on the anxiety generated by a "Country-Dance, Rout, or Cabal of Negroes" held on a Saturday night outside the city of Charles Town. The estimated sixty slaves involved in this activity alarmed one white witness who wrote, "Whenever or wherever such nocturnal rendezvouses [sic] are made, may it not be concluded, that their deliberations are never intended for the advantage of the white people." This event took on the air of a carnival or Pinkster celebration with its inversion of social roles and power relationships. The onlooker noted that the nocturnal activities included "the men copying (or taking off) the manners of their masters, and the women those of their mistresses." While the witness alludes to the frequency of these gatherings, there is no way of measuring how representative this "rendezvous" was. A clear association of dance with slave resistance and recalcitrance, however, was evident in colonial South Carolina and demonstrates at least one of the possible impacts West-central African culture had on the colony.[45]

Dance was a multifaceted and multifunctional tool in the ethos of various African groups brought to the Americas. Often, dance had a spiritual and religious significance, epitomized in the ubiquitous ring-shout Africans and their descendants have engaged in since colonial times. The ring-shout, while heavily associated with West-central Africa, has been linked by Sterling Stuckey to other circular dances present among a variety of Atlantic African groups. With a strong resonance in the Kongo cosmogram, this counter-clockwise dance was both an elaborate prayer to the ancestors and a recognition of the four major "moments" of the life cycle—birth, adolescence, elder-hood, and afterlife. Both the ring-shout and the Kongo cosmogram it was likely based on embodied the notion of spiritual trans-migration, a concept found among several African groups present in South Carolina, including Akan-speakers, Igbo-speakers, and the West-central African groups.[46]

There is no direct evidence suggesting that the rebels at Stono engaged in the ring-shout; however, by singing, dancing, and beating drums, they were likely evoking the power of African gods and the ancestors to aid them against their enemies, not simply celebrating their victory "over the whole Province" as the contemporary eyewitness asserted.[47] Dancing to worship the ancestral spirits and various deities can be found among Africans throughout the African diaspora.[48] Thus, even if all the rebels in the Charles Town conspiracy or the Stono revolt were not "Angolan" or West-central African, dancing would have served as a cultural bridge allowing other African ethnicities to participate in this collective act.

Another important "cultural bridge" would be the drum. The ubiquity of drums throughout Atlantic Africa meant that for many African slaves in South Carolina and other locales in the Americas, drums had a cultural significance that transcended ethnic differences. Authorities in South Carolina recognized the link between drums and resistance and prohibited the manufacture or use of drums by slaves.[49]

Slaves involved in the Charles Town plot and the Stono revolt could have also used dance and drums for military purposes. John Thornton contends that slaves involved in the Stono revolt may have received military training in Kongo and Angolan armies in the eighteenth century. By the early eighteenth century, large-scale military campaigns were increasingly commonplace in the Kongo kingdom and other polities in this region of Africa. The obvious result of the increasing number of wars in West-central Africa would be a large number of well-trained, captured enemy soldiers who were sold into slavery. West-central African armies also had access to firearms and, similar to Gold Coast militaries, began to utilize them increasingly as primary weapons during the early eighteenth century. This type of military experience, according to Thornton, would explain why the Stono rebels acquitted themselves well during their engagement with the militia.[50]

In addition, armies representing West-central African polities used colorful banners, drums, and a type of "martial" dance, all of which were integral to the military cultures in this region. West-central African armies used banners, flags, and drums in a sophisticated system of battlefield signals.[51] Though the use of these items could have been in imitation of colonial militias, the dancing points to a definite African background. As Thornton points out, "Although European and Euro-American armies and militias marched, flew flags, and beat drums as they approached combat, they did not dance. Military dancing was part of the African culture of war. In African war, dancing was as much a part of military preparation as drill was in Europe. Before 1680, when soldiers fought hand to hand, dancing was a form of training to quicken reflexes and develop parrying skills. Dancing in preparation for war was so common in Kongo that "dancing a war dance" (*sangamento*) was often used as a synonym for "to declare war" in seventeenth-century sources."[52] Martial dances in West-central African militaries prefigured the emergence of an African martial art found in Brazil and known as *capoeira*. Like South Carolina, Brazil was the destination of a great number of West-central African slaves, some of whom intertwined dance with resistance. Brazil, therefore, is a useful parallel for analyzing cultural developments and slave resistance in colonial South Carolina.

As Philip Morgan contends, "Obviously, North American slavery varied a great deal from its Latin American equivalents; but when it is remembered that approximately two-thirds of the slave population of South Carolina at mid-century were Africans, then the potential for parallels should not be lightly dismissed."[53] Since so many South Carolina Africans were from West-central Africa, Brazil represents the colony's best Latin American analogue. By triangulating the cultural activities of slaves in Brazil and South Carolina, a common source of these phenomena in West-central African cultures becomes even more likely. In this way, the presence of conjure in colonial New York City or dance in colonial Carolina takes on a much larger significance.

The practice of *capoeira* in Brazil was actively disguised as a dance so that West-central African slaves and others could openly practice and hone their skills without fear of detection. Though the origins of *capoeira* may date back to the seventeenth century, the earliest documentary reference to this practice in Brazil appeared in a series of newspaper columns in the 1770s. In the eyes of the white Brazilian elite, *capoeira* was simply a form of entertainment. When performed, *capoeira* involves a ring of singers and instrument players who encircle the fighters. The *capoeristas* in the ring were not "fighting" in the language of this practice; instead they engaged in a *jogo*, or game. In fact, unlike other martial arts one does not fight in *capoeira*, but instead euphemistically plays *capoeira* "games." The practice was actively masked by the use of deceptive language and form. Brazilian plantation owners were as blind as their North American counterparts to the inner worlds of their African and African American slaves.[54]

The oldest and most prevalent variation of this art is called "*capoeira* Angola," which implies strong West-central African ties. The body movements characterizing this martial art—including a variety of kicks, leg sweeps, cartwheels, and jumps—have definite Angola coast antecedents. African slaves imported into Guadeloupe and Martinique created similar cultural links between dance and resistance. These French Caribbean islands imported a large number of West-central Africans and, not surprisingly, a dance-like martial art known as *ladya* developed in both locales. It mirrors *capoeira* in almost every way, from the ring of singers and musicians to the complex array of kicks and cartwheels. Practitioners of *ladya*, similar to *capoeiristas*, create illusions of weakness and use deceit as a tool to vanquish opponents. Both *ladya* and *capoeira* are similar to another cultural form typically associated with West-central Africans—the ring-shout. Combatants performing in these martial art forms encircle each other in a counter-clockwise direction before engaging in ritual battle.[55]

In the sixteenth and seventeenth centuries, European visitors were amazed by the physical prowess of West-central African soldiers. Based on these perceptions, Thornton contends, "the physical agility of central African soldiers was notable . . . and required arduous physical training that was constantly renewed, especially in special military reviews and dances where virtuosity were displayed." With their alleged abilities to dodge arrows and javelins in flight, as well as their prowess in hand-to-hand combat, West-central African soldiers commanded physical abilities that could easily prefigure the development of martial arts in the Americas. The *nsanga* (sangamento)— or armed war dance—was so essential to West-central African military culture that it was almost always performed before military campaigns.[56]

One distinct example of a West-central African martial art would be the *ngolo*. In analyzing African-derived martial art forms, T. J. Desch Obi observes that "as a combat system, the art of *ngolo* and its cognates utilized kicks and powerful headbutts for attack and acrobatic evasions for defense. These attributes were developed in a number of training exercises, one of which was the ritual practice with a partner inside a circle of singers." In almost every way, the *ngolo* of West-central Africa mirrors *capoeira* and *ladya*— the formation of a circle of singers and musicians, the complex array of kicks and leg sweeps, and the active role of deception and trickery.[57]

Even if slaves in colonial South Carolina were not performing a variant of *ngolo*, that they chose to incorporate dance with resistance in ways similar to their Brazilian and French Caribbean counterparts implies that these actions shared similar cultural roots. Indeed, South Carolina was home to two distinct expressive forms that bear West-central African imprints. The first is "knocking and kicking," a unique nineteenth- and twentieth-century martial art found in South Carolina and other regions of the U.S. South. It parallels the form and practice of *ngolo*, *capoeira*, and *ladya*. Like other West-central African martial practices, knocking and kicking included a series of kicks, headbutts (knocking), and a deceptive dance-like form. As Obi contends, "Moves like the cross step, Bantu style cartwheels and the dynamic kicks of the art make knocking and kicking a dance of unmistakably African origin. On the occasions of these performances, the rhythms of drums, clapping, or pounding sticks were accompanied by a quill."[58] Thus, knocking and kicking may very well be linked to the same cultural matrix that produced *ngolo*, *capoeira*, and *ladya*, and which determined the actions of slave rebels in eighteenth-century South Carolina.

The second expressive form which likely had its origins in West-central African culture was a unique dance characteristic of nineteenth- and twentieth-century South Carolina. According to Robert Farris Thompson, the Juba was "a dance which, in its angulations, kicking patterns, and timing" had analogues in dance styles of the Kongo kingdom. Charleston, South Carolina, the final destination of thousands of West-central Africans, would become so associated with this dance that the Juba became known as the "Charleston" by the early twentieth century. With its emphasis on kicks and other leg motions, this dance is similar in form to *ngolo* and its various Atlantic World variants. Even the word "Juba" has a West-central

African origin, meaning "to beat time in a rhythmic pattern." In a typical performance, older black men would rhythmically "pat juba" by slapping their hands on their thighs—in imitation of the drum—while others would perform the dance. Both the "patters" and dancers would sing as an integral part of the Juba dance. By combining "drumming," singing, as well as elaborate and competitive dances, the Juba resembled West-central African military dances and derivative martial arts. The Juba was also characteristic of the various dance styles inspired by West-central African cultural elements performed at the aptly named "Congo Square" in New Orleans during the early nineteenth century. Many of the Congolese from West-central Africa arriving in Louisiana after 1800 were transshipped there from South Carolina, which demonstrates the levels of interconnectedness throughout the Western Hemisphere and the Atlantic World.[59]

### Conjure and Poison

The ever-present conjurer can be found in the South Carolina colonial records in association with various acts of rebellion, day-to-day resistance, and even activities that were accommodationist in nature. As Peter Wood notes, "Some of the Negroes listed by the name 'Doctor' in colonial inventories had no doubt earned their titles."[60] Peter the Doctor and Doctor Harry of eighteenth-century New York City had a number of counterparts in South Carolina. Slaves from different ethnic backgrounds and geographic origins adopted the title "Doctor" and were able to hold a significant amount of influence over other slaves and, at times, even whites.

In the case of one alleged slave conspiracy uncovered near Cooper River in 1749, James Akin—owner of most of the 104 slaves involved in this plot— recorded some vital evidence relayed to him by a loyal slave. At a meeting of slave conspirators held in late December 1748, one of the slaves reportedly said "let the fire kindle as fast as it will, he will Engage by his *obias* to stiffle and put it out."[61] According to Philip Morgan, this is the first direct reference to Obeah, an Akan or Igbo practice involving conjure and other spiritual abilities, to appear in mainland North American colonial records. In an October 1749 *South Carolina Gazette* slave runaway advertisement, Jacob Martin sought the return of "an Ebo negro fellow named Simon, well known in town and country, and pretends to be a doctor." Sometime before April 1764, a Gambian-born doctor cured a fellow slave of an unusual swelling.[62]

Conjure may have been one way that Akan, Igbo, and Gambian slaves in South Carolina were able to bridge the cultural gulf that stood between them and the West-central Africans.[63] Evidence of cultural affinities between African ethnolinguistic groupings suggests that "tribal" groups could find common cultural ground and thus combine their forces against common foes. Slave conjurers served as one of these cultural commonalities and helped forge a more unified response to oppression by a heterogeneous slave population.

The practice most commonly associated with slave conjurers in colonial South Carolina was poisoning. As early as the 1720s, white colonists viewed the use of poison as one of the more dangerous forms of slave resistance. Rev. Richard Ludlam reported in 1725 the treacheries "by secret poisonings and bloody insurrection" of some slaves being exposed to the Christian catechism.[64] This was followed by an August 1741 report appearing in the *South Carolina Gazette* of a man claimed to be a "Negro Doctor" who had allegedly administered a quantity of poison to a white infant. In 1747, another "Negro Doctor" named Jack was accused of poisoning three people—two slaves and the wife of his owner. After being detained and searched, Doctor Jack was found to have toxic herbs and roots in his pockets. The "horrid practice of poisoning White people" led to a number of slaves being burned, gibbeted, and hanged according to a 1749 *Gazette* editorial.[65]

Not all conjurers used their skills for destructive purposes however. "Caesar's Cure" was first reported in the *South Carolina Gazette* in 1733. "Doctor" Caesar Norman was a former slave who created antidotes to poison and snake bites. In March 1750, the General Assembly heard direct evidence that Caesar had "cured several Persons who had been long ill of a lingering Distemper, attended with intollerable Pains in the Stomach and Bowels." Even after employing skilled white physicians, John Cattell, Henry Middleton, and a Mr. Gaillard continued to suffer from this unknown ailment until Caesar's cure was applied. The assembly requested that Caesar divulge his methods, and he willingly complied.[66] His cure for poison, which illustrates Caesar's knowledge of roots and plants, required the following steps and ingredients:

> Take the Roots of Plantane and wild Hoare-hound, fresh or dried, three Ounces; boil them together in two Quarts of Water to one Quart, and strain it; of this Decoction let the Patient take one third Part three Mornings, fasting successively . . .

For Drink during the Cure, let them take the following, Take of the Roots of Golden Rod, six Ounces, or in Summer two large Handfuls of the Roots and Branches together, and boil them in two Quarts of Water . . . to this Decoction, after it is strained, add a Glass of Rum or Brandy.[67]

Caesar was a prototypical "root doctor" with vast knowledge of the healing properties of roots, herbs, tree barks, and plant leaves. The source of this knowledge was revealed in the correspondence of Dr. Alexander Garden, a notable Charles Town physician, who stated that Caesar was "a native African." As a reward for his various cures, Caesar would receive his freedom and an annual stipend of £100 for life from the General Assembly.[68]

White Carolinians believed that slaves first acquired their knowledge of poisons and cures from Africa. Within nine months of his arrival in South Carolina in 1752, Dr. Garden reported "the Negroe slaves here seem to be but well acquainted with the Vegetable poisons (whether they gain that knowledge in this province or before they leave Africa I know not, tho' I imagine the Latter)."[69] African herbology applied in the Americas because of similar environmental conditions and the purposeful and accidental transplanting of African herbs, plants, and food crops. In *Working Cures*, Sharla Fett contends that "some West African captives undergoing the terror of the transatlantic crossing may have worn strings of red and black wild licorice seeds and thus brought the licorice plant to the Caribbean. The roots of the licorice plant served as a common medicine aboard slave vessels, and West African descendants in the Caribbean continued to use wild licorice medicinally for coughs and fevers. African grasses crossed the Atlantic with slavers who discarded on American shores the straw used to line the putrid holds of slave ships. In addition, benne (sesame) seeds, yams, okra, and black-eyed peas originated in Africa and were later grown by enslaved Africans for food. Some of these cultivated foods served medicinal purposes in the New World as well."[70] In addition, Africans adopted aspects of Native American herb lore and created poisons and remedies based on plants indigenous to North America.

Whites' anxiety about being poisoned by slaves was epitomized in the 1740 Slave Act, which made the administering of poison a felony punishable by torture and execution. Both the actual practice of slave poisonings and white fears associated with this act were to increase after 1749. In that year Rev. William Cotes of St. George's Parish reported that slaves were frequently using poison as a method of resistance: "A horrid practice of poisoning their Masters, or those set over them, having lately prevailed among them. For this practice, 5 or 6 in our Parish have been condemned to die, altho 40 or 50 more were privy to it."[71] In 1751, lawmakers passed additional clauses to the Slave Act of 1740, entitled "An Act for the Better Ordering and Governing Negroes and other Slaves in this Province," to address the issue of poisoning. In this addendum, the General Assembly noted that "the detestable crime of poisoning hath of late been frequently committed by many slaves in this Province, and notwithstanding the execution of several criminals for that offence, yet it has not been sufficient to deter others from being guilty of the same."[72]

The new legislation stipulated that any slave convicted of making, carrying, or using poison would be executed. A reward of £4 was to be given to informants identifying any slave who possessed poisonous substances. Three additional clauses were aimed specifically at conjurers and their abilities to pass on their vast knowledge of roots and plants to apprentices. The first clause stated "that in case any slave teach or instruct another slave in the knowledge of any poisonous root, plant, herb, or other poison . . . shall, upon conviction thereof, suffer death as a felon." Another clause sought "to prevent, as much as may be, all slaves from attaining the knowledge of any mineral or vegetable poison . . . it shall not be lawful for any physician, apothecary or druggist, at any hereafter, to employ any slave or slaves in the shops or places where they keep their medicines or drugs." Lastly, "no negroes or other slaves (commonly called doctors,) shall hereafter be suffered or permitted to administer any medicine, or pretended medicine, to any other" or suffer no more than fifty lashes.[73]

These laws failed to curb the activities of slave spiritualists. In 1761, for example, the South Carolina Gazette reported that "the negroes have again begun the hellish practice of poisoning."[74] In August 1769, the Gazette detailed a specific account of poisoning. In this account, Dolly, a slave owned by James Sands, and a slave named Liverpool who was claimed to be a "Negro Doctor" conspired to poison the infant of Mr. Sands "which died some time since, and attempting to put her master out of the world the same way." Both slaves were burned alive—Dolly for administering the poison and Liverpool for making and furnishing her with the poisonous compound.[75] Not all suspected poisoners were executed however. The 1772 report of an anonymous visitor to South Carolina described "daily instances of the most execrable villains being sold, or sent out of the province . . . even for the horrid crime of administering poison which is an evil of the first magnitude."[76]

While white Carolinians may have indeed viewed poisoning as an "evil of the first magnitude," they could recoup any potential financial losses by selling these dangerous elements in the slave community to other regions of the Americas. The practice of selling rebellious slaves to other colonies was long-standing among planters in the Caribbean; economically, it was a most viable solution to the constant and persistent problem of slave resistance. The frequency of resistive acts shows that restrictive laws, cruel punishments, public torture, and execution were not effective means in preventing slave rebelliousness. Planters and lawmakers alike wanted to find ways either to reap a financial benefit, however minor, from the continued presence of rebellious slaves or to preserve the provincial treasury by avoiding reimbursing slave owners whose slaves were executed.

### Flight, Ethnicity, and Community Formation

One pattern of resistance associated with West-central Africans, at least in the minds of white colonists, was their tendency to abscond. Running away in groups was quite frequent among West-central Africans. Three fugitives ran away from Mr. Paine's plantation on Wando Neck in January 1733. "Hector, Peter and Dublin, all of Angola, and speak but very little English" took with them axes and hoes and escaped by way of canoe. These three slaves were quite prepared for the harsh realities facing them and would have been capable of independent subsistence and survival.[77] In another case, two men "one named Will the other Tom, Angola Slaves; bought about 2 Months ago of Joseph Wragg" escaped together from the plantation of William Donning.[78] As reported in the March 30, 1738, edition of the *South Carolina Gazette*, "3 Angola Negro Men, named Harry, Cyrus and Chatum, they have been in the Country three Years, and speak little English, they are branded BG on the right or left Breast" left Benjamin Godin's plantation.[79]

"Two Angola Negro Men," a *Gazette* runaway advertisement begins, "one named Ben the other Symon," absconded from Richard Wright's plantation in June 1738. In November of the same year another group of Angolan slaves left James Bulloch's plantation near Pon Pon Bridge: "3 new Angola Negro Men, they speak little or no English . . . branded upon their right Breasts just above the nipple B, and are named Fellow, Edinburgh, and Humphry."[80]

In February 1740, the *Gazette* issued advertisements for groups of "Angolan" slaves who left plantations owned by Peter Seccare and James Cochran.[81] This trend of Angolans leaving in groups would continue throughout the colonial era. Two West-central African men escaped from James Island in 1741. In 1748, Moses and Sampson escaped from Daniel Bourget on a canoe headed south from Charles Town. Both men had so recently arrived from West-central Africa, that the runaway advertisement lists their "country names," Monvigo and Goma. Abraham Swadler advertised the loss of three "Angolan" men in September 1752. Three Angolan slaves left their master, John Bulline, in August 1760 and carried "with them an old gun with a small quantity of ammunition."[82] Both Francis LeJau in 1762 and Francis Roche in 1765 advertised the loss of two Angolan "new negroes." In November 1763, seven Angolans, six men and one woman, all fled their master. Five Angolans—four men and one woman—absconded from their plantation in August 1771.[83]

West-central Africans were not the only slaves attempting to escape from bondage in homogeneous groups. Three Igbo men escaped together from two different plantations according to a June 1733 runaway advertisement. In October 1758, Thomas Boone advertised the loss of seven Igbos—five men and two women—from his plantation in the Pon Pon District. Though Igbo were typically associated with suicide and other acts of self-destruction, they appear in disproportionately high numbers in runaway notices.[84] Akan- and Mande-speaking Africans also managed to form runaway enclaves. Two Akan-speaking "Coromantee" slaves escaped from Benjamin Smith in 1761. John Geurard requested the return of two men, both from the Gold Coast, in a 1763 advertisement. Mande-speaking Gambians appeared in a number of advertisements also. In March 1753, four Gambian men, two of whom were noted to have "country marks" on both sides of their faces, left Daniel Heyward's plantation. "Five Gambia new negro men and a boy" left Thomas Heyward's plantation on November 5, 1760. Within days of being disembarked from Captain Watt's slave ship, three Gambian men escaped a plantation at Horse-Savannah on November 19, 1761.[85]

Perhaps the most obvious reason Africans took flight in homogeneous groups is because they had shared cultural understandings and shared visions of community that predated their arrival in the Americas. The five Angolan slaves who left John Vermounet's plantation in St. James Parish in August 1784 epitomize this view. Not only did they leave in a group, but also each of them took "a blanket, kettle, and hoe."[86] These items, as Gomez argues, imply that they sought to establish a viable community outside the purview of white control. Maroonage among escaped African slaves has a long history dating back to the first Spanish settlement in South Carolina. Herbert Aptheker points to the existence of over fifty maroon societies at various times between 1672 and 1864 in isolated mountains, forests, and swamps of the slave South.[87]

In June 1711, white colonists in South Carolina were "in great fear and terror" over the activities of several maroons who attacked, robbed, and plundered plantations and houses.[88] The governor of South Carolina offered a reward in September 1733 for the capture or death of "several Runaway Negroes who are near the Congarees, & have robbed several inhabitants thereabouts."[89] Additional evidence of maroon communities existing in colonial South Carolina can be found in an anonymous letter appearing in a 1772 edition of the *Gazette*. A white witness, in describing a "Country-Dance" of slaves five miles outside Charleston, notes: "They had also their private committees; whose deliberations were carried on in too low a voice, and with so much caution, as not to be overheard by the others . . . Not less than 12 fugitive slaves joined their respectable company before midnight, 8 of whom were mounted on good horses; these, after delivering a good quantity of Mutton, Lamb, and Veal, which they brought with them, directly associated with one or other of the private consultators; and went off about an hour before day, being supplied with liquor, &c. and perhaps having also received some instructions."[90]

An August 1768 letter from Charleston mentions is a conflict between white colonists and a community of maroons described as "a numerous collection of outcast mulattoes, mustees, and free negroes."[91] The heterogeneous nature of this specific maroon community finds parallels in the patterns of slave runaways. In one case, reported in January 1738, two Africans absconded together—Levi "an Angola Negro . . . the other an Ebo Negro, named Kent." Likewise, two more slaves left their plantations in March 1743. They were named "Cyrus and Caesar, the former is an Ebo, and the other an Angola." One runaway advertisement appearing in the *Gazette* in March 1748 reports that Prince, a twenty-six-year-old Angola slave, absconded with "an Ebo Wench, aged about 19 years, named Lydia." On February 19, 1753, Josiah Perrey reported the escape of two slaves—Ismael, "an Angolan fellow," and Plymouth, "an Ebo negro."[92]

Despite the appearance from these runaway advertisements, Angolan and Igbo slaves did not have some special affinity for each other. Gomez, for example, contends that slaves from multiple ethnolinguistic groups running away together is a significant part of the transition "away from ethnicity toward race."[93] It was also part of the transition away from "Africans" and toward "African Americans." Confirmation of this can be found in slave advertisements in which members of different African ethnic groups sought to join forces and escape together. In June 1738, Richard Wright sought the return of five men—two American-born slaves, two Angolans, and one Mande-speaking "Bambra" (Senegambian) slave. Another group of five slaves, including three American-born, an Angolan, and an Akan, successfully escaped from James White's plantation on November 16, 1755. "Guiney born" Ben managed to escape with his Igbo wife, Linda, and their child from James Reid's plantation in 1759. In July 1760, four slaves—two Guinea born, one Igbo, and an American-born biracial woman—absconded from John Martin. One Igbo from Calabar joined a group of seven Akan-speaking "Coromantee" in a mass escape from Thomas Middleton's plantation in Prince William's Parish on November 18, 1761.[94]

The ability of West-central Africans; Igbos and others from Biafra, Akan, and Bambara; and American-born slaves to take flight together in heterogeneous groups, to form family units, and to create maroon communities implies a process of cultural transformation that prefigures similar developments during the 1822 Denmark Vesey conspiracy.[95] Aside from the obvious "cultural bridges" created by dance, drums, and conjure, African groups in colonial South Carolina all faced the same type of oppression and a common foe. Thus, both political conditions and cultural similarities combined to create a new set of identities among African- and American-born slaves.

Individually, runaways represented the most recalcitrant of the enslaved population. The *South Carolina Gazette* reported on May 10, 1735, the story of a West-central African slave held by Thomas Diston of Charles Town who had "run away Saturday the 3d instant from the Plantation."[96] The disaffection with his condition was such that he risked the extreme punishments outlined by the 1712 Slave Act and its subsequent amendments. In 1737, the 1712 Act was further amended to create a more systematic means to discipline runways. This new law mandated the following punishments for runaways: "Every slave of above sixteen that shall runaway from his master, mistress or overseer, and shall continue in the space of twenty days at one

time, shall . . . for the first offense, be publicly and severely whipped not ex-
ceeding 40 lashes; and in case the master, mistress, overseer, or head of the
family shall neglect to inflict such punishment of whipping, upon any negro
or slave that shall run away, for the space of ten days upon complaint made
thereof, within one month . . . said justice of the peace shall by his warrant
directed to the constable, order the said negro or slave to be publicly and
severely whipped."⁹⁷

Slaves running away a second time were to be branded on the right
cheek with the letter "R." For the third offense, one ear was to be cut off.
On certain occasions, slave runaways were executed, especially if they had
designs to escape to St. Augustine. On March 3, 1743, Lieutenant Governor
William Bull introduced a slave woman named Sabina Ladson to the Commons House of Assembly so that she would receive an award for betraying
a runaway plot. According to this entry in the Commons journal, Sabina
had "discovered the Design of several Negroes to desert to St. Augustine
whereupon one of them was tried and executed."⁹⁸

Despite the passage of various restrictive laws and associated draconian
punishments, instances of slave runaways persisted. One example was the
case of a slave named London who escaped from Arthur Bull in January
1754. The runaway advertisement noted that London's country name was
"Apee" and that "he came from St. Croix last year . . . and has several bullet scars in his arms and under the waistband of his breeches." In addition
to having these battle scars and signs of previous torture, Apee also "took
a gun; shot pouch, and some powder and shot with him" perhaps to ensure his freedom from bondage. The next year, Francis Roche placed an
advertisement for the return of Cuffee who escaped from a plantation near
Cooper River. Having very likely been involved in resistive behavior in the
past, Cuffee's main identifying mark was the fact that "all of his toes [were]
burnt off."⁹⁹

Another example appears in the slave runaway advertisement issued by
Captain Thomas Buckle on November 23, 1769. The previous week a slave
named Quako had escaped from Buckle's ship, a schooner named *Margaret*. The captain listed Quako's identifying marks as "his nose slitted, and
both of his Ears cropped"—grisly signs of his frequent attempts to abscond
from his master or otherwise protest his enslavement.¹⁰⁰ Though Appee,
Cuffee, and Quako may or may not have been part of the Akan-speaking
continuum of violent resistance in the Americas, their presence in South

Carolina demonstrates how connected North America was to phenomena occurring throughout the Atlantic World.

The ability to speak in "good" English has often been used as a gauge by a number of scholars to evaluate how acculturated slaves were becoming in North American colonies.[101] In August 1735, a West-central African named Soho who "speaks very little english, mark'd all over his breast his country mark" escaped his master, David Mongin, of Charles Town. The description of Soho is in contrast to that of two slaves who escaped in 1736. One Angola slave named Dick who "speaks good English" escaped from John Edwards of Edisto Island in May 1736.[102] Also in May 1736, the *South Carolina Gazette* reported "run away about 11 months ago an Angola Negro Man named Sampson, speaks English."[103] The ability to escape slavery successfully was perhaps enhanced by the ability to speak English. This skill alone was not a true indicator of which slaves were "acculturated" or "creolized." Atlantic Africans tended to be multilingual people, and this facility with language allowed them to learn English without necessarily being culturally assimilated.[104]

Some slaves actively "code-switched," sliding in and out of pidgin and "good" English when the circumstances warranted. This was the case of a young Angola slave named Ned, who escaped from his master at Ashley-Ferry in October 1746. According to his master, John Gordon, Ned "speaks good English when he pleases."[105] Subterfuge of this nature was prevalent throughout the colonial and antebellum eras in South Carolina. Obviously this was one way in which slaves could create illusive means of communicating and resist exposing their inner thoughts and critiques of slave life to white planters.

In sum, the slaves in colonial South Carolina found many ways to form links and connections that bridged cultural gaps, helped forge a common worldview, and facilitated collective acts of resistance. While dance, drums, conjure, and flight bound slaves together on the earthly plane, the graveyard was a location that brought them together even in death. At numerous gravesites throughout South Carolina, burial customs bearing strong African imprints are prevalent. According to Robert Farris Thompson, "The fusion of slaves from the Gold Coast, the Congo-Angola area, and other parts of the Guinea Coast in Southern slavery could mean the reinforcement of the African notion that the funeral is the climax of life and the dead should be honored by having their possessions placed upon the top of their graves."[106] Placing broken pottery and personal items on graves were ubiquitous practices in the colonial, antebellum, and post–Civil War South. The maintenance of uniquely African burial customs proves that slaves in South Carolina, similar to their counterparts in colonial New York City, did not suffer through a "spiritual holocaust." Indeed, the graveyard as cultural bridge and liminal space was a powerful force in shaping a shared "African American" consciousness.

PART TWO

# African American Resistance in Antebellum America

# CHAPTER 4

# "We Will Wade to Our Knees in Blood"
## Blacksmiths and Ritual Spaces in Gabriel Prosser's Conspiracy

### Slave Imports in Colonial Virginia

The colony of Virginia experienced a very different pace of development in comparison to both New York and South Carolina. From the very inception of the latter two colonies, African slaves were present in large numbers and played key roles in the early economies of both regions. In Virginia, however, there was a slow transition to an African slave labor force only after decades of trial and error with other forms and sources of labor. Africans first appeared in Virginia in August 1619 when a Dutch warship unloaded twenty West-central Africans in exchange for food. Whether they were actually slaves or servants is difficult to answer definitively. Despite the problem of determining the precise label to attach to these first Africans, their overall numbers before 1660 demonstrate that Virginians had yet to conclude that Atlantic Africa would be their primary source for forced labor. The numbers of Africans in Virginia increased slowly over the decades following 1620. By 1649, one report estimates that the African population was only about three hundred strong.[1]

By 1675 the African population had increased to two thousand, marking the beginning of a decided shift from white indentured servants to enslaved Africans. Slavery was officially written into the statute law of Virginia after 1660 and, from that point forward, imported Africans were automatically defined as slaves. The legalization of slavery coincided with the sharp decrease in the number of white indentured servants in the 1660s. African imports steadily increased to meet the labor demand and, by the early 1680s, the black population was between three and four thousand. At the turn of the century, the black population was estimated at ten thousand representing a threefold increase over the span of two decades. The majority of the seventeenth-century imports originated from the Caribbean, but this pattern was to change during the eighteenth century. Many slaves could be purchased legally from Barbados, which became, according to one contemporary account, the source of the vast majority of slaves entering Virginia before 1680. Planters primarily acquired slaves from British Caribbean plantations or the Dutch, so most Africans entering the colony during the late seventeenth century were originally from the Gold Coast, the Bight of Biafra, and West-central Africa.[2]

Between 1700 and 1750, more than 45,000 Africans were imported into Virginia, where the total enslaved population was approximately 100,000 by the mid-eighteenth century. The majority of these slaves came directly from Africa, as evidenced in records kept by the Royal African Company. In the period between June 1698 and December 1708 a total of 6,607 Africans entered Virginia, with only 236 coming from the British Caribbean. This count includes Africans entering the colony via Royal African Company ships and various "separate traders" or private merchants representing recorded slave trading vessels not controlled or owned by the company. The slave trade monopoly held by the Royal African Company ended with the passage of the Act of 1698, which allowed any subject of the crown to trade for slaves in Atlantic Africa. This act rapidly increased the imports of Africans into the colonies, and planters in both the British Caribbean and the Chesapeake could count on a constant supply of fairly cheap labor as a result. In the three decades before the passage of the Act of 1698, the Royal African Company was not keeping up with Virginia's increasingly heavy demand for African labor. In the 1670s, about one thousand Africans were imported on company ships. Between a thousand and fifteen hundred entered Virginia in the 1680s. The 1690s witnessed a marked decline of Royal African Company imports. Of fifty-four company slave ships sent to the Americas between October 25, 1693, and February 15, 1699, only one was consigned to Virginia. The Royal African Company, which held a monopoly on the importation of slaves into the British colonies from 1672 until 1698, only sent 7,248 Africans directly from Africa to Virginia before 1691.[3]

Virginia planters often resorted to both private traders and trade with Barbados to ensure a steady flow of slaves. They were among many who praised the passage of the Act of 1698. The various "separate traders," as the company designated them, transported nine times more Africans to Virginia than the Royal African Company had over the same period between

1698 and 1708. The success of "free trade" permanently undermined the company's ability to monopolize the slave trade, even after the expiration of the Act in 1712.[4]

Free trade meant that an ever-increasing percentage of Africans entering Virginia came directly from Africa. Another reason for the rising presence of slaves directly from Africa was that many Caribbean slaves were sold to mainland colonies as a result of being involved in various acts of resistance. In 1751 Charles Steuart, a factor responsible for selling several cargoes of slaves in Virginia in the 1750s, noted that even small boys from Africa "will sell considerably better than the best West India Negroes, for it is generally supposed that they are ship'd off for great crimes." Another slave factor, Thomas Ringgold of Maryland, informed a correspondent in Barbados that "I shant be able to sell any of ye [Negro] people in general and fearful of them being Rogues and will not give ye price of new Negroes [directly from Africa] for them."[5] This preference for slaves imported from Africa became firmly engrained in import duties by the mid-eighteenth century. In 1759, Virginia imposed a 20 percent tax on slaves coming in from Maryland, North Carolina, and the Caribbean while direct imports from Africa were taxed at 10 percent—a policy that would last until the Revolutionary War.[6]

Between 1710 and 1769, of the 52,504 slaves imported into Virginia, roughly 86 percent were brought directly from Africa. The proportion of slaves imported directly from Africa continued to increase up to the Revolutionary War. In another tabulation of African imports, Susan Westbury estimates that between 1727 and 1775 about 91 percent of slaves entering Virginia came directly from Africa. This heavy importation of Africans occurred despite the fact that most slave ships entering Virginia in that period came from either the Caribbean or nearby North American colonies. These local trade ships rarely unloaded more than a few dozen slaves at a time while the comparatively smaller number of ships from Africa unloaded full cargoes of slaves.[7]

In comparison to South Carolina or Jamaica, the pattern of Virginia slave imports demonstrates some unique ethnic trends. Unlike South Carolina's trade pattern, which was heavily skewed toward slave imports from West-central Africa and Upper Guinea (Senegambia and Sierra Leone), Virginians imported an excessively large number of Africans from the Bight of Biafra (see table 4.1). In the 1700s, roughly 45 percent of Africans from identifiable regions and embarking on ships headed to Virginia came from the Bight of

TABLE 4.1. Enslaved Africans Imported into the British Americas, 1701–1800

| Coastal Region of Origin | Virginia | South Carolina | Jamaica | British North America/ United States |
|---|---|---|---|---|
| Senegambia | 17.1% | 24.9% | 1.8% | 24.4% |
| Sierra Leone | 3.2 | 12.1 | 3.5 | 9.6 |
| Windward Coast | 4.7 | 9.2 | 5.2 | 7.7 |
| Gold Coast | 8.3 | 13.3 | 28.9 | 11.7 |
| Bight of Benin | 2.2 | 2.3 | 11.2 | 3.1 |
| Bight of Biafra | 45.1 | 11.3 | 34.5 | 20.9 |
| West-central Africa | 17.2 | 26.4 | 14.5 | 21.4 |
| Southeast Africa | 2.3 | 0.3 | 0.1 | 1.1 |
| Unknown | 39.1 | 21.3 | 31.0 | 30.3 |

Source: Eltis, Behrendt, Richardson, and Klein, The Trans-Atlantic Slave Trade.
Note: Percentages do not include unspecified destinations.

Biafra.[8] In addition, due to links with Jamaica and Barbados via the lucrative reexport trade, Virginians likely imported an even larger number of Bight of Biafra imports than previously thought. When combining the numbers of slaves imported directly from Africa to those transshipped from the British Caribbean, more than half of all Africans entering Virginia during the eighteenth century were from the Bight of Biafra. By no stretch of the imagination then was this trade as "random" as Philip Morgan claims; nor were the resulting cultural outcomes as "mangled" as Sidney Mintz contends.[9]

Lorena Walsh shows that during the eighteenth century fully nine of ten enslaved Africans were disembarked in Virginia directly from Africa or were transshipped from Jamaica or Barbados after "a brief period of recuperation from their transatlantic ordeal." Using both the Du Bois institute database and records from the British Naval Office, she concludes that two dominant trade import patterns emerged in the Chesapeake. In the upper Chesapeake (Maryland and northern Virginia), slaves from Upper Guinea and the Gold Coast predominated. By comparison, the lower Chesapeake—the region under study in this chapter—received a larger number of Africans from the Bight of Biafra and West-central Africa.[10] This higher percentage of Igbo and other Biafrans entering Virginia in the eighteenth century contrasts the significant opposition to the importation of this group in South Carolina and other British colonies. The concentration of Igbos and other Biafrans in the slave population would later give significant shape to Virginia's slave culture.

## The Biafra Majority in the Lower Chesapeake: Ethnic Preferences and Stereotypes

The English, in general, felt that Africans from Calabar or the Bight of Biafra were among the worst possible laborers. A large number of planters, ship captains, and factors shared this opinion. In 1749, one English commentator claimed that those "who live idle in their own Country, and are in general of a lazy Disposition, and tender Constitution" such as Angolans and Calabars were not in high demand in the British sugar colonies. These groups were either transshipped to other colonies, including North America, or sold in Barbados or Jamaica at an average of ten to twelve pounds less than Gold Coast or Bight of Benin imports. Another commentator in 1757 remarked that the worst slaves "are reckon'd those of Calabar, Congo, Angola, & c."[11] South Carolinians were especially opposed to buying slaves from Calabar and the Bight of Biafra. John Guerard of that colony claimed in 1752 that "I would chuse all Men of Gambia or windward Coast, in failure of which Angolas, but no Bite or Callabarrs, which may be cheaper than the last."[12]

Biafran imports were often much cheaper than other Africans. In 1755, Igbo slaves sold in Charleston for only £270 while Africans from others regions cost £300.[13] Henry Laurens—the noted slave merchant of colonial South Carolina—claimed in 1755 that very few Calabar Africans could be sold in the Charleston slave market when others were available. He then recommended the importation of a "few fine Negro Men, not Callabars."[14] In a letter to Richard Oswald dated May 17, 1756, Laurens also noted that "slaves from the River Gambia are preferr'd to all others with us save the Gold Coast, but there must not be a Callabar among them."[15]

Much of this prejudice against Igbos and others from the Bight of Biafra was due to their alleged propensity to commit suicide. Guerard complained, "As to bite Slaves, I protest against them at any Rate there has been so many instances of their Distroying themselves that none but the Lower sort of People will Medle with them."[16] South Carolina planters who did purchase Calabar slaves were advised to buy only "young People from 15 to 20" who were typically "not accustom'd to destroy themselves" like their older compatriots. Based on this assumption, Henry Laurens advised that Bight of Biafra slaves under the age of fourteen should be the only Africans from that region purchased by Low Country planters.[17] In another assessment by ship captain John Adams, who made ten visits to the Niger River delta between 1786 and 1800, the Igbo were considered to be "naturally timid and desponding, and their despair on being sent on board a ship is often such, that they use every stratagem to effect the commission of suicide, and which they would often accomplish, unless narrowly watched."[18]

Though Vincent Carretta has recently raised doubts about the veracity of Olaudah Equiano's account, this narrative does include verifiable facts and perhaps epitomizes an "authentic" Igbo account of enslavement, the Middle Passage and transshipment.[19] Kidnapped in 1756 at the age of eleven, Equiano survived the harrowing Middle Passage experience and arrived in Barbados. He apparently embarked on a ship in the Bight of Biafra with other Igbo-speakers, for it was among some of his "own nation" that young Equiano found some degree of comfort. The "brutal cruelty" and "savage manner" of the European crew and the "intolerably loathsome" conditions on this ship confirmed his belief that he had indeed been handed over to evil spirits and demons who intended to eat him. This apparently was a ubiquitous belief among captives from the Bight of Biafra who witnessed the various horrors and inhumane abuses made famous by the traffickers in human flesh. It was in this horrid context that two of his countrymen, "who were chained together . . . preferring death to such a life of misery, somehow made through the nettings and jumped into the sea." Equiano himself noted "I now wished for the last friend, death, to relive me."[20] At least according to this account, the alleged Igbo propensity for suicide was directly related to the savage treatment they received at the hands of European shippers.

Despite Equiano's claim that "West India planters prefer the slaves of Benin or Eboe . . . for their hardiness, intelligence, integrity and zeal," that he was immediately transshipped to Virginia after a brief stay in Barbados provides sufficient evidence to the contrary. Before they were disembarked, the ships crew "got some old slaves from the land" to calm the new arrivals and to dispel their fears of white cannibalism. In Barbados, Equiano and the other Igbo arrivals were told by the "old slaves" that many of their country people were already there, a fact that brought a great amount of ease. After staying in Barbados for only "a few days," he and a few of his countrymen were shipped to Virginia. Unlike his encounters in Barbados, Equiano writes that his group was greeted in Virginia by only "a few of our native Africans, and not one soul who could talk to me." He was to stay in Virginia for less than a year before being purchased by Michael Henry Pascal, a British naval officer.[21] Equiano's experiences demonstrate the influx of Igbo-speakers into the British Caribbean and their propensity for suicide, which predisposed planters in Barbados and Jamaica to reexport Bight of Biafra imports to colonies like Virginia.

Philip Curtin contends that the much higher number of Africans imported into Virginia from the Bight of Biafra was due to the strong prejudice against these enslaved Africans by South Carolina and Jamaican planters; since Africans from the Bight of Biafra tended not to sell well in either Charleston or Kingston, Curtin concludes that they "may well have been sold in the nearest convenient market," which in this case would be Virginia. More recently, Lorena Walsh and Stephen Behrendt have shown that this peculiar pattern might be due to the fact that "British merchants employed ships of varying tonnage (and hence slave-carrying capacity) in different African markets." Ships with larger capacities were typically sent to the biggest slave buying markets in the Americas in order to quickly sell their cargoes and maximize profits. Thus, the large capacity ships exporting Africans from the Gold Coast, the Bight of Biafra, and West-central Africa were the majority of the ships entering Jamaica, Barbados, or other large markets in the British Americas. The refuse slaves, in this case the imports from the Bight of Biafra and West-central Africa, were then transshipped to North America. More highly prized Africans from Upper Guinea routinely embarked on smaller capacity ships and were sent to marginal markets like South Carolina and the Upper Chesapeake. This fully explains the paradoxical trade pattern that saw the "least desired ethnic groups [sent] to the best markets while . . . slaves from the most desired groups [were sent] to more marginal ports."[22]

Whatever the explanation for the import patterns, that Virginia would bring in ever increasing numbers of Igbos and other Africans from the Bight of Biafra becomes crucial in understanding the cultural patterns that appeared there. While the alleged Igbo propensity for suicide is well documented, the martial and religious beliefs they brought with them were also important determinants of their activities. These African groups came from regions of West Africa where important metalworking, water ritual, burial, and other traditions were present. These beliefs strongly influenced the worldview of those who joined Gabriel Prosser's 1800 plot.

*Restrictive Legislation and Slave Resistance, 1663–1791*

Virginia was the site of the first known conspiracies involving African laborers to occur in the history of British North America. Two relatively minor disturbances occurred in the 1640s. Though details of a plot in 1663 are lacking, we know it occurred in Gloucester County and included both white indentured servants and enslaved blacks. This biracial plot was betrayed by a white servant, leading to the executions of the plot's leaders.[23]

By the last three decades of the seventeenth century, Virginia slaves made several efforts to create maroon communities. In 1672, a group of escaped slaves created one such rebellious enclave, engaging in a series of armed raids on neighboring plantations. In direct response, the House of Burgesses enacted legislation that stated: "Forasmuch as it hath beene manifested to this grand assembly that many negroes have lately beene, and now are out in rebellion in sundry parts of the country, and that noe means have yet beene found for the apprehension and suppression of them from whom many mischiefs of very dangerous consequences may arise to the country if either other negroes . . . should happen to fly forth and joyne with them." They ordered the capture or death of those slaves involved in activities of this sort. The inability of colonial officials to effectively prevent the rise of rebel communities forced the House of Burgesses to issue additional legislation in June 1680 which ordered the hunting down and killing of maroons in the colony. During the same year, legislators in Virginia moved to ban public gatherings where slaves "played on their Negroe drums." Drums of apparently African manufacture had been used by slaves as a means of communication and could potentially assist in plans for rebellion.[24]

Westmoreland and other Northern Neck counties reportedly witnessed a large-scale slave conspiracy in October 1687. Rebels had planned to kill whites and escape from the region, but their plan was discovered and the leaders were eventually executed. Once again, colonial lawmakers tried to quash the possibility of future resistive activities. Because it was determined by contemporary witnesses that the plot was formed during an unsupervised slave funeral, the legislature banned public slave funerals. It also ordered a special court, which was to include three council members living in Westmoreland, in order to conduct a speedy trial. As Philip Schwarz contends, "The 1687 plot moved the government to create a special court and perhaps even helped to inspire the 1692 institution of the oyer and terminer courts."[25]

In 1709, another alleged conspiracy caught the attention of whites in Virginia—though records of it were seemingly suppressed by the courts and other colonial authorities. This conspiracy involved both slaves and Native Americans in Surry, James City, and Isle of Wright counties. According to a March 24, 1709, special court investigation of the plot, the combatants planned to escape from Virginia, killing any whites who stood in their way. Three slaves—Scipio Edwards, Salvadore Jackmans, and Tom Shaw Thompson —were considered the leaders of the "great numbers of ye said negroes and Indian slaves" apparently involved in the conspiracy. According to a April 4, 1710, report issued by the lieutenant-governor of Virginia to the Lords of Trade, two of the leaders involved in this plot were sentenced to execution. In June, both Scipio and Salvadore were publicly hanged and quartered. As revealed in a statement from the Lords of Trade, the public nature of the executions and bodily mutilations was meant to "serve as an example to deter any attempt of the like nature for the future."[26]

The 1720s witnessed no fewer than three conspiracies, resulting in a series of very restrictive laws. The first plot, occurring in 1722, was alleged to have included slaves from as many as three different Virginia counties. Three slave men—Will Throckmorton, Sam Burwell, and Sam Richardson —were found guilty on November 2, 1722, of unlawful assembly and conspiracy to "kill murder & destroy very many" whites in the region. Each of the leaders received a three-year sentence or was subject to transportation out of Virginia according to the whims of his master. The extent of this conspiracy may have been quite widespread. According to one secondary account, as many as two hundred slaves were involved in this plot, and they sought to "cutt off their masters, and possess themselves of the country." On December 20, 1722, Lieutenant-Governor Hugh Drysdale predicted accurately when he claimed the main consequence of this plot would be the "stirring upp the next Assembly to make more severe laws for the keeping of their slaves in greater subjection."[27]

Within five months of Dyrsdale's statement, another plot was discovered among slaves living in Middlesex and Gloucester counties. An unknown number were involved, but as many as seven enslaved men were found guilty and sentenced to transportation from the province. Before the beginning of the 1723 session of the General Assembly, Dyrsdale warned that the current laws "seem very deficient in the due punishing any Intended Insurrection of your Slaves . . . you are too well acquainted with the Cruel dispositions of those Creatures . . . to let Slipp this faire Oppertunity of makeing more proper Laws against them." Following Drysdale's lead, the assembly quickly enacted a law that made it a capital crime for six or more slaves to "consult, advise, or conspire" with the intent to rebel and kill whites. Despite the long history of servile recalcitrance in colonial Virginia, this was the first law that allowed for the execution of slave rebels and conspirators.[28]

As a result of the various efforts by enslaved blacks to resist bondage, the Virginia assembly began to enact a series of laws that sought to restrict slaves even further. One example is the 1727 law that prohibited slaves from gathering in large numbers, especially during Christmas, Easter, and Whitsuntide celebrations. A law passed in 1748 prohibited the creation and use of poisons by slaves on penalty of immediate execution. With additional conspiracies occurring in 1729, 1730, 1732, 1750, 1767, 1776, 1781, 1782, 1785, and 1791, it was painfully obvious to Virginia lawmakers that legislation could never cure slaves of their resistive proclivities. The worst was yet to come. During the decade between 1792 and 1802, white Virginians would witness unprecedented slave resistance, both in frequency and scope.[29]

### Gabriel Prosser's Plot in History and Historiography

Northampton, a county that had roughly equal numbers of slaves and whites in 1790, witnessed a major slave conspiracy on May 5, 1792.[30] On that day, Lieutenant Smith Snead of the Northampton militia received a letter from six local residents informing him of an impending slave revolt. In response to this alarm, Snead requested much-needed military supplies from the governor.[31] Another letter dated May 17, 1792, reveals specific details about the plot: "Several alarming accounts have been received in town, of a very dangerous Insurrection among the Negroes in the Eastern shore of Virginia;— Reports state, That about two weeks ago, the Negroes in that part of the State, to the amount of about 900, assembled in different parts, armed with muskets, spears, clubs &c and committed several outrages upon the inhabitants . . . Celeb, a negro, the property of Mr. Simkins, was to command this banditi . . . A barrel of musket balls, about 300 spears, some guns, powder, provisions, &c have already been discovered and taken; the spears, it is said, were made by a negro blacksmith on the Eastern shore."[32]

This plot allegedly included slaves from Norfolk and Portsmouth as well. The rebels were to explode the ammunition depot in Norfolk and kill as many of the city's inhabitants as they could. An anonymous slave revealed

the plot to local officials and the captured ringleaders were hanged. For pre-
cautionary purposes, the county of Northampton increased patrols and limited the movement of slaves. These militia patrols became new targets for
slave resentment. One militia unit on patrol duty was assaulted by six slaves
armed with clubs. The patrol escaped unharmed, but five of the attackers
were tried and executed for their actions.[33] Many of the details pertaining
to this conspiracy remain unclear, but the presence and involvement of a
blacksmith in the preparation of this revolt is highly significant.

According to both Michael Mullin and Douglas Egerton, the presence of
blacksmiths and other skilled artisans in this and other slave revolts implies
that these slaves were "highly acculturated." Mullin makes this argument
in two separate works—*Flight and Rebellion* and *Africa in America*. In the first
effort, he observes that in the case of Gabriel's 1800 conspiracy, the core
leaders were "a small group of relatively assimilated slave artisans."[34] These
men were American born, literate, probably Christian, and heavily influenced by the radical political doctrine generated by the American Revolution. These combined factors contributed to the development of a plot that
was, according to Mullin, "exceptionally political in character."[35] Unlike
Denmark Vesey or Nat Turner, who both relied in varying degrees on religion or magic, Gabriel's plot "lack[ed] a sacred dimension, was without a
Moses, and thus without a following."[36]

In Mullin's interpretation, since these few slaves had been inspired by
revolutionary ideology, had acquired an "intelligent demeanor," and had
advanced in the occupational hierarchy, they were better able to "outwardly"
resist the slave regime. According to this view, unassimilated Africans
tended to be illiterate, unskilled laborers who relied on conjure and other
spiritual means to "inwardly" resist their oppressed condition. The natural
disjuncture between the enlightened few and the benighted many very likely
meant that Gabriel had, in this view, a limited numbers of followers.[37]

Despite the problematic overtones of this argument, Mullin reproduces
the alleged dichotomy between the assimilated artisan and the spiritually
inspired field hand in his 1994 work *Africa in America*.[38] Again it is the "as-
similateds" who are able to utilize their "artful" demeanors and occupational skills to facilitate resistance. The "ingenuity and resourcefulness that
flowed from the social and psychological compensations of their tasks and
rank" gave them a decided advantage over the field hands. These were the
key factors in determining who would be part of the leadership in Gabriel's

plot and why the conspiracy gained only a few adherents. Mullin argues that an unbridgeable divide separated the creolized leadership from the African masses.[39]

Douglas Egerton's 1993 work entitled *Gabriel's Rebellion: The Virginia Slave Conspiracies of 1800 and 1802* follows Mullin's interpretations quite closely. Egerton's Gabriel was not a man inspired by religion or spirituality but was instead an urban artisan who employed the language of republicanism.[40] Egerton echoes both Arna Bontemps and Mullin when he adds that "Gabriel, unlike Nat Turner, neglected to cast his appeals in messianic terms or to imply that he was the man chosen to bring on the day of jubilee."[41] This failure was ultimately due to the fact that Gabriel's "association with politicized white artisans pulled him away from the religious traditions of the quarters."[42]

In Egerton's view, this plot was more class revolt than potential slave rebellion. Highly politicized urban artisans, black and white, joined together against those who lived from the toil of others—merchants, bankers, and speculators. Many of these mechanics formed and joined Democratic-Republican societies that typically adhered to an egalitarian interpretation of the American Revolution. It would be in this volatile environment that Gabriel gained his political consciousness. Egerton writes, "From Gabriel's limited urban perspective, it appeared that the white mechanics he labored alongside were preparing for battle in a political cause, and that cause was his as well."[43] He transforms Gabriel into a Jeffersonian Republican, a conclusion that is tenuous at best.

According to Egerton, Gabriel simply did not know that Virginian Republicans were typically slaveholding planters and that the revolutionary rhetoric sought the equality of white males only. "It appears that the Republican planters played no part in his thinking," Egerton adds, "for he never identified them, or even whites in general, as enemies."[44] In this view, Gabriel in fact had much more in common with white mechanics than with black field hands. He had a consciousness based primarily on class and thus reserved the word "enemy" for the exploitative merchants only. This startling conclusion is based largely on a single comment Ben Prosser made during the trials following disclosure of the plot. Egerton does not include the direct quote in his work, but it can readily be found in the voluminous documents generated by the courts.[45]

On October 6, 1800, during the trial of Gabriel, Ben Prosser testified "if the white people agreed to their freedom they would then hoist a white flag, and he would dine and drink with the merchants of the city on the day when it should be agreed to."[46] This is the only comment in the testimony given that day by Ben pertaining to merchants. It is difficult, if not impossible, to conclude from this statement that Gabriel singled out the merchants of Richmond as his sole enemies. On the contrary, Ben asserts later that "none were to be spared of the whites except Quakers, Methodists, and French people."[47] In other words, not even the mechanics and artisans that Gabriel was supposedly in allegiance with were to be spared the collective wrath of slaves. Egerton does make note of this statement but still manages to fit it within his interpretation. Essentially, he takes the quote out of context emphasizing only that "Gabriel warned that 'Quakers, Methodists, and French people' were not to be harmed." By beginning the quote at that point, he avoids dealing with the fact that Gabriel had also commanded "none were to be spared of the whites," which completely undermines Egerton's view of an interracial class revolt.

Gabriel and the other slaves involved in this plot had no problems identifying whites in general as their enemies. This is not to deny the active involvement of whites in other examples of slave resistance. Biracial elements were readily evident in the 1741 New York conspiracy and a number of attempts at servile resistance in Virginia between 1640 and 1676 (and 1859 for that matter). There is, however, no evidence of biracial collaboration in Gabriel's plot. In the trial record, comments such as "he would join him to fight the white people," "he would enlist with Gabriel to fight the white people," or "the prisoner proposed to join and fight the whites" are frequent. Aside from the exemptions noted, whites in general were readily viewed as the targets for violent retribution during the planned insurrection. Gabriel's views regarding whites were further exposed during an October 1799 conflict he had with Absalom Johnson—a white overseer working for Colonel Nathaniel Wilkinson's plantation. After Johnson accosted a slave named Jupiter Wilkinson for allegedly stealing a hog from his master's plantation, Gabriel and his brother Solomon confronted the overseer. While Solomon threatened to destroy Johnson "or his property by Fire or other ways," Gabriel physically assaulted him and bit off a large portion of his left ear. All three slaves—Jupiter, Solomon, and Gabriel—

were later found guilty of conspiring to kill the whites of Richmond within one year of this altercation. More importantly, once the plans for rebellion were formed, the slave conspirators identified Johnson as one of the first white men they would kill. This 1799 confrontation and the various comments made in the trial record demonstrates that Gabriel did not view men like Johnson as anything but mortal enemies, despite any similarities in their respective social standing.[48]

In both Mullin's and Egerton's treatment of the 1800 plot, there seems to be a shared sentiment that slaves possessing blacksmith skills must have received that knowledge from European or Euro-American artisans. This conclusion may be plausible in the case of Gabriel, who was actually trained in America.[49] But for other slave artisans, having skills of this nature should not necessarily be a measure of the degree of assimilation or acculturation. Ironworking in Atlantic Africa dates back as early as 600 B.C. The earliest known iron smelting in West Africa took place in central Nigeria, home of many of the Igbo and others who were to become one of the largest African-born segments of Virginia's slave population. At a site discovered in eastern Nigeria in the 1960s, archaeologists uncovered iron implements, including blades, nails, rods and rings, made by the Igbo-Ukwu sometime between the eighth and eleventh centuries A.D., and similar findings have been made throughout Igboland. In southeastern Nigeria, a number of iron-smelting furnaces well over two thousand years old have been found.[50]

The ancient tradition of metalworking in West Africa led to blacksmiths having spiritual influence in a number of societies.[51] However, a lack of knowledge among American historians about Africa's historical and cultural contributions has led to faulty and defective analyses of how outlandish Africans were transformed into intelligent, assimilated, and skilled artisans in North America. The idea of neolithic Africans being introduced to "modern" European technology greatly overstates the case. No matter how well intentioned, these treatments are decidedly ethnocentric.

Perhaps the best recent treatment of Gabriel's plot can be found in James Sidbury's 1997 work, Ploughshares into Swords. Sidbury's Gabriel is not depicted simply as an assimilated slave. Of course, Gabriel was literate, but literacy was an important tool that enslaved blacks utilized to guarantee their freedom; it was not necessarily a measure of how "American" they were becoming. Being able to write gave slaves the very practical ability to produce passes to facilitate safe travel. This ability alone, therefore, cannot be accurately used to gauge the degree of assimilation. We also know, as Sterling Stuckey has shown, that slave folk tales with African values of profound import were conveyed in English, a language that helped to preserve such concepts.[52]

In addition, Sidbury points out that the prominent role that blacksmiths were to play in Gabriel's revolt demonstrates a plausible African cultural link. The Yoruba *orisha* known as Ogun was both a blacksmith and a warrior, and Yoruba-speakers accorded all blacksmiths a high degree of reverence. Though admittedly very few Virginian slaves were Yoruba-speakers, Sidbury adds that "blacksmiths also played prominent roles in the cosmology of the neighboring Igbo, the people most frequently sold into the colony." While much of this case ends up being based on inferential evidence, Sidbury does open the possibility of African cultural connections that were alive in Gabriel's Virginia. He concludes that blacksmiths brought a sense of cultural authority with them across the Atlantic which would have been of value to those assuming leadership roles in slave revolts.[53]

### Details of Gabriel Prosser's 1800 Plot

By early summer, the conspiracy of 1800 was in its formative stages. Gabriel; his two brothers, Solomon and Martin; and Jack Ditcher were among the initial leaders of the planned revolt. According to the trial testimony, the plot seems to have been originally formulated by Jack. Ben Prosser testified on October 9, 1800, that "Gabriel informed him that [Jack] was the first person from whom he received information of the insurrection intended by the Negroes."[54] Initially, Gabriel was not even the leader of the revolt. Again, Ben Prosser's testimony reveals that "Gabriel was appointed Captain at first consultation respecting the Insurrection, and afterwards when he had enlisted a number of men appointed General."[55] Even though Jack was the first to devise the slave plot, Gabriel became the "general" of the conspiracy. Jack was physically more imposing and older than Gabriel and might have seemed better suited to lead the slave insurgents.[56] Jack felt that he, not Gabriel, should be the general of the rebellion. According to Ben, Jack would often visit the blacksmith's shop that Gabriel, Solomon, and Ben worked at to "raise and enlist men and contend for command with Gabriel."[57]

This struggle over leadership reached its apex three weeks before the planned revolt. Many of the leaders and other enlisted men met at a spring near the plantation of William Young. According to Ben, it was at this

meeting that Jack "applied to many who had agreed to engage in the insurrection, to give him the voice for General." When the votes were tallied,
"Gabriel had by far the greater number." Jack was later elected as Gabriel's
second-in-command and captain of the cavalry.[58]

Why did the enlisted slaves choose Gabriel over Jack? Surely the slaves
did not choose "Gabriel's brains over Ditcher's brawn," as Egerton explicitly concludes.[59] It would seem the field slaves, who were well represented
among the enlisted men, would have been highly suspicious of an assimilated slave espousing the rhetoric of artisan republicanism. What freedom
can be found in an ideology that embraces the planter class? Would potential conspirators follow someone who allegedly had more in common with
white mechanics than with field hands? That Gabriel was literate and an
artisan would not seem to sway the sentiments of slaves decidedly in his
favor; in this regard; he would lack the credibility and authenticity they may
have sought in a general. The most plausible reason that Gabriel became
the leader of the rebellion was his employment and embodiment, conscious
or not, of cultural metaphors and cultural spaces that enslaved Igbos and
others would find familiar and inspirational.

The role that metalworkers played in the planning of this revolt was
central. Their most practical function was making weapons to be used during the revolt. Ben Prosser testified that Solomon, Gabriel's older brother,
"made a number of swords" in preparation of the rebellion.[60] On one occasion, Solomon was commissioned to transform two scythe blades into
four swords. On another, Issac Allen asked Solomon to make him a sword
because, as Ben Prosser testified, he was "determined not to serve the white
man another year." Solomon agreed to fashion a sword for Isaac but only after he received a scythe blade from him. He then showed Isaac some "handles
which he had for the swords."[61] In his own confession, Solomon states that
Gabriel "applied to me to make scythe-swords, which I did to the number
of twelve."[62] These scythe-blade swords were to serve as the primary weapons for the slave rebels until the weapons caches in Richmond were taken.

While Solomon had the task of fashioning the blades, Gabriel utilized
his own skills to craft handles for the swords. With the aid of his other
brother Martin, Gabriel also fashioned some five hundred bullets. Though
Gabriel felt that Martin was too old to fight, his eldest brother did volun-
teer to "run bullets and keep them in bullets." Ben Prosser further adds
that Gabriel "had twelve dozen swords made, and had worn out two pair of

bullet moulds in running bullets, and pulling a third pair out of his pocket, observed that was nearly worn out." The confession of Ben Woolfolk reveals another example of Gabriel's ability as a blacksmith. One slave insurgent named Gilbert had somehow secured a pistol "but it was in need of repair; he gave it to Gabriel, who was [to] put it in order for him."[63]

Knowing that he could not forge enough weapons for all the enlisted slaves, Gabriel made careful note of where arms were stored in Richmond. Jupiter, the slave of Colonel Wilkinson, had agreed to give Gabriel the colonel's key to one of Richmond's arms caches.[64] But before Richmond could be successfully taken, Gabriel and his men needed more weapons with which to fight. Gabriel proved to be very resourceful in this regard by enlisting the aid of yet another blacksmith, Thornton Thilman. This blacksmith was appointed or elected as another important leader of the slave army and, according to Ben's testimony, "was to go under the name or title of Colonel."[65] Ben testifies further that Thornton stated "they need not provide arms for his men, for he would do that himself, and pointed to some scythe blades then in the shop, which he said would make to answer the purpose." Like Solomon and Gabriel, Thornton had the ability to transform scythe blades into swords. In addition, he made a number of bullets and even produced a sample of his work to demonstrate to Ben the process of making cartridges.[66]

While blacksmiths played important leadership roles in this conspiracy, the blacksmith's forge served a multitude of functions during the planning phases of the revolt. First, it was the place that Solomon, Gabriel, and Thornton fabricated most of the arms the conspirators were to use. Second, Gabriel utilized the blacksmith shop on Thomas Prosser's plantation as both a recruiting station and meeting place. In Ben Prosser's testimony on October 9, 1800, it is revealed that the shop was where Jack "would raise and enlist men."[67] Finally, on the night that the revolt was to occur, "the place of meeting was near Prosser's Blacksmith's shop in the woods."[68]

The revolt was to take place Saturday, August 30, 1800, at midnight. The rebellion was set for that month primarily because a number of soldiers had recently been discharged, leaving Richmond relatively vulnerable to attack. Gabriel's followers were first to be provisioned with weapons forged by the blacksmiths and acquired from two slaves who had access to armories in the city. The first whites to be killed were to be those on the Prosser and Wilkinson plantations, including Absalom Johnson, the white overseer

Gabriel had assaulted the year before. After the combatants killed Prosser's family and Johnson, the neighboring planters were to be attacked as well. The next stage involved a group of fifty combatants who were to set fire to the southern end of Richmond to serve as a decoy. While the whites attended the blaze, more slaves would enter the city to seize additional arms and ammunition. At this time, the greatest amount of killing was to commence, with all whites except Quakers, Methodists and French to be put to death. Other whites who agreed to the end of slavery would have at least an arm amputated. Even blacks who did not support the cause were to be killed. After Richmond was taken, the rebels would attack one of two neighboring towns, either Hanover Town or York, and Gabriel had ultimately "intended to subdue the whole of the country where slavery was permitted."[69]

On the day of the intended rebellion, two slaves owned by Mosby Sheppard—Tom and Pharoah—betrayed the plot to their master, and Sheppard managed to inform Governor James Monroe of the impending danger. Immediately, Monroe ordered nearby militia units to guard the capitol building, the penitentiary, the magazine, and the major roads leading to Richmond. In addition, the governor received permission to use the federal armory at Manchester and informed every militia commander in the state about the rebellion. Even with these swift and decisive actions on the part of Monroe, Richmond may not have been spared if not for an unforeseen event that destroyed all hopes of a successful revolt. Just after sunset, the area around Richmond witnessed a deluge of epic proportions. The enormous amount of rainfall washed away bridges and flooded some of the major roads between Prosser's plantation and the capital. As one contemporary noted, when the bridge over Brook Swamp was destroyed by the torrential rain, "the africans were of necessity to pass, and the rain had made the passage impracticable."[70]

It is questionable whether the 650 militiamen Monroe called upon could have successfully repulsed the full force of Gabriel's army. Several hundred slaves armed with clubs, scythe-swords, knives, and guns reportedly assembled at the rendezvous location six miles outside Richmond. The attack was delayed because the rain made it impossible for all the combatants to meet. During the delay, a number of slaves were arrested and Gabriel went into hiding. While attempting to escape the area on a schooner named *Mary*, he was captured in Norfolk on September 25, 1800. After the trials, which lasted from September 8 to November 22, thirty-five slaves were executed, ten were banished from the state, six were pardoned, four somehow managed to escape prison, and one committed suicide. While the actual number of those actively involved in the conspiracy will never be known, the count was likely less than the ten thousand Gabriel claimed and significantly more than the fifty slaves officially charged with conspiracy.[71]

### Technospiritual Forces and Concepts among West African Imports into Virginia

Among Yoruba-speakers in the western portion of the Niger River Delta, the ancient god Ogun, the deity of iron, warfare, and hunting, was a central figure in their religious practice.[72] In the words of Robert Farris Thompson, Ogun "lives in the flames of the blacksmith's forge, on the battlefield, and more particularly on the cutting edge of iron."[73] Through a combination of military conquest and relatively benign cultural diffusion, the influence of the Yoruba orisha, or deities, spread over much of the region west of the Niger river. In the kingdom of Dahomey, Ogun became Gû, the god of iron and war among the Fon. Among the Edo in Benin, Ogun appears again as a blacksmith, hunter, and warrior. In these regions, blacksmiths were highly respected mainly because, according to Margaret Thompson Drewal, "working with iron, man thus partakes of Ogun's dynamic force."[74] Blacksmiths were, in effect, earthly embodiments of Ogun. They wielded powerful technospiritual forces and, because blacksmiths created the instruments necessary for hunting and war, they seemingly controlled life and death. Enslaved Africans exported from the Bight of Benin would have been familiar with these concepts and would have accorded blacksmiths like Gabriel, Solomon, and Thornton a great degree of respect.

Though Bight of Benin imports represented about 2 percent of Africans from identifiable regions entering eighteenth-century Virginia, this small number was augmented by Saint-Domingans entering the state in the wake of the 1791 slave revolt there. Beginning in 1793, large groups of French colonists escaping Saint-Domingue were landing in Norfolk. Though no records exist detailing the actual number of Saint-Domingue slaves entering Virginia between 1793 and 1800, the number was certainly in the hundreds. These immigrants would have likely been exposed to vodun, a discrete system that emerged in Saint-Domingue from a confluence of Dahomean, Fon, Aja, Ewe, Yoruba, Kongo, and Angolan beliefs. The god Ogun was also present in this belief system.[75]

The influence of Ogun worship spread to regions east of the Niger River delta, which included the Bight of Biafra. This cultural diffusion was due, in part, to the rise of a series of conquest states between 1400 and 1700, including the Edo kingdom of Benin, the Fon kingdom of Dahomey, and the Yoruba kingdom of Oyo. Benin even established tributaries in the heart of Igboland, according to Equiano's narrative and other historical accounts.[76] Among a number of Calabar or Bight of Biafra groups, including the Igbo, the Igala, the Idoma, and others in the eastern portion of the Niger River delta, Ogun does not appear as a specific deity but rather as a ritual practice associated with blacksmiths. The absence of Yoruba and Edo *orisha* among the Igbo and others may be due to the fact that, according to Robert Armstrong, "pantheons are more typical of hierarchical organized states than of stateless societies."[77]

The Idoma concept of *ògwú* is of extreme importance among warriors and hunters. When a hunter has destroyed a fierce beast or a warrior has slain an enemy, he must then go through a ceremony called *èögwóönà*, which washes from the face of the killer *ògwú*, a combination of pride and battle rage. One reason for this ceremony, according to Armstrong, is "that without it, the spirit of the slain enemy or animal may trouble the victorious warrior or successful hunter, and he may cause trouble at home."[78] This cleansing ceremony is performed by a blacksmith at a metal forge. Similarly, among the Igala, there is the concept of *ògú*, which parallels *ògwú* in form and meaning. *Ògú* refers primarily to battle rage, or the "near-mad behavior of a successful killer," and it requires the water of a blacksmith's forge to cool down the enraged warrior.[79]

The Igbo and others exported from Biafra therefore had similar ideas to those in from the Bight of Benin about the link between blacksmiths, killing, and cleansing. Among the Igbo, the word *ògbú*, "killer," is conjectured to be the linguistic base from which various cognates like *ògú*, *ògwú*, and ultimately Ogun derive both their meaning and phonetic similarities. The Igbo shared the belief that those dealing in death—hunters and warriors—had to be cleansed or "cooled" in the waters of a blacksmith's forge. Because of these cultural connections, Armstrong has concluded "these must be regarded as an ancient set of culture words associated with the spread of the cult-like syndrome of ideas, probably westward from Igbo to Yoruba and Fon."[80]

Some verification that such ritual beliefs reached Virginia via Igbo slaves can be found in Equiano's autobiographical account. Born in the Igbo village of Essaka, he was seized at age ten by African slave traders. After being sold to a planter in Virginia in 1756, Equiano was to stay there for less than a year. A contemporary of Gabriel's parents, Equiano recounts: "The natives of this part of Africa are extremely cleanly. This necessary habit of decency was with us a part of religion, and therefore we had many purifications and washings . . . Those that touched the dead, at any time, were obliged to wash and purify themselves before they could enter a dwelling-house, or touch any person or anything we eat."[81] Though no specific mention is made regarding blacksmiths, Equiano emphasizes a purification process similar to the ones associated with hunters and warriors. It could well be that this is the same ceremony performed to wash pride, battle rage and "killing" off the faces of those who deal in death.

In addition to ògbú and other concepts connected to Ogun, the Igbo developed an entire complex of practices and beliefs regarding blacksmiths. Owing to the ancient nature of ironworking in this region, the complexity of these traditions should come as no surprise. During the eighteenth and nineteenth centuries, three major centers of ironworking emerged in Igboland—Awka, Abiriba, and Nkwerre. In each town, blacksmiths formed an endogamous group of itinerant craftsmen. During a six- to eight-month period every year, small groups of blacksmiths traveled throughout Igboland plying their trade. The secrets of ironworking were closely guarded, and the Igbo highly revered these traveling blacksmiths.[82]

Igbo blacksmiths were associated with spiritual powers as well. The smiths of Awka, for example, used their seasonal travels as an opportunity to inform others about the powerful oracle located in their town. According to one oral tradition, the smiths of Awka were directly descended from a man named Awka—the first blacksmith who was instructed in this divine craft by the Igbo creator god Chukwu. Perhaps because their trade was so closely linked to spiritual forces, Igbo blacksmiths were known to produce protective charms and amulets and, in some cases, even erected religious shrines.[83] They therefore were understood by many in the Bight of Biafra and the Niger River delta to command technospiritual forces that could possibly prove useful to slave rebels in the Americas.

Evidence of both African-born blacksmiths and identifiably African styles of metalworking in Virginia indicate the correlating transmission of concepts connected to particular Atlantic African spiritual beliefs. In two separate slave runaway advertisements in the *Virginia Gazette*, mention is made of Africa-born blacksmiths. On January 10, 1771, James Walker posted a notice for the return of Sam, a thirty-two-year-old from Africa who was "a tolerable blacksmith." Sam, however, had been in Virginia for nineteen years by the time this advertisement was published. Thus it is questionable whether he gained his knowledge of the trade in West Africa.[84] In another instance, Edmund Ruffin placed a runaway advertisement in January 1776 for "Lewis, an outlandish, short, thick fellow, remarkably bow-legged, an excellent wheelwright and wagon maker, and a very good blacksmith."[85] It is likely that African-born metallurgists brought both the requisite technical expertise and uniquely African metaphysical understandings of their craft to eighteenth-century Virginia.

African styles of metalworking in Virginia were found in a set of metal spoons excavated at Kingsmill Plantation in Williamsburg, Virginia. The spoons have identifiable African iconographic symbols carved on them, possibly reflecting a specific West-central African cosmological belief.[86] The discovery of a wrought-iron figure excavated from a blacksmith shop and slave quarters in Alexandria, Virginia, is the most striking example of African metalworking styles appearing in North America (see fig. 4.1). The figure, which dates back to the late eighteenth century, bears strong similarity to Ogun and Gû iron statues crafted in West Africa by Fon, Yoruba and Edo blacksmiths. John Michael Vlach identifies the piece as similar to wrought-iron figures made by Mande-speaking blacksmiths from Upper Guinea.[87]

Mande-speakers and others from Senegambia made up roughly 17 percent of all enslaved Africans sent from identifiable ports in Atlantic Africa to Virginia during the eighteenth century. Like the Igbo and others from Biafra, they also brought with them particular understandings of the spiritual powers of blacksmiths. According to two separate European witnesses who visited the Bamana region during the nineteenth century, there was a great degree of association between blacksmiths and conjurers among the Mande. In many cases, Mande smiths were viewed as priests with the uncanny ability of bridging technology to sorcery. These smith-priests were responsible for making protective amulets

FIGURE 4.1. Wrought iron statue, Alexandria, Virginia, ca. late eighteenth century.

and weapons forged in wrought iron and imbued with a technospiritual force known as *nyama*. The case of an elderly Mande blacksmith named Niany is quite instructive. As detailed in an 1840s travel account by Anne Raffenel, Niany was described as a combination of smith, priest, doctor, spirit medium, and exorcist. In other words, blacksmiths among Mande-speakers held an elevated spiritual position similar to their counterparts among ethnic groups living in the Niger delta.[88]

If any Mande were involved in Gabriel's conspiracy, they would have probably accorded blacksmiths respect and reverence. Considering the combined influx of enslaved Africans from Biafra, Senegambia, Benin, and Saint-Domingue, some two-thirds of all enslaved imports entering Virginia in the late eighteenth century came from societies with rich metalworking traditions (see table 4.1). These groups found in the role of the blacksmith, a powerful combination of martial, technological, and spiritual mastery, which explains the elevated position of metalworkers in a number of Atlantic African societies. Perhaps then, the leadership roles assumed by African and African American blacksmiths in Virginia were direct results of these cultural realities.

*Bridges, Springs, and Rivers: Ritual Spaces in Gabriel's Conspiracy*
Important spaces in the forming of the rebellion were areas such as bridges, spring, and rivers, which were near or adjacent to waterways. In the trial of a slave named Frank, John Price stated, "Gabriel asked [Frank] to join him . . . Those who were to join were to stand up; the prisoner stood up. They were to meet at Young's spring afterwards to confer on the same subject."[89] The testimony given again by John on October 6, 1800, during the trial of Gabriel reveals what happened during the meeting planned at Young's spring, just three weeks before the uprising. He mentions that Gabriel "gave a general invitation to the negro men to attend the Spring . . . when there he mentioned the Insurrection, and proposed that all present should join them in the same, and meet in 3 weeks for the purpose of carrying the same into effect."[90] This would be the same meeting at which Gabriel became the overwhelming choice as general of the rebellion. Details of the plans for the rebellion also were formed at Young's spring.[91]

Another important recruiting meeting, which occurred two weeks before the planned insurrection, took place at Littlepage's Bridge, yet another association with a waterway. On this occasion, the slaves assembled for a Sunday religious service at the bridge. After the sermon, several slaves gathered by a spring a short distance away to discuss the conspiracy. Ben Woolfolk testified that "on his way to Caroline he fell in with [Thilman's Dick] at the bridge called Littlepage's. He enquired about the business and how they were to get arms, which being mentioned, he said he would certainly attend at the time and place appointed."[92] It was at this meeting that the blacksmith Thornton made his first appearance in the plot. According the Ben Woolfolk, Thornton "was damned glad to hear [the rebellion] would take place soon." Woolfolk added that "Thornton with other slaves, came to the spring and there said he would be sure to bring his men at the appointed time."[93] The conspirators were to further solidify their plans, elect more leaders, and recruit additional slaves on this eventful day. During the meeting at Littlepage's Bridge, the slave insurgents chose Brook's Bridge as the final rendezvous site for the rebellion.

Igbo and others from Biafra saw waterways as important cultural symbols and ritual spaces. During the early nineteenth century, the Efik of Calabar worshipped a number of ndem, or river gods and goddesses. Devotees would dress in white and perform religious rites at rivers or other bodies of water; after being possessed by river spirits, they engaged in emotional and expressive dancing. In assessing the early-nineteenth-century variant of this ritual practice, Rosalind Hackett notes that "Ndem are always prayed to for blessings, fertility and forgiveness and for the special protection which they are believed to extend to the people of Calabar."[94] The Igbo also believed that rivers, springs, and other bodies of water contained protective spirits. During the late nineteenth and early twentieth century, the Igbo paid homage to a number of water deities and held particular bodies of water as sacred spaces. These Owo Amapo, or water spirits, dwell in rivers, pools, and springs and were both feared and respected by the Igbo in the Niger delta.[95]

Certain cleansing and purification rites were common in the worship of Igbo water spirits and in other West African river cults. The cleansing and purification rites discussed by Equiano suggest that the Igbo likely maintained the belief in the spiritually restorative power of cleansing by water in Virginia. In this context, it is ironic that water, in the form of a deluge, was the principal cause for the conspiracy's failure.[96]

African river cults and water spirits, along with the various baptismal rites associated with their worship, were important to many Atlantic African groups. Similar concepts were prevalent among the Yoruba of the Niger River delta, the Akan of the Gold Coast, and the BaKongo of West-central Africa. These common practices linked Africans from different cultural enclaves and allowed for the creation of a more unitary ethos. This set of beliefs regarding water rites, according to Melville Herskovits, explains why the Baptist Church became such an influential factor in black religious life in the South.[97] Herskovits adds that the popularity of the Baptist Church by the nineteenth and twentieth century should not be surprising since the "predisposition of these Africans toward a cult [the Baptist Church] which, in emphasizing baptism by total immersion, made possible the worship of the new supernatural powers in ways that at least contained elements not entirely unfamiliar."[98] In other words, the seeming Christianization of American slaves was facilitated by the lasting presence of West African religious traditions and practices. Practices that superficially appear to be "Christian" may in reality be linked to West and West-central African ritual beliefs.

African cultural concepts, then, may have influenced the planned revolt in the form of blacksmith forges and waterways serving as primary congregation locations for the slave conspirators. It is plausible, therefore, that the slaves chose Gabriel as their general because he held both the mundane and metaphysical powers associated with blacksmiths in Atlantic Africa. His ability to craft arms, though extremely important, could not have been the sole factor in explaining why he became the leader of the plot. In the confession of Ben Woolfolk, it is revealed that Jack Ditcher also produced arms: "he had got 50 spiers or bayonets fixed at the end of sticks." Though he was not a metalworker, Jack carved spears and used rope to fix knives to the ends of wooden poles.[99]

As a blacksmith, Gabriel would have been a potent spiritual and martial symbol among a sizable number of slaves in Virginia in 1800. It is, therefore, not surprising that it was at a spring that the enlisted men picked him as their leader. Apparently Gabriel was thought to be an important bearer of African culture, one who had the ability to craft the weapons of war and, consequently, might have been thought to possess the ritual powers held by blacksmiths. For the Igbo and others involved in this conspiracy, it was the powerful mixture of familiar symbols and spaces that gave them a decided advantage in their endeavor to overthrow the slave regime in Virginia.

*Spirituality, Conjure, and Poisoning in Virginia, 1745–1800*
The fact that slaves, during the planning of the 1800 Virginia revolt, held religious and secular ceremonies at springs and bridges implies that these spaces held some ritual power in the minds of African- and American-born slaves. The slaves made an elaborate oath at Littlepages' Bridge in which they shook hands and stated, "here are our hands and hearts, we will wade to our knees in blood sooner than fail in the attempt."[100] Other relevant Atlantic African religious practices and beliefs were present in Virginia during the time of Gabriel's planned revolt. One proof of this appears in the excavation of an eighteenth-century burial site in James City County, Virginia. Sometime between 1700 and 1750 an unknown black woman was buried in the Utopia quarter cemetery with a clay tobacco pipe under her left arm. Two other adults were buried with tobacco pipes and an adolescent was interred with a bead necklace made from amethyst-colored glass. These practices had parallels among a number of African ethnic groups, but they have particularly strong resonance with Igbo notions of death and burial. The spiritual beliefs of the slaves buried in James City County may have had Igbo origins; as Equiano recounts, "Though we had no places of public worship, we had priests and magicians . . . Most of their implements and things of value were interred with them. Pipes and tobacco were also put into the graves with the corpse, which was always perfumed and ornamented, and animals were offered in sacrifice to them."[101]

There is every reason to believe, given the influx of Igbos and other African groups into Virginia, that not a few slaves following Gabriel's lead in 1800 believed in the power of those professing the ability to conjure. The most direct example of this appears in the trial of George Smith. In his testimony against George, Ben Woolfolk revealed that he intended to "go down as far as the pipeing tree, to enlist men, partially the *Outlandish* people, because they were supposed to deal with witches and wizards, and of course useful in armies to tell when any calamity was about to befall them."[102] The ubiquity of these esoteric and spiritual practices in Virginia slave communities is readily observed in runaway advertisements and court proceedings during the eighteenth century.

Mention of conjurers, root doctors, and others claiming command of spiritual forces abound in the records. In 1745, an enslaved woman from Orange County named Eve was burned alive after poisoning her master, Peter Montague. She placed an unknown toxin in Montague's milk in August, causing her master to slowly die after four months of agony. Dangerous examples like this prompted lawmakers to pass a special law in October 1748: "Whereas many negroes, under pretence of practising physic, have prepared and exhibited poisonous medicines, by which many persons have been murdered, and others have languished under long and tedious indispositions, and it will be difficult to detect such pernicious and dangerous practices, if they should be permitted to exhibit any sort of medicine, *Be it therfor enacted* . . . That if any negroe, or other slave, shall prepare, exhibit, or administer any medicine whatsoever, he, or she so offending, shall be ajudged guilty of felony, and suffer death." This law had little effect on slave behavior. As Philip Schwarz demonstrates, more slaves were tried for poisoning than any other offense between 1740 and 1785.[103]

In Cumberland County, a slave named Peter Harrison was convicted and sentenced to execution for the poisoning of a white man in January 1763. The 1760s were an especially troubling time for whites in Alexandria and Cumberland counties due to a wave of alleged poisonings. In 1767, a group of slaves in Alexandria administered poison that was likely prepared by a conjurer to several overseers as part of a planned rebellion. While they managed to kill an unknown number of overseers with the poison, four of the conspirators were captured, publicly executed, and had their severed heads placed atop the county courthouse. In another case reported in newspapers in Georgia and Pennsylvania between 1767 and 1768, eight slaves in Alexandria were found guilty of conspiring to poison a number of whites. In 1769 alone, three slaves were accused of poisoning two white men in Cumberland County.[104]

On November 4, 1763, Alexander Marshall published a notice in the *Virginia Gazette* for Sambo, "a stout likely Negro fellow . . . [who] pretends to be a doctor." Another mention of a conjurer appears in a trial record ten years later. In this particular case, a slave named Sharper was accused of procuring poisonous substances from an elderly "Negroe Doctor or Conjuror" in order to "destroy White people." In a runaway advertisement dated July 28, 1775, a "Coromatee" slave woman named Nanny absconded with "a free negro fellow, who pretends being a doctor." A Spotsylvania County court found an enslaved man named Obee guilty of administering poisonous substances on July 29, 1778. His name, as Philip Morgan conjectures, could have possibly been derived from the esoteric practice of Obeah. In an advertisement dated March 4, 1789, Austin Brockenbrough sought the return of Romeo, who was "fond of prescribing and administering to sick negroes, by which he acquired the nick-name of Doctor among them." Romeo apparently absconded along with the aptly named Juliet—a female slave belonging to Benoi Williams. Long before he left with his female companion, Romeo was known for his doctoring and his manufacture of passes and certificates of freedom for other escaping slaves.[105]

In a 1791 case, two slave blacksmiths in Spotsylvania claimed to have been unduly influenced by a "Negro wench, or Conjuror" when they attempted to poison their master. In the same year, court testimony reveals the story of Ben, a slave "pretend[ing] to be a Cungerer & forting teller," who had paying customers both white and black. Three years later in Powhatan County, three slaves who reportedly killed a white overseer relied on the services of Pompey, a slave "reputed among the Negroes as a Conjurer." Pompey had consulted with the three men and his alleged powers allowed them to plan the murder in secrecy.[106] Again, the ubiquity and widespread belief in conjure among the enslaved in Virginia demonstrates, at the very least, the African origins of this practice. As we have seen in colonial New York and South Carolina, conjurers were a cultural bridge that linked Africans from a variety of ethnic groups. Irrespective of the particular ethnic mix in Gabriel's Virginia, the presence of conjurers held much shared cultural meaning for both the African- and American-born slaves involved in the conspiracy.

That those in the Biafran majority in the Lower Chesapeake region were familiar with the creation and use of poison is verified in Equiano's account of the spiritual practices of his homeland. He notes that the "priests and magicians, or wise men" were acquainted with the production of both poisons and cures. While Equiano notes that "[t]he natives are extremely cautious about poison," the presence of "magicians" in his village helped alleviate these fears. "These magicians were also our doctors and physicians . . . and were very successful in healing wounds and expelling poisons. They had likewise some extraordinary method of discovering jealousy, theft, and poisoning; the success of which, no doubt, they derived from their unbound influence over the credulity and superstition of the people. I do not remember what those methods were, except that, as to poisoning, I recollect an instance or two, which I hope it will not be deemed impertinent here to insert, as it may serve as a kind of specimen of the rest, and is still used by the negroes in the West Indies." Equiano goes on to describe a particular instance in which a young woman died from poisoning. After "doctors" performed an investigation, involving the use of the woman's corpse, they were able to discover the identity of the poisoner and get the perpetrator to confess to the crime.[107]

Both conjure and poison were integral elements to the Igbo socioreligious matrix. As "Igbos" and "Mandes" were transformed into enslaved "Africans," and then into "African Americans," elements from a variety of socioreligious matrices were blended together to form a more unified whole. The result would be a syncretic set of values and beliefs that became the basis of an African American cultural identity. In a recent discussion of slave religion and culture in eighteenth-century Virginia and South Carolina, Philip Morgan contends, "North American plantation slaves generally could not practice 'African Religion,' nor did they appropriate only those values that could be absorbed into their 'Africanity.' This is to make excessive claims for the autonomy of slaves and the primacy of their African background."[108] In the cases of eighteenth-century New York, South Carolina, and Virginia, it is quite clear from the available evidence that the African backgrounds of the enslaved populations were fundamental—if not absolutely essential—to their identity, culture, and consciousness. African- and American-born slaves were neither *tabula rasas* nor victims of a collective spiritual holocaust. Instead, they crafted a dynamic and functional culture, despite the denial of their humanity and the severe limitations on their freedom. In this process of cultural transformation, resistance in its multitude of forms was one of the prime movers.

# CHAPTER 5

# "I Will Gather All Nations"

## Ethnic Collaboration in Denmark Vesey's Charleston Plot

And they utterly destroyed all that was in the city, both man and woman, young and old . . . with the edge of the sword.

JOSHUA 6:21

Behold, the day of the Lord cometh, and thy spoil shall be divided in the midst of thee. For I will gather all nations against Jerusalem to battle; and the city shall be taken.

ZECHARIAH 14:1–2[1]

## Fluctuations and Trends in the Slave Trade into South Carolina, 1740–1776

Serving in its principal role as the main entry point for many Georgia, South Carolina, and North Carolina slaves, the city of Charleston was a key commercial center in the Atlantic trade network. Daily auctions of African- and American-born slaves held on Vendue Range Street, near the aptly named Exchange building, were so common that by 1790 the city of Charleston began to assume a distinctly African flavor. Its 16,341 total residents made it the fourth largest urban region in North America at the time of the first federal census in 1790. Of that total number, 8,252 were free and enslaved blacks, giving the city the highest concentration of Africans and their descendants in urban North America. Rice, indigo, and Sea Island and short-staple cotton cultivation fueled Charleston's booming export market, but it was the trade in black flesh that made everything possible. By 1800, this commercial capital of the South stood on the brink of a new century with unlimited economic opportunities and the ever-present fear, and real possibility, of servile revolt.[2]

Throughout the eighteenth century in South Carolina, the importation of slaves was periodically ended or severely limited to adjust to fears of insurrection or other unrelated political and economic factors. Major fluctuations in South Carolina's slave imports began soon after the Stono revolt of 1739. Only after slave traders in Bristol, England, protested did prohibitive import duties (imposed in 1740) end and the trade in Africans to South Carolina recommence. Three prohibitive duties on African slaves were enforced in South Carolina between 1741 and 1769 as a direct response to fears of slave revolts. In 1770, Parliament's various tax laws led North American colonists to support a general nonimportation policy. South Carolina temporarily suspended the African slave trade for one full year. The trade began again at a tremendous pace in 1773, bringing some 8,050 Africans to Charleston on forty-two separate slave ships in that one year alone. South Carolina would again be forced to do without steady imports of slaves during the course of the American Revolution.[3]

Given the various prohibitions, it is remarkable that between 1760 and 1774, nearly 42,000 Africans were legally imported into South Carolina. The beginning of the American Revolution changed this trend. In 1775 the Continental Congress resolved to "neither import nor purchase, any slave imported after the first day of December next; after which time we will wholly discontinue the slave trade."[4] Of course this decision to completely end the slave trade was reversed after the war, but the legal trade would come to an end by January 1, 1808.

## Rebellious Influences from Abroad: The Aftermath of the 1791 Saint-Domingue Revolt

Postrevolutionary South Carolina faced a precarious situation in guaranteeing a constant flow of slave imports from Africa, but in all cases, definite commercial gain was weighed against the increasing possibility of slave rebellion. Even though the South Carolina General Assembly officially suspended the slave trade with Africa from 1787 until 1800, more than 14,000 slaves were either imported from abroad or brought into the state by white migrants. White migrants bringing slaves into South Carolina in the early 1790s included French refugees fleeing Saint-Domingue after the successful slave rebellion led by Toussaint L'Ouverture. About 500 refugees entered Charleston in 1792, beginning a trend that lasted until 1795. Immediately, local officials began searching all incoming vessels from Saint-Domingue to prevent the illegal immigration of Africans from the former French Caribbean colony. It was assumed that slaves and free blacks from Saint-Domingue would bring with them an infectious revolutionary fervor. This fear of imported rebelliousness began to be realized in 1793. One concerned white noted, "The NEGROES have become very insolent, in so much that the citizens are alarmed and the militia keep a constant guard. It is said that the St. Domingo negroes have sown these seeds of revolt, and that a magazine has been attempted to be broken open."[5] In the same year, Thomas Jefferson delivered a warning to the governor of South Carolina regarding two Saint-Domingue free blacks who were headed to Charleston "with a design to excite an insurrection among the negroes."[6]

With disclosure of the Garvin conspiracy in Richmond, Virginia, in 1793, South Carolinians had further cause for alarm. On August 8, 1793, an anonymous letter was found in Richmond which detailed plans for a massive slave revolt. It was later reported that the letter was written by the conspiracy's leader, a black itinerant preacher named Garvin. The plan allegedly sought to create simultaneous rebellions in Virginia and South Carolina and to use fire as a means of resistance because "the Negroes of Cape Francois have obtained their liberties by this method." It was also assumed by authorities in Virginia and South Carolina that the numerous slaves imported from Saint-Domingue would collaborate with American-born slaves in this endeavor.[7] This possible evidence of cross-cultural collaboration may have set an important precedent for future efforts by enslaved Africans and African Americans in South Carolina.

In response to these disturbances, Governor William Moultrie of South Carolina ordered all free blacks who had arrived from Saint-Domingue in the twelve months prior to October 1793 to leave within ten days. State authorities would confine those who did not depart when ordered. The justification for expelling free Saint-Dominguan blacks was voiced in 1793 by a white Charlestonian using the pseudonym "Rusticus." Rusticus wrote, "It may be true that the generality of those admitted [into South Carolina] were not immediately concerned in the revolt . . . but they had witnessed all the horrors of the scene—they saw the dawning hope of their countrymen to be free." In 1794, the state legislature created the Militia Act to further secure against servile revolt. This act required the enlistment into a militia unit of all able-bodied white males between the ages eighteen and forty-five. Due to lingering fears about the 1791 Saint-Domingue revolution, South

Carolinians engaged in additional preemptive actions. Definitive evidence linking Domingan refugees to the renewed spirit of rebellion in South Carolina required an immediate and decided response.[8]

After the panic created by the alleged Garvin conspiracy in Richmond, fires threatened Charleston every year from 1795 to 1798. The 1796 blaze was allegedly set by a Saint-Domingue slave. On November 14, 1797, five "French Negroes" were captured and charged with plotting to kill whites and conspiring to set fire to Charleston. All five were found guilty, three were executed on December 2, 1797, and the remaining two were banished from the state. Soon after the sentences were carried out, local planters petitioned state lawmakers in December 1797 to create in Charleston a permanent guard detail composed of infantry and cavalry.[9] This did not sufficiently hinder the activities of Saint-Domingue slaves, however, as another slave arsonist conspiracy was revealed early in 1798. According to local authorities, "French Negroes [were] to fire the City, and to act here as they had formerly done at St. Domingo." This plot was the work of between ten to fifteen Saint-Domingue slaves led by Figaro and Jean Louis; the two leaders were executed and the others were jailed.[10]

On May 5, 1798, many concerned white Charlestonians met at St. Michael's Church to discuss what they thought to be an imminent attack and invasion from Saint-Domingue. Then, in 1799, South Carolina congressman Robert G. Harper received information that substantiated this fear of invasion from the former French Caribbean colony. He discovered a plot allegedly initiated by a Haitian military leader named Hedouville. The Haitian army had supposedly been "preparing to invade the southern states from St. Domingo, with an army of blacks; which was to be landed . . . to excite an insurrection among the negroes . . . to subjugate the country by their assistance, and then plunder and lay it waste." These fears, real and imagined, haunted the city of Charleston at the beginning of the nineteenth century. As a result of the threat of slave revolt, the state again passed major prohibitive legislation in 1800 and 1801. Nevertheless, Saint-Domingue and Haiti would remain ominous symbols in the memories of white Charlestonians as late as 1822.[11]

The act of 1800 banned the foreign import of Africans and limited the number of slaves brought into South Carolina from other states to ten per owner. This act also required that these "domestically imported" slaves must have been owned for at least two years and could not be sold for two years after entry into the state. Thus, planters from other states attempting to sell unruly and rebellious slaves in the South Carolina market faced formidable barriers. The 1801 act was even more restrictive; it stipulated that no more than two slaves could be imported by owners from other states. In addition, these slaves had to be for personal use and thus could not be sold at all. With the foreign trade suppressed and domestic trade slowing to a trickle, the viability of slavery as a consistent and long-term source of agricultural labor in South Carolina seemed in serious doubt.[12]

## African Ethnicity and Slave Imports, 1776–1807

The Philadelphia Constitutional Convention in 1787 had ensured a federally mandated end to the African slave trade by January 1, 1808. South Carolina planters decided that continued prosperity was well worth the risk of increasing the likelihood of slave rebellion, and the 1808 deadline inaugurated an unprecedented push for the expansion of slave imports. Between 1776 and 1807, more than 56,000 enslaved Africans entered South Carolina to labor primarily on plantations outside Charleston and on the Sea Islands. Of that total, an estimated 47,000 were imported between 1801 and 1807 alone. This was a massive and unprecedented influx of forced labor; in comparison, North America as a whole imported some 67,000 enslaved Africans between 1776 and 1807. Taking as a reasonable approximation Philip Curtin's estimate of 399,900 total slave imports into British North America, this would mean that one out of seven of all slaves imported into North America arrived in South Carolina in the three decades preceding 1807.[13]

Even after the federally mandated end of the slave trade, Africans were brought into southern ports through clandestine means as late as the 1860s. While Curtin estimates that more than 50,000 Africans were imported into North America between 1808 and 1861, an unknown number were smuggled by land and ship throughout the era of the slave trade.[14] Although significant numbers of Africans were imported after 1808, the legal ending of the slave trade had obvious implications for the continued transmission of African cultures into North America. The direct line of cultural contact between Africa and North America was formally severed, and, in some real sense, Africans in America were placed on a faster track to becoming "African American" in identity, consciousness, and culture.

It was not an instantaneous transformation, as is shown by African practices and beliefs enduring among South Carolina's black residents as late as the twentieth-first century.[15] This powerful cultural legacy was significantly influenced by slaves from three separate cultural regions of Atlantic Africa: Upper Guinea (Senegambia and Sierra Leone), West-central Africa, and the Bight of Biafra. Denmark Vesey and other leaders actively recruited from these three groups during the 1822 conspiracy. While people from Upper Guinea and West-central Africa were among the most favored by Carolina planters and thus represent a large percentage of Africans imported into the colony/state, the Igbo and others from the Bight of Biafra represented just over 5 percent of all Africans entering South Carolina before 1807 (see table 5.1).[16] Despite this disparity in numbers, the Igbo and other Biafran imports had a discernible influence on the nature of slave culture throughout nineteenth-century South Carolina. In combination, these three African groups influenced and shaped significantly slave resistance and culture in postrevolutionary South Carolina.

TABLE 5.1. Enslaved Africans Imported into South Carolina and the United States

| | SOUTH CAROLINA | | UNITED STATES | |
|---|---|---|---|---|
| Coastal Region of Origin | 1776–1800 | 1801–25 | 1776–1800 | 1801–25 |
| Senegambia | 15.7% | 7.5% | 20.8% | 6.8% |
| Sierra Leone | 18.3 | 13.8 | 22.3 | 13.2 |
| Windward Coast | 2.4 | 5.2 | 4.7 | 5.0 |
| Gold Coast | 38.2 | 15.0 | 31.8 | 13.8 |
| Bight of Benin | * | 1.9 | 11.2 | 1.8 |
| Bight of Biafra | 5.1 | 6.5 | 3.0 | 6.3 |
| West-central Africa | 20.1 | 48.1 | 17.1 | 51.0 |
| Southeast Africa | * | 2.0 | 0.1 | 2.0 |
| Unknown | 18.8 | 26.1 | 28.5 | 26.0 |

Source: Eltis, Behrendt, Richardson, and Klein, The Trans-Atlantic Slave Trade.
Note: Percentages do not include unspecified destinations.
* No recorded voyages from this particular coastal region.

## Details of the 1822 Denmark Vesey Conspiracy

On May 25, 1822, the discovery of a planned revolt in Charleston sent shock waves through the slaveholding South. Peter Prioleau, a slave belonging to Col. John Prioleau, was sent to the fish market by his mistress and received intelligence that a sizable group of slaves were planning for revolt.[17] While in town, he had met a slave named William Paul who reportedly asked him, "Do you know that something serious is about to take place?" Peter, according to his trial testimony, asked William to explain himself. "We are determined to shake off our bondage, and for this purpose we stand on a good foundation, many have joined," was the response. This information shocked Peter, who cut short the conversation and immediately sought the aid of a free black man by the name of William Pencell. Pencell advised Peter to reveal the conspiracy to his master. The colonel, however, was out of town, so Peter informed his mistress and her son about his earlier conversation with William Paul. When Colonel Prioleau returned on May 30, 1822, he notified James Hamilton, the intendant of Charleston, about the alleged conspiracy, which soon led to the complete unraveling of the plot.[18]

By informing a house slave about the planned rebellion, William Paul had committed a cardinal sin in the eyes of the other conspirators. One prominent rebel leader, Peter Poyas, had specifically warned slaves to "take care you don't mention [the plot] to those waiting men who receive presents of old coats, etc., from their masters, or they'll betray us."[19] As a result of his error in judgment, William was arrested on May 30 and, fearing for his life, implicated Mingo Harth and Peter Poyas as co-conspirators and leaders of the rebellion. These men were arrested on May 31, but because they maintained their silence and composure, both were released the same day. William, however, remained in custody as late as June 8. Fearing what he thought to be his imminent execution at the gallows, William made additional revelations about the plot, saying that he had been aware of it for some time and "that it was very extensive, embracing an indiscriminate massacre of the whites, and that the blacks were to be headed by an individual, who carried about him a charm which rendered him invulnerable."[20]

Even after this admission, it was not until June 14 that William's information was confirmed by Charleston city officials. Major John Wilson— commander of a local militia company—visited Charleston city intendant Hamilton and presented him with additional proof of a large-scale slave conspiracy. His wife's slave George had told Major Wilson that a "public disturbance was contemplated by the blacks . . . the succeeding Sunday, the 16th, at twelve o'clock at night . . . the period fixed for the rising, which, if not prevented, would inevitably occur at that hour." George, described later as an American-born "dark mulatto" blacksmith, voluntarily served as a spy, and the intelligence he relayed to his master was particularly damaging for the conspirators' plans. The leaders of the plot had tried to recruit him earlier, which gave George access to critical conspiracy details. This information also became a useful means for the politically ambitious Major Wilson to discredit his chief rival—Thomas Bennett, then governor of South Carolina. The revelation that a number of Bennett's slaves were involved in the conspiracy contributed to Wilson's defeat of Bennett during the 1824 gubernatorial election.[21]

On June 14, 1822, Hamilton communicated the plans for the revolt to Governor Bennett, who immediately acted to ensure the security of Charleston. Within one hour, the governor ordered the city's militia commanders to meet at the intendant's residence to lay out an array of defensive measures. At this meeting, officials decided that five military companies under the command of Col. Robert Hayne were to patrol city streets and guard against insurrection. In addition, the number of watchmen manning signal stations around Charleston was doubled, and for two or three full days, men were kept busy repairing weapons and making cartridges. On the night of the planned rebellion, the rebels discovered Colonel Hayne's troops and a sizable contingent of volunteers patrolling the area surrounding Charleston. City officials quickly and effectively insured the safety of the city, and, as one resident noted much later, "when morning dawned without any alarm having been given, there was a general feeling of relief but the anxiety and suspense were not dissipated for some time."[22] The rebel leaders—Denmark Vesey, Monday Gell, and Peter Poyas—decided to delay the revolt, but ten more slaves were arrested on June 18, and full disclosure of the plot soon followed.[23]

The plan reportedly included between 6,600 and 9,000 slaves divided into six attack groups. According to the confession of John Enslow—an enslaved African-born cooper—the original plan called for five of these groups to storm Charleston on July 16, 1822, capturing weapons caches and killing all whites they found. The essential elements of the plan were repeated in the testimony of several informants. After the main guard houses, arsenals, a naval store, and the city magazine were taken, the rest of the city would be set on fire to create an additional distraction. The sixth unit of rebels were initially to patrol the city's streets on horseback and would later be used to recruit more slaves from the surrounding countryside. By mid-June, some 500 weapons had been reportedly crafted, bought, or stolen. The conspirators made note of stores containing firearms and ammunition, while slaves who were expert horse handlers and riders were actively recruited in the hundreds.[24]

The rebels even included a barber who volunteered to craft wigs and mustaches to conceal the identities the conspirators so they could impersonate whites to facilitate their nighttime mobility. Charleston resident John Potter wrote, "I must confess if one of these fellows had made his way to my bedroom, in the dead of the night dressed out in his *Wig, Whiskers,* and *Whitened* face—that I might have been appalled." Once the city was completely captured, the rebels planned to plunder Charleston's banks for gold and silver specie and set sail for Haiti where they hoped to receive asylum.[25] The revelations made by William and George completely undermined these plans, and, with the arrests of key figures on June 18, all hopes of a revolution ended.[26]

## Denmark Vesey: Historical and Historiographical Context

The trials of the captured conspirators began on June 19. Denmark Vesey, leader of the insurgent army, was arrested soon after.[27] Details of his early life were revealed to court officials during testimony. At the age of fourteen, Denmark was one of 390 slaves Capt. Joseph Vesey transported onboard a Massachusetts brig named the *Prospect* from St. Thomas to Cape Francois, Saint-Domingue, in October or September 1781. During the passage to Saint-Domingue, young Denmark—nicknamed Telemaque by the crew— was distinguished for his "beauty, alertness, and intelligence" and became a "pet" onboard the ship. Once the ship arrived at Cape Francois, Captain Vesey, "having no use for the boy," sold him and returned to St. Thomas. Allegedly subject to periodic epileptic fits, however, young Denmark was judged unsound by the French sugar planter who purchased him, and he was returned to Captain Vesey sometime after April 23, 1782.[28]

Denmark likely lived with Captain Vesey in Norfolk, Virginia, until the British completed their evacuation of Charleston in 1782. Having mastered French, creole Danish, and English, young Denmark proved useful as a shipmate on Captain Vesey's voyages. Denmark traveled extensively and may have visited West Africa on more than one occasion. By 1783 Captain Vesey settled in Charleston, and Denmark remained his slave until 1799. In that year Denmark won a $1,500 prize in the East Bay Street lottery. On December 31, 1799, thirty-three-year-old Denmark petitioned for his freedom. He paid Captain Vesey $600 to be released from service and used the rest of his lottery earnings to open a carpentry shop in downtown Charleston. As a carpenter, Denmark Vesey entered the city's sizable class of free black skilled professionals. He utilized his considerable talents as a carpenter to amass a great deal of wealth. It was reported that by 1822, he owned property worth about $8,000. Although contemporary accounts note that Vesey owned as many as three houses in Charleston, no proof exists to confirm this claim. He did, however, rent a house from a Dr. Trezevant on 20 Bull Street according to an 1821 city directory.[29]

In 1819, free black men engaged in more than thirty different professional occupations in Charleston. By 1820 Charleston's free black population was 3,165 and steadily increasing. The nature of urban slavery allowed a number of slaves also to engage in highly skilled occupations. In Charleston the relative lack of available white labor enhanced occupational opportunities for free and enslaved blacks. As evident in Gabriel's Virginia, occupational status is a poor indicator of the level of acculturation or the level of acquiescence to the harsh realities of slavery. Despite that he was a successful free black professional, Denmark Vesey orchestrated the largest slave conspiracy in North American history. In doing so, he actively utilized his understanding of pan-African cultural phenomena and intercultural connections to his advantage.[30]

Not much is known regarding Vesey's ethnic background. David Robertson has recently forwarded the possibility that he was a Muslim from the Western Sudanic region of Upper Guinea. While admitting that "Vesey's own relationship with, or sympathies toward, Islam remain unknown," Robertson adds "Vesey, in apparent accordance with Islamic practices and teaching, accepted polygamy and scorned those blacks who drank intoxicating beverages." He goes on the postulate that the date chosen for the planned rebellion and even the numbers he picked in winning the lottery that paid for his freedom had numerological meanings linked directly to Islam. The date for the rebellion, July 14, 1822, according to Robertson was representative of the Prophet Muhammad's name. Also this day, "reckoned by the Islamic lunar calendar, marked the last two months of that Islamic year, Dhu al-Qa'dah and Dhu al-Hijah, respectively." The etymological base for Dhu al-Hijah—Hijrah—means "to migrate, withdraw, or to make an exodus" in Arabic, which was exactly what the rebels had planned once Charleston was destroyed.[31]

Lastly, because Denmark chose the numbers 1–8–8–4 to win the East Bay Street lottery, Robertson draws another tenuous link to the Islamic faith. "It is perhaps of significance that the first, eighth, and fourth letters respectively of the Arabic alphabet spell a word of significance in the Islamic faith, rendered as *add-th* in English." With some additional manipulation, Robertson derives the word *haddith*, which was one of a number of phrases the Prophet Muhammad would say after prayer. Robertson uses creative data and flawed interpretive approaches to support these conclusions, and there simply is not enough solid evidence to bolster such claims.[32]

Aside from Robinson's largely unfounded speculation that Denmark Vesey was a Muslim of Mande origin, there is a stronger possibility that he was either an Akan or was born to Akan-speaking parents. Captain Vesey bought Denmark in 1781 on the Danish Caribbean island of St. Thomas. While we do know with some certainty that he was born in 1767, it is not known where Denmark was from originally—leaving open the possibility that he was either from Africa or Danish St. Thomas. During the eighteenth century, some 41 percent of imports from identifiable regions embarking on ships sent to the Danish Virgin Islands were from the Gold Coast. Other enslaved groups brought to the Danish Virgin Islands in large numbers included those from West-central African (21 percent), the Bight of Biafra (21 percent), and the Windward Coast (7 percent). While Douglas Egerton claims that Denmark was "evidently of Ashanti descent," there simply is no reliable way to verify his ethnicity as Akan or to show that he was specifically from the kingdom of Asante.[33]

While Denmark's ethnicity is uncertain, much has been written about the implications of his socioeconomic status in the shaping of the 1822 plot. That many of the conspiracy's leaders were urban artisans has prompted Richard Wade to contend that "there is persuasive evidence that no conspiracy in fact existed, that, at the most, it was a vague and unformulated plan in the minds or on the tongues of a few colored townsmen."[34] According to Wade, the nature of urban slavery "proved inhospitable to conspiracies because it provided a wider latitude to the slave."[35] This relative sense of freedom, in addition to the well-organized police forces in the major cities, would sufficiently deter those seeking to engage in resistive acts. Yet examples of slave uprising and plots in North American urban areas obviously show that even an increase in the relative freedom enjoyed by urban slaves did not alter their determination to seek true liberty. Even quasi-free blacks, like Denmark Vesey, understood that their liberty would always be limited and threatened as long as slavery existed in North America. In some very real sense, free blacks were simply slaves without masters.[36]

More recently, Michael P. Johnson has joined Wade in questioning the existence of the 1822 conspiracy. In challenging the "heroic" interpretation of Vesey and his followers, Johnson contends that the true conspiracy was concocted by court officials and "unwitting" modern historians who "failed to exercise due caution in reading the testimony of witnesses." Sounding proper cautionary notes similar to those heard in the debate surrounding the 1741 New York conspiracy, Johnson aims the bulk of his criticism at three 1999 works on the Vesey plot—Douglas Egerton's *He Shall Go Out Free*, Edward Pearson's *Designs against Charleston*, and David Robertson's *Denmark Vesey*. He accuses these works, particularly Pearson's edited volume, of "unrelenting carelessness" and "interpretive improvisation," among other charges. Johnson does raise a valid point when he contends that historians need "to read evidence with renewed skepticism."[37]

Johnson's lengthy review essay rightly calls attention to the problems in the court proceedings, the active shaping of court documents, the use of coerced testimony, and the possible flaws among modern historians' interpretations. However, as Douglas Egerton notes in his rebuttal, "Johnson cites only two contemporaneous sources beyond the trial transcripts and the *Official Record* . . . yet dozens of letters and documents exist to prove that . . . Richard Wade and Michael Johnson are wrong." Both Egerton and Robertson point to the letters of Mary Beach—ignored in Johnson's critique—which further corroborate the existence of a real conspiracy and Vesey's leadership.[38] Johnson also does not fully account for the cultural continuities and significant amounts of ethnographically consistent material evident in the court records and other contemporary accounts. Why would court officials go so far as to concoct a story that included the inner workings of Gullah culture or the existence of ethnic enclaves in Charleston? A closer examination of the trial record, and its references to culture and ethnicity, demonstrates the development and persistence of specific African and creole enclaves and the veracity of the trial testimony and other sources of evidence.

### Conjure, Charms, and Gullah Resistance

Denmark's plan epitomizes how African culture and pan-African connections shaped conspiracies and, in a more general sense, became facilitating factors in slave resistance. One of the most effective and ubiquitous of these links was the various Afro-Atlantic religious impulses that helped inspire slave revolts throughout the Americas.[39] Denmark's plan to destroy Charleston was bolstered by three men who claimed to wield uncanny spiritual forces. An African-born conjurer named Gullah Jack Pritchard was one of the central figures in the 1822 conspiracy. Having served as a "doctor" in Charleston for fifteen years, Jack's reputation as a mystic "who can't be killed, shot or caught" allowed him to sway enslaved Africans of all nationalities who respected him as conjurer and "general" of the conspiracy. Claimed in court records to have been "Angola" born, Jack's ability to influence Africans from a number of ethnic groups was perhaps the source of his true power.[40]

As a member of a cohort of Gullahs, Jack brought from his West-central African homeland esoteric spiritual practices familiar to the numerous Africans from this region. West-central Africans represented 48 percent of all slaves from identifiable regions on ships headed to South Carolina between 1801 and 1825 (see table 5.1). Zaphaniah Kingsley—a slave trader and planter residing near St. John's River in East Florida—reports that Jack also brought his "conjuring implements with him in a bag which he brought on board the ship and retained them." Kingsley asserts that Jack was sold as a prisoner of war near the East African port town of Zanzibar, though there is no other confirmation for this claim. He also states that "Jack the Conjurer" was originally from a kingdom or town known as "M'Choolay Moreema"—a place where "a dialect of the Angola tongue is spoken." This "Angola" dialect was no doubt one of many Bantu variants spoken widely throughout much of West-central and East Africa. While there is no way of knowing for certain what specific location in Africa Jack was from, we can say definitively that he identified with Gullah culture and this connection allowed him to sway the actions of others.[41]

According to court testimony and other contemporary sources, even American-born slaves greatly feared Gullah Jack's powers as a conjurer. Intendant Hamilton remarked that "Even the negroes who were born in this country seem to have spoken of his charmed invincibility with a confidence which looked much like belief."[42] In his most crucial role, Jack was to distribute charms to slave combatants which were said to render them invincible. This particular activity was mirrored in a number of slave rebellions and conspiracies throughout the Atlantic world. That not one slave questioned the validity of Jack's powers during the course of the trials is singular testament to the continuing connection they had to African spiritual beliefs and values.

For Gullah Jack's conjurations to work, slaves had to first fast on corn and peanuts the night before the revolt. The following morning, the rebels were to place Jack's charms, consisting of crab claws—or what the conspirators referred to as "Cullahs"—in their mouths in order to be rendered invulnerable. These talismans had one severe limitation, however; one anonymous witness noted that "his charms would not protect him from the treachery of his own color."[43] Jack also presided over a ceremony in which a small group of conspirators ate a half-cooked fowl to solidify their bond. Oathing ceremonies of this sort were common features of slave rebellions and conspiracies in the Americas.[44]

Gullah Jack's role as a recruiter was equally significant. The fear inspired by his abilities often was sufficient inducement for slaves to join the plot. During the trial of Julius Forrest, for example, Harry Haig testified that Jack had "charmed" both men into joining the conspiracy and that even after Jack was arrested, Haig felt that he was somehow "bound up and had not the power to speak one word about [the conspiracy]." The influence Jack held over these men and others was due perhaps to his threat to kill anyone who betrayed the planned revolt. In Jack's own trial, George Vanderhorst literally begged the court to send him out of state because he considered his life "in great danger from having given testimony." A presiding judge mentioned later that "it was not without considerable difficulty that the Court satisfied him that he need no longer fear Jack's conjurations (as he called them)."[45]

The dread inspired by Jack's ability as a conjurer was not limited to blacks alone. One of his contingency plans, in case the rebellion failed, was so frightening that all mention of it was intentionally omitted from the version of the trial record made publicly available by judges Lionel Kennedy and Thomas Parker. Henry Haig, one of the conspirators who turned state's witness, told the court that Jack "was going to give me a bottle with poison to put into my Master's pump and into as many pumps as he could about town, and he said he wanted to give other bottles to those he could trust to."[46] These unpublishable words reveal the real worries of white Charlestonians; militia companies and federal troops could probably defeat an army of enslaved rebels, but there was no legitimate means of preventing slaves from poisoning the city's water supply.

Due to his considerable influence, Jack was able to recruit enough slaves to lead an entire unit, known as the Gullah Company. As revealed by court officials during Gullah Jack's trial, this unit was to "kill the City Guard, and take all the arms in the Arsenal" during the outbreak.[47] Leading up to the appointed date for the rebellion, the Gullah Company met on a monthly basis from December 1821 until June 1822 to solidify their plans and involve more recruits from slaves living along the coast and on the sea islands. To find additional enlistees for his company, Jack was sent by Monday Gell—a noted harness-maker and fellow leader of the plot—to get the support of slaves living in the countryside on the outskirts of Charleston. Jack returned having reportedly enlisted some 6,000 slaves from Goose Creek and Dorchester counties.[48]

One of Jack's recruits in the Gullah Company was Tom Russel—a blacksmith who specialized in making edged tools. According to the testimony of Harry Haig, when Jack was asked what he would do about weapons, he replied "he would have some arms made at the Blacksmith's."[49] Mirroring the importance metal workers played in Gabriel Prosser's conspiracy, at least five slave blacksmiths made weapons for use in the 1822 plot. Tom Russel, Jim Bennett, Perault Strohecker, and an anonymous slave blacksmith who was to make daggers were all involved in providing arms for the combatants.[50] Another slave named Jacob Stagg volunteered to make swords out of scythe blades for use by Monday Gell's "Ebo" Company.[51]

Six spearlike weapons were crafted at Tom's shop and later transported to Gullah Jack. Not only was Tom an expert blacksmith and Jack's second-in-command, he was also a conjurer in training. According to Henry Haig's July 10 testimony, "Tom Russel the Blacksmith and Jack are partners, Jack learnt him to be a Doctor . . . Jack said Tom was his second and when you did not see him, and see Tom, you see him."[52] Thus, Tom served as a vehicle of Jack's mystical powers, allowing for tighter control over slaves involved in the plot. Obviously, Tom was a vital asset to Jack's Gullah Company.

The fact that Tom was indeed Gullah is made evident in the trial testimony. Not only did he voluntarily join Gullah Jack's company, but James Mall, described by the court as a white young man, testified that "Gullah Jack was frequently at [Tom's] Shop and they frequently talked together in Gullah *so that I could not understand them.*"[53] This unique dialect became an effective language of subversion as enslaved Africans actively code-switched when in the presence of whites to maintain secret communication. The use of Gullah dialect in this manner creates what James C. Scott refers to as a "hidden transcript." By speaking Gullah, slaves could safely criticize and mock slaveholders and, in this particular instance, make plans to rebel against white authority while in the very presence of their enemies.[54] Whites were not the only ones unable to decipher this unique form of Africanized English. During the trial of Nero Haig, Perault Strohecker testified that during an organizing meeting in May 1822, "Nero and [Gullah] Jack spoke some time together in the Gullah language." After this particular exchange was over, Nero translated portions of the conversation to Perault, an enslaved Gambian.[55]

The origins of Gullah dialect has been a topic of scholarly inquiry for the past half century. From the pioneering work of Lorenzo Turner in the 1940s to the more recent scholarly contributions of Margaret Washington, Peter Wood, Daniel Littlefield, and Michael Gomez, the various debates regarding the origin and nature of Gullah culture are well beyond the scope of this study. However, regarding the 1822 Charleston conspiracy, Gomez recently noted that Gullah Jack's company was composed of "Congolese-Angolan and/or Gola members of the slave community in the Charleston area and their descendants."[56] With distinct influences from and connection to West-central Africans, and the Gola and the Kissi from Sierra Leone and Liberia, respectively, evidence suggests that this unique culture and dialect is a blend of two or more distinct African cultural enclaves. Gullah was, therefore, the epitome of the intragroup syncretism that Gomez describes in his keen analysis of the African "sociocultural matrix" that developed in the North American context.[57]

As one of the earliest population groups in South Carolina, West-central Africans greatly influenced the nature of Gullah culture. Winifred Vass and Lorenzo Turner in separate studies made note of a number of Bantu linguistic elements in Gullah dialect. The more recent work of Washington, Wood, and Littlefield has shown that Sierra Leonians—brought to South Carolina because of their expertise in rice cultivation—were imported in increasingly large numbers in the decades before and after the American Revolution. This new wave of importation allowed for a fusion of West-central African Bantu and Sierra Leonian Gola-speakers and added new dimensions to Gullah dialect and culture. Though Gullah Jack Pritchard was of possible West-central African origin, the scholarly convention of referring to his Gullah band as "Angolan" simplifies a rather complex cultural reality.[58]

An elderly blind preacher named Philip was the third conjurer connected with the plot. During the planning phases, Monday Gell and Peter Poyas brought William Garner to Philip's house on Elliott Street. William, who worked as a cart driver, was recruited primarily because of his skills as a horseman and his access to a dozen or more horses from his mistress's stables. Monday Gell testified that on this particular occasion, Philip asked William "why he was so timorous," and quoting from biblical scripture, added "let not thy heart be troubled neither be afraid."[59] William Garner later testified that the old man's inquiries "alarmed him much as Philip was blind."[60] The preacher was not completely without sight, however. Court officials made note that Philip was born with a layer of skin, known as a caul, covering his face. According to the folk traditions of enslaved Africans throughout the Americas, the caul or veil was a sign that an infant would eventually be able to communicate with ghosts and predict future events. Philip testified that having been born with a caul allowed him to "foresee events . . . He said he possessed a Gift—a species of second sight—which came to him after prayer or in dreams."[61]

Philip was never tried, even though the court later determined that this "High Priest of Sedition" played a role in the plot. Trial testimony confirms that conspirators frequently gathered at his residence and his words often reassured frightened recruits. It was, in fact, his claims to predict the future which ultimately spared him the wrath of the court. Due to his alleged second sight, Philip predicted the ultimate failure of the conspiracy and attempted to dissuade recruits, telling the rebels to "to give up the business" because "white people could fire five times while they fired once."[62] Despite his rather ambiguous role, Philip's presence is definitive proof of the numerous pan-African influences in Vesey's plot.

The nearly identical meaning of the caul among Africans in the kingdom of Dahomey, the Gold Coast, Dutch Guyana, Jamaica, Haiti, and the American South "as a sign dey will be bery wise an kin talk wid duh spirits" fully demonstrates that enduring African spiritual concepts and pan-African cultural links informed the actions of slaves in Vesey's South Carolina. According to Melville Herskovits, there were certain aspects of abnormal births, including the caul, which "among African folk [are] regarded as special types of personalities whose spiritual potency calls for special treatment." These notions were ubiquitous features of Southern African American culture as late as the 1930s and beyond. The numerous interviews performed by the Georgia Writers' Project during the Great Depression illuminate the continuing significance of the caul. Martha Page of Yamacraw, Georgia—an early twentieth-century community of ex-slaves from coastal South Carolina and Georgia—stated "I dohn mine ghos, cuz I caahn see em as I wuzn bawn wid a caul." From the same community, Carrie Hamilton revealed that "I wuz bawn wid a caul an wuz diffrunt frum duh res. Ebry now an den I see ghos."[63] Those born with this gift believe they can see the unseeable because of their direct connection to a spirit world distinctly defined by West and West-central African parameters.

### Ethnic Enclaves and the 1822 Conspiracy

In addition to the central role of conjure and other African spiritual components, additional pan-African elements influencing this conspiracy demonstrate a level of intercultural collaboration ignored by many previous scholars of the 1822 plot. Along with Jack Pritchard's Gullah Company, Denmark Vesey also relied upon aid from the "French band" in formulating his plot. This band, which "had been ready a long time," was composed of about 300 slaves who fled Saint-Domingue with their masters in the wake of the 1791 uprising led by Toussaint L'Ouverture.[64] The trials of two of these "French Negroes," Louis Remoussin and Joe Jore, reveal that this French band was thoroughly armed in the weeks before the outbreak. William Colcock mentioned in his trial testimony that "Pompey Haig told me that there were some black Frenchmen very skillful in making swords and spears, such as they used in Africa."[65] Once the rebellion was to begin, they were to raid a Mr. Duquereron's store near the Inspection, "break the door open and get arms."[66] Similar to the members of the Gullah society, the Saint-Domingue slaves also used a subversive language, in this case Creole French, to help plan the revolt while maintaining a high level of secrecy. Perault, a French-speaking slave who turned state's witness, testified that when Louis and Joe would communicate, "the conversation was in Creole French."[67]

Haiti influenced other crucial areas of the conspiracy. Vesey was reported to have read "passages in the newspapers that related to Santo Domingo" as a means of encouraging his fellow conspirators and enlistees.[68] One newspaper article Vesey used related the story of the Haitian defeat over an invading Spanish army. Taking advantage of Spanish military weaknesses in the Dominican Republic, President Jean-Pierre Boyer of Haiti successfully invaded the Spanish territory and abolished slavery there. This news emboldened Saby Gailliard enough to claim "if he had many men he could do the same too, as he could whip 10 white men himself."[69]

Having spent some time earlier in his life in Saint-Domingue, Vesey learned French and used it as a tool to facilitate resistance. During the planning of the rebellion, Vesey reportedly drafted two letters requesting military aid from Haiti. One of the letters was to be carried by a ship's steward whose brother was allegedly a general in the Haitian military. The other, addressed directly to President Boyer of Haiti, was to be conveyed via a ship's cook. Despite that he was not in direct contact with Haitian officials, Vesey and other leaders frequently claimed that armies from both "Santo Domingo and Africa would come over and cut up the white people" to further inspire fellow conspirators. In this light, Denmark's fluency in French cannot be used as a measure of assimilation or acculturation. Instead, this ability allowed him to draw on additional pan-African connections, increasing the confidence of enlistees and offering Denmark a greater chance of success in this plot.[70]

In addition to Gullah and Domingan elements, other more directly African elements were present in the conspiracy. Monday Gell, described in the trial transcript as "an Ebo . . . having been in the country fifteen or twenty years," was leader of an entire company of Igbo slaves.[71] Though he turned state's witness and provided some rather damaging testimony during the trials, Monday was one of the key leaders and recruiters of the plot. Monday was a noted and respected harness-maker who kept his own shop on Meeting Street in downtown Charleston and enjoyed the relative freedom of being a highly skilled slave. It was at his shop that Tom Russel, the blacksmith-conjurer working with Gullah Jack's Company, stored six pike-head spears. Reflecting the limited numbers of Igbo and others from Biafra entering South Carolina during the slave trade, Monday's "Ebo" Company had only forty-two enlistees. In comparison, Jack reportedly recruited thousands into his Gullah Company, and the French Band numbered in the hundreds. Also, not all of the forty-two members of Monday's Company were actually Igbo. Perault, a French-speaking slave who turned state's witness, was one of the non-Igbo members of Monday's company. He was originally a Gambian Mande-speaker born near Gorée. This reality may reflect how flexible African or African American identity was becoming in the antebellum South or that, as shown in chapter 3 and in the work of Michael Gomez, certain African ethnic groups may have had natural affinities for each other.[72]

Akan-speakers were another African group whose presence can be found in the records generated by the Charleston courts. Two men with Akan day-names were arrested in connection with the conspiracy—Cuffy

Graves and Quash Harleston. South Carolina imported very few Akan-speakers, and it is entirely likely that these two individuals simply had Akan day-names but were not Akan-speakers themselves. This is especially true in the case of the popular name "Cuffee," which, while Akan in origin, was used quite frequently in North American slave communities with few, if any, Akan-speaking elements.[73]

Arrested on July 11, 1822, Cuffy Graves was soon after released due to a lack of sufficient evidence to bring him to trial. Though he was found not guilty by the court, a free black man named Quash Harleston was transported out of "the limits of the United States" on July 29, 1822.[74] It is unknown exactly where Quash was sent, but it is possible he followed the same route as his close companion Prince Graham; one of two other free black men to be found guilty during the court proceedings, on July 21, 1822, Prince was sentenced to permanent banishment from South Carolina. The court record reveals that Prince made a request to be "transported to Africa on board a vessel which sailed from Charleston." His request was honored and, after serving a month in the Charleston workhouse, Prince sailed aboard the *Dolphin* to Liberia.[75]

Africans from Senegambia and Sierra Leone, were another segment of South Carolina's slave population playing an integral role in the events unfolding in 1822. Imported in large numbers due to their expertise in rice cultivation, Africans from the Western Sudan were to have a profound impact on cultural developments throughout the region. Two Gambian-born slaves involved in the conspiracy—Mingo Harth and Perault Strohecker—engaged in activities bearing a strong cultural stamp from their West African places of origin. Identified by his first name as possibly a Gambian-born Mande-speaker, Mingo eventually became one of the most important figures in the conspiracy.[76] Perault, according to his brief biography detailed in the court proceedings, was a Mande-speaker born in the Western Sudanic region near Gorée. Both men were expert horse handlers and had the responsibility of either recruiting for or leading the slave cavalries. Monday Gell testified that Mingo "was to take his master's horse and act as a horseman during the fight."[77] In the trial of Mingo's younger brother, Isaac Harth, Monday further claimed that Isaac "said also, that he belonged to the horse company. Mingo told me that his brother was one too."[78] The horse company Mingo led was composed primarily of stable workers from three different stables throughout the city.[79]

Perault was a member of another horse company connected, as mentioned earlier, to Monday Gell's group of Igbos. He worked as a stable hand, and his role in the conspiracy was to "get horses to send men into the country," probably to recruit more slaves after the rebellion commenced. On several occasions, Perault hired his horses out to slaves who were sent into the country to enlist more volunteers. From June 6 to June 16, Jack Glenn, Scipio Simms, and Agrippa Perry all requested horses from Perault for the purpose of going "into the country to get men to join this insurrection."[80]

During the outbreak of violence, the various horse companies were to "Go about the streets and prevent the whites from assembling." Gaining access to horses was not a major problem as the conspirators had four ready sources. First, Charleston's draymen and carters often had access to horses day and night; they were therefore valuable targets for recruitment efforts. The second source was the slave butchers, who for undisclosed reasons "could with ease provide themselves with horses." The third and fourth sources were revealed in the trial of Peter Poyas, in which the anonymous Witness No. 5 testified "there are the public Livery Stables, where we have several candidates [for recruitment] and the waiting men belonging to the white people of the Horse Companies will be told to take away their master's horses."[81] Understanding the strategic importance represented by having use of a cavalry, Vesey actively recruited men with some experience with horses. Smart Anderson confessed that "the old man (meaning Vesey) told him to get some draymen who had horses, if you hear of a good rider make him Captain of Troop." In this manner, Vesey ultimately recruited about a hundred draymen to serve in the slave cavalry during the revolt.[82]

Evidence, however circumstantial, suggests that three additional men may have also been Gambian horse handlers. The first, a drayman named Peter Cooper, was described as an elderly "Guinea" Negro by Monday Gell. The term "Guinea" lacks geographic specificity, but it would definitely include the Western Sudan region, which was home to numerous expansionist polities. The second possible Gambian was a drayman named Caesar Smith. In his second confession on July 13, 1822, Bacchus Hammet describes Caesar as "a tall negro, an African, who is an intimate acquaintance of Perault's, and who is often at the stable where Perault keeps his horses." That he was a very close associate of a known Mande-speaking Gambian and also shared an affinity for horses suggests that Caesar was Gambian as well. Another slave mentioned in court testimony may have been a Gambian

Muslim. Though Billy Purse was never directly implicated in the plot, Perault testified on August 6, 1822, that Billy "carried a Book to Monday Gell which he stated came from Africa." In all likelihood, this was a copy of the Holy Quran.[83]

That as many as three enslaved Gambians—Mingo, Isaac and Perault—were intimately involved with recruiting for, leading, or joining the slave cavalry demonstrates an important continuity of Gambian military culture in North America. From as early as 1100 A.D., the Mande and other Gambian groups were renowned in the Western Sudan for being fierce horse warriors. Between 1100 and 1500 A.D., Gambian cavalry forces swept across an extensive territory in the sahel, savanna, and woodland areas of the Western Sudan and became primarily responsible for the rise of the Mali and Songhai empires. The unique disease ecology created by trypanosomiasis-infected tsetse flies contained the spread of horse warrior empires, as well as the horses themselves, to the region north of the Upper Guinea coastal rivers. Even as late as the mid-nineteenth century, horse warriors continued to be a determining factor in warfare and state formation in the Western Sudanic region of Upper Guinea. Gambian horsemen were infamous among Europeans around the Atlantic World for three centuries prior to the Vesey conspiracy. As John Thornton has shown, the Hispaniola slave revolt of 1522 involved Gambian-born Wolofs who had "knowledge of horses and how to stand up to cavalry charges." Not only did they use successful tactics to repulse a Spanish cavalry, but they developed their own group of horse warriors and continued to harass the sugar planters of Hispaniola for two decades. Friar Balthasar Barreira, a Portuguese Jesuit priest visiting the Gambia region, noted "because the Mandingas are fine horsemen, wherever they are living they help kings in their wars, acting always as the vanguard."[84]

It is entirely possible that Perault was formerly a member of a Gambian cavalry unit. In his revealing biography included in the trial extracts, the court recorded the following details about his prior exploits: "Perault was born at Jumba in Africa, about a week's travel from Goree. Mamadu, his father, who is wealthy and owns about 60 working hands, trades to Hassou with tobacco and salt in exchange for which he receives gold; to which place Perault accompanied him six times. Perault was engaged in three battles against the people of Hassou, who do not cultivate their lands, but made predatory incursions into the cultivated territories of their neighbors.

Perault also fought twice against the people of Darah, but in the second battle he was taken prisoner and carried to that place."[85] He therefore spent a portion of his early life in military service during a period in which Mande-speaking horse warriors were engaging in numerous clashes in Upper Guinea. After his capture, Perault was traded to a European ship captain and arrived in Charleston at some point between 1804 and 1807. By mentioning the Hassou (Hausa), the Hausa kingdom of Darah (Daura), the westward salt trade and his origins in proximity to Gorée, Perault was almost certainly from the town of Gumbu—a northern sahelian settlement located in the middle Niger River Valley which specialized in the trade of rock salt from the Idjil mines during the eighteenth and nineteenth centuries. If Perault was not a horse warrior, he likely became familiar with the use of horses as he accompanied his father on his salt-trading ventures.[86]

Confirmation that Gambian horse warriors were indeed present among North American slaves can be found in the story of Abd Rhama Ibrahima, a Mande-speaking Muslim prince and former soldier. Living in Futa Jallon, Ibrahima was the son of a Fulbe king and was a high-ranking officer in his father's army. In 1788, at the age of twenty-six, he led a group of horse warriors in an attack on the "Hebohs" near Rio Pongas. He was captured following a Heboh ambush, enslaved by his former enemies, and sold to European slave traders. After spending forty years as a slave in the West Indies and Natchez, Mississippi, he was recognized by a white man he had known in West Africa. Ibrahima's master manumitted him, and in 1828 he returned to Africa where he died months later. His story, detailed in Terry Alford's *Prince among Slaves*, attests to the presence and influence of Gambian horsemen in North American history.[87]

Along with their aptitude in rice cultivation, Gambians also were highly prized by South Carolina planters because of their expertise in handling horses and livestock. As Peter Wood notes, "People from along the Gambia River, a location for which South Carolina slave dealers came to hold a steady preference, were expert horsemen and herders."[88] This strong association made between Western Sudanic Africans and horses prompted Wood to suggest that even the word "cowboy" may have originated as a result and was first applied to these Gambian horsemen in South Carolina.[89]

Along with the obvious African influences and the appearance of particular African ethnic enclaves, there was a correlating fear among the rebels in Denmark Vesey's conspiracy of those slaves who were born in North

America and seemed to lack a direct link to Africa. In one case, William Paul was informed by a French-speaking slave that "I was Country born I should not know anything of what was going on 'till the horn blew and [the revolt] broke out."[90] This marked distrust of "countryborns" is clear in the trial of Pierre Lewis. In his testimony against Pierre, Charles Drayton claimed that "Pierre Lewis told me that something serious would happen, but that I was a countryborn, and he was afraid to trust me."[91] He testified on another occasion that Joe Jore, a member of the French Band, typically spoke to him using subtle parables because he "did not know how to trust countryborns."[92] Eventually, Charles was allowed to join and even lead his own army; he was given command over the country-born company. This initial lack of confidence was perhaps well founded, as it would be Charles Drayton, along with two others, who received pardons in exchange for the testimony they provided during the court proceedings.[93]

Even some African-born men were not trusted by the rebel leaders. The most heinous charge against George Parker, in the eyes of Denmark Vesey and Monday Gell, was that "he was an African, but they alleged against him, that he did not associate with his countrymen."[94] Unlike Charles Drayton, George was never allowed to join and actively participate, and his suspect character "convinced the Court of the wisdom and circumspection displayed by the leaders of the conspiracy in excluding him from their ranks."[95] The leaders even developed a means to encourage seemingly trustworthy but reluctant African-born slaves to join the rebellion. In the trial of Peter Poyas, the unnamed slave of Col. George Cross testified that Peter threatened him by saying "if I would not join he would turn all my Country people against me." This prospect was so frightening to this witness that he immediately told Peter, "if so, I'll join you." According to a statement given by Colonel Cross, this unnamed slave—known in the published trial record as Witness no. 10—was indeed born in Africa. Cross had apparently "owned him since 1806 or 1807 when he brought him out of an African Ship." Thus Peter's threat was very real.[96]

Whether born in Africa or America, house servants or "waiting men who receive presents of old Coats from their masters" could not be trusted by the conspirators either.[97] After all, it was house servant Peter Prioleau who, after William Paul attempted to enlist him, informed his mistress and ultimately played a key role in unraveling the conspiracy. Although a number of the rebel leaders were skilled slaves or free blacks, this status did not signify greater cultural assimilation or political conformity. Their actions and words reflect a consciousness shaped tremendously by an appreciation and understanding of African cultural values. The main dichotomy existing in their minds was not between skilled and unskilled, or even city and country slaves, but between those who positively identified themselves as African and those who did not. Rebel leaders in the Americas who fully grasped this concept and used it to their advantage were seemingly more successful in inspiring collective resistance. Even more effective were those who could connect the various African ethnicities with the "country-born" population to create a unified front against oppression.

Another group seemingly despised and distrusted by the conspirators were black members of white and biracial churches in Charleston. According to Governor Bennett, while "members of an irregular Association which called itself the African Church" were intimately associated with the conspiracy, "very few, indeed, of the religious Negroes, in *regular* churches among us, were drawn into the Plot; and in some churches there were not any on whom a charge of criminality has been proven." The reasons were quite evident to Bennett: "It would seem that the conspirators were afraid to trust them; For since the plot has been discovered, voluntary information has been given, that Attempts not then understood, were made to feel the Pulse of some of them, by artful, different approaches which not being countenanced were laid aside."[98]

For whatever reason, it seemed to the conspirators that blacks who attended white or biracial churches would not be inclined to join their movement. This perhaps is further proof that some identification with Africa was a requirement for being included in the destructive plans. Though mostly Christian in outlook, members of the African Methodist Episcopal (A.M.E.) churches in Charleston not only identified in a positive way with the African past, they also identified with a denomination that supported resistance to white racism and oppression.

### The Legacies of the Vesey Conspiracy

After the trials, thirty-five men were executed, thirty-two were banished from the state, and fifty-three were either acquitted or discharged. Denmark Vesey was hanged on July 2, 1822, along with five followers. The extremity of the punishments and doubts about the conspiracy's existence prompted criticism of South Carolina officials from around the country. An acerbic response to a New York editor's critique appeared in the August 12, 1822, edition of the *Charleston Courier*: "Mr. Stone, of the N. York *Commercial Advertiser*, appears to have forgotten ... that in the year 1741, in the city of New-York, *thirteen Negroes were* BURNT ALIVE *for insurrectionary efforts*."[99]

Fear-stricken whites in Charleston sought to suppress the spirit of insurrection among the slave populace. Their vigilante activities included the hanging death in August 1822 of three black men at the hands of a white mob. This act was allegedly in retaliation for a nonfatal attack by the three slaves on a white mail deliverer.[100] Other citizens tried more legal means to achieve the same goal. One group petitioned the state legislature to forcibly export all free blacks from the state, limit the freedoms given to black mechanics and other professionals, prohibit blacks from owning property, and prevent blacks from learning to read and write.[101] However extreme these may seem, many of the proposed restrictive measures became state law by January 1823.

The widespread nature of this conspiracy, in combination with public pressure, prompted South Carolina lawmakers to create preemptive legislation. One ordinance, ratified by the Charleston city council on August 6, 1822, prohibited the ownership of boats by free or enslaved "persons of colour." This was a direct response to Vesey's plan to ship conspirators to safety, freedom, and asylum in Haiti. This was the first of many legal measures which sought to limit the potentially dangerous connections between blacks in North America and Haiti.[102]

On December 1, 1822, the state legislature passed a measure requiring that free black males over the age of fifteen have a white guardian or be sold into slavery. That three free black men were found guilty in connection with the plot signaled to white Charlestonians that the relative freedoms enjoyed by that sector of society had to be thoroughly curtailed. Charleston's city council sought to create a 150-man slave patrol and even petitioned the state legislature for $100,000 to erect a "Citadel" to protect life and property in the city.[103] Other restrictive laws passed by the state in December 1822 provided that: "No free Negro or person of color who left the state would be allowed to return. Every free male Negro between the ages of fifteen and fifty, who was not a native of or had not resided in the state for the preceding five years, would have to pay a tax of $50 a year ... No person could hire from any male slave or slaves of their time; slaves permitted by their owners to hire out their time were made subject to seizure and forfeiture."[104] Combined, these measures addressed many of the concerns white Charlestonians had about free blacks and the relative freedoms enjoyed by skilled slaves.

In November 1822, Thomas Pinckney—former Revolutionary War soldier and Charleston resident during Denmark's conspiracy—published an analysis of the causes of the 1822 plot. In "Reflections, Occasioned by the Late Disturbances in Charleston," Pinckney blamed the slave conspiracy on northern abolitionists, the lack of restrictions on free and enslaved blacks, the disparity between the white and black populations and "the example of St. Domingo, and (probably) the encouragement received from thence." Regarding the connection to Haiti, he lamented: "Nothing effectual can be done by us to obviate the influence of the example of St. Domingo, so long as it retains its condition. It would be difficult also to prevent encouragement being offered from thence, because we cannot cut off the direct communication, neither, if this were practicable, would it avail while the circuitous intercourse through the Northern States must remain open."[105]

Though Pinckney felt there was no effective means of solving the problem posed by Haitian influences, within a month of the publication of his "Reflections," state lawmakers began to redress this specific concern. On December 21, 1822, the legislature passed the "Negro-Seaman's Act" as a viable means of cutting off any further rebellious influences from entering Charleston. This act stipulated that "free Negro employees on any vessel coming into a South Carolina port would be Imprisoned until the vessel was ready to depart, with the captain required, under pain of fine or imprisonment, to pay the expenses of detaining his employees and to take them away from the state upon leaving; otherwise they would be deemed 'absolute slaves' and be sold."[106] In addition, blacks from Mexico, the West Indies, or South America were prohibited from entering the state. Within weeks, dozens of black seamen were jailed in Charleston. This act created a tense diplomatic impasse between the United States and Britain, which sought to protect its citizens from being imprisoned and enslaved due to South Carolina's "obnoxious law."[107]

Although the Negro Seamen Act was deemed unconstitutional by a federal court the next year, a group of politically influential Charlestonians known as the South Carolina Association successfully petitioned for the act's reinstatement. Whites in Charleston feared that free black seamen might "corrupt our . . . slave population." Between 1829 and 1832, Florida, Georgia, and North Carolina passed their own Negro Seamen Acts, which sought to quarantine or imprison free black sailors. By 1830, South Carolina, North Carolina, and Georgia sought to further strengthen the restrictions on black sailors in light of the publication and distribution of David Walker's inflammatory *Appeal*. Evidence that Walker's pamphlet—which advocated the justifiable use of violence by enslaved blacks—was being circulated widely throughout the South as a result of the activities of black sailors led to a more thorough enforcement of the Negro Seamen Acts.[108]

Ever since 1791 this fear of imported slave discontent weighed heavily on South Carolina's lawmakers. Charlestonians now hoped that along with the 1808 federal ban on the slave trade, the Negro Seamen Act and the renewed limitations on black immigration from the Caribbean and Latin America would forever sever any potentially disruptive pan-African connections. Many planters realized in the wake of the tumultuous events of 1822 that Vesey's conspiracy represented something extremely unsettling for the continuation of white hegemony in the slave South. Simply put, the earlier efforts to "randomize" Africans on slave ships and auction blocks had utterly failed to prevent collaboration and resistance. Denmark Vesey, in his keen wisdom, created a confluence of African cultures and understood much of what concerned and inspired slaves, whether country born or African. Not surprisingly, he claimed that "country born, Africans and all kinds joined [the plot]," a statement which epitomizes Vesey's particular genius as a leader.[109]

This type of pan-African sentiment was also reflected in one of Vesey's favorite biblical passages: "For I will gather all nations against Jerusalem to battle; and the city shall be taken."[110] Akan, Igbo, Gambian, Gullah, French-speaking Domingan, and English-speaking American-born slaves combined in this effort to caste off the shackles of bondage. Given the numerous links between various African groups, Denmark's conspiracy epitomized a reality that transcended any assumed or real ethnic boundaries and allowed for, and even facilitated, resistance. This conclusion finds resonance in the work of Michael Gomez who notes "Vesey sought to elevate a single status, a lone condition, that of blackness, of descent from Africa."[111] The intersection of various African cultures and the acknowledgment of pan-African connections during the course of this plot were means to the end of creating a unitary black consciousness in North America. Indeed, a plausible conclusion would be that Vesey's plot had, as its very foundation, a pan-Africanist consciousness.

# CHAPTER 6

# "I Was Ordained for Some Great Purpose"
## Conjure, Christianity, and Nat Turner's Revolt

Looking back at the turbulent history of slavery in the plantation South, Rev. Charles C. Jones, writing in 1842, exposed the fears many antebellum southerners had regarding the influence of what he referred to as "teachers, doctors, prophets, conjurers" in influencing the actions of slaves: "Ignorance and superstition render them easy dupes to . . . artful and designing men . . . On certain occasions they have been made to believe that while they carried about their persons some charm with which they had been furnished, they were *invulnerable*. They have, on certain other occasions, been made to believe that they were under a protection that rendered them *invincible* . . . They have been known to be so perfectly and fearfully under the influence of some leader or conjurer or minister, that they have not dared disobey him in the least particular."[1]

These "artful and designing men" and women on plantations throughout the Americas were as ubiquitous as the individual and group acts of slave resistance they inspired. They served as conduits for powerful spiritual forces beyond the comprehension of many modern observers and were, therefore, believed to be integral to the success of a number of slave resistance movements. The mystical powers they claimed to control made them formidable and respected figures among enslaved Africans. As John Blassingame notes, "in many instances, the conjurer had more control over the slaves than the master had."[2]

These spiritualists evoked fear and awe, something readily measured by the words and actions of slaves and their holders. Henry Clay Bruce, who spent twenty-nine years of his life as a slave in Missouri, Virginia, and Mississippi, recalled numerous "conjurors, who succeeded in duping their fellow-slaves so successfully, and to such an extent that they believed and feared them almost beyond their masters."[3] Among slaves, conjurers were respected not solely because of the dread they inspired. In the words of W. E. B. Du Bois, African spiritualists had multifaceted functions in the slave community; at any given time, the conjurer could be "the healer of the sick, the interpreter of the Unknown, the comforter of the sorrowing, the supernatural avenger of wrong."[4] It would be through many of these roles that conjurers helped to encourage slave resistance throughout the Americas.

Conjurers very often were leaders or major figures in slave rebellions. Claiming command over esoteric forces, they were seen as integral to the success of slave revolts. Peter the Doctor who rubbed powder onto the bodies of slaves to render them invulnerable during the 1712 New York City revolt. Utilizing similar spiritual powers, Obeah doctors inspired revolts through-out the Caribbean during the eighteenth and nineteenth centuries. During the initial phases of the 1791 Saint-Domingue revolution, a vodun priest by the name of Boukman sacrificed a pig to ensure the success of that rebellion. In addition, conjurers and other African spiritualists were present in a variety of conspiracies and plots including important examples in New York City in 1741, Richmond in 1800, and Charleston in 1822. In these cases, the power of conjure was revered by both African- and American-born slave insurgents in similar fashion. They believed, with little question, the ability of these spiritualists to determine the outcome of events through arcane means.

This evidence runs counter to the claims of Eugene Genovese, who argues that the presence of Caribbean conjurers as revolutionary leaders "could not be reproduced in the United States, except on a trivial scale, be-cause the necessary revolutionary conjuncture did not exist. The conjurers of the Old South were accommodationists in the same sense as were the black preachers."[5] Despite a general tendency by Genovese and other American historians to view the experiences of North American slaves as unique or ex-ceptional, the widespread belief in conjuration proves that this was a shared Atlantic World phenomenon. Concepts of American "exceptionalism" are not nuanced enough to account for the many connections and parallels that exist in the Western Hemisphere, especially in the case of slavery.

There is sufficient evidence that slave conjurers played an important role in a number of mass rebellions and conspiracies. Far from being the accom-modationists discussed by Genovese, North American conjurers in several instances served as a revolutionary vanguard inspiring and encouraging resistive behavior among their fellow slaves. What Sterling Stuckey refers to as the "conjuror's doctrine of invincibility" became one of the most useful tools spiritualists used to foment rebellion. Examples of this doctrine abound in Jamaica, New York, South Carolina, and other locales throughout the Americas. The ubiquity of the belief that conjurers could render slave insurgents invulnerable underscores both the connections that tie North America to the rest of the Atlantic World and the truly revolutionary potential of these esoteric practices.[6]

"Revolutionary" examples like Peter the Doctor, Doctor Harry, Gullah Jack, and perhaps Nat Turner provide effective foils to Genovese's interpretation of North American conjurers. In each case, these men were involved in concerted efforts to violently overturn the power relationship between slaves and masters. They were the very definition of revolutionaries. While the goals of the rebellions varied—from the establishment of an ethnic polity to asylum in an existing black republic—it cannot be said that these men actively worked with whites to make slaves more tractable and pliant. Instead, they were cut from the same mold as Boukman Dutty of Saint-Domingue or the rebel Obeah doctors in the British, Danish, and Dutch Caribbean.

In other instances, conjurers engaged their powers for lesser acts of resistance, navigated and bridged any remaining cultural differences between enslaved African Americans, and embodied an emerging community consciousness that led to an African American outlook. There are examples of conjurers acting as accommodationists, but they are far outweighed by the number of accounts showing the connection between African-inspired esoteric beliefs and acts of slave resistance. Doctor Caesar, inventor of the famous antidote for poison known as "Caesar's Cure," was one conjurer who plied his trade for the benefit of white authorities in colonial South Carolina. However, even his form of accommodation did not imply a reactionary consciousness or political conformity to white supremacy.[7]

*Conjurers and Day-to-Day Resistance*
Aside from their presence in the trial records of slave revolts and conspiracies, conjurers also appear in a number of slave narratives, runaway notices, interviews, biographies, and autobiographies as agents in day-to-day forms of resistance. Through these sources, there is ample proof that conjurers were an ever-present factor in the lives of the majority North American slaves. No less an authority than William Wells Brown, a man who spent

a significant portion of his life in bondage, once noted that "nearly every large plantation . . . had at least one, who claimed to be a fortune-teller, and who was regarded with more than common respect by his fellow-slaves."[8] Speaking on the widespread appeal of conjuration in South Carolina in the early 1800s, Charles Ball added that slaves "are universally subject to the grossest and most abject superstition, and uniformly believe in witchcraft, conjuration, and the agency of evil spirits in the affairs of human life."[9] These statements show not only that conjurers were ubiquitous but also that belief in their abilities and powers encompassed a large portion of the slave populace.

A conjurer named Sandy Jenkins of Easton, Maryland, created a shaping impression on Frederick Douglass's early life. After receiving a savage beating from Edward Covey, a man "who enjoyed the execrated reputation, of being a first rate hand at breaking young negroes," Douglass turned to Sandy for aid. Sandy was "not only a religious man, but he professed to believe in a system for which I have no name. He was a genuine African, and had inherited some of the so called magical powers, said to be possessed by African and eastern nations." Sandy instructed Douglass to find the root of a particular herb in the forest which had mystical powers of protection. After undisclosed preparations, Sandy told him to wear the root on his right side because "it would be impossible for Covey to strike a blow; that with this root . . . no white man could whip [him]."[10]

To Douglass, talk of magically endowed herbs and roots was "very absurd and ridiculous, if not positively sinful." His statements were guided by his acceptance of Christianity and can be viewed as an appeal to both his writing audience and his fellow abolitionists. One of the abolitionists' key arguments was that few slaves received true Christian instruction, something they measured by the persistence of "heathen" or "savage" African religious practices in the plantation South. Despite Douglass's obvious disdain for conjure due to an alleged "positive aversion to all pretenders to 'divination,'" he still wore the root and perhaps believed in Sandy's esoteric abilities.

In August 1834, a confrontation Douglass had with Covey involved a protracted wrestling bout between the two that rendered the former Negro-breaker "as gentle as a lamb" for the next six months that Douglass lived with him.[11] Although Douglass never fully acknowledged it, the root in his right pocket was certainly a factor in his new spirit of assertiveness and resistance.

In another case, William Webb, a conjurer living in Kentucky, became concerned about the cruel treatment slaves faced on a neighboring plantation. After secretly meeting with the slaves, Webb urged them to gather roots that he placed into bags. The slaves then walked around their own quarters a few times and positioned the bags in front of their master's abode during the morning hours. The intention was to induce the master to dream about his slaves gaining retribution for past wrongs. Shortly after, the master reportedly began to treat the slaves decidedly better and Webb's influence over the slaves was to increase dramatically as a result.[12]

Items placed into bags and used for protective charms, similar to the ones prepared by both Sandy Jenkins and William Webb, were generally known as "hands" or "jacks." A typical hand or jack could contain roots, seeds, barks, insects, human hair and finger nail clippings, graveyard dirt (gopher powder), horse shoe nails, hog bristles, salt, red pepper, and other essential substances. Henry Clay Bruce observed that "these conjurors claimed to be able to bury a hand or a jack under the master's door step, which would prevent him from whipping a particular slave while it was there."[13] The leather bag an elderly slave gave Louis Hughes combined roots, nuts, pins, and other items and had the ability to prevent the wearer from being beaten. Hughes added that "it was the custom in those days for slaves to carry voodoo bags," a tradition "handed down from generation to generation; and . . . it was still very generally and tenaciously held to by all classes."[14]

In a case related to Henry Clay Bruce by a female slave from Amelia County, Virginia, a conjurer was said to have been employed to aid about thirty slaves who were fearing their imminent sale to the cotton fields of Alabama in the year 1800. Hearing of a conjurer living ten miles away from the plantation, the slaves pooled their resources to pay him ten dollars to set a hand or jack on their master. After receiving his payment, the conjurer "went to the front door steps of the great house about twelve o'clock that night, dug a small hole under the ground step, took from his pocket a little ball, talked to it a while in a whisper, then kissed it and put it in the hole, and covered it carefully and came away."[15] The key was insuring that the master actually stepped over the hand; if that did not occur, then all the conjurer's preparations and incantations would have been wasted. Fortunately for those slaves, the next morning they "saw [the master] come down the steps and walk around a while, then go back over this particular step." The slaves were never sold to Alabama.[16]

According to fugitive slave Henry Bibb, the general prescription for dealing with an abusive master was "some kind of bitter root," which slaves were to chew and spit in the direction of their masters. Along with the root were "certain kinds of powders, to sprinkle about their master's dwellings. This is all done for the purpose of defending themselves in some peaceable manner."[17] After a conjurer gave Bibb the protective powders and roots, he did not receive a whipping for leaving the plantation without permission. Bibb firmly trusted in the powers conveyed to him, claiming that he had "great faith in conjuration and witch-craft," which led him to believe that he could do what he pleased without getting flogged.[18] Thus emboldened, he left the plantation again without his master's permission. Upon his return, Bibb stated his master would punish him for absconding, but he added: "I did not believe that he could do it, while I had the root and dust."[19]

Bibb's master was so enraged at his slave's "saucy" retorts that he "grasped a handful of switches and punished [him] severely, in spite of all [his] roots and powders." Despite the seeming failure of the charms of protection, Bibb was to consult yet another conjurer, who gave him a concoction composed of fresh cow manure, red pepper, and hair from a white man's head to safeguard Bibb from further abuse by his master. That Henry Bibb continued to believe in conjure even after protective charms did not work shows how much sway this practice had in the slave community.[20] Even the failure of these charms to protect slaves from their masters or from other whites could be explained without disturbing the foundations of these spiritual beliefs. Henry Clay Bruce claimed that if a slave with a protective hand or jack "got whipped, and so reported to the old conjuror, he would promptly claim one of three things, either that someone removed the jack, or that the fellow had failed to carry out instructions, or had no faith in the jack, and therefore was deserving of punishment."[21]

Conjurers also had the reported ability to foretell the outcome of future events, including rebellions and runaway attempts. This gift was said to have saved Philip, the blind South Carolina preacher, from execution in the trials following the Denmark Vesey conspiracy. Philip predicted the disastrous outcome of the plot and discouraged slaves from continuing on their ill-fated path. Similarly, Frederick Douglass received a warning from Sandy Jenkins, who informed him about a series of dreams he had while slaves on the plantation were plotting a mass escape. Sandy's interpretation of the dreams did not bode well for the conspirators, and he told Douglass "dare is sumpon in [that dream], shose you born; dare is, indeed, honey."[22] Despite these warnings, the slaves continued their plans. On the morning of the escape, Douglass himself had a premonition: "I had a sudden presentiment, which flashed upon me like lightning in a dark night . . . I instantly turned to Sandy Jenkins, who was near me, and said to him, 'Sandy, we are betrayed; something just told me so.'" Sandy replied to Douglass "Man, dat is strange; but I feel just as you do." Within minutes the plan was revealed and the slaves were placed into custody.[23]

At times, the predictions of slave fortune tellers had positive outcomes. Uncle Frank of St. Louis, Missouri, described by William Wells Brown as a slave who "was very distinguished (not only among the slave population, but also the whites) as a fortune-teller," predicted that Brown would successfully escape bondage. After being paid a fee of twenty-five cents, Uncle Frank gazed into a gourd filled with water and immediately relayed the results. Brown would later query "whether the old man was a prophet, or the son of a prophet, I cannot say; but there is one thing certain, many of his predictions were verified."[24]

In a more famous case, Harriet Tubman had frequent premonitions and visions while helping slaves escape from bondage. Sarah Bradford, Tubman's biographer, remarked that "she is the most shrewd and practical person in the world, yet she is a firm believer in omens, dreams, and warnings." Tubman reportedly had dreams that foretold her flight from bondage, helped her avoid pursuers during her missions in the South, and predicted the Civil War and the eventual emancipation of all slaves three years before these events actually occurred. According to Tubman, her father was the source of these abilities because he had an uncanny skill of predicting the weather and he reportedly foretold the Mexican-American War.[25]

### Nat Turner in History and Historiography

Based on evidence derived from trial records, slave narratives, interviews and other sources, we can describe a "typical" slave conjurer. They were often isolated ascetics, living on the margins of the slave community and wrapped in mystery. Their elevated status on the plantation and their mastery over mystical forces made them simultaneously feared and respected. These spiritualists claimed to possess a variety of uncanny powers, including the ability to communicate with the spirit world and the power to heal the sick; many claimed to possess "second sight" or the ability to foretell future events through interpreting visions and dreams. Their command of esoteric forces and other-worldly knowledge allowed them to gain influence over slaves, and they played central roles in various acts of slave resistance from mass revolts to day-to-day forms. In terms of their collective belief in conjure and magic, North American slaves shared similar cultural experiences with Africans and their descendants throughout the Atlantic World. Far from being accommodationists, North American conjurers were vital in the creation of a resistive and unifying consciousness among fellow enslaved Africans and African Americans.

On all of the above counts, slave rebel Nat Turner fits very closely this description of the typical slave conjurer. Yet he explicitly professed a strong abhorrence of conjure. In his own words, transcribed by Thomas Gray, Nat confessed: "Knowing the influence I had obtained over the minds of my fellow servants (not by the means of conjuring and such like tricks—for to them I always spoke of things with contempt) but by the communion of the Spirit whose revelations I often communicated to them, and they believed and said my wisdom came from God."[26] Based on these words, a number historians have claimed that Nat Turner's spiritual inspiration had purely Christian roots. Beginning with the work of William S. Drewry in 1900, the historical Nat Turner was transformed into something he perhaps was not. In his work entitled *The Southampton Insurrection*, Drewry refers to Nat as "a careful student of the Bible, a Baptist Preacher."[27] U. B. Phillips continued this trend by referring to Nat Turner as "a Baptist exhorter" who "had heard voices from the heavens commanding him to carry on the work of Christ."[28] Kenneth Stampp also refers to Nat as "a Baptist exhorter by avocation," and Herbert Aptheker claims that he "was a religious leader, often conducting services of a Baptist nature and exhorting his fellow workers."[29] Aside from minor references to the mystical elements of Nat's visions and his communion with spirits, these scholars share the consensus that Nat was simply a Christian preacher inspired by religious zeal to kill the whites of Southampton County, Virginia.

Perhaps W. E. B. Du Bois captured best the meaning and significance of Nat Turner when he noted "as bard, physician, judge, and priest, within the narrow limits allowed by the slave system, rose the Negro preacher, and under him the first church was not at first by any means Christian nor definitely organized; rather it was an adaptation and mingling of heathen rites among the members of each plantation, and roughly designated as Voodooism." In essence, between conjure and Christianity was a temporal and religious middle ground inhabited by numerous slave exhorters, preachers and prophets—like Nat Turner—who bridged the two spiritual worldviews while not completely belonging to either. To view Nat Turner as either a Christian preacher or a conjurer is to lose sight of the fact that he was an example of the transition Du Bois eloquently describes when he noted that "association with the masters, missionary effort and motives of expediency gave these rites an early veneer of Christianity, and after the lapse of many generations the Negro church became Christian."[30]

With Christianity as slightly more than a veneer, a strong undercurrent of African spiritual values would guide Nat Turner's actions. This is similar to Theophus Smith's contention that Nat represented a particular phase of "magical shamanism" that "features ostensibly the repression of conjure but (precisely thereby) the return of conjurational impulses via biblical symbolism and Christian theological discourse."[31] Nat Turner, therefore, may have "read" and interpreted Christianity through the lens of conjure. This fusion of values may well be a prime example of the creation of an African American consciousness and religious worldview.

### Southampton before Nat's Rebellion

Comprising some 600 square miles between Sussex County and the North Carolina border, the tidewater county of Southampton was the site of one of the most bloody slave insurrections in the history of North America. According to the 1830 census, there were 7,756 slaves in the county, nearly 1,200 more than the number of whites. Combining the enslaved and free black populations, Southampton was 60 percent African American on the eve of Nat Turner's revolt. According to Herbert Aptheker, the large slave population in the county at the time was due to economic depression in the cotton-producing lower South, which slowed rather dramatically the pace of the internal slave trade. Between 1808 and 1860 more than a million slaves were sold to the lower South from upper South states like Virginia, in response to the huge demand for labor following the end of the African slave trade. Economic depression in the lower South in the 1830s caused demand for upper South slaves to slow to a trickle. Profits generated by cotton cultivation were much more attractive than the revenues generated by tobacco or the internal slave trade. As a result, a sizable number of Virginia planters were compelled to move to the new cotton-producing regions of the lower South—especially Georgia and Alabama.[32]

Southampton County also had 1,745 free blacks, the third highest total out of thirty-nine other Tidewater counties in 1830. During the course of the trials associated with Nat Turner's insurrection, at least four free men of color—Arnold Artis, Thomas Hathcock, Exum Artist, and Isham Turner— were implicated in the uprising. Court transcripts for three of the four were either lost or destroyed during the Civil War. The fourth man, Arnold Artis, had all charges dropped.[33] These men may have been implicated unjustly. But if they did take part, then in their minds, the difference between being quasi-free and a slave was marginal at best. If their freedom was truly meaningful, there would be too much to lose for those engaging in such a dangerous venture as a servile rebellion.

There were no doubt a complex array of reasons that explain the involvement of Denmark Vesey and other free blacks in slave conspiracies or revolts. Just five months prior to the rebellion, the Virginia legislature passed a law that made illegal "all meetings of free negroes or mulattoes, at any school-house, church, meeting house or other place for teaching them reading or writing." Violations of the new law were punishable by twenty lashes for blacks and a fine of $50 for whites. This was a direct result of the publication and dissemination in the South of David Walker's *Appeal*. In addition, the legislature stipulated that any newly freed blacks remaining in the state would be sold into slavery. This new law ran contrary to previous legislation, which forced manumitted blacks to leave Virginia on gaining free status.[34] This law and others reaffirmed to free blacks the precarious nature of their "freedom" and made clear that their fate was symbiotically tied to that of their comrades in bondage. Forced separation from family, the inability of some to earn living wages, and the stifling pressure of white supremacy could compel people to involve themselves in risky ventures, which may well have been the case for at least three of the four free men who were tried for their connection to the Southampton tumult.

### Nat Turner's Life and Death

Among the 7,756 slaves of Southampton County in 1830 was one Nat, owned by Benjamin Turner. Born on October 2, 1800, Nat's birth and early life were foreshadowings of his future. As Herbert Aptheker notes, the year

1800 was a momentous one in the history of slave rebellion. It was the year Gabriel Prosser formed his conspiracy near Richmond, Virginia. That same year, Denmark Vesey gained his freedom after winning the East Bay lottery in Charleston. In addition, Nat's birth inspired his parents and others to believe that he "was intended for some great purpose," due to certain marks on his head and chest.[35] He was destined for greatness very early in life.

Described as a small man with "distinct African features," Nat always saw himself as different from other slaves. Perhaps this was due to the fact that he could read and write, abilities he gained with remarkable ease. Or, perhaps, the distance that grew between Nat and his fellow slaves was due to the influence of his reportedly African-born mother, who convinced him as a child that he had special powers of clairvoyance and divination. Whatever the case may be, it is quite clear that Nat inhabited a space separate from, but at the same time symbiotically linked to, that of slaves around him.[36]

Two of the most important influencing forces in Nat's life were his paternal grandmother "who was very religious" and his father who, along with his mother, taught Nat how to read.[37] At some point in Nat's early life, his father successfully escaped from the plantation. Though his final destination is unknown, Nat's father likely became an inhabitant of the nearby Dismal Swamp. Extending twenty-five miles east of Southampton into North Carolina, this fifteen-mile wide wetland region was the destination and home of hundreds of slave runaways and outlyers. Perhaps his father was among the "band of lurking assassins" reported in a May 12, 1823, edition of the *Norfolk Herald*. This group of Dismal Swamp maroons plagued southern Virginia in the decades preceding Nat's revolt: "Their first objective is to obtain a gun and ammunition, as well to procure game for subsistence as to defend themselves from attack, or accomplish objects of vengeance."[38]

Sometime between 1821 and 1822, Nat Turner escaped from his master, Samuel Turner. It was at this time that he again came into contact with what he referred to as "the Spirit." His first contact with this noncorporal entity came several years earlier at an undeterminable point, and from that time on Nat was in frequent communion with this supernatural entity.[39] After Nat's escape attempt, the Spirit informed Nat that he should return to his earthly master, apparently because he had a greater task to accomplish later in life. Nat returned to the plantation after being missing for thirty days. Upon his return, Nat recollected that "the negroes found fault, and murmured against me, saying that if they had my sense they would not serve any master in the world."[40]

Almost a decade after his escape attempt, Nat revealed the details of a plan he had been crafting for at least three years. Henry, Hark, Nelson, and Sam became his first converts and they chose July 4, 1831, to put their deadly plans into effect. The five conspirators met and formulated the plan but failed to forge a consensus, and Nat's untimely illness forced the band to change the date on which the revolt was to be launched. They waited until August 13, 1831, for a heavenly sign to appear; it came in the form of a deep sky-blue tint in the rising and setting sun.[41] The next Saturday, Nat along with Henry and Hark decided to prepare a dinner on Sunday, August 21, for the men who joined the rebel band. Nat later told Thomas Gray, "Hark, on the following morning brought a pig, and Henry brandy, and being joined by Sam, Nelson, Will and Jack, they prepared in the woods a dinner, where, about three o'clock I joined them."[42] After being joined by another slave named Austin sometime later that evening, this band of eight men began their destructive work at about 2:00 A.M. By the morning of August 23, 1831, Nat's band, which by this point numbered some seventy men, had cut a bloody swath across Southampton, leaving fifty-seven white men, women, and children dead. Militia units from Virginia and North Carolina, as well as federal troops, were called in to quell the insurrection and by the morning of August 24, 1831, the whites of Southampton had largely survived the bloodiest slave rebellion in U.S. history.[43]

After his capture on October 30, 1831, Nat was tried and sentenced to be executed on November 11, 1831. In total, sixteen were executed and twelve were transported from Virginia. As many as a hundred slaves reportedly died in the wake of the rebellion. The case against Nat Turner generated two important documents that unlock several mysteries regarding the causes of the revolt. This first document was the "confession" dictated to Thomas Gray from November 1–3. Gray, a slaveholding attorney, was no doubt hostile to what Nat Turner's revolt represented. His editorial comments reveal both a deep-seated animosity and a begrudging admiration of Nat. Despite the fact that Gray's interpretation of the events may have colored certain aspects of the confession, Nat Turner's undeniable voice, as black preacher in the tradition identified by Du Bois, is still present in this document.[44] The other item that helps create a more complete picture of Nat Turner, and further illustrates some of the African dimensions of the revolt, is the actual trial record. Additional details about Nat are revealed through the court proceedings, which very clearly demonstrate that he was heavily influenced by African cultural undercurrents.

However, due to the nature of this revolt, the trial record is not as useful as the records generated by the Gabriel Prosser and Denmark Vesey conspiracies. The relatively spontaneous nature of the planning and actual revolt, that there were no lengthy meetings or massive recruiting efforts, means that the collective voice of the slaves involved is relatively limited in the record of the proceedings. In addition, slave testimony was actively paraphrased, abbreviated, and edited by court officials. Since the revolt was formulated in the mind of one man, this increases exponentially the value of Nat's confession. What is not revealed in the court record can be found, in full detail, in this key historical document.

*African Spirituality and Folk Culture in Shaping Nat Turner's World*
African cultural influences helped shape the course of Nat's life. Having been born with special marks on his head and chest, Nat remarked that his father and mother greatly influenced his estimate of himself, saying that he "was intended for some great purpose."[45] The marks, which Gray described as "a parcel of excrescences," appear to have been signs to his parents that Nat would later develop supernatural powers.[46] Nat thought his parents' assumptions were correct: "Being at play with other children, when three or four years old, I was telling them something, which my mother overhearing, said it had happened before I was born—I stuck to my story, however, and related somethings which went, in her opinion to confirm it—others being called on were greatly astonished, knowing that these things had happened, and caused them to say in my hearing, I surely would be a prophet, as the Lord had shewn me things that had happened before my birth."[47]

Slave conjurers were often born with distinguishing marks and features or born under special circumstances. According to Newbell Niles Puckett, the typical conjurer was "in many cases a person [who was] 'born different,'" which destined him to develop supernatural powers. Being born with birth marks, a caul, or other distinguishing features often made certain children likely candidates to be future root doctors or conjurers. In his observations of black "hoodoo doctors," Puckett further claimed:

In Africa the witch-doctor is usually selected because of some physical or mental peculiarity which shows him to be possessed of a spirit. I have noticed that the American witch-doctor is also possessed of unusual mentality and often shows physical peculiarities as well. Miss Owen mentions a "Witcheh-man" as having a whopple-jaw, a hare-lip, a lop-side, a crooked leg, one eye like fire and the other eye dead. Ed Murphy, a Mississippi conjure-doctor . . . has three birthmarks on his left arm, a "luck mole" on his right arm, he is "chicken-breasted," was born with a caul on his face . . . His face shows considerable personality, and these traits, coupled with his habit of living off by himself and attending to his own business, give him a tremendous influence with the Negroes of that locality.[48]

Though Nat was not born with a caul or veil, his distinguishing congenital marks gave him attributes associated with the caul. As Puckett notes, "a child born with a 'veil' over his face will have good luck, will be able to communicate with ghosts, and tell fortunes."[49] Nat was not only clairvoyant but was also, as mentioned earlier, in frequent communication with a supernatural entity he referred to as "the Spirit." However deeply suffused with Christianity his language became, he affirmed African spiritual values throughout his life.

### Nat Turner as Christian Prophet and Conjurer

Always at a distance from other slaves and keeping himself cloaked in an enigmatic shroud, young Nat Turner was admired by blacks and whites alike. In his own words "having soon discovered to be great," he thought he "must appear so, and therefore studiously avoided mixing in society, and wrapped [himself] in mystery," devoting much of his time to prayer and fasting.[50] It was in the midst of prayer that Nat first came into contact with supernatural forces. The spirit implored him to "Seek ye the kingdom of Heaven and all things shall be added unto you." When asked by Gray what he meant by "the Spirit," Nat replied, "the Spirit that spoke to the prophets in former days."[51] This allusion to biblical prophets supports the view that Nat had qualities of a "Baptist exhorter."[52]

Sometime in 1825, Nat's influence became so powerful that both slaves and whites came to him for spiritual guidance. It was in that year that Nat baptized Etheldred T. Brantley, a white Virginian. After Brantley suffered through skin eruptions and unusual bleeding, Nat prescribed nine days of praying and fasting, which ultimately cured him of his ailments. After ceasing his "wickedness," Brantley "was baptised by the Spirit."[53] Baptism by total water immersion is a phenomenon found in a number of Atlantic African belief systems. Among Fon, Yoruba, Edo, Akan, and BaKongo speakers, water baptismal rites were prevalent, which helps explain why, according to Melville Herskovits and Albert Raboteau, North American slaves tended toward the Baptist faith. Herskovits notes, "the slaves, then, came to the United States with a tradition which found worship involving immersion in a body of water understandable, and encountered this belief among those whose churches and manner of worship were least strange to them." Raboteau, though very cautious of the generalizations made by Herskovits, does agree with him in part. Also, aside from the Methodists, the Baptists were among the few denominations actively appealing to slaves in the antebellum South.[54]

There were significant parallels between the practice of slave conjurers and Nat's reported abilities. In fact, slave conjurers possessed many of Nat Turner's attributes; they too were often wrapped in mystery and lived the lives of ascetics. Constantly preparing cures, poisons, protective charms, and mystical "hands" meant a certain amount of social space between conjurers and the rest of the slave populace was necessary. Despite the central roles they played on the plantation, they typically lived on the margins of slave society. Their considerable influence over whites and blacks meant that both groups would often come to slave conjurers for spiritual guidance and aid. Paralleling Nat's influence over Brantley, the two conjurers discussed by William Wells Brown, Dinkie and Uncle Frank, often provided aid to local whites by utilizing their esoteric powers of divination and fortune-telling.[55]

Nat was fully convinced that the influence he gained over others was due to his communion with the Spirit and "not by the means of conjuring and such like tricks."[56] Though he definitely did not see himself as a conjurer, Nat's actions and beliefs prove otherwise. His communion with the Spirit reached its apex between 1825 and 1828. The nature of communication with the Spirit would change over time. Initially the Spirit would recite biblical passages to Nat, but later the communication would come primarily in the form of visions and omens. As Nat recalled, "I had a vision—I saw white spirits and black spirits engaged in battle, and the sun was darkened—the thunder rolled in the Heavens, and blood flowed in streams."[57] After receiving this vision, Nat withdrew further from contact with other slaves, in order to dedicate more of his time communicating with the Spirit. This continuous communion would reveal to Nat "the knowledge of the elements, the revolution of the planets, the operation of tides, and changes of the season."[58]

As claimed in his confession, Nat discovered drops of blood on corn stalks in the fields in addition to hieroglyphic symbols and numbers written on leaves in the woods. In an article appearing in The Constitutional Whig on September 26, 1831, an anonymous writer provided more detail about these signs and visions: "[Nat] traced his divination in characters of blood, on leaves alone in the woods; he would arrange them in some conspicuous place, have a dream telling him of the circumstances; and then send some ignorant black to bring them to him, to whom he would interpret their meaning. Thus, by means of this nature, he acquired an immense influence . . . I have in my possession, some papers given up by his wife, under the lash—they are filled with hieroglyphical characters, conveying no definite meaning. The characters on the oldest paper, apparently appear to have been traced with blood; and the figures 6,000, 30,000, 80,000, &e."[59] That this article appeared a full month before Nat was captured on October 30, 1831, implies that its author truly gained insights and evidence bearing on Nat Turner's motivations from those he had actual influence over. The meaning of the symbols and numbers will forever remain unclear. What is obvious however is that these visions and signs, which motivated Nat's revolt, had little to do with Christianity. Also, if the evidence presented by the anonymous writer in The Constitutional Whig has any validity, it demonstrates that Nat did gain influence over slaves because of his alleged clairvoyant and fortune-telling abilities, even if those abilities were manufactured or faked, as the writer of the article suggests.

On May 12, 1831, Nat had the most important revelation in his contact with the Spirit. In his confession, he described in full detail this incident: "I heard a loud noise in the heavens, and the Spirit instantly appeared to me and said the Serpent was loosened, and Christ had laid down the yoke he had borne for the sins of men, and that I should take it on and fight against the Serpent, for time was fast approaching when the first should be last and the last should be first . . . And by signs in the heavens that it would make known to me when I should commence the great work—and until the first sign appeared, I should conceal it from the knowledge of men." So Nat would wait from May 1828 until February 12, 1831, to receive the sign which came to him in the form of a solar eclipse.[60]

For the first time in three years, he communicated the plan to slaves in whom he had the greatest confidence. After falling ill, Nat awaited another sign, which came in the form of a blue sun. His knowledge of, and perhaps command over, the heavens would continue even after his death. In one apocryphal account of Nat's execution, William Drewry alleged that "upon the scaffold Nat declared that after his execution it would grow dark and rain for the last time. It did actually rain, and there was for some time a dry spell. This alarmed many of the whites as well as the negroes." Though this story may be questionable, Drewry was able to interview older inhabitants of Southampton who still had memory of family tales about Nat's revolt. This story also demonstrates the lasting imprint Nat Turner made on the minds of whites in Southampton County.[61] Indication that Nat professed some ability to control heavenly phenomena can be found in the trial records. On November 5, 1831, the Court of Oyer and Terminer heard evidence that Nat claimed "command over the clouds which he had been entertaining as far back as 1826."[62] The abilities to predict, interpret, and even control heavenly phenomena are powers typically associated with slave conjurers, further linking his actions to this practice.

Another ability that gained Nat considerable influence among slaves was his skill in curing diseases. Not only did he successfully cure Ethelred Brantley of his ailments, but according to the trial records Nat could "by the imposition of his hands cure disease—That he related a particular instance in which it was believed that he had in that manner effected a cure upon one of his comrades."[63] Whether or not Nat saw himself as a conjurer, the ability to cure ailments would secure for him a great amount of influence among his fellow slaves.

Comparing the actions of Nat Turner to some of his contemporaries perhaps clarifies his image and the significance of his actions and beliefs. If one were to construct a spectrum of slave spiritual practices, on one end would be Sandy Jenkins who lived in Maryland in the 1830s. Born in Africa, Sandy used his knowledge of herbs and roots to make protective charms, which proved quite useful to Frederick Douglass. Like Nat Turner, Sandy had dreams or visions, which, it was thought, enabled him to foretell events.[64] On the other end of this spectrum of spiritualists would be another Maryland slave, Harriet Tubman, who was born in America and eventually escaped from slavery in 1849. Though her worldview was more or less Christian, she shared many attributes with Nat Turner. They both had visions about future events.[65] They both had the ability to cure disease.[66] Both were in constant communion with spiritual forces.[67] Nat would fall closer to Harriet Tubman's end of the spectrum, but both figures would represent the transitional stage between the African conjurer and the slave preacher outlined by Du Bois in 1903.

The particular African cultural antecedents that may have shaped Nat's spiritual beliefs are impossible to discern from this vantage point. The elements of his practice that may have been identified at an earlier point as Igbo, Mande, or Akan were now part of a uniquely African American cultural matrix.[68] As direct contact with Africa was effectively severed after 1808, slaves created specific cultural mechanisms to maintain a connection to both their African cultural antecedents and to each other. The primary "mechanisms" were the various cultural bridges connecting African- and American-born slaves. These bridges helped slaves separated by hundreds or thousands of miles maintain a shared worldview and a relatively shared consciousness; hence, they helped Africans from different ethnic enclaves find commonality and engage in collaborative resistance efforts while simultaneously creating the bases for an African American culture and consciousness. Nat, therefore, stood firmly on the conceptual middle grounds between an African cultural matrix and an African American one; between the African divine priest and the Baptist preacher; and between conjure and Christianity.

Nat Turner's use of spiritual notions and values familiar to both African- and American-born slaves explains, in part, his appeal and influence over others. One possible example of how widespread the values he expressed were in the antebellum South can be found in his confession. When asked by Gray if he had anything to do with the simultaneous uprising in North Carolina, Nat denied any knowledge of that revolt but added, "I see sir, you doubt my word; but can you not think the same ideas, and strange appearances about this time in the heaven's might prompt others, as well as myself, to this undertaking."[69] By September, authorities in Sampson County, North Carolina, had uncovered a plot organized by an enslaved man named Dave. Scheduled to take place on October 1, 1831, the plan included a coordinated attack on Wilmington by two armies of slaves with the intent to kill all whites and to free the enslaved populace. With the arrest of Dave, disclosure of the plot followed. A month later, the discovery in Richmond County, North Carolina, of a cache of iron spearheads provided substantiation for the conspiracy.[70]

Delaware, Georgia, Louisiana, and Kentucky would experience conspiracy scares or attempted revolts between August and September 1831. It was assumed by contemporaries that Nat Turner had something to do with all of the uprisings, but it was more likely that another force (or set of forces) explains these simultaneous occurrences.[71] Again, according to Nat, slaves in North Carolina, Virginia, and other states viewing the same heavenly phenomena might have similar interpretations about their meaning. But what could possibly explain the existence of this shared cultural consciousness across hundreds of miles? Before and for some time after 1808, one could argue that ethnic concentrations as a result of regional import patterns might explain cultural affinities among slaves in a particular locale. Decades after the close of the slave trade, the principal conduit of this shared consciousness would have to be slave folklore—a force that had the power to bridge physical and cultural gaps separating slaves. Moreover, folklore is the principal means by which one can understand the slave ethos or value system. Thus, it was a key cultural bridge, one that, more than any other indicator, reflects the emergence of a common political and cultural consciousness among free and enslaved African Americans.

# Coda: Folklore and the Creation of an African American Identity

As Michael Gomez describes in *Exchanging Our Country Marks*, the transition from an African matrix of cultures and values to an African American one, while difficult to trace, certainly occurred sometime after the arrival of the first Africans in British North America in 1619. In the course of this dynamic and prolonged process, Igbos, Akans, Mandes and others developed a more unified sense of culture and ethnicity. Their many cultural bridges and shared cultural spaces had already forged a sense of unity and allowed for acts of collaborative resistance. In essence, the rebellions, conspiracies, and day-to-day resistance by enslaved Africans (and African Americans) in North America were crucial in the creation of African American culture and consciousness.[1]

The end of the slave trade into North America also facilitated this process of transformation; once the influx of Africans ended, so too did the umbilical links to specific African cultural roots. While their African cultural and sociopolitical backgrounds continued to inform the world views of enslaved African Americans, the hostile environments they faced and various contacts with European and Euro-American cultures also played roles in this transformative process. What resulted was a unique ethos with broad and relatively fluid parameters. However defined, this new culture had its roots firmly planted in African soil.

In studies of creolization, scholars have typically placed more emphasis on the synthesis of monolithic "African" and "European" cultural milieus.[2] Creolization undoubtedly did occur in North America. However, more attention should be placed on the process by which Africans from different ethnolinguistic groups combined to become African American, a phenomenon that has been practically ignored until Sterling Stuckey's *Slave Culture*.

Despite the seemingly denuding affects of slavery, the enslaved African did not emerge from the experience as either a Sambo or a *tabula rasa*. Instead he or she developed a consciousness that was shaped by resistance and a distant connection to Africa. At times, resistance was itself a conscious opposition to acculturation, as Gomez aptly contends in his work.[3] The African American consciousness that arose out of this dynamic process was transmitted to North American slaves, over space and time, through their folkloric traditions.

In Stuckey's assessment, slave folklore still remains a viable means of further understanding the slave ethos—"a life style and set of values . . . which prevented [slaves] from being imprisoned altogether." Indeed, it seems that folklore was one of the key mechanisms that helped produce a uniquely "African American" outlook and worldview. It had the potential of combining elements from a variety of African cultures and allowing for the creation of a unitary outlook.[4]

In terms of the origins of the African American folklore, Lawrence Levine, while acknowledging the possibility of African influences, contends that "regardless of where slave tales came from, the essential point is that . . . slaves quickly made them their own and through them revealed much about themselves and their world."[5] Because of the difficulty involved in tracing the ultimate origins of the tales, and due to inadequate indices of African tale types and motifs, Levine essentially calls for a reorientation of the folklore debate. Instead of concentrating so much scholarly effort on the origins question, he feels that an analysis of the meaning and function of folk tales should take precedence.[6]

However, if Stuckey is correct that folk songs and tales are a viable means of assessing the slave ethos, then the question of origins is fully intertwined with the meaning and function of slave folk tales. There were reasons why Africans chose to create and tell those stories that have much to do with circumstances and conditions unique to their homelands. If these stories were meant to convey assessments of power and oppression, and if they functioned as tools of education and empowerment, then their ultimate origin would matter a great deal. If the meaning and the function of the folklore are defined by African parameters, then Africans may have special understandings of the songs, stories, and characters that became integral components of their folk culture. Hence, there must also be reasons why Africans adapted and modified these stories to the new realities they faced in the Americas. Folklore facilitated the creation of a unitary cultural and political outlook among African American slaves, a phenomenon that would be difficult, if not impossible, to explain if their folk tales and songs had primarily European origins.

## Animal Trickster Folk Tales as a Discourse of Resistance

In his discussion of animal tricksters in Black Culture and Black Consciousness, Lawrence Levine makes mention of some traditional interpretations of Brer Rabbit. It has been generally held that these animal trickster stories gave slaves a sort of psychic relief and were metaphorical assaults on the powerful. The central trickster character often was a relatively weak animal using wit and cunning instead of force to vanquish more powerful foes. In this specific sense, scholars and African American storytellers have agreed that Brer Rabbit represented the enslaved, while the more powerful animals like Brer Wolf, Brer Bear, Brer Tiger, and Brer Gilyard symbolized the oppressive planter aristocracy.[7] In the words of former slave Prince Baskin, one of the South Carolina storytellers whose tales Abigail Christensen collected, "You see, Missus, I is a small man myself; but I aint nebber 'low no one for to git head o' me. I allers use my sense for help me 'long; jes' like Brer Rabbit." As Christensen accordingly concluded that indeed "the Rabbit represents the colored man."[8] In a similar vain, Simon Brown—an ex-slave from Virginia—admitted to his mentee Rev. William Faulkner: "Now, I was too smart to ever go hungry or to get a whipping. I was too much like Brer Rabbit. I used my head the same way he did. I out-smarted big old Brer Bear time and again."[9] Slaves easily associated themselves with the trickster-hero character.

Levine believes that these metaphorical meanings were sometimes significant, but in other instances he contends that the roles played by the animals were completely different. Brer Rabbit and the other animals may have represented whites, hence the tales reflected how slaves viewed and critiqued white society. Levine further argues that prior assumptions identifying animal tricksters with the slaves ignore "much of the complexity and ambiguity inherent in these tales."[10] Thus he calls for relaxing the "orthodoxy" that the trickster and the slave are one. These stories, according to Levine, had amoral and irrational aspects. The animals rarely perform acts of altruism and friendship, rather using violence and duplicity to get their way.[11] Yet when referring to the tales themselves, one gets a completely different picture. Acts of community building, civil protest, and resistance to oppression undermine the notion that slave folklorists envisioned Brer Rabbit as white.

In several of the stories Brown told Faulkner, Brer Rabbit emerges as a helpful and altruistic friend of the smaller animals. In "Brer Tiger and the Big Wind," Brer Rabbit tricks Tiger so that other animals will not starve to death. In "Brer Possum and Brer Snake," Brer Rabbit helps his friend who is about to be devoured by a snake. Similar tales of Brer Rabbit's moral, altruistic, and perhaps heroic exploits can be found in Brown's tales: "Brer Rabbit's Protest Meeting" depicts Brer Rabbit leading the short-tailed animals in protest. In "Brer Rabbit Rescues His Children" and "Who Got Brer Gilyard's Treasure," Brer Rabbit assumes the role of epic hero as he rescues his children, steals treasure, and slays the dragonlike monster known as Brer Gilyard.[12] Some of the dominant motifs in these specific stories told by Brown include sharing, unity, and the importance of kinship. Similar motifs are found in "The Dance of the Little Animals," a Bur Rabbit Tale collected by E. C. L. Adams in South Carolina. Bur Rabbit saves the smaller animals from Bur Fox by getting a pack of hounds to chase him around a tree stump.[13]

In the various stories collected by Abigail Christensen, Brer Rabbit again emerges as a defender of the weak and helpless. In "De Rabbit, De Bear An' De Locus' Tree," Brer Rabbit tricks Brer Bear into thinking that an enormous storm is sweeping through the woods. Bear urges Rabbit to fasten him to a tree, which Rabbit does, leaving Bear's greedily hoarded food for other animals to eat. Typically, the famous Tar Baby story begins with Brer Rabbit stealing fish or food crops from Brer Wolf, as in the version Prince Baskin told Adams. In "Br'er Rabbit An' Br'er Wolf Plant Pertater An' Hunt Honey," Rabbit manages to steal a bag of potatoes, four loaves of bread, and a barrel of honey from Wolf to feed to his family.[14] While Brer Rabbit's actions may not always be altruistic, they are quite practical. In the end, Rabbit manages to fool the wealthier, more powerful dupes and his reward is the ability to provide sustenance to his kin.

Levine seems to exaggerate the notion that Brer Rabbit is capable of acts of senseless cruelty, noting that in one story "Rabbit *coolly* sacrifices his wife and little children in order to save himself from Wolf's vengeance."[15] Levine appears to have seriously misread the tale. In the variation of the story to which Levine refers, Rabbit does not "coolly" sacrifice his family to save himself; they are killed by Brer Wolf as they seek to avoid asphyxiation. The tale recorded by Christensen as "De Reason Br'er Rabbit Wears a Short Tail" demonstrates that Brer Rabbit tries to save his family:

> Well, Wolf da cut brush wid 'e hatchet tell 'e hab 'nuff; den 'e buil' a fire right close ter de doo' so de win' carry de smoke all tru de crack in de house, an den' 'e t'row black pepper in de fire tel de smoke mos' strangle Br'er Rabbit an' dem . . .
>
> When Br'er Rabbit an' dem couldn't stan' de smoke no longer, dey climb out on de roof o' de house. But dey 'fraid for go down, dey 'fraid Wolf . . .
>
> Well, de smoke ben bery bad. Br'er Rabbit an' all, dey da cough, cough. 'Pear like dey can't stan' it much longer. Dey hab one leetle daughter, an' bimeby him say, tel 'e pa, "Pa, I can't hang on no longer. Dis smoke is too bad."
>
> "My chile you mus' hol' on. Aint you see dat man down dere gwine kill you ef you drop down?" . . . she aint hab strengk for to hol' on no longer, an' she 'blige for le' go an' drop down . . .
>
> Wolf da catch um an' cut off 'e head.[16]

One by one his four children and his wife fall to their deaths. Rabbit's pleas for them to hold on indicate that he does not want his family to die at the hands of Wolf. Using this story as an example of how cruel and self-serving Brer Rabbit can be severely stretches logic. In some important ways, this story fully reflects the slave consciousness and strong aversion to greed found in many of the Brer Rabbit tales. Wolf's murderous rage in this story is sparked by the fact that Rabbit has fooled him out of a tub of fish with which Rabbit fed his family. Instead of being a tale of selfish indulgence, this story embodies selfless sacrifice, and thus, at best, Levine's reading and use of this tale is questionable.[17]

Levine's conclusion that animal trickster folk tales were "a prolonged and telling parody of white society" and that slaves were intentionally mocking the immorality and hypocrisy of white society is interesting if faulty. He bases this interpretation on the fact that Brer Rabbit, at times, engages in acts of abject evil, which in some sense would make the trickster and other animals reflect white planter society.[18] Following this logic, the entire range of stories about human tricksters—John the Slave, High John the Conqueror, and Stagolee—would have to be reenvisioned as a form of "white-faced" minstrelsy because these characters, following the lead of animal tricksters, were also ambiguously depicted by black storytellers. Human tricksters, especially in the so-called "Bad Nigger" tales, sometimes used deception and brute force.[19] It is clear however, that despite their "bad" qualities and capacity for evil, black folklorists always associated human tricksters with African Americans.[20] What Levine essentially does is confine his interpretations of animal tales to a rigidly Manichean model. Perhaps slaves did not view their world in terms of rigid dichotomies; rather they fully understood the ambiguities inherent in the human condition. Brer Rabbit was both good and evil, a multidimensional and multifaceted personality. Indeed, he embodied the broad outlines of the slave psyche.

Levine mentions several of Brown's tales in which central characters fight over access to food. As Faulkner notes, "vegetables and the pig offered a slave a chance to have a little extra food for his family during the winter."[21] Yet cruel masters and overseers sometimes found out about these extra efforts and destroyed or confiscated the food. It this context Brown told a story about Brer Rabbit stealing a cow from Brer Bear.[22] These types of stories underscore the notion that the slaves fully identified with the trickster and that the stories closely mirrored their social conditions. These stories also conveyed survival tactics and encouraged subversive activities, which helped maintain enslaved communities.

Furthermore, these tales demonstrate a particular set of sociopolitical concerns associated with the rural peoples of Atlantic West Africa. If Brer Rabbit and other animal trickster characters are predated by African analogues, and if tales in Africa and the Americas serve some of the same functions and have similar meanings, then there would have to be some common social, political, and environmental circumstances in Africa and in the Americas. Well before rural Africans became victims in the Atlantic slave trade, many had already experienced oppression from powerful African political and economic elites. As John Thornton and many others have shown, polities in Atlantic Africa developed unique systems of land tenure in which rural villagers paid tribute or rent in kind to a mostly urban-dwelling elite. Expansive city-states and kingdoms often established tributaries in smaller polities or rural villages which helped produce agricultural surpluses.[23]

Thus, control over the production and distribution of food was one of the key power-relationships binding peasants to the numerous polities in Atlantic Africa. Failure to pay tribute, personal debt, military service, or involuntary involvement in war led to many rural villagers becoming slaves in the Americas.[24] The folklore they created, therefore, may have been a full reflection of conditions and concerns in Atlantic Africa. This memory of social power and oppression in the African context, as Suzanne Preston

Blier demonstrates, led to the production of art embodying images of shock and horror in Atlantic African societies—principally those influenced by vodun—and American communities.²⁵ According to her, these artistic representations, or *bocio*, often bound in chains and other restrictive devices, embodied in specific Atlantic African societies status and power distinctions between "commoners versus royalty, popular versus elite, slaves versus slave owners."²⁶ Blier adds: "Through juxtaposed themes of peasantry and princedom, official and contraband, concealment and display, a range of contrasting and competing social values come into play. Themes of inversion and carnivalesque reversal also are central to *bocio* conceptualization. In referencing the chaos, incongruity, and disorder of everyday life, these works challenge the status quo."²⁷ This idea leads to the tantalizing possibility that Carnival, Pinkster, Mardi Gras, and other Africanized celebrations in the Americas, as well as the production of "voodoo" dolls and animal trickster tales, reflected a "peasant" consciousness and a series of critiques by enslaved Africans of oppressive power. While oppression was a constant in their lives, the face of the oppressors changed radically when Africans arrived in the Americas.

If the animal trickster was truly a metaphor for slaves in North America, then it has to follow that Brer Rabbit, Anansi the Spider, and others had been reflections of African rural peasants at some earlier point. Perhaps this explains why even the empowered and oppressive animals in the Brer Rabbit tales are referred to as "Brer" and "Sis," terms that imply a definite kinship association. Terms like these may have been employed initially to represent other Africans who were in a position to enforce hegemonic rule over their own people. Their "brothers" and "sisters" participated in their debasement in West and West-central Africa and sold them to European trading interests. The enemies depicted in African American trickster tales were not simply race rivals; they were also class enemies, depicted in the stories as greedy, abusive, and powerful brutes. Not only were African peasants and North American slaves clearly aware of their degraded status, but they identified their enemies and various means to address their oppression. In this sense, these tales reflect a unique cultural and sociopolitical consciousness that was as African as it was nonelite.

The dupes or victims of the animal trickster's schemes in Atlantic African folktales have been variably described as large and powerful, if dim-witted and greedy.²⁸ That the dupes are typically larger, more powerful animals reflects a shared social consciousness on both sides of the Atlantic. That the acquisition of food was a theme common in trickster tales demonstrates a critique of hegemony and hierarchy shared by American slaves and African peasants. This largely follows the insightful analysis of John Roberts, who states, "The similarities between trickster traditions throughout Africa and those found among people of African descent throughout the New World, even on the surface level, would seem to suggest that similar concerns at some level very likely played a role in the perpetuation of similarly structured tales among African people, even those geographically and culturally removed from the continent."[29]

The resistive consciousness fostered by African and African American folklore is singular proof that slavery did not have the power to create a class of "prepolitical" and "proto-nationalist" ciphers.[30] Brer Rabbit becomes, in this way, the fictional counterpart of the slave conjurer. Though Brer Rabbit typically uses trickery and cunning—as opposed to magical and spiritual forces—to aid the dispossessed, both the trickster and the conjurer found ways to empower the powerless throughout the Atlantic world.

*Flying Africans: Tales of Rebellion and Spiritual Transmigration*
Slaves in the Sea Islands of South Carolina and Georgia frequently told "flying African" tales. Stories of this type were passed down as late as the 1930s, and many examples were recorded in the WPA study of cultural survivals in coastal Georgia entitled *Drums and Shadows*. One ex-slave informant, Emma Monroe of Tin City, reported that "Duh ole folks use tuh tell us chillun duh story bout people dat flied off tuh Africa. I blieb um bout flyin."[31] Another Tin City resident, Paul Singleton, similarly testified that "Muh daddy use tuh tell me duh time bout folks wut could fly back tuh Africa. Dey could take wing an jis fly off."[32] Children of the Sea Islands heard these stories so often from their parents that very few could claim ignorance of the flying African phenomenon. Gene Tattnall, an ex-slave living on Wilmington Island, stated "Long as I kin membuh, missus, I been heahin bout dat. Lots uh slaves wut wuz brung obuh frum Africa could fly . . . Dey dohn lak it heah an dey tink dey go back tuh Africa. One by one dey fly up in duh eah an all fly off an gone back tuh Africa."[33] Tales of this sort are unique to the Americas. Shaped by the particular circumstances of American bondage, these flight stories, even if lacking direct African analogues, are intrinsically

linked to Atlantic West and West-central African metaphysical and spiritual understandings.[34]

Ex-slave Wallace Quarterman of Darien, Georgia, related the following story to a WPA interviewer in the 1930s: "deys all African . . . Dey go 'quack, quack, quack,' jis as fas as a hawse kin run, an muh pa say, 'Ain no good tuh lissen tuh um.' Dey git long all right but yuh know dey wuz a lot ub um wut ain stay down yuh . . . duh obuhseeuh an Mr. Blue put um in duh fiel, but he couldn do nuttn wid um. Dey gabble, gabble, gabble, an nobody couldn unduhstan um an dey didn know how tuh wuk right. Mr. Blue he go down one mawnin wid a long whip fuh tuh whip um good . . . he whip um good an dey gits tuhgedduh an stick duh hoe in duh fiel an den say 'quack, quack, quack,' and dey riz up in duh sky an tun heself intuh buzzards an fly right back tuh Africa."[35] Typically in these stories, African-born slaves had the ability to take flight and could only perform the feat if certain criteria were met. They had to truly believe in this power before flight was possible, and the flight was frequently preceded by the chanting of magical words. Jack Wilson, an ex-slave from Old Fort, Georgia, reported: "Some hab magic powuh wut come tuh um frum way back in Afirca. Muh Mothuh use tuh tell me bout slabes jis brung obuh frum Africa wut hab duh supreme magic powuh. Deah wuz a magic pass wud dat dey would pass tuh udduhs. Ef dey belieb in dis magic, dey could scape an fly back tuh Africa."[36]

In a similar story told by Rosa Grant of Possum Point, she related how her great-grandmother was captured in Africa and brought into bondage in the Sea Islands of Georgia. After being there for some time, Grant's great-grandmother "stretch uh arms out—so—an rise right up an fly back tuh Africa." Because her grandmother was American-born, "she try and try doin duh same way but she ain nebuh fly. She say she guess she jis wuzn bawn wid duh powuh."[37] Again, a typical theme in stories of this type is that only African-born slaves possessed the ability to take flight.

Another story found in the Sea Islands regarding a return to Africa would be the "Ibo Landing" account. At some indeterminate point before the end of the slave trade, a pivotal event occurred at Dunbar Creek on St. Simons Island. Floyd White, an ex-slave resident of St. Simons testified "Heahd bout duh Ibo's Landing? Das duh place weah dey bring duh Ibos obuh in a slabe ship an wen dey git yuh, dey ain lak it an so dey all staht singin an dey mahch right down in duh ribbuh tuh mahch bach tuh Africa, but dey ain able tuh git deah. Dey gits drown."³⁸ This story of mass suicide represents a particularly Igbo spiritual and metaphysical conceptualization. The Igbos who entered the river did not believe they were committing suicide. Instead they were, in a very real sense, returning home. The Igbo were among many West African groups that adhered to a belief in transmigration, that upon death the spirit is, in the words of G. T. Basden, "reborn at an appointed season and will resume [its] life in this world."³⁹ This fact is corroborated by one famous Igbo ex-slave, Olaudah Equiano. In discussing the spiritual beliefs of his homeland, Equiano recounted that some of the Igbo from his province "believe[d] in the transmigration of souls."⁴⁰

The "Ibo Landing" account reveals that Sea Island flight stories may also have deeper spiritual meanings. Perhaps the tales were also metaphorical stories of suicide or death by other means. This would allow for an understanding of why only African-born slaves could fly back to Africa. Charles Ball, who spent a significant portion of his life as a slave in South Carolina, noted "[Africans] are universally of the opinion, and this opinion is founded in their religion, that after death they shall return to their own country, and rejoin their former companions and friends, in some happy region, in which they will be provided with plenty of food, and beautiful women, from the lovely daughters of their own native land." If the soul of a deceased individual returns to former companions and friends, then the souls of African-born slaves would have to "fly" or "swim" across the Atlantic to get back home. This was an impossible feat for slaves born in the Americas. Their families and friends were in the Western Hemisphere, not Africa, and thus they did not have the ability to take flight. The phenomenon of flying Africans is absent in African folklore for similar reasons. If the individual dies in Africa, the spirit has no need to fly because it is already home. Though rooted in African metaphysical understandings, this orientation is uniquely African American and perhaps, in other ways, epitomizes the creolization process. In a very real sense, the point at which Africans could no longer take flight was the point when African Americans were born.⁴¹

Transmigration and similar concepts of spiritual renewal are evident in a variety of Atlantic West African societies. In addition to Igbo beliefs, the concept of *Sankofa* among the Akan and the BaKongo cosmogram reflected in the ring-shout demonstrate notions of spiritual rebirth. Stories of flight represent the creation of an "African American" consciousness. Combining spiritual understandings central to Igbo, Akan, and BaKongo beliefs in order to cope with North American bondage is evidence that slaves success-fully crafted a more unitary cultural identity.[42] If the flight stories, like the "Ibo Landing" incident, were metaphorical accounts of suicide, then they are also reflected a consciousness of resistance.

*Memory and Resistance: Historical Rebel Leaders in Folklore*
While no North American slave rebellion can be deemed "successful," the memories and legacies of these examples of resistance lived on in folklore and folk songs. Perhaps the most instructive illustration of this is "Uncle Gabriel." This banjo song, composed sometime before 1855, ex-plains the story of Gabriel Prosser:

Oh, my boys I'm bound to tell you;
Oh! Oh!
Listen awhile, and I will tell you;
Oh! Oh!
I'll tell you little 'bout Uncle Gabriel;
Oh, boys, I've just begun.
Hard times in old Virginny.
Oh, don't you know old Uncle Gabriel?
Oh! Oh!
Oh, he was a darky General,
Oh! Oh!
He was the chief of the insurgents,
Way down in Southampton.
Hard times in old Virginny.
It was a little boy betrayed him,
Oh! Oh!
A little boy by the name of Daniel
Oh! Oh!
Betrayed him at the Norfolk landing;
Oh, boys I'm getting done.
Hard times in old Virginny.
Says he, How d'ye do, my Uncle Gabriel?
Oh! Oh!
My name it is Jim McCullen;
Some they calls me Archy Mullin.
Hard times in old Virginny.
They took him down to the gallows,
Oh! Oh!

They drove him down with four grey horses,
Oh! Oh!
Brice's Ben, he drove the wagon,
Oh, boys, I am most done.
Hard times in old Virginny.
And there they hung him, and they swung him,
Oh! Oh!
And that was the last of the darkey General;
Oh, boys I'm just done.
Hard times in old Virginny.[43]

While the creator of this song may have confused some of the details of Gabriel's plot with Nat Turner's revolt, clearly both remained part of the collective memory of enslaved and free black communities throughout the nineteenth-century South. Indeed, Gabriel was "chief of the insurgents" and was captured after attempting to escape Richmond by way of ship. But the song's lament that "they hung him, and they swung him . . . And that was the last of the darkey General" strikes a uniquely African American chord. While one can certainly question whether this was truly the "last" of Gabriel if he was still being memorialized as late as 1855, the line's finality of this sentiment implies some significant distance from the beliefs in transmigration that had been so ubiquitous in enslaved communities.[44] It is important to note that these values did not completely disappear. Another folk song recorded sometime during the late nineteenth to early twentieth century, details the continuing memory of Nat Turner and even hints at his life after death:

You mought be rich as cream
And drive you coach and four-horse team,
But you can't keep de world from movin' round
Nor Nat Turner from gainin' ground.

And your name it mought be Caesar sure,
And got you cannon can shoot a mile or more,
But you can't keep de world from movin' round
Nor Nat Turner from gainin' ground.[45]

Both songs together represent how complex the emerging African American culture was. In embracing Christian notions of death while maintaining connections to spiritual transmigration, the dynamism of African American culture is quite apparent.

A paradigm shift was occurring which signaled the creation of a matrix of new forms, modes, and beliefs. When Africans stopped flying home, when the ring shout was more of a dance than an elaborate prayer, and when the last of General Gabriel had been seen (even though Nat Turner was still gaining ground), an African American identity, consciousness, and orientation effectively replaced African ones. Perhaps nothing epitomizes this transformative process more than blues music, which was a natural outcome of tales and songs of lament and sorrow. While certain elements of this expressive form are identifiably African, the content of blues songs voices sociopolitical concerns that are, in a number of ways, uniquely American.

# Notes

INTRODUCTION

1. Arna Bontemps, *Black Thunder, Gabriel's Revolt: Virginia, 1800* (1936; reprint, Boston: Beacon Press, 1968), xxvi–xxvii.

2. Michael Mullin, *Africa in America: Slave Acculturation and Resistance in the American South and the British Caribbean, 1736–1831* (Chicago: University of Illinois Press, 1994), 228.

3. Bontemps, *Black Thunder*, xxvi, 52.

4. Ulrich B. Phillips, *American Negro Slavery* (1918; reprint, Baton Rouge: Louisiana State University Press, 1966), 291, 339, 454–58.

5. Ibid., 458–63.

6. Eugene Genovese, "Herbert Aptheker's Achievement," in Gary Y. Okihiro, ed., *In Resistance: Studies in African, Caribbean, and Afro-American History* (Amherst: University of Massachusetts Press, 1986), 22–25.

7. Herbert Aptheker, *American Negro Slave Revolts* (1943; reprint, New York: International Publishers, 1993), 12–13.

8. Ibid., 139.

9. Stanley Elkins, *Slavery: A Problem in American Institutional and Intellectual Life* (1959; reprint, New York: Universal Library, 1963), 91; Aptheker, *American Negro Slave Revolts*, 1.

10. Kenneth Stampp, *The Peculiar Institution* (1956; reprint, New York: Vintage Books, 1989), vii.

11. Gerald W. [Michael] Mullin, *Flight and Rebellion: Slave Resistance in Eighteenth-Century Virginia* (London: Oxford University Press, 1972), 35–37, 56, 81–82.

12. Mullin, *Africa in America*, 268–69, 230.

13. Eugene Genovese, *From Rebellion to Revolution: Afro-American Slave Revolts in the Making of the Modern World* (Baton Rouge: Louisiana State University Press, 1979), 5, 7–8, 18–19, 26.

14. Ibid., 26.

15. Elkins, *Slavery*, 91; Richard Dunn, *Sugar and Slaves: The Rise of the Planter Class in the English West Indies, 1624–1713* (Chapel Hill: University of North Carolina Press, 1972), 236.

16. Michael Gomez, *Exchanging Our Country Marks: The Transformation of African Identities in the Colonial and Antebellum South* (Chapel Hill: University of North Carolina Press, 1998), 149–153.

17. David Eltis, Stephen Behrendt, David Richardson, and Herbert Klein, eds., *The Trans-Atlantic Slave Trade: A Database on CD-ROM* (Cambridge: Cambridge University Press, 1999).

18. Lorena Walsh, "The Chesapeake Slave Trade: Regional Patterns, African Origins, and Some Implications," *William and Mary Quarterly*, 3rd ser., 58 (January 2001): 139–69.Walsh notes that the Biafran imports tended to be concentrated in the Lower Chesapeake region.

19. Gomez, *Exchanging Our Country Marks*, 4.

20. Sterling Stuckey, *Slave Culture: Nationalist Theory and the Foundation of Black America* (New York: Oxford University Press, 1986), 10–11, 95–97.

21. Gomez, *Exchanging Our Country Marks*, 55.

22. David Northrup, "Igbo and Myth Igbo: Culture and Ethnicity in the Atlantic World, 1600–1850," *Slavery and Abolition* 21 (2000): 1–20.

23. Douglas B. Chambers, "Ethnicity in the Diaspora: The Slave-Trade and the Creation of African 'Nations' in the Americas," *Slavery and Abolition* 22 (December 2001): 26.

24. Sidney Mintz and Richard Price, *The Birth of African-American Culture: An Anthropological Perspective* (Boston: Beacon Press, 1976), 2.

25. John Thornton, *Africa and Africans in the Making of the Atlantic World, 1400–1680* (New York: Cambridge University Press, 1992), 206.

26. Gomez, *Exchanging Our Country Marks*, 5.

27. Sterling Stuckey, "Through the Prism of Folklore: The Black Ethos in Slavery," *Massachusetts Review* 9 (Summer 1968): 417–37.

## 1. FIRES OF DISCONTENT, ECHOES OF AFRICA

1. William Renwick Riddell, "The Slave in New York," *Journal of Negro History* 13 (January 1928), 54–55; Winthrop Jordan, *White Over Black: American Attitudes Toward the Negro, 1550–1812* (New York: W. W. Norton, 1968), 83; Joyce Goodfriend, *Before the Melting Pot: Society and Culture in Colonial New York City, 1664–1730* (Princeton: Princeton University Press, 1992), 9, 111; Edgar McManus, *A History of Negro Slavery in New York* (Syracuse: Syracuse University Press, 1966), 2–6; John Thornton, "The African Experience of the '20. and Odd Negroes' Arriving in Virginia in 1619," *William and Mary Quarterly*, 3rd ser., 55 (July 1998): 421; Peter Wood, *Strange New Land: Africans in Colonial America* (New York: Oxford University Press, 2003), 18–19, 23.

2. David Kobrin, *The Black Minority in Early New York* (Albany: University Press of the State of New York, 1971), 1–3; Goodfriend, *Before the Melting Pot*, 8–10; McManus, *Negro Slavery in New York*, 2–3.

3. K. G. Davies, *The Royal African Company* (New York: Atheneum, 1970), 8–12; Edwin Morgan, *Slavery in New York* (New York: New York City History Club, 1897), 3–6.

4. Riddell, "The Slave in New York," 55.

5. Ibid., 53–57; Thornton, *Africa and Africans*, 63–65; Charles R. Boxer, *The Dutch Seaborne Empire, 1600–1800* (New York: Oxford University Press, 1965), 21–29; Davies, *The Royal African Company*, 8–9.

6. Quoted in Morgan, *Slavery in New York*, 3.

7. E. B. O'Callaghan, ed., *Documents Relative to the Colonial History of the State of New York* (Albany: Weed, Parsons, and Company, 1858), 1:154; Morgan, *Slavery in New York*, 4–7; Riddel, "The Slave in New York," 54–56.

8. O'Callaghan, *Documents*, 2:213, 223, 222, 521. In a list of free African landowners in Manhattan from 1643 to 1664, the following names appear: Garcia D'Angola, Simon Congo, Paulo

D'Angola, Anthony Congo, Francisco D'Angola, Domingo Angola, Anthony van Angola, Lucie D'Angola, Catalina van Angola, Laurens van Angola, and Assento Angola. In addition, a number of these free African landowners had Spanish or Portuguese surnames which would likely mean they were plundered from Spanish and Portuguese ships or were acquired in peaceful trade from Spanish America or Brazil. Ultimately, the vast majority of these Africans were clearly from West-central Africa. See Howard Dodson, Christopher Moore, and Robert Yancy, *The Black New Yorkers: The Schomburg Illustrated Chronology* (New York: John Wiley and Sons, 2000), 15–16.

9. E. B. O'Callaghan, ed., *Voyage of the Slavers St. John and Arms of Amsterdam* (Albany: J. Munsell, 1867), 13.

10. Elizabeth Donnan, ed., *Documents Illustrative of the History of the Slave Trade to America* (Washington, DC: Carnegie Institution, 1932), 3:418.

11. Davies, *The Royal African Company*, 12, 15. Six years later, Portugal expelled the Dutch from Brazil signaling the beginning of the end of Dutch dominance in the Atlantic World.

12. Ibid., 8, 12, 240; Philip Curtin, *The Atlantic Slave Trade: A Census* (Madison: University of Wisconsin Press, 1969), 208; Christopher DeCorse, *An Archaeology of Elmina: Africans and Europeans on the Gold Coast, 1400–1900* (Washington, DC: Smithsonian Institution Press, 2001), 7. For an overview of the Dutch slave trade, see Johannes Menne Postma, *The Dutch in the Atlantic Slave Trade, 1600–1815* (Cambridge: Cambridge University Press, 1990).

13. Davies, *The Royal African Company*, 12; Michael Kammen, *Colonial New York: A History* (New York: Charles Scribner's Sons, 1975), 71–72.

14. Jordan, *White Over Black*, 83–85, 103; J. Franklin Jameson, ed., *Narratives of New Netherland, 1609–1664* (New York: Charles Scribner's Sons, 1909), 89. Goodfriend, *Before the Melting Pot*, 13, 16.

15. McManus, *Negro Slavery in New York*, 3.

16. Kobrin, *Black Minority in Early New York*, 4; Kammen, *Colonial New York*, 72; McManus, *Negro Slavery in New York*, 6.

17. Goodfriend, *Before the Melting Pot*, 111; Mary Booth, *History of the City of New York* (New York: W. R. C. Clark, 1867), 1:356; Joel Tyler Headley, *The Great Riots of New York, 1712–1873* (New York: Bobbs-Merrill Company, Inc., 1970), 26.

18. Goodfriend, *Before the Melting Pot*, 8–10, 13, 61, 112–114, 134. James G. Lydon "New York and the Slave Trade, 1700–1774," *William and Mary Quarterly*, 3rd ser., 35 (1978): 388; Darold Wax, "Preferences for Slaves in Colonial America," *Journal of Negro History* 58 (October 1973): 372; Evarts Greene and Virginia Harrington, *American Population before the Federal Census of 1790* (Gloucester, MA: Peter Smith, 1966), 94–102; Gary Nash, *The Urban Crucible: Social Change, Political Consciousness, and the Origins of the American Revolution* (Cambridge, MA: Harvard University Press, 1979), 14–15.

19. Donnan, *Documents Illustrative of the History of the Slave Trade*, 3:435.

20. Jordan, *White Over Black*, 67, 83–84; Morgan, *Slavery in New York*, 7–8.

21. Riddell, "The Slave in New York," 56, 66.

22. Morgan, *Slavery in New York*, 12–13.

23. Stampp, *The Peculiar Institution*, 192, 206–8, 218–19.

24. O'Callaghan, *Documents*, 3:374; Oscar Williams, *African Americans and Colonial Legislation in the Middle Colonies* (New York: Garland, 1998), 45.

25. O'Callaghan, Documents, 5:138.

26. Williams, African Americans and Colonial Legislation, 46–47; Riddell, "The Slave in Early New York," 68; Edwin Olson, "The Slave Code in Colonial New York," Journal of Negro History 29 (April 1944): 156.

27. Morgan, Slavery in New York, 13; Williams, African Americans and Colonial Legislation, 46; Riddell, "The Slave in New York," 68.

28. E. B. O'Callaghan, ed., Laws of His Majesties' Colony of New York As They Were Enacted by the Governor, Council and General Assembly in Divers Sessions, the First of Which Began April 9th, 1691 (Albany: Weed, Parsons and Company, 1849), 1:520; A. Judd Northrup, Slavery in New York: A Historical Sketch (Albany: New York State Library Bulletin History no. 4, 1900), 260–61

29. O'Callaghan, Laws of New York, 1:521, 588; Williams, African Americans and Colonial Legislation, 47.

30. Riddell, "The Slave in New York," 68–69; Northrup, Slavery in New York, 260–61; Aptheker, Slave Revolts, 168–69.

31. O'Callaghan, Documents, 5:39; Aptheker, Slave Revolts, 169, 72. Aptheker notes an earlier instance of slave rebelliousness in colonial New York. Lord Cornbury issued a proclamation to the justices of the peace in July 1706 regarding a group of "riotous" slaves in Kings County. Though Lord Cornbury commissioned them to "fire on them, kill, or destroy them, if they cannot otherwise be taken," no other specific mention of this incident can be found in the records of colonial New York.

32. Aptheker, Slave Revolts, 169.

33. Williams, African Americans and Colonial Legislation, 49; Riddell, "The Slave in New York," 69–70.

34. O'Callaghan, Documents, 5:341

35. Reverend John Sharpe, "Journal of Reverend Sharpe," Pennsylvania Magazine of History and Biography 40 (January–October 1916): 421; James Grant Wilson, ed., The Memorial History of the City of New-York: From Its First Settlement to the Year 1892 (New York: New York History Company, 1892), 2:139–40; Headley, Great Riots, 26–28; Riddell, "The Slave in New York," 72.

36. Though not as well documented as other slave rebellions and conspiracies, the 1712 revolt did generate a number of contemporary accounts. Among those records are:

(1) Court records from the Municipal Archives of the City of New York: (a) Engrossed "Minutes of the Court of Quarter and General Sessions, begun August 7th Anno 1694," 212–46, 248; (b) Engrossed "Minutes of the Supreme Court of Judicature," Book 2 (June 6, 1710–June 5, 1714); (c) "Minutes of the Court of General and Quarter Sessions of the Peace" (1683–1742); (d) Rough "Minutes Book of the Court of General Sessions" (1705–1714), 39–40, 48–50; (e) "Court of General Sessions Minutes" (February 1683–August 1760); and (f) "Supreme Court Minute Books" (October 1691–October 23, 1739).

(2) Documents from the New-York Historical Society Collection: (a) "Trials of Slaves at the City Hall, NY," in Daniel Parish, ed., Transcripts of Material on Slavery in the Public Record Office in London (1690–1750), Mss. Collection; (b) "Coroner's Inquisition and Jury Finding on the Death of William Asht, April 9, 1712" and "Coroner's Inquisition and Jury Finding on the Death of Augustus Grasset, April 9, 1712."

(3) The April 7–14 and April 14–21, 1712, editions of the Boston News-Letter.

(4) A letter written by Reverend John Sharpe on June 23, 1712, published in *The New York Genealogical and Biographical Record* 21 (1890): 162–163. This letter was based on Sharpe's interview of one of the slaves involved in the conspiracy, thus offering the only account with information directly from the accused. The recipients of Sharpe's letter created their own account of the 1712 revolt, which appears in David Humphreys, *An Account of the Endeavours Used by the Society for the Propagation of the Gospel in Foreign Parts* (London: Society for the Propagation of the Gospel in Foreign Parts, 1830), 2:8–10.

(5) A letter written by Governor Robert Hunter on 23 June 1712 to the Lords of Trade, published in O'Callaghan, *Documents*, 5:341–42.

37. *Boston News-Letter*, April 7–14, 1712. Emphasis added.

38. *Boston News-Letter*, April 14–21, 1712.

39. John Sharpe, "The Negro Plot of 1712," *The New York Genealogical and Biographical Record* 21 (1890): 162–63. Emphasis added.

40. Ibid., 163; John Sharpe, "Reverend John Sharpe's Proposals for Erecting a School, Library, and a Chapel at New York," New-York Historical Society Collections, Revolutionary Papers, 3:352–53; Kenneth Scott, "The Slave Insurrection in New York in 1712," *New-York Historical Society Quarterly* 45 (January 1961), 65–66; Engrossed "Minutes of the Court of Quarter and General Sessions, begun August 7th Anno 1694," Municipal Archives of the City of New York; Rough "Minutes Book of the Court of General Sessions" (1705–1714), Municipal Archives of the City of New York. There is a small discrepancy in Sharpe's accounts of his interview with Robin. In his letter to the Society for the Propagation of the Gospel in Foreign Parts, he claims that the interview took place on the third day of Robin's sentence. In the document known as "Rev. John Sharpe's Proposals," he claims to have seen Robin "after he had hung five days." Other than that minor difference, both accounts agree on the content of Robin's confession.

41. O'Callaghan, *Documents*, 5:341. Emphasis added.

42. The Gold Coast, as defined by the English in the eighteenth century, included the coastal region between Assini in the west and Lake Volta in the east, an area roughly coterminous with the southern portion of modern-day Ghana. Curtin, *Atlantic Slave Trade*, 128.

43. E. Kofi Agorsah, "Archaeology and Resistance History in the Caribbean," *African Archaeological Review*, 11 (1993): 178–80.

44. Ibid.; Thornton, *Africa and Africans*, 185–86; Basil Davidson, *The African Slave Trade* (Boston: Little, Brown and Company, 1980), 72; Monica Schuler, "Ethnic Slave Rebellions in the Caribbean and the Guianas," *Journal of Social History* 3 (summer 1970): 375; Melville Herskovits, *The Myth of the Negro Past* (Boston: Beacon Press, 1941), 35; Ray Kea, *Settlements, Trade, and Polities in the Seventeenth-Century Gold Coast* (Baltimore: Johns Hopkins University Press, 1982), 15, 69, 147; Davies, *Royal African Company*, 9, 40, 42, 265.

45. Thornton, *Africa and Africans*, 196; Monica Schuler, "Akan Slave Rebellions in the British Caribbean," *Savacou* 1 (1970): 9–11; Lydon, "New York and the Slave Trade," 376–377, 380; Eltis et al., *The Trans-Atlantic Slave Trade*.

46. See Orlando Patterson, *The Sociology of Slavery: An Analysis of the Origins, Development, and Structure of Negro Slave Society in Jamaica* (Cranbury, NJ: Associated University Press, 1967), 120.

47. Schuler, "Ethnic Slave Rebellions," 375; Chambers, "Ethnicity in the Diaspora," 27, 29–33; Ray Kea, "'When I Die, I Shall Return to My Own Land': An 'Amina' Slave Rebellion in the

Danish West Indies, 1733–1734," in John Hunwick and Nancy Lawler, eds., *The Cloth of Many Colored Silks: Papers on History and Society Ghanaian and Islamic in Honor of Ivor Wilks* (Evanston, IL: Northwestern University Press, 1996), 159, 161–62; John Thornton, "The Coromantees: An African Cultural Group in Colonial North America and the Caribbean," *Journal of Caribbean History* 32 (1998): 161–78; Thelma Foote, "'Some Hard Usage': The New York City Slave Revolt of 1712," *New York Folklore* 18 (2001): 149–50.

48. Davies, *Royal African Company*, 224–26, 233; Curtin, *Atlantic Slave Trade*, 150; Hugh Thomas, *The Slave Trade: The Story of the Atlantic Slave Trade, 1440–1870* (New York: Simon and Schuster, 1997), 349.

49. Trevor Burnard and Kenneth Morgan, "The Dynamics of the Slave Market and Slave Purchasing Patterns in Jamaica, 1655–1788," *William and Mary Quarterly*, 3rd ser., 58 (January 2001): 205–7, 209, 210; Eltis et al., *The Trans-Atlantic Slave Trade*; Lydon, "New York and the Slave Trade," 383–84; Patterson, *Sociology of Slavery*, 134; David Eltis, "The Volume and Structure of the Transatlantic Slave Trade: A Reassessment," *William and Mary Quarterly*, 3rd ser., 58 (January 2001): 36; Colin Palmer, *Human Cargoes: The British Trade to Spanish America, 1700–1739* (Urbana: University of Illinois Press, 1981).

50. Burnard and Morgan, "Slave Purchasing Patterns in Jamaica," 215–16; Eltis, "Volume and Structure of the Transatlantic Slave Trade," 36–37; Eltis et al., *The Trans-Atlantic Slave Trade*; Mintz and Price, *The Birth of African-American Culture*, 2, 7–9.

51. Burnard and Morgan, "Slave Purchasing Patterns in Jamaica," 218.

52. Patterson, *Sociology of Slavery*, 134, 137–38; Eltis, "Volume and Structure of the Transatlantic Slave Trade," 46, 40.

53. Lydon, "New York and the Slave Trade," 383; Eltis, "Volume and Structure of the Slave Trade," 39–40; Eltis et al., *The Trans-Atlantic Slave Trade*.

54. Wax, "Preferences for Slaves," 384.

55. Quoted in ibid., 385.

56. Daniel Littlefield, *Rice and Slaves: Ethnicity and the Slave Trade in Colonial South Carolina* (Baton Rouge: Louisiana State University Press, 1981), 11–14

57. Donnan, *Documents Illustrative of the History of the Slave Trade*, 2:354.

58. Edward Long, *The History of Jamaica* (1774; reprint, London: Frank Cass, 1970), 2:470.

59. Ibid.; Philip Curtin, *Two Jamaicas: The Role of Ideas in a Tropical Colony, 1830–1865* (Westport, CT: Greenwood Press, 1955), 24.

60. Sharpe, "The Negro Plot," 162.

61. Ibid.

62. Scott, "The Slave Insurrection," 51–52, 58–60, 62–67; Engrossed "Minutes of the Court of Quarter and General Sessions, begun August 7th Anno 1694," Municipal Archives of the City of New York.

63. Ibid.; O'Callaghan, *Documents*, 5:367, 342; "Trials of Slaves at the City Hall, NY," in Daniel Parish, ed., *Transcripts of Material on Slavery in the Public Record Office in London (1690–1750)*, New-York Historical Society.

64. O'Callaghan, *Documents*, 5:371.

65. Scott, "The Slave Insurrection," 67–68; Sharpe, "The Negro Plot," 162–63; Goodfriend, *Before the Melting Pot*, 126–27.

66. Humprheys, *Endeavours Used by the Society for the Propagation of the Gospel*, 9–11.

67. Sharpe, "The Negro Plot," 163; Sharpe, "Rev. Sharpe's Proposals," 353.

68. Goodfriend, *Before the Melting Pot*, 117; Graham Russell Hodges, *Root and Branch: African Americans in New York and East Jersey* (Chapel Hill: University of North Carolina Press, 1999), 89; "Court of General Sessions Minutes" (February 1683–August 1760), Municipal Archives of the City of New York. Despite the obvious possibility of an intimate relationship between the two, Sarah could have been a client requesting spiritual consultations with the renowned doctor.

69. Schuler, "Akan Slave Rebellions," 12, 15–16; Long, *The History of Jamaica*, 2:451–54.

70. Long, *The History of Jamaica*, 2:451–52; Schuler "Ethnic Slave Rebellions," 383. Emphasis added. In a 1789 report, specific mention is made of Obeah doctors and their mystical powders: "The influence of the Professors of that art was such as to induce many to enter into that rebellion on the assurance that they were invulnerable, and to render them so, the Obeah man gave them a powder with which they were to rub themselves." Quoted in Joseph Williams, *Voodoos and Obeahs: Phases of West India Witchcraft* (New York: Dial, 1932), 116.

71. This pattern finds parallels among twentieth-century Dutch Guianan maroons who have maintained a number of Akan beliefs and customs. Anthropologists Melville and Frances Herskovits write "In the Saramacca bush the role of the *Kromanti* group (the Obeah sorcerers) is in all respects akin to that of the Asafotche companies of the Gold Coast today . . . In both instances they have magic to help them in war. In both instances this magic includes powers which endow the members with resistance to bullets, and to all things that cut or lacerate." Melville Herskovits and Frances Herskovits, *Rebel Destiny: Among the Bush Negroes of Dutch Guiana* (New York: Whittlesey House, 1934), 350.

72. O'Callaghan, *Documents*, 5:341.

73. Scott, "The Slave Insurrection," 63–65; "Coroner's Inquisition and Jury Finding on the Death of William Asht, April 9, 1712," New-York Historical Society; "Coroner's Inquisition and Jury Finding on the Death of Augustus Grasset, April 9, 1712," New-York Historical Society; Parish Transcripts, New-York Historical Society; "Court of General Sessions Minutes" (February 1683–August 1760), Municipal Archives of the City of New York.

74. Robert Weir, *Colonial South Carolina* (Millwood, NY: Kto Press, 1983), 184; John Inscoe, "Carolina Slave Names: An Index to Acculturation," *Journal of Southern History* 49 (November 1983): 535; Peter Wood, *Black Majority: Negroes in Colonial South Carolina from 1670 through the Stono Rebellion* (New York: W. W. Norton, 1974), 182.

75. N. O. Anim, *Sub-Sahara Africa Forum 9: Names as a Factor in Cultural Identity Among the Akan, Ga, and Ewe Tribes of Ghana* (Pretoria, RSA: Unit for Development Analysis, 1991), 2–3. This particular naming practice was obviously kept intact by many Akan-speakers in the Western Hemisphere, including those in North America. Take, for example, the case of a twenty-six-year-old slave named Quash of Mountholly, New Jersey. In 1777, his master issued a fugitive advertisement in *The New-Jersey Gazette*, stating that Quash "may probably change [his name] to YERRAH." Quash was likely continuing the Akan naming practices so ubiquitous in the Gold Coast and in the American regions which imported Akan-speakers in large numbers. See Graham Hodges and Alan Brown, eds., *"Pretends to Be Free": Runaway Slave Advertisements from Colonial and Revolutionary New York and New Jersey* (New York: Garland, 1994), 209.

76. Scott, "The Slave Insurrection," 53, 57, 62–65; "Coroner's Inquisition and Jury Finding on the Death of William Asht, April 9, 1712," New-York Historical Society; "Minute Book of the Court of General Sessions" (1705–1714), Municipal Archives of the City of New York; "Supreme Court Minute Books" (October 1691–October 23, 1739), Municipal Archives of the City of New York. The rough minutes transcribed in the "Minutes Book of the Court of General Sessions" include sections entitled "Evidence for Dom Regina" not found in the "Court of General Sessions Minutes" (February 1683–August 1760), the "Minutes of the Court of General and Quarter Sessions of the Peace" (1683–1742), or the Engrossed "Minutes of the Court of Quarter and General Sessions, begun August 7th Anno 1694." These evidence sections are simply lists of informants providing testimony on given dates. Tracing slave informants—who are listed without surnames—is a relatively simple matter in this record.

77. Schuler, "Akan Slave Rebellions," 9.

78. Kwame Gyekye, *An Essay on African Philosophical Thought: The Akan Conceptual Scheme* (New York: Cambridge University Press, 1987), 73–75.

79. Basil Hedrick and Jeanette Stephens, *It's a Natural Fact: Obeah in the Bahamas* (Greely: University of Northern Colorado, Museum of Anthropology, 1977), 8; Ivor Morrish, *Obeah, Christ, and Rastaman* (Cambridge: James Clarke and Co., 1982), 22–23; Williams, *Voodoos and Obeahs*, 120–22.

80. Williams, *Voodoos and Obeahs*, 120–21.

81. Hedrick and Stephens, *Obeah in the Bahamas*, 9; Robert July, *A History of the African People* (New York: Charles Scribner's Sons, 1980), 144; Thornton, *Africa and Africans*, 189.

82. Jerome S. Handler and Kenneth M. Bilby, "On the Early Use and Origin of the Term 'Obeah' in Barbados and the Anglophone Caribbean," *Slavery and Abolition* 22 (2001): 87–100; Douglas Chambers, "'My Own Nation': Igbo Exiles in the Diaspora," *Slavery and Abolition* 18 (1997): 72–97. I was perhaps overly hasty in criticizing Handler and Bilby's presentation at the 2000 Association for the Study of the Worldwide African Diaspora meeting regarding the multiple origins of Obeah. The likelihood that Obeah is a syncretic blend of Akan, Igbo, and West-central African beliefs seems more and more plausible as my knowledge of this practice advances.

83. Chambers, "My Own Nation," 88.

84. Handler and Bilby, "The Early Use and Origin of the Term 'Obeah,'" 91; Schuler, "Ethnic Slave Rebellions," 374–85; Schuler, "Akan Slave Rebellions," 15–23; Eltis et al., *The Trans-Atlantic Slave Trade*.

85. Molesworth to Blathwayt, November 2, 1685, W. Noel Sainsbury et al., eds., *Calendar of State Papers, Colonial Series, America and the West Indies* (London, 1862) quoted in Barbara Klamon Kopytoff, "The Early Political Development of Jamaican Maroon Societies," *William and Mary Quarterly*, 3rd ser., 35 (April 1978): 298n.

86. Quoted in Koptyoff, "Jamaican Maroon Societies," 298. Emphasis added.

87. David Dalby, "Ashanti Survivals in the Language and Traditions of the Windward Maroons of Jamaica," *African Language Studies* 12 (1971): 48; Karla Gottlieb, *"The Mother of Us All": A History of Queen Nanny Leader of the Windward Jamaican Maroons* (Trenton, NJ: Africa World Press, 2000), 24. The vast majority of Maroon leaders had Akan day-names or names that reflected a Gold Coast origin.

88. Gottlieb, *The Mother of Us All*, 10, 25, 44, 52, 58; Mullin, *Africa in America*, 59–60; Martha Warren Beckwith, *Black Roadways: A Study of Jamaican Folk Life* (1929; reprint, New York: Negro Universities Press, 1969), 191–92; Orlando Patterson, "Slavery and Slave Revolts: A Socio-Historical Analysis of the First Maroon War, 1655–1740," *Social and Economic Studies* 18 (September 1970): 302; Koptyoff, "Jamaican Maroon Societies," 300; Michael Craton, *Testing the Chains: Resistance to Slavery in the British West Indies* (Ithaca, NY: Cornell University Press, 1982), 81.

89. Quoted in David Barry Gaspar, *Bondsmen and Rebels: A Study of Master-Slave Relations in Antigua* (Durham: Duke University Press, 1985), 246–47; David Barry Gaspar, "The Antigua Slave Conspiracy of 1736: A Case Study of the Origins of Collective Resistance," *William and Mary Quarterly*, 3rd ser., 35 (April 1978): 322; Schuler, "Akan Slave Rebellions," 21.

90. Mullin, *Africa in America*, 58–59.

91. Long, *The History of Jamaica*, 2:416–17. Though Long uses Myal and Obeah as interchangeable concepts, they were actually polar opposites in practice. Whereas Obeah was typically characterized as the use of spiritual forces to provide protection or to harm others, Myalism was associated with healing and curative powers. Seen another way, Obeah was defined in the West African and Euro-American context as witchcraft while Myalism was the functional equivalent of an anti-witchcraft/anti-sorcery cult. See Patterson, *The Sociology of Slavery*, 185–88.

92. Long, *The History of Jamaica*, 2:417–18.

93. Schuler, "Akan Slave Rebellions," 16; James Patrick Hubbard, "Ashanti Military Affairs in the Nineteenth Century" (M.A. thesis, University of Wisconsin, Madison, 1969), 11–13.

94. Willem Bosman, *A New and Accurate Description of the Coast of Guinea, Divided into the Gold, the Slave, and the Ivory Coasts* (1705; reprint, London: J. Knapton, D. Midwinter, B. Lintot, G. Strahan, J. Rand, E. Bell, 1721), 155–56.

95. Helaine Minkus, "Causal Theory in Akwapim Akan Philosophy," in Richard A. Wright, ed., *African Philosophy: An Introduction* (Washington, DC: University Press of America, 1977), 116–17; Robert Fisher, *West African Traditions: Focus on the Akan of Ghana* (Maryknoll, NY: Orbis Books, 1998), 111–12.

96. Minkus, "Causal Theory in Akwapim Akan Philosophy," 116–17.

97. Sharpe, "The Negro Plot," 162.

98. Schuler, "Akan Slave Rebellions," 21; Gaspar, *Bondsmen and Rebels*, 244, 321.

99. Gaspar, *Bondsmen and Rebels*, 240–44; quoted in Schuler, "Akan Slave Rebellions," 21–22. In this particular case, a significant Akan presence is evident. Not only did many of the rebels have Akan day-names, but Secundo's name also has Gold Coast origins. Secundo was likely named after *Sekondi*—a major commercial region to the west of Cape Coast Castle.

100. Quoted in Gaspar, *Bondsmen and Rebels*, 240. Emphasis added.

101. W. C. Westergaard, "Account of the Negro Rebellion on St. Croix, Danish West Indies, 1759," *Journal of Negro History* 11 (January 1926): 55, 57.

102. Schuler, "Akan Slave Rebellions," 23; Westergaard, "Account of the Negro Rebellion," 58–60.

103. Quoted in Williams, *Voodoos and Obeahs*, 163.

104. Quoted in Mullin, *Africa in America*, 41.

105. Long, *The History of Jamaica*, 2:465; Schuler, "Ethnic Slave Rebellions," 384. Long asserts that "With good reason therefore it was suspected, by many persons in St. Mary's, that

these deserters, who had taken the *fetishe*, or oath, which they regard as inviolable, would dissemble their genuine sentiments for the present, and wait a favourable opportunity to execute their bloody purposes."

106. Long, *The History of Jamaica*, 2:473.

107. Bosman, *A New and Accurate Description*, 124. Though Bosman does not reveal the specific ingredients of the "oath draught," he does hint that oathing materials could include "Earth, Oil, Blood, the Bones of Dead Men and Beasts, Feathers, [and] Hair" (126).

108. J. K. Fynn, *Asante and Its Neighbours, 1700–1807* (London: Longman, 1971), 58.

109. Hubbard, "Ashanti Military Affairs," 11–13. Though in use in the nineteenth century, the Great Oath of the Asante (or *Ntam Kese*) referenced by Hubbard actually has its origins in the early eighteenth century. When Osei Tutu—one of the greatest kings in Asante history—died in 1717, the Great Oath was, according to Fynn, "intended not only to assure the Asante that Osei Tutu's spirit continued to guide the nation, but also to reunite and rekindle their fighting spirit to achieve the purposes for which the Asante Union had been called into being." Even before 1717, oaths were essential elements of Akan statecraft. See Fynn, *Asante and Its Neighbours*, 58, 60.

110. Mullin, *Africa in America*, 68.

111. Gaspar, *Bondsmen and Rebels*, 245. Grave dirt had a similar importance in nineteenth- and twentieth-century examples of African American folk culture. Zora Neale Hurston mentions "All over the South and in the Bahamas the spirits of the dead have great power . . . frequently graveyard dust is required in the practice of hoodoo, goofer dust as it is often called." See Zora Neale Hurston, *Mules and Men* (Bloomington: Indiana University Press, 1963), 205, 234; Newbell Niles Puckett, *Folk Beliefs of the Southern Negro* (Chapel Hill: University of North Carolina Press, 1926), 102, 189, 194, 196, 206, 208, 210, 220, 232, 235, 239, 246–48, 275, 286, 290, 525.

112. Quoted in Mullin, *Africa in America*, 67.

113. Bosman, *A New and Accurate Description*, 125.

114. Williams, *Voodoos and Obeahs*, 111.

115. Quoted in ibid., 164; Mullin, *Africa in America*, 176; Hedrick and Stephens, *Obeah in the Bahamas*, 12–14. Even during the twentieth century, Obeah was prohibited throughout the British Caribbean. Those found guilty of practicing Obeah could be imprisoned or fined as late as 1971.

116. Quoted in Williams, *Voodoos and Obeahs*, 183; Mullin, *Africa in America*, 183; Hesketh Bell, *Obeah: Witchcraft in the West Indies* (1889; reprint, Westport, CT: Negro University Press, 1970), 15–16. An inspection of a nineteenth century Obeah-man's home and personal effects in Grenada reveals many of the same items used by Obeah doctors of a previous era:

> The dirty little room was littered with the Obeah man's stock in trade . . . In every corner were found the implements of his trade, rags, feathers, bones of cats, parrots' beaks, dogs' teeth, broken bottles, grave dirt, rum, and egg-shells. Examining further, we found under the bed a large *conarie* or earthen jar containing an immense number of round balls of earth or clay of various dimensions, large and small, whitened on the outside and fearfully and wonderfully compounded. Some seemed to contain hair and rags and were strongly bound round with twine; others were made with skulls of cats, stuck round with human or dogs' teeth and glass beads, there were also a lot of egg-shells and numbers of little bags filled with farrago and rubbish. In a little tin canister I found the most valuable

of the sorcerer's stock, namely, seven bones belonging to a rattlesnake's tail . . . so highly valued are they as amulets or charms—in the same box was about a yard or rope, no doubt intended to be sold for hangman's cord, which is highly prized by the negroes, the owner of a piece supposed to be able to defy bad luck.

117. Jon Butler, *Awash in a Sea of Faith: Christianizing the American People* (Cambridge, MA: Harvard University Press, 1990), 129–30, 155, 157. This likely explains Butler's brief discussion of the 1712 revolt and the specific role played by Peter.

118. Butler, *Awash in a Sea of Faith*, 153, 159. Butler discusses, "the rich religious systems of Akan, Ashanti, Dahoman, Ibo, and Yoruba societies—to name only some of the major sources of African religion in America." Oddly, by referring to "Akan" and "Ashanti" religious systems as if they are somehow unrelated, Butler confuses the issue. Since the Asante are a subgroup of Akan-speakers, there is no major disjuncture between these two religious systems. It only seems logical that in order for one to make such conclusions, a better understanding of the nature of these allegedly "destroyed" religious systems would be necessary.

119. Morgan, *Slavery in New York*, 22; Michael Blakey "The New York African Burial Ground Project: An Examination of Enslaved Lives, A Construction of Ancestral Ties," *Transforming Archaeology* 7 (1998): 53; Sherrill Wilson, *New York City's African Slaveowners: A Social and Material Culture History* (New York: Garland, 1994), 47; Hodges, *Root and Branch*, 15.

120. Sharpe, "Rev. Sharpe's Proposals," 255; Goodfriend, *Before the Melting Pot*, 122.

121. David Valentine, *Manual of the Common Council of New York* (New York: D.T. Valentine, 1865), 567; Blakey, "Burial Ground Project," 53; Joyce Hansen and Gary McGowan, *Breaking Ground, Breaking Silence: The Story of New York's African Burial Ground* (New York: Henry Holt, 1998), 53, 66, 68; Wilson, *New York City's African Slaveowners*, 47.

122. Edward Kaufman, ed., *Reclaiming Our Past, Honoring Our Ancestors: New York's 18th Century African Burial Ground and the Memorial Competition* (New York: African Burial Ground Coalition, 1994), 6; Wilson, *New York City's African Slaveowners*, 48; Cheryl La Roche and Michael Blakey, "Seizing Intellectual Power: The Dialogue at the New York African Burial Ground," *Historical Archaeology* 31 (1997): 94–95; Michael Blakey, "The Study of New York's African Burial Ground," in Sheila Walker, ed., *African Roots/American Cultures: Africa in the Creation of the Americas* (New York: Rowman and Littlefield, 2001), 225; Kwaku Ofori-Ansa, "Identification and Validation of the Sankofa Symbol," *Update: Newsletter of the African Burial Ground and Five Points Archaeological Projects* 8 (1995): 6.

123. Hansen and McGowan, *Breaking Ground*, 55–56; Adolph Agbo, *Values of Adinkra Symbols* (Kumasi, Ghana: Ebony Designs and Publications, 1999), 3, 31; Kwaku Amoako-Attah Fosu, *Handicrafts of Ghana* (Kumasi, Ghana: Centre for National Culture, 2001), 15, 36. See also Fynn, *Asante and Its Neighbours*, 138–39, and T. C. McCaskie, *State and Society in Pre-Colonial Asante* (Cambridge: Cambridge University Press, 1995), 82–83.

124. Agbo, *Values of Adinkra Symbols*, 1; Amoako-Attah Fosu, *Handicrafts of Ghana*, 10; Fynn, *Asante and Its Neighbours*, 138–39; McCaskie, *State and Society in Pre-Colonial Asante*, 82–83.

125. Blakey, "Burial Ground Project," 55–56; Hansen and McGowan, *Breaking Ground*, 47–48.

126. Bosman, *A New and Accurate Description*, 221.

127. Hansen and McGowan, *Breaking Ground*, 40–42, 44; Robert Farris Thompson, "African Influence on the Art of the United States," in Armstead Robinson, Craig Foster, and Don-

ald Ogilvie, eds., *Black Studies in the University: A Symposium* (New Haven: Yale University Press, 1969), 122, 124, 127, 149, 167; Blakey, "Burial Ground Project," 53. The broken stoneware pottery found at the burial site may have been the kiln refuse from two nearby pottery factories established during the 1740s.

128. Blakey, "Burial Ground Project," 57; Blakey, "Study of New York's African Burial Ground," 229; Hansen and McGowan, *Breaking Ground*, 68; Bruce Frankel, "Black Cemetery in NYC New Key to Colonial Times," *USA Today* September 15, 1992.

129. Ross Jamieson, "Material Culture and Social Death: African-American Burial Practices," *Historical Archaeology* 29 (1995): 52–53; Christopher DeCorse, "Culture Contact, Continuity and Change on the Gold Coast, A.D. 1400–1900," *African Archaeological Review* 10 (1992): 163–96; Kaufman, *Reclaiming Our Past*, 8; Hansen and McGowan, *Breaking Ground*, 9, 13; Morgan, *Slavery in New York*, 22 Agorsah, "Archaeology and Resistance," 183. Agorsah suggests that although the use of coffins reflect European influences, the Asante were using them in burials by the late seventeenth century.

130. *Minutes of the Common Council of the City of New York, 1675–1776* (New York: Dodd, Mead, 1905), 3:296.

131. *Minutes of the Common Council*, 4:88.

132. Morgan, *Slavery in New York*, 22.

133. Ibid., 16; Scott, "The Slave Insurrection," 49; Sharpe, "The Negro Plot," 163.

134. Littlefield, *Rice and Slaves*, 10.

135. Gomez, *Exchanging Our Country Marks*, 117.

136. Quoted in Patterson, *The Sociology of Slavery*, 196.

137. Quoted in Kea, "When I Die, I Shall Return to My Own Land," 159–60.

138. Ibid., 187, 160.

139. Long, *The History of Jamaica*, 2:473.

140. Patterson, *The Sociology of Slavery*, 196.

141. Quoted in Schuler, "Akan Slave Rebellions," 11.

142. Ibid., 15–16.

143. Ibid., 16; Bosman, *A New and Accurate Description*, 124–25.

144. Kea, *Settlements*, 158; John Thornton, *Warfare in Atlantic African, 1500–1800* (London: University College London Press, 1999), 61–63.

145. Bosman, *A New and Accurate Description*, 156–57.

146. Kea, *Settlements*, 11, 131.

147. Ibid., 131, 139.

148. Sharpe, "The Negro Plot," 162–63. Emphasis added.

149. Riddell, "The Slave in New York," 71.

150. In similar fashion, John Thornton demonstrates that African military training was important in the events leading up to the Stono Rebellion, the Haitian Revolution, and the various Akan-inspired rebellions in the British Caribbean. See John Thornton, "African Dimensions of the Stono Rebellion," *American Historical Review* (October 1991): 1101–13; "African Soldiers in the Haitian Revolution," *Journal of Caribbean History* 25 (1991): 58–80; and "War, the State, and Religious Norms in 'Coromantee' Thought: The Ideology of an African American Nation," in Robert Blair St. George, ed., *Possible Pasts: Becoming Colonial in Early America* (Ithaca, NY: Cornell

University Press, 2000), 196–98. Peter Wood cites similar evidence of the presence of Gold Coast soldiers in the Americas in *Black Majority*, 126–27.

151. Kea, "When I Die, I Shall Return to My Own Land," 174–80.

152. Thornton, *Warfare in Atlantic African*, 142.

153. *New-York Weekly Journal*, March 7, 1737.

154. Sterling Stuckey, "The Skies of Consciousness: African Dance at Pinkster in New York, 1750–1840," in *Going through the Storm: The Influence of African American Art in History* (New York: Oxford University Press, 1994), 55, 59; Hodges, *Root and Branch*, 24–25, 88. In similar fashion, both governors and kings were elected by enslaved and free African-Americans in New England colonies and states during the annual "Election Day" celebrations of the eighteenth and nineteenth centuries. See Shane White, "'It Was a Proud Day': African Americans, Festivals, and Parades in the North, 1741–1834," *Journal of American History* 81 (June 1994): 17, 20, 42; Shane White, "Pinkster: Afro-Dutch Syncretization in New York City and the Hudson Valley," *Journal of American Folklore* 102 (January–March 1989): 72–73; Edwin Olson, "Social Aspects of the Slave in New York," *Journal of Negro History* 26 (January 1941): 71.

155. In an early-nineteenth-century description of Pinkster festivities in Albany, New York, Dr. James Eights notes the following: "They had a chief,—Old King Charley. The old settlers said Charles was a prince in his own country . . . [H]e was nearly barelegged, wore a red military coat trimmed profusely with variegated ribbons, and a small black hat with a pompon stuck on one side." Routinely dressed as a British soldier, King Charles was described as an "Angolan" who was brought to Albany in the early 1700s. The fact that Burial #6 at the African Burial Ground contained the skeletal remains of man who apparently was wearing a British Naval long coat prompted Sterling Stuckey to surmise that he could have been a Pinkster king presiding over the celebration in eighteenth-century New York City. Dr. James Eights, "Pinkster Festivities in Albany Sixty Years Ago," quoted in Alice Morse Earle, *Colonial Days in Old New York* (New York: Charles Scribner's Sons, 1896), 196–97; David Steven Cohen, *The Dutch-American Farm* (New York: New York University Press, 1992), 162–163; Shane White, "It Was a Proud Day," 20, 22–24; Hansen and McGowan, *Breaking Ground*, 8–11; *New York Times*, August 9, 1992; Stuckey "The Skies of Consciousness," 77; Sterling Stuckey, "African Spirituality in Colonial New York," in Carla G. Pestana and Sharon Salinger, eds., *Inequality in Early America* (Hanover, NH: University Press of New England, 2000), 175.

156. Perhaps the best evidence for this is the fact that both the Nanny and Moore Town maroons of Jamaica and the Saramaka maroons of Suriname used a system of matrilineal descent very similar to the one that exists in Akan culture. Likewise, Kea discusses the attempt to create an "Amina" Akan-speaking polity in the Danish West Indies Island of St. John. See Kenneth Bilby and Filomina Chioma Steady, "Black Women and Survival: A Maroon Case," in Filomina Chioma Steady, ed., *The Black Woman Cross-Culturally* (Rochester, VT: Shenkman Books, 1985), 461; Richard Price, *Saramaka Social Structure: Analysis of a "Bush Negro" Society* (Rio Piedras: University of Puerto Rico, 1973), 45–46; Kea, "When I Die, I Shall Return to My Own Land," 160, 182–83.

157. Chambers, "Ethnicity in the Diaspora," 25–39; Douglas Chambers, "The Significance of Igbo in the Bight of Biafra Slave-Trade: A Rejoinder to Northrup's 'Myth Igbo,'" *Slavery and Abolition* 23 (2002): 101–20; Thornton, "The Coromantees," 161–78; Chambers, "My Own Nation," 72–97.

## 2. "ONLY DRAW IN YOUR COUNTRYMEN"

1. Lydon, "New York and the Slave Trade," 382–384; McManus, *Negro Slavery in New York*, 25–28; Hodges, *Root and Branch*, 74.

2. Hodges, *Root and Branch*, 79–80; Northrup, *Slavery in New York*, 274; Lydon, "New York and the Slave Trade," 385; McManus, *Negro Slavery in New York*, 28. As McManus notes, the demand for adults imported from Africa was so limited that one governor of New York recommended that traders should sell these slaves in the southern colonies.

3. Donnan, *Documents Illustrative of the History of the Slave Trade*, 2:446.

4. Williams, *African Americans and Colonial Legislation*, 63.

5. Donnan, *Documents Illustrative of the History of the Slave Trade*, 2: 446–47.

6. Ibid., 447; Lydon, "New York and the Slave Trade," 386. The loophole that allowed ship captains to disembark slaves in New Jersey for sale in New York in order to avoid paying duties was fixed in the Duty Act of 1753. This new law accounted for slaves imported overland in the collection of duties by New York officials. By the 1750s, efforts were made to force slave buyers to pay the import duties in order to undermine efforts by shippers to smuggle slaves into the colony. See Lydon, "New York and the Slave Trade," 385–86.

7. McManus, *Negro Slavery in New York*, 24–25; Lydon, "New York and the Slave Trade," 385.

8. Quoted in Riddell, "The Slave in New York," 79–80; O'Callaghan, *Documents*, 6:34, 5:935–36; Lydon, "New York and the Slave Trade," 385.

9. Mary Booth, *History of the City of New York* (New York: W. R. C. Clark, 1867), 1:356–57; Nash, *Urban Crucible*, 68; Gary Nash, *Red, White and Black: The Peoples of Early North America* (1974; reprint, Upper Saddle River, NJ: Prentice Hall, 2000), 153, 177.

10. Goodfriend, *Before the Melting Pot*, 117–18; Hodges, *Root and Branch*, 74–75. Both Goodfriend and Hodges assume that nuclear families were the only stable family structures among black New Yorkers. This is a problematic conclusion considering the polygamous, matrifocal, and extended family structures which were characteristic of a number of eighteenth-century Atlantic African societies.

11. Goodfriend, *Before the Melting Pot*, 116.

12. Ibid., 117; Hodges, *Root and Branch*, 70–71.

13. Riddell, "The Slave in New York," 82; McManus, *Negro Slavery in New York*, 101–4; Kenneth Porter, "Relations between Negroes and Indians," *Journal of Negro History* 17 (1932): 308; Hodges, *Root and Branch*, 52.

14. Hodges, *Root and Branch*, 131; McManus, *Negro Slavery in New York*, 105; Peter Linebaugh and Marcus Rediker, *The Many-Headed Hydra: Sailors, Slaves, Commoners, and the Hidden History of the Revolutionary Atlantic* (Boston: Beacon Press, 2000), 179–84.

15. McManus, *Negro Slavery in New York*, 105–6; Hodges, *Root and Branch*, 130–31, 96–97; Thomas J. Davis, ed., *The New York Conspiracy by Daniel Horsmanden* (Boston: Beacon Press, 1971) xiii, xv, 67, 69, 82, 93–94, 120, 161.

16. Davis, *The New York Conspiracy*, 67, 93; Hodges, *Root and Branch*, 97.

17. McManus, *Negro Slavery in New York*, 106.

18. *Minutes of the Common Council of the City of New York, 1675–1776* (New York: Dodd, Mead and Company, 1905), 4:86.

19. Ibid., 86–89; Williams, *African Americans and Colonial Legislation*, 76–77.

20. Davis, *The New York Conspiracy*, 13–15, 446, 448; Stokes, *Iconography*, 4:565; Thomas J. Davis, *A Rumor of Revolt: The "Great Negro Plot" in Colonial New York* (Amherst: University of Massachusetts Press, 1985), 5–6.

21. Davis, *The New York Conspiracy*, 14–15, 67; Isaac Newton Phelps Stokes, *The Iconography of Manhattan Island, 1498–1909* (New York: Arno Press, 1967), 4:565.

22. Davis, *Rumor of Revolt*, 6; Davis, *The New York Conspiracy*, 446–47.

23. Davis, *Rumor of Revolt*, 6–7; Davis, *The New York Conspiracy*, 447.

24. Davis, *The New York Conspiracy*, 443–45, 448–49; Davis, *Rumor of Revolt*, 6–8.

25. Joseph Cephas Carroll, *Slave Insurrections in the United States, 1800–1865* (1938; reprint, New York: Negro Universities Press, 1968), 26–29; Thomas J. Davis "The New York Slave Conspiracy of 1741 As Black Protest," *Journal of Negro History* 56 (1971), 18–19; Booth, *History of the City of New York*, 1:357; T. Wood Clarke, "Negro Plot of 1741," *New York History Quarterly* 25 (April 1944): 168.

26. Headley, *Great Riots*, 29; Davis, *The New York Conspiracy*, 27, 64.

27. Headley, *Great Riots*, 29–30; Leopold Launitz-Schurer Jr., "Slave Resistance in Colonial New York: An Interpretation of Daniel Horsmanden's New York Conspiracy," *Phylon* 41 (1980): 137; Thomas J. Davis, "Slavery in Colonial New York City" (Ph.D. diss., Columbia University, 1974), 122; Davis, *The New York Conspiracy*, 30–31; Davis, *Rumor of Revolt*, 21.

28. Davis, *The New York Conspiracy*, 28–29, 89, 103–4.

29. Ibid., 94–96; Davis, *Rumor of Revolt*, 88.

30. Davis, ed., *The New York Conspiracy*, 65–67; Clarke, "Negro Plot of 1741," 169.

31. Davis, "The New York Slave Conspiracy of 1741 As Black Protest," 21–22; Davis, "Slavery in Colonial New York City," 123–24; Davis, *The New York Conspiracy*, 90.

32. Davis, *The New York Conspiracy*, 90–92, 111, 118, 121, 128, 132, 173, 182, 196, 210, 268.

33. Ibid., 101, 103, 258.

34. Ibid., 103.

35. Ibid., 15, 21, 443.

36. Ibid., 60–61, 160–61, 224, 284–85.

37. Ibid., 224, 268–69, 271; Davis, *Rumor of Revolt*, 276. For reactions to the various wars involving Spain and France in New York City, see *New-York Weekly Journal*, February 2, 16, 23; March 6; and April 6, 1741.

38. Davis, *The New York Conspiracy*, 350–51; Davis, *Rumor of Revolt*, 211–12.

39. Davis, *The New York Conspiracy*, 60, 302–6; Davis, *Rumor of Revolt*, 185.

40. Davis, *The New York Conspiracy*, 59, 91.

41. Ibid., 43–44, 283, 285, 296–97, 342–43, 350–51; Davis, *Rumor of Revolt*, 212, 218, 226–27, 234.

42. Davis, *The New York Conspiracy*, 155.

43. Ibid., 167–68.

44. Ibid., 94, 129, 468, 471; Aptheker, *Slave Revolts*, 194–95; *Boston News-Letter* (May 7–14, 1741), 1–2; Carroll, *Slave Insurrections in the U.S.*, 29–30. Caesar and Prince were executed earlier on May 11 for the burglary at Hogg's shop and were not tried for their involvement in the planned insurrection. This was because "It was thought proper to execute them for the rob-

bery, and not wait to bringing them to a trial for conspiracy, though the proof against them was strong and clear concerning their guilt as to that also . . . this earnest example and punishment might break the knot, and induce some of them to unfold this mystery . . . it is probable, that with some it had this effect." See Davis, *The New York Conspiracy*, 66.

45. For more recent assessments, see Aptheker, *Slave Revolts*, 192–94; Davis, *A Rumor of Revolt*; Davis "The New York Slave Conspiracy," 17–30; and Launitz-Schurer, "Slave Resistance in Colonial New York," 137–52.

46. Launitz-Schurer, "Slave Resistance in Colonial New York," 139; Davis, *Rumor of Revolt*, 265–66.

47. Davis, *Rumor of Revolt*, 266.

48. George Washington Williams, *History of the Negro Race in America from 1619 to 1880* (New York: G. P. Putnam's Sons, 1883), 1:144–71.

49. Walter F. Prince, "The Great Conspiracy Delusion: A Sketch of the Crowning Judicial Atrocity of American History," New Haven, Connecticut *Saturday Chronicle* (June 28–August 23, 1902), 1–3. A typewritten copy of the article is available at the New York Historical Society.

50. George Washington Williams was the first scholar of the 1741 conspiracy to compare it to the Salem hysteria, but he also makes a significant error in his assessment. He claims that "there is nothing in this country to equal it, except it be the burning of the witches of Salem." However, even the accused witches of Salem did not have to suffer the torture of death by burning. This was a punishment used almost exclusively for slave arsonists and rebels in the British Americas. For Williams however, the most accurate comparison to be made would be with the 1679 Popish plot in England, and, thus, his initial error does not completely undermine his analysis. See Williams, *History of the Negro Race in America*, 144.

51. Prince, "The Great Conspiracy Delusion," 4–5.

52. Roi Ottley, *Black Odyssey: The Story of the Negro in America* (New York: C. Scribner's Sons, 1948), 29.

53. Clarke, "The Negro Plot of 1741," 167, 170–171. A number of these issues were mentioned in Williams's analysis of the 1741 trials.

54. Ibid., 176, 177–79. Horsmanden eventually began to question the veracity of some of Burton's claims: "we could not but be Shockt, the persons mentioned being beyond Suspition; thence been raised against [Burton] and now, by Some, She must be esteemed a person of no Credit . . . the things She Says, cannot but Stagger ones belief in Some measure." See "Daniel Horsmanden to Cadwallader Colden, 7 August 1741," in *Collections of the New-York Historical Society for the Year 1918: The Letters and Papers of Cadwallader Colden* (New York: New-York Historical Society, 1918), 2:226–27.

55. McManus, *Negro Slavery in New York*, 126–31.

56. Ferenc M. "Szasz, The New York Slave Revolt of 1741: A Re-examination," *New York History Quarterly* 48 (1967): 216–17, 220, 226–27.

57. Launitz-Schurer, "Slave Resistance in Colonial New York," 137, 142–43, 148, 152.

58. Aptheker, *Slave Revolts*, 192–93.

59. Davis, *Rumor of Revolt*, 255.

60. Ibid., 259–60.

61. Davis, *The New York Conspiracy*, 288; Davis, *Rumor of Revolt*, 173.

62. Davis, *The New York Conspiracy*, 284; Davis, *Rumor of Revolt*, 169.

63. Davis, *The New York Conspiracy*, 460. Davis, *Rumor of Revolt*, 173. This corroborating testimony came from two slaves who did not previously know each other, yet both confessed similar things about Harry's role in the conspiracy.

64. Davis, *The New York Conspiracy*, 274, 284–85.

65. Ibid., 273–75.

66. Ibid., 275–76.

67. Ibid., 456–57, 461.

68. Ibid., 461. Emphasis added.

69. Carl Bridenbaugh, *Cities in the Wilderness: The First Century of Urban Life in American, 1625–1742* (New York: Alfred A. Knopf, 1968), 374; Aptheker, *Slave Revolts*, 192.

70. Davis, *The New York Conspiracy*, 286, 288, 294, 310, 318, 325–26.

71. Ibid., 468–73, appendix "List of Negroes Committed on Account of the Conspiracy."

72. Ibid., 118.

73. "Guinea" is a broad geographic region encompassing portions of West Africa's Atlantic coast. Depending on the century, the word "Guinea" could refer to different coastal areas. In the sixteenth century, Guinea generally meant the entire coastal region of West Africa from Senegal to Angola. By the eighteenth and nineteenth centuries, Guinea referred to the coastal region from the Sierra Leone River to the Bight of Benin. Importantly, this area encompasses the Gold Coast. Curtin, *Atlantic Slave Trade*, 104.

74. Davis, *The New York Conspiracy*, 461, appendix "List of Negroes Committed on Account of the Conspiracy." The names of the seventeen slaves being transported to Hispaniola were Bastian, Bridgewater, Caesar, Deptford, Dick, Diego, Jack, Jonneau, London Kelley, London Wyncoop, Prince, Sandy, Sarah, Sterling, Tom, Will (or Gill) and Tickle.

75. Ibid., 463.

76. Gaspar, *Bondsmen and Rebels*, 28–37, 221–22. The names of the other twelve slaves banished to North America from Antigua in 1737 were: Triblin, Jemmy (2), Tom, Quamina (2), Quaco, Ingham, Otta, Peter, Cuffee, and George. Also, several Antigua slaves banished to St. Croix eventually led another Akan rebellion in 1759, hence Will's role in the 1741 New York City conspiracy is likely part of a continuum of Akan rebelliousness to enslavement in the Americas.

77. Davis, *The New York Conspiracy*, 304–5, 265–66, 322; Kea, "'When I Die, I Shall Return to My Own Land,'" 174–80.

78. Davis, *The New York Conspiracy*, 277–78, 463–64, appendix "List of Negroes Committed on Account of the Conspiracy."

79. Ibid., 87, 120.

80. Ibid., 159–61. This particular meeting was corroborated in the confessions of Jack Sleydall, Cajoe Gomez, William Kane, Pedro De Peyster, and Cato Shurmur, See Davis, *The New York Conspiracy*, 164–65, 238, 249–51, 252–53, 285.

81. Ibid., 239.

82. Ibid., 99–100.

83. Ibid., 100–101.

84. Ibid., 265–66.

85. Kea, "'When I Die, I Shall Return to My Own Land,'" 160.

86. Ibid., 159, 160, 165, 169–70, 182, 186–89. Kea identifies this polity as possibly being Akwamu, which was defeated by a confederation of neighboring states, led by Akyem, in 1730.

87. Gaspar, "The Antigua Slave Conspiracy," 316, 319–22; Gaspar, *Bondsmen and Rebels*, 240–44.

88. Gaspar, "The Antigua Slave Conspiracy," 322.

89. Gaspar, *Bondsmen and Rebels*, 28–37, 221–22; *New-York Weekly Journal*, March 7, 1737; Schuler, "Akan Slave Rebellions," 21–22.

90. Quoted in Schuler, "Akan Slave Rebellions," 22.

91. Davis, *The New York Conspiracy*, 464.

92. Quoted in Gaspar, *Bondmen and Rebels*, 24.

93. Kea, "'When I Die, I Shall Return to My Own Land,'" 159–60.

94. Davis, *The New York Conspiracy*, 199, 204, 239, 278,

95. Quoted in Linebaugh and Rediker, *The Many-Headed Hydra*, 176.

### 3. DANCE, CONJURE, AND FLIGHT

1. Wood, *Black Majority*, 4; Aptheker, *Slave Revolts*, 163.

2. Wood, *Black Majority*, 5–6, 13–20; Weir, *Colonial South Carolina*, 47–49.

3. Wood, *Black Majority*, 13; Converse D. Clowse, *Economic Beginnings in Colonial South Carolina, 1670–1730* (Columbia: University of South Carolina Press, 1971), 3.

4. Wood, *Black Majority*, 27–28.

5. Clowse, *Economic Beginnings*, 55–56.

6. Wax, "Preferences for Slaves," 372–73.

7. Ibid., 388; Wood, *Black Majority*, 55; Curtin, *Atlantic Slave Trade*, 144–45; Herskovits, *Myth of the Negro Past*, 48.

8. Wax, "Preferences for Slaves," 388.

9. Quoted in ibid., 376–79.

10. Eltis et al., *The Trans-Atlantic Slave Trade*; Wood, *Black Majority*, 301–4, 333–41; Margaret Washington Creel, "*A Peculiar People*": *Slave Religion and Community-Culture Among the Gullahs* (New York: New York University Press, 1988), 30–31; Gomez, *Exchanging Our Country Marks*, 135; Elizabeth Donnan, "The Slave Trade into South Carolina before the American Revolution," *American Historical Review* 33 (1927–1928): 817; Wax, "Preferences for Slaves," 390–91; Thornton, "African Dimensions of the Stono Rebellion," 1103–4.

11. Joseph Miller, *Way of Death: Merchant Capitalism and the Angolan Slave Trade, 1730–1830* (Madison: University of Wisconsin Press, 1988), 77, 88, 90; Joseph Miller, "Central Africa during the Era of the Slave Trade, c. 1490s-1850s," in Linda Heywood, ed., *Central Africans and Cultural Transformations in the American Diaspora* (New York: Cambridge University Press, 2002), 28, 37.

12. For a more detailed account, see Wood, *Black Majority*, and Judith Carney, *Black Rice: The African Origins of Rice Cultivation in the Americas* (Cambridge: Harvard University Press, 2001).

13. Gomez, *Exchanging Our Country Marks*, 135–37.

14. Littlefield, *Rice and Slaves*, 10; Washington, "*A Peculiar People*," 35–36; Burnard and Morgan, "Slave Purchasing Patterns in Jamaica," 215–16; Eltis, "Volume and Structure of the Transatlantic Slave Trade," 36–40.

15. Littlefield, *Rice and Slaves*, 13.

16. Quoted in Wax, "Preferences for Slaves," 391–92.

17. That Angolans were heavily prized in Brazil is evident in the following seventeenth century saying: "Without sugar there is no Brazil and without Angola there is no sugar." James Duffy, *Portuguese Africa* (Cambridge: Harvard University Press, 1961), 138–39. By the eighteenth century, as Portugal began to develop trade in Lower Guinea, Angolans were no longer as esteemed, and the new preference was for "Sudanese" or Lower Guinea Africans including the Yoruba, Fon, and Edo. See Littlefield, *Rice and Slaves*, 14–15.

18. Quoted in Wax, "Preferences for Slaves," 390.

19. W. Robert Higgins, "Charleston: Terminus and Entrepot of the Colonial Trade," in Martin Kilson and Robert Rotberg, eds., *The African Diaspora: Interpretive Essays* (Cambridge: Harvard University Press, 1976), 119–20.

20. Records in the British Public Records Office Relating to South Carolina (South Carolina Department of Archives and History, Columbia), 8:24–27.

21. Aptheker, *Slave Revolts*, 175; Phillips, *American Negro Slavery*, 473; Carroll, *Slave Insurrections in the U.S.*, 17; Benjamin Brawley, *A Social History of the Negro Being a History of the Negro Problem in the United States* (New York: MacMillan, 1921), 40; Harvey Wish, "American Slave Insurrections before 1861," in John Bracey, August Meier, and Elliott Rudwick, eds., *American Slavery: The Question of Resistance* (Belmont, CA: Wadsworth, 1971), 26; Joshua Coffin, *An Account of Some Principal Slave Insurrections* (New York: American Anti-Slavery Society, 1860), 11. Aptheker warns that "no contemporary account resembling this has been seen. Coffin is unreliable in several other instances and it is probable he is in error here." It should be noted that Aptheker's discussion of an account given by E. C. Holland regarding another South Carolina slave revolt is prefaced by the statement that Holland likely "had access to materials destroyed during the Civil War." This statement was offered to explain why Holland's account of the 1730 Charleston conspiracy included details not corroborated by extant primary sources. See Aptheker, *Slave Revolts*, 175n, 180n.

22. Coffin, *Some Principal Slave Insurrections*, 13; Edward Clifford Holland, *A Refutation of the Calumnies Circulated Against the Southern and Western States Respecting the Institution and Existence of Slavery Among Them* (New York: Negro University Press, 1969), 68–69, 81; Wish, "American Slave Insurrections," 26–27; Wood, *Black Majority*, 237.

23. *Boston News-Letter*, October 15–22, 1730. Emphasis added.

24. Holland, *Refutation of the Calumnies*, 68–69. Emphasis added.

25. Ibid., 69.

26. Aptheker, *Slave Revolts*, 180–181n.

27. Bernhard A. Uhlendorf, trans. and ed., *The Siege of Charleston With an Account of the Province of South Carolina: Diaries and Letters of Hessian Officers from the von Jungkenn Papers in the William L. Clements Library* (Ann Arbor: University of Michigan Press, 1938), 323. Aptheker has doubts about the existence of this plot as well, noting that "no confirmation whatsoever has been seen . . . it seems likely that [it is] erroneous." See Aptheker, *Slave Revolts*, 184.

28. Aptheker, *Slave Revolts*, 184–87; Coffin, *Some Principal Slave Insurrections*, 14; Quoted in Allen Candler, ed., *The Colonial Records of the State of Georgia: Stephen's Journal, 1737–1740* (Atlanta: Franklin Printing and Publishing Company, 1906), 4:275–76, 18:135; Jane Landers, "Gracia

Real de Santa Teresa de Mose: A Free Black Town in Spanish Colonial Florida," *American Historical Review* 95 (February 1990): 17–19; Ralph Betts Flanders, *Plantation Slavery in Georgia* (Cos Cob, Connecticut: John E. Edwards, 1967), 24; David Duncan Wallace, *The History of South Carolina* (New York: American Society, Inc., 1934), 1:372; Cooper, ed., *The Statutes at Large of South Carolina* (Columbia: A. S. Johnson, 1838), 3:525; McCord, ed., *The Statutes at Large of South Carolina* (Columbia: A. S. Johnson, 1840), 7:414.

29. "Letter of William Bull to the Duke of Newcastle, 5 October 1739," in *South-Carolina Historical Society Collections* (Charleston: South-Carolina Historical Society, 1858), 2:270.

30. Aptheker, *Slave Revolts*, 187–89; Alexander Hewatt, *An Historical Account of the Rise and Progress of the Colonies of South Carolina and Georgia* (London: St. Paul's Church-Yard, 1779), 2:72–73; Wish, "American Slave Insurrections," 26; Wood, *Black Majority*, 314–319; *Boston News-Letter*, November 1–8, 1739; Newton Mereness, *Travels in the American Colonies* (New York: Macmillan Company, 1916), 222–23.

31. Aptheker, *Slave Revolts*, 187–89; Wood, *Black Majority*, 314–19.

32. Mereness, *Travels in American Colonies*, 223.

33. Wood, *Black Majority*, 132.

34. *South Carolina Gazette*, August 6–13, 1737.

35. Joseph Holloway, ed., *Africanisms in American Culture* (Bloomington: Indiana University Press, 1991), 6–7; Wood, *Black Majority*, 131; Gomez, *Exchanging Our Country Marks*, 136.

36. Allen Candler and William Northen, eds., *The Colonial Records of the State of Georgia* (Atlanta: Chas P. Byrd, State Printer, 1913), 233. The same letter appears in "Extract of a Letter from South Carolina, Oct. 2nd," *The Gentleman's Magazine and Historical Chronicle* 10 (1740): 127–28.

37. Candler and Northen, *Colonial Records of Georgia*, 234. Emphasis added.

38. Wallace, *The History of South Carolina*, 1:373; Walter B. Edgar, ed., *The Letterbook of Robert Pringle, Vol. One: April 2, 1737–September 25, 1742* (Columbia: University of South Carolina Press, 1972), 163; J. H. Easterby, ed., *The Colonial Records of South Carolina: The Journal of the Commons House of Assembly, September 12, 1739–March 26, 1741* (Columbia: Historical Commission of South Carolina, 1952), 480; "Constables Bill, January 29, 1740/41," *The Magazine of American History with Notes and Queries* 25 (1891), 85–86.

39. Wallace, *The History of South Carolina*, I, 373; Records in the British Public Records Office Relating to South Carolina, 20: 300.

40. Darold Wax, "'The Great Risk We Run': The Aftermath of the Slave Rebellion at Stono, South Carolina, 1739–1745," *Journal of Negro History* 67 (Summer 1982): 142.

41. Aptheker, *Slave Revolts*, 189; Wax, "The Great Risk We Run," 142; *Boston Weekly News-Letter*, July 3–10, 1740; Easterby, *Journal of the Commons House of Assembly, September 12, 1739–March 26, 1741*, 378.

42. Easterby, *Journal of the Commons House of Assembly, September 12, 1739–March 26, 1741*, 68.

43. McCord, *The Statutes at Large of South Carolina*, 7:397–417. The 1740 Act was reprinted in the *South Carolina Gazette* in the aftermath of the 1822 Denmark Vesey conspiracy. See *South Carolina Gazette*, August 24, 1822.

44. Aptheker, *Slave Revolts*, 191.

45. *South Carolina Gazette*, September 17–24, 1772; Weir, *Colonial South Carolina*, 190.

46. Gomez, *Exchanging Our Country Marks*, 112, 117–21, 133–34, 146–49.

47. Stuckey, *Slave Culture*, 12–14; Thompson, *Flash of the Spirit* (New York: Vintage Books, 1983), 103–14; Candler and Northern, *Colonial Records of Georgia*, 234–35; John Blassingame, *Slave Community: Plantation Life in the Antebellum South* (New York: Oxford University Press, 1972), 23.

48. Georgia Writers' Project, *Drums and Shadows: Survival Studies Among the Coastal Negroes* (Athens: University of Georgia Press, 1940), 209. Of nineteenth-century Gold Coast Africans, Rattray notes that dancing "invariably has a religious significance." Also Talbot states that among the Africans of Southern Nigeria, "dance was developed as a method of worship, of attaining union with [the deities]." Quoted in *Drums and Shadows*, 209.

49. H. M. Henry, *The Police Control of the Slave in South Carolina* (New York: Negro Universities Press, 1968), 150.

50. Thornton, "African Dimensions of the Stono Rebellion," 1112.

51. Ibid.; John Thornton, "Art of War in Angola," *Comparative Studies in Society and History* 30 (April 1988): 366. Thornton states, "The armies were divided into 'various bodies' . . . and each body had its own standards and flags. There was then a complex system of signals, broadcast by drums and trumpets of various sizes, which soldiers could understand over the din of battle."

52. Thornton, "African Dimensions of the Stono Rebellion," 1112.

53. Philip Morgan and George Terry, "Slavery in Microcosm: A Conspiracy Scare in Colonial South Carolina," *Journal of Social History* (Summer 1982): 167.

54. J. Lowell Lewis, *Ring of Liberation: Deceptive Discourse in Brazilian Capoeira* (Chicago: University of Chicago Press, 1992), 18–29, 38, 86–87, 135; Robert Farris Thompson, "Tough Guys Do Dance," *Rolling Stone* (March 24, 1988), 138, 140.

55. Lewis, *Ring of Liberation*, 20, 25; Bira Almeida, *Capoeira: A Brazilian Art Form* (Berkeley: North Atlantic Books, 1986), 16; Thomas Obi Desch, "Knocking and Kicking, *Ladya*, and *Capoeira*: Resistance and Religion in the African Martial Arts of the Black Atlantic" (M.A. thesis, University of California, Los Angeles, 1994), 18, 32–45, 58, 63. Also, Lewis points to the existence of an Afro-Cuban martial art known as *maní* which involved "acrobatic, mock combat set to music." Like Brazil and South Carolina, Cuba also witnessed a large number of imports from West-central Africa. See Lewis, *Ring of Liberation*, 20.

56. Thornton, *Warfare in Atlantic Africa*, 105; T. J. Desch Obi, "Combat and the Crossing of the Kalunga," in Heywood, *Central Africans and Cultural Transformations*, 359–60.

57. Obi, "Combat and the Crossing of the Kalunga," 357–58. Scholars have claimed that the *ngolo* was actually a "zebra" dance performed by young men during the female initiation ceremony. For those voicing concern over this interpretation, see Lewis, *Ring of Liberation*, 25–26; Nestor Capoeira, *Capoeira: Roots of the Dance-Fight-Game* (Berkeley: North Atlantic Books, 2002), 295–98.

58. Lewis, *Ring of Liberation*, 20, 227n; Obi, "Combat and the Crossing of the Kalunga," 362; Obi, "Knocking and Kicking, *Ladya*, and *Capoeira*," 21–22, 27–31. Oral testimony from Louisiana, South Carolina, Georgia, and Alabama support the continuing existence of this art in the twenty-first century South.

59. Holloway, *Africanisms*, xviii, 150, 215–17; Blassingame, *Slave Community*, 36–39; Gomez, *Exchanging Our Country Marks*, 137. Though Gomez demonstrates that the majority of slaves

in Louisiana were Congolese and not Angolan, they still had Western Bantu cultural origins. Three separate descriptions of early nineteenth-century slave dances in New Orleans reveal strong evidence of Bantu cultural elements. In 1808, Christian Schultz discovered "twenty different dancing groups of the wretched Africans, collected together to perform their worship after the manner of their country. They have their own national music, consisting for the most part of a long kind of narrow drum of various sizes." The drums described by Schultz are almost certainly conga drums. More revealing is Benjamin Latrobe's 1819 description. He witnessed about 500 slaves in New Orleans dancing in groups, beating conga drums, and playing stringed instruments and calabashes. Finally, Isaac Holmes's 1821 report regarding New Orleans slave dances notes "the general movement is in what they call the Congo dance; but their music consists of nothing more than [a drum] on which they beat; this, and the singing or vociferation of those who are dancing, and those who surround the dancers, constitute the whole of the harmony."

60. Wood, *Black Majority*, 289.

61. Quoted in Morgan and Terry, "Slavery in Microcosm," 129–30. Emphasis added.

62. *South Carolina Gazette*, October 2–9, 1749; Philip Morgan, *Slave Counterpoint: Black Culture in the Eighteenth-Century Chesapeake and Low Country* (Chapel Hill: University of North Carolina Press, 1998), 626.

63. This mention of Akan/Igbo conjure in colonial South Carolina could also imply that planters with previous personal experience with slaves from the British Caribbean may have used the word "Obeah" to cover a wide range of esoteric African spiritual practices. In similar fashion, *vodun*—a specific spiritual belief and practice developed by the Fon, Edo, and others near the Bight of Benin—is currently used as a generic term for African magical and mystical practices.

64. Frank Klingberg, *An Appraisal of the Negro in Colonial South Carolina: A Study in Americanization* (Philadelphia: Porcupine Press, 1975), 46.

65. *South Carolina Gazette*, August 15, 1741; Morgan, *Slave Counterpoint*, 616; *South Carolina Gazette*, October 30, 1749. For discussions of slave conjure and poisoning in colonial South Carolina, see Wood, *Black Majority*, 289–92; Morgan, *Slave Counterpoint*, 612–30.

66. *South Carolina Gazette*, March 31–April 6, 1733; Wood, *Black Majority*, 289; Easterby, *Journal of the Commons House of Assembly March 28, 1749–March 19, 1750*, 478–480.

67. Easterby, *Journal of the Commons House of Assembly March 28, 1749–March 19, 1750*, 479.

68. Wood, *Black Majority*, 289, 291; Wallace, *The History of South Carolina*, 373; Morgan, *Slave Counterpoint*, 617.

69. Quoted in Morgan, *Slave Counterpoint*, 617; Wood, *Black Majority*, 291.

70. Sharla Fett, *Working Cures: Healing, Health, and Power on Southern Slave Plantations* (Chapel Hill: University of North Carolina Press, 2002), 63.

71. Quoted in Klingberg, *Appraisal of the Negro*, 89.

72. McCord, ed., *The Statutes at Large of South Carolina*, 7:422–23.

73. Ibid.; Wood, *Black Majority*, 290.

74. *South Carolina Gazette*, January 17–24, 1761; Aptheker, *Slave Revolts*, 197; Wallace, *The History of South Carolina*, 374.

75. *South Carolina Gazette*, August 1–8, 1769.

76. *South Carolina Gazette*, September 17, 1772.

77. *South Carolina Gazette*, February 2–9, 1733–1734.

78. *South Carolina Gazette*, February 5–12, 1737.

79. *South Carolina Gazette*, March 23–30, 1738.

80. *South Carolina Gazette*, December 7, 1738.

81. *South Carolina Gazette*, February 2–9, 1740; *South Carolina Gazette*, February 9–16, 1740.

82. Lathan Windley, ed., *Runaway Slave Advertisements: A Documentary History from the 1730s to 1790, Volume 3, South Carolina* (Westport, CT: Greenwood Press, 1983), 45, 115, 186.

83. Windley, *Runaway Slave Ads*, 239, 218, 253, 303.

84. *South Carolina Gazette*, June 9–16, 1733; *South Carolina Gazette*, October 2–6, 1758; Philip Morgan, "Colonial South Carolina Runaways: Their Significance for Slave Culture," in Gad Heuman, ed., *Out of the House of Bondage: Runaways, Resistance and Marronage in Africa and the New World* (London: Frank Cass and Company Limited, 1986), 62. Though Igbos were only 11 percent of all African imports into South Carolina, they represented 10 percent of all slave runaways appearing in notices between 1732 and 1782.

85. *South Carolina Gazette*, October 31–November 7, 1761; *South Carolina Gazette*, December 17–24, 1763; *South Carolina Gazette*, January 15–22, 1754; *South Carolina Gazette*, November 8–15, 1760; *South Carolina Gazette*, October 31–November 7, 1761.

86. *South Carolina Gazette*, August 5–12, 1784.

87. Herbert Aptheker, "Maroons Within the Present Limits of the United States," in Paul Finkelman, ed., *Rebellions, Resistance, and Runaways Within the South* (New York: Garland Publishing, 1989), 65–66; Herbert Aptheker, *To Be Free: Pioneering Studies in Afro-American History* (New York: Citadel Press, 1948), 11–15; Gomez, *Exchanging Our Country Marks*, 139.

88. Holland, *Refutation of the Calumnies*, 63.

89. Aptheker, *To Be Free*, 12.

90. *South Carolina Gazette*, September 17–24, 1772.

91. Candler, *Colonial Records of the State of Georgia*, 292–93.

92. *South Carolina Gazette*, January 12–19, 1738; *South Carolina Gazette*, April 4, 1743; *South Carolina Gazette*, March 14–21, 1748; Windley, *Runaway Slave Ads*, 118, 140.

93. Gomez, *Exchanging Our Country Marks*, 180.

94. Windley, *Runaway Slave Ads*, 33, 137, 185.

95. In that antebellum plot discussed in a later chapter, Igbo, Gambian, and "Gullah" slaves, among others, planned to work in concert to overthrow the slave regime.

96. *South Carolina Gazette*, May 3–10, 1735.

97. Sirmans, *Colonial South Carolina*, 96; Howell, *Police Control of the Slaves*, 34; Williams, *History of the Negro Race*, 1:294–96; *South Carolina Gazette*, April 4, 1737.

98. Daniel Meaders, "South Carolina Fugitives as Viewed Through Local Colonial Newspapers With Emphasis on Runaway Notices, 1732–1801," *Journal of Negro History* 60 (April 1975): 289; Easterby, *Journal of the Commons House of Assembly, September 14, 1742–January 27, 1744*, 263–64; *South Carolina Gazette*, April 4, 1737.

99. Windley, *Runaway Slave Ads*, 136, 138–39.

100. Ibid., 283.

101. For examples of this argument, see Lathan A. Windley, *A Profile of Runaway Slaves in Virginia and South Carolina from 1730–1787* (New York: Garland Publishing, 1995), 71–74; Mullin, *Flight and Rebellion*, 83.

102. *South Carolina Gazette*, May 15–22, 1736.

103. *South Carolina Gazette*, May 29–June 5, 1736.

104. Thornton, *Africa and Africans*, 185–91, 207–8, 211–18; David Dalby adds "a pattern was thus established whereby the main burden of communication between Black and White was to be shouldered by Black people." This pattern in the Americas was prefigured much earlier during early contacts between Atlantic Africans and Europeans. As early as the fifteenth and sixteenth centuries, the "burden" of language was on African merchants and traders who already had a long tradition of multilingualism. David Dalby, "Black Through White: Patterns of Communication" (Bloomington, IN : African Studies Program, 1978), 5.

105. *South Carolina Gazette*, October 18, 1746.

106. Thompson, "African Influence on the Art of the United States," 150.

## 4. "WE WILL WADE TO OUR KNEES IN BLOOD"

1. Nash, *Red, White and Black*, 175; Jordan, *White Over Black*, 73.

2. Nash, *Red, White and Black*, 175; Jordan, *White Over Black*, 73; T. H. Breen, "A Changing Labor Force and Race Relations in Virginia, 1660–1710," in *Shaping Southern Society* (New York: Oxford University Press), 120, 132; Edmund Morgan, *American Slavery, American Freedom* (New York: W. W. Norton and Company, 1975), 299, 305–6, 422–23; Davies, *Royal African Company*, 359–60; Eltis et al., *The Trans-Atlantic Slave Trade*.

3. Davies, *Royal African Company*, 142–43; Wax, "Preferences for Slaves," 372; Morgan, *American Slavery, American Freedom*, 305, 308. Morgan reports more precisely that 38,418 slaves entered Virginia between 1708 and 1750.

4. Davies, *Royal African Company*, 135–37, 142–43; Morgan, *American Slavery, American Freedom*, 306–7; Donnan, *Documents Illustrative of the History of the Slave Trade*, 4:89, 172–73.

5. Quoted in Wax, "Preferences for Slaves," 377.

6. Ibid., 388.

7. Susan Westbury, "Slaves of Colonial Virginia: Where They Came From," *William and Mary Quarterly* 42 (1985): 228–37; Herskovits, *Myth of the Negro Past*, 46–47; Curtin, *Atlantic Slave Trade*, 143–44; Susan Westbury, "Colonial Virginia and the Atlantic Slave Trade" (Ph.D. diss., University of Illinois at Urbana-Champaign, 1981), 88–89.

8. Eltis et al., *The Trans-Atlantic Slave Trade*; Curtin, *Atlantic Slave Trade*, 156–57, 188–89; Herskovits, *Myth of the Negro Past*, 47; Donnan, "The Slave Trade Into South Carolina," 821; Wax, "Preferences for Slaves," 391; Thornton, *African and Africans*, 189–190.

9. See Philip Morgan, "The Cultural Implications of the Atlantic Slave Trade: African Regional Origins, American Destinations and New World Developments," *Slavery and Abolition* 18 (April 1997): 138–39. Sidney Mintz quoted in Morgan, "Cultural Implications of the Slave Trade," 142.

10. Walsh, "The Chesapeake Slave Trade," 144–46.

11. Quoted in Wax, "Preferences for Slaves," 391, 392.

12. Quoted in ibid., 394.

13. Donnan, "The Slave Trade Into South Carolina," 821.

14. Quoted in Wax, "Preferences for Slaves," 395.

15. George Rogers Jr. et al., eds., *The Papers of Henry Laurens* (Columbia: University of South Carolina Press, 1968), 2:186.

16. Quoted in Wax, "Preferences for Slaves," 394–95.

17. Littlefield, *Rice and Slaves*, 10.

18. Quoted in Elizabeth Isichei, *Igbo Worlds: An Anthology of Oral Histories and Historical Descriptions* (Philadelphia: Institute for the Study of Human Issues, 1978), 12.

19. See Vincent Carretta, "Olaudah Equiano or Gustavus Vassa? New Light on an Eighteenth-Century Question of Identity," *Slavery and Abolition* 20 (December 1999): 96–105. The evidence Carretta presents is not completely convincing in this regard. The case mostly hinges on a 1759 baptismal record at St. Margaret's church in Westminster which states that "Gustavus Vassa" was born in Carolina in either 1746 or 1747.

20. Chambers, "My Own Nation," 72–73; Adam Potkay and Sandra Burr, eds., *Black Atlantic Writers of the 18th Century* (New York: St. Martin's Press, 1995), 167, 179, 185–88.

21. Potkay and Burr, eds., *Black Atlantic Writers*, 171, 189–92.

22. Curtin, *Atlantic Slave Trade*, 156–58, 161; Walsh, "Chesapeake Slave Trade," 154–55.

23. Aptheker, *Slave Revolts*, 164–65. In 1640, two white servants and a black servant escaped from their master but were eventually captured. The 1644 example was mentioned in the Minutes of the Council and General Court of Virginia. On September 3, 1644, the council noted that a group of black servants were "riotous and rebellious in conduct." Seven days later, the council reported the arrest of an unknown number of assailants guilty of rebellion. See Aptheker, *Slave Revolts*, 165n; Philip Schwarz, *Twice Condemned: Slaves and the Criminal Laws of Virginia, 1705–1865* (Baton Rouge: Louisiana State University Press, 1988), 68–69; H. R. McIlwaine et al., eds., *Minutes of the Council and General Court of Colonial Virginia 1622–1632, 1670–1676* (Richmond, 1979), 502.

24. Aptheker, *Slave Revolts*, 165–66; Schwarz, *Twice Condemned*, 69–70; Anthony S. Parent, "'Either a Fool or a Fury': The Emergence of Paternalism in Colonial Virginia Slave Society" (Ph.D. diss., University of California, Los Angeles, 1982), 95–96, 163–65; William W. Hening, ed., *The Statutes at Large, Being a Collection of All the Laws of Virginia*, 13 vols. (Richmond, 1809–1823), 2:209, 481; 4:128–29.

25. Aptheker, *Slave Revolts*, 166; Schwarz, *Twice Condemned*, 70; Philips, *American Negro Slavery*, 472; Westmoreland County Court Order Book (1676–1689), 644; H. R. McIlwaine, *Executive Journals of the Council of Colonial of Virginia* (Richmond, 1925–1966), 1:85–87.

26. Aptheker, *Slave Revolts*, 169–70; H. W. Flournoy, ed., *Calendar of Virginia State Papers and Other Manuscripts* (Richmond: Virginia State Library, 1890) (herafter *CVSP*), 1:129; McIlwaine, *Executive Journals*, 3:234–35; Schwarz, *Twice Condemned*, 86–87; Parent, "Either a Fool or a Fury," 167–71.

27. Aptheker, *Slave Revolts*, 176–79; Carroll, *Slave Insurrections*, 17; Coffin, *Some Principal Slave Insurrections*, 11; Schwarz, *Twice Condemned*, 88.

28. Hening, *Statutes at Large*, 4:126; Schwarz, *Twice Condemned*, 88; Aptheker, *Slave Revolts*, 177–78; Phillips, *American Negro Slavery*, 472–73.

29. Parent, "Either a Fool or a Fury," 174; Hening, *Statutes at Large*, 4:105; Schwarz, *Twice Condemned*, 86–88, 97, 171, 189; Aptheker, *Slave Revolts*, 179–80, 198–99, 204, 206–7, 210–11.

30. Northampton had 3,181 whites and 3,244 slaves in 1790. Aptheker, *Slave Revolts*, 210n.

31. *CVSP*, 5:534–35. Snead writes "by the enclosed letter you will perceive that the people of this country are much alarmed with apprehension of an Insurrection of the slaves, and have applied to me as County Lieutenant, to secure them from the danger . . . The gentlemen . . . have requested me to make application to Your Excellency for one hundred weight of powder, and four hundred of lead."

32. Aptheker, *Slave Revolts*, 211; *The Boston Gazette and the Country Journal*, June 18, 1792.

33. Aptheker, *Slave Revolts*, 211–12; *CVSP*, 5:542, 546–47, 555, 625; Carroll, *Slave Insurrections*, 42–43.

34. Mullin, *Flight and Rebellion*, viii.

35. Ibid., 140.

36. Ibid.

37. Ibid., 162

38. Mullin never fully explains why assimilated slaves had an "intelligent demeanor" while the newly imported Africans were incapable of that feat.

39. Mullin, *Africa in America*, 215–17, 230–32. He does manage to refrain from characterizing the assimilated slaves as "intelligent" in this work.

40. Douglas Egerton, *Gabriel's Rebellion: The Virginia Slave Conspiracies of 1800 and 1802* (Chapel Hill: University of North Carolina Press, 1993), 20. Egerton adds that "freedom would be his only religion."

41. Ibid., 51, 38–41.

42. Ibid., 52.

43. Ibid., 38–40. There is a major incongruence in the rhetoric of Jeffersonian Republicanism. If those who lived from the toil of others were truly to be considered political and class enemies, then Jefferson as a tobacco planter becomes a rather ironic espouser of "Republican Virtue." This paradox is ignored by Egerton and others. It also seems ironic that Gabriel would have supported the Democratic-Republican societies since they had no real critique concerning the legitimacy of human bondage.

44. Ibid., 41.

45. Ibid., 38–41; *CVSP*, 9:164.

46. *CVSP*, 9:164; James Sidbury, *Ploughshares into Swords: Race, Rebellion, and Identity in Gabriel's Virginia, 1730–1810* (New York: Cambridge University Press, 1997), 88n. At no point in the trial records are white merchants singled out as enemies or white artisans referred to as allies.

47. *CVSP*, 9:165; Egerton, *Gabriel's Rebellion*, 51.

48. *CVSP*, 9:141, 142, 145, 146, 147, 149, 152, 159, 134, 168–69; Philip Schwarz, "Gabriel's Challenge: Slaves and Crime in Late Eighteenth-Century Virginia," *The Virginia Magazine of History and Biography* 90 (July 1982): 283–84, 302, 305; Henrico County Order Book (1799–1801), 94–95. Though Gabriel went before a court of oyer and terminer and was found guilty, he did not suffer physical punishment as a result of the assault. Instead, the court determined that Gabriel was "entitled to the benefit of Clergy" and was released back to his master. Solomon's case was dismissed, and Jupiter received thirty-nine lashes after being found guilty of theft.

49. Though there is some conjecture that since Gabriel and his brother Solomon were blacksmiths, they likely learned this trade from their father, who could possibly have entered

Virginia directly from Africa. The endogamous nature of iron-working knowledge in Gabriel's family has parallels among occupational castes in Atlantic Africa, and especially among the Igbo. See Sidbury, *Ploughshares into Swords*, 85, and Egerton, *Gabriel's Rebellion*, 21.

50. Thornton, *Africa and Africans*, 46; Thompson, *Flash of the Spirit*, 3–61; Francoise Germaix Wasserman, "On Myth and Practice of the Blacksmith in Africa," *Diogenes* 78 (1972): 87–122; Elizabeth Isichei, *The Ibo People and the Europeans: The Genesis of a Relationship to 1906* (New York: St. Martin's Press, 1973), 21–22, 25; Thurstan Shaw, *Unearthing Igbo-Ukwu: Archaeological Discoveries in Eastern Nigeria* (Ibadan: Oxford University Press, 1977), 21, 28, 34, 64–65, 72, 91–92, 100, 105; Thurstan Shaw, *Igbo-Ukwu: An Account of Archaeological Discoveries in Eastern Nigeria* (Evanston: Northwestern University Press, 1970), 97–103, 262. At Ezira, a location near Igbo-Ukwu, a number of iron implements were uncovered, including a sword and iron gongs.

51. Sidbury, *Ploughshares into Swords*, 84–85; Sandra Barnes, ed., *Africa's Ogun: Old World and New* (Bloomington: Indiana University Press, 1997), 42–43.

52. Sidbury, *Ploughshares into Swords*, 62, 84; Stuckey, *Slave Culture*, 5–11.

53. Sidbury, *Ploughshares into Swords*, 84–85.

54. *CVSP*, 9:159.

55. Ibid., 164.

56. In the reward proclamation issued by Gov. James Monroe on September 9, 1800, Gabriel, aged twenty-four, is described as "a Negro of brown complexion about 6 feet 3 or 4 inches high, a bony face, well made, and very active, has two or three scars on his head, his hair very short." The twenty-eight-year-old Jack was described by a contemporary source as 6'5", "straight made and perhaps as strong a man as any in the state." Ibid., 151, 160, 1; Aptheker, *Slave Revolts*, 219–20; "Gabriel's Rebellion," *Henrico County Historical Society Newsletter* (November 1996), VHS; Virginius Dabney, "Gabriel's Insurrection," *American History Illustrated* 11 (July 1976): 27.

57. *CVSP*, 9:151, 160, 165.

58. Ibid.

59. Egerton, *Gabriel's Rebellion*, 66. Egerton adds, "most likely [Ditcher's] lack of literacy and a trade had led Gabriel to regard him less highly than he did men like Sam Byrd." This statement is quite curious when one considers that Ditcher was named second-in-command of the rebellion by Gabriel and was one of the most effective recruiters.

60. *CVSP*, 9: 141.

61. Ibid., 170.

62. Ibid., 141–42, 147.

63. Ibid., 145, 151, 164–65.

64. Solomon states, "every Sunday [Gabriel] came to Richmond to provide ammunition and to find where the military stores were deposited." Ibid., 147–49.

65. Ibid., 168.

66. Ibid.

67. Ibid., 149, 159.

68. Ibid., 141.

69. Ibid., 141, 142, 147, 151, 152, 165; Dabney, "Gabriel's Insurrection," 27; William Radford to John Preston, September 14, 1800 in the Preston Family Papers, VHS.

70. Quoted in Aptheker, *Slave Revolts*, 221; Dabney, "Gabriel's Insurrection," 28.

71. Aptheker, *Slave Revolts*, 221–25.

72. Harold Courlander, *Tales of Yoruba Gods: Myths, Legends and Heroic Tales of the Yoruba People of West Africa* (New York: Crown Publishers, 1973), 237.

73. Thompson, *Flash of the Spirit*, 52.

74. Thornton, *Africa and Africans*, 190; Barnes, ed., *Africa's Ogun*, 142, 29–30, 39–42, 51.

75. James Sidbury, "Saint Domingue in Virginia: Ideology, Local Meanings, and Resistance to Slavery, 1790–1800," *Journal of Southern History* 63 (1997): 538–41; Susan Branson and Leslie Patrick, "Saint-Domingan Refugees of Color in Philadelphia," in David Geggus, ed., *The Impact of the Haitian Revolution in the Atlantic World* (Columbia: University of South Carolina Press, 2001), 193; Gomez, *Exchanging Our Country Marks*, 55.

76. Barnes, *Africa's Ogun*, 39–41; Potkay and Burr, *Black Atlantic Writers*, 167; Elizabeth Isichei, *A History of the Igbo People* (London: MacMillan Press Ltd., 1976), 51–54. During the sixteenth century, Benin expanded into western Igboland, establishing major tributaries in the Igbo towns of Onitsha and Oguta located east of the Niger River.

77. Barnes, *Africa's Ogun*, 30–31.

78. Ibid., 29–32.

79. Ibid., 31–32.

80. Ibid., 32–34.

81. Potkay and Burr, *Black Atlantic Writers*, 174–75.

82. Isichei, *A History of the Igbo People*, 29–31; Isichei, *Igbo Worlds*, 27, 52–53, 56; G. T. Basden, *Among the Ibos of Nigeria* (London: Frank Cass and Co. Ltd., 1966), 77, 318, 321.

83. Basden, *Niger Igbos*, 77; Isichei, *Igbo Worlds*, 52–53; P. Amaury Talbot, *Tribes of the Niger Delta, Their Religions and Customs* (London: Sheldon Press, 1923), 277.

84. *Virginia Gazette*, January 10, 1771.

85. *Virginia Gazette*, January 6, 1776. The term "outlandish" refers to an African-born slave. It also implies a recently imported African. Lewis was likely heeding the proclamation issued in November 1775 by the Royal Governor of Virginia, Lord Dunmore, which granted freedom to any slave escaping from an American owner to join the British. See Mullin, *Flight and Rebellion*, 120–21, 124, 131–36.

86. Leland Ferguson, *Uncommon Ground: Archaeology and Early African America, 1650–1800* (Washington: Smithsonian Institution Press, 1992), 117. African-born blacksmiths and African metallurgical technologies were also shaping influences in the British Caribbean. Not only did African blacksmiths labor at important iron foundries in Jamaica, but their technical expertise proved pivotal for English planters and maroon rebels there. See Candice Goocher, "African Metallurgy in the Atlantic World," *The African Archaeological Review* 11 (1993): 197–215, and "African Hammer, European Anvil: West African Iron Technology in the Atlantic Trade Era," in Bassey W. Andah, ed., *Cultural Resource Management: An African Dimension* (Ibadan, Nigeria: Wisdom Publishers Ltd., 1990) 200–208.

87. John Michael Vlach, *By the Work of Their Hands: Studies in Afro-American Folklife* (Ann Arbor: UMI Research Press, 1991), 25–27.

88. Curtin, *Atlantic Slave Trade*, 157; Patrick R. McNaughton, *The Mande Blacksmiths: Knowledge, Power, and Art in West Africa* (Bloomington: University of Indiana Press, 1993), 8, 20–21, 49–64.

According to a refrain in a popular twentieth-century Mande masquerade celebration song, "Real smiths are the masters of sorcery."

89. CVSP, 9:145.

90. Ibid., 165.

91. Ibid., 159.

92. Ibid., 158, 166.

93. Ibid., 168.

94. Rosalind I. J. Hackett, *Religion in Calabar: The Religious Life and History of a Nigerian Town* (New York: Mouton De Gruyter, 1989), 28–31.

95. Francis Arinze, *Sacrifice in Ibo Religion* (Ibadan: Ibadan University Press, 1970), 14–15; Talbot, *Tribes of the Niger River Delta*, 32–62. There is no historical confirmation that these practices predate the twentieth century.

96. Potkay and Burr, *Black Atlantic Writers*, 169, 171, 174–75.

97. Melville Herskovits notes "in ceremony after ceremony witnessed among the Yoruba, the Ashanti, and in Dahomey, one invariable element was a visit to the river or some other body of 'living' water . . . for the purpose of obtaining the liquid indispensable for the rites." Similar river cults can be found in a variety of American locales including Haiti, Brazil, Cuba, Guyana, and Jamaica. See, e.g., Curtin, *Two Jamaicas*, 164–65, and Herskovits, *Myth of the Negro Past*, 233.

98. Herskovits, *Myth of the Negro Past*, 233.

99. CVSP, 9:151.

100. Ibid., 149.

101. Thompson, "African Influence on the Art," 122, 124, 127, 149, 167; Lorena S. Walsh, *From Calabar to Carter's Grove: The History of a Virginia Slave Community* (Charlottesville: University Press of Virginia, 1997), 106–7; Potkay and Burr, *Black Atlantic Writers*, 175; Sylvia Frey, *Water from the Rock: Black Resistance in a Revolutionary Age* (New Jersey: Princeton University Press, 1991), 40–41. Frey notes the "minimal African influence" and the "forced extinction of African practices" at burial grounds in the Chesapeake between the late seventeenth and early nineteenth centuries. The excavations in James County and Frey's own discussion of internment items in slave burials at Williamsburg, Virginia, and Catoctin Furnace, Maryland, offer sufficient evidence to the contrary.

102. CVSP, 9:153. Emphasis added.

103. Schwarz, *Twice Condemned*, 92, 95–97; Morgan, *Slave Counterpoint*, 612, 613n; Hening, *Statutes at Large*, 6:105. Morgan reports that at least 175 slaves were brought before twenty-two different Virginia county courts between 1700 and 1780.

104. Schwarz, *Twice Condemned*, 102, 108–9; Morgan, *Slave Counterpoint*, 612–13; *Pennsylvania Gazette*, December 31, 1767; *Georgia Gazette*, March 30, 1768.

105. *Virginia Gazette*, November 4, 1763; *Virginia Gazette*, July 28, 1775; *Virginia Independent Chronicle*, March 4, 1789; Morgan, *Slave Counterpoint*, 620; Fett, *Working Cures*, 162; Aptheker, *Slave Revolts*, 198–99.

106. Morgan, *Slave Counterpoint*, 616; CVSP, 5:333, 338.

107. Potkay and Burr, *Black Atlantic Writers*, 175.

108. Morgan, *Slave Counterpoint*, 657–58. Oddly, Morgan cites Stuckey as an advocate of this sort of claim. While one of the main contentions of *Slave Culture* is that African culture—and

the ring shout in particular—helped shape African-American (or slave) culture and consciousness, it is a bit misleading to characterize the interpretation in this manner. Obviously, newly imported Africans did not simply forget the religious beliefs that sustained them through the horrors of the Middle Passage. One can even contend that first and second generation enslaved African Americans maintained core principles taught to them by their African parents or grandparents. Hence, the notion that slaves during the eighteenth century almost instantly adopted Christianity is untenable. On the nature of nineteenth-century slave religion, however, Stuckey explicitly states: "In fact, the great bulk of slaves were scarcely touched by Christianity, their religious practices being vastly more African than Christian. The slave preacher on the plantation was able to relate to slave communities touched by Christianity and to those with little or no Christian characteristics, the latter because otherwise he could have had no credence whatsoever among the majority of his people." Syncretism was a process that took place over time. On these concepts, Morgan agrees more with Stuckey then he thinks. See Stuckey, *Slave Culture*, viii–ix, 35, 37.

## 5. "I WILL GATHER ALL NATIONS"

1. According to court justices Lionel Kennedy and Thomas Parker, these two verses were among the biblical passages used by Denmark Vesey to rally slaves to his cause. John O. Killens, *The Trial Record of Denmark Vesey* (Boston: Beacon Press, 1970), 11; Robert S. Starobin, ed., *Denmark Vesey: The Slave Conspiracy of 1822* (Englewood Cliffs: Prentice-Hall, 1970), 21–22; Edward Pearson, ed., *Designs against Charleston: The Trial Record of the Denmark Vesey Slave Conspiracy of 1822* (Chapel Hill: University of North Carolina Press, 1999) 80–81, 329; Thomas Wentworth Higginson, *Black Rebellion: A Selection from Travelers and Outlaws* (1889; reprint, New York: Arno Press, 1969), 224.

2. Walter Fraser, *Charleston! Charleston! The History of a Southern City* (Columbia: University of South Carolina Press, 1989), 119, 178, 188; Frey, *Water From the Rock*, 213; George Rogers, *Charleston in the Age of the Pinckneys* (Norman: University of Oklahoma Press, 1969), 141; John Lofton, *Insurrection in South Carolina: The Turbulent World of Denmark Vesey* (Yellow Springs, Ohio: Antioch Press, 1964), 6–7.

3. Donnan, "The Slave Trade into South Carolina," 807, 822–23, 827; Aptheker, *Slave Revolts*, 190–91; Rogers, *Age of the Pinckneys*, 141; Lofton, *Insurrection in South Carolina*, 7, 14.

4. Donnan, "Slave Trade into South Carolina," 828; Weir, *Colonial South Carolina*, 178.

5. Quoted in Aptheker, *Slave Revolts*, 96–97; Lofton, *Insurrection in South Carolina*, 69.

6. Albert E. Bergh, ed., *The Writings of Thomas Jefferson* (Washington: Thomas Jefferson Memorial Association, 1905), 275–276; Bernard Powers, *Black Charlestonians: A Social History, 1822–1885* (Fayetteville: University of Arkansas Press, 1994), 28.

7. Frey, *Water from the Rock*, 230; CVSP, 6:436–38, 453, 470, 475. Lt. Col. Thomas Newton of the Norfolk, Virginia, militia noted that Saint-Domingue slaves "would be ready to operate against us with the others." See Thomas Ott, *The Haitian Revolution, 1789–1804* (Knoxville: University of Tennessee Press, 1973), 54. Beyond a small handful of references, no other corroboration for this plot exists.

8. Aptheker, *Slave Revolts*, 96–97, 217–18, 237; Rogers, *Age of the Pinckneys*, 142; Fraser, *Charles-*

ton! 182–183; Frey, *Water from the Rock*, 213; Lofton, *Insurrection in South Carolina*, 72; Powers, *Black Charlestonians*, 28.

9. Henry, *Police Control of the Slave*, 150; Fraser, *Charleston!* 185; Aptheker, *Slave Revolts*, 97; Rogers, *Age of the Pinckneys*, 142.

10. St. George Chronicle and Grenada Gazette, February 23, 1798; Aptheker, *Slave Revolts*, 96–97; Powers, *Black Charlestonians*, 28–29; Marina Wikramanayake, *A World in Shadow: The Free Black in Antebellum South Carolina* (Columbia: University of South Carolina Press, 1973), 160.

11. Aptheker, *Slave Revolts*, 217–18, 237; Powers, *Black Charlestonians*, 286n; C. L. R. James, *Black Jacobins* (New York: Vintage Books, 1963), 202; Elizabeth Donnan, ed., "Papers of James A. Bayard 1796–1815," in *Annual Report of the American Historical Association* (Washington: Government Printing Office, 1913), 2:11.

12. Aptheker, *Slave Revolts*, 236.

13. Fraser, *Charleston!* 119; Rogers, *Age of the Pinckneys*, 142; Donnan, "Slave Trade into South Carolina," 828; Powers, *Black Charlestonians*, 3; Curtin, *Atlantic Slave Trade*, 87–89; Eltis et al., *The Trans-Atlantic Slave Trade*. Curtin's estimate excludes Africans entering French, Spanish, and American Louisiana. According to the Du Bois institute dataset, which is based on roughly 70 percent of all slave-trading voyages, 270,976 enslaved Africans disembarked in North America during the entire period of the slave trade.

14. Curtin, *Atlantic Slave Trade*, 74–75. Curtin is partly corroborated by the Du Bois institute slave trade dataset which records that 49,583 enslaved Africans disembarked in North American ports between 1801 and 1867. See Eltis et al., *The Trans-Atlantic Slave Trade*.

15. One small example of this continuity would be the sweet grass baskets any modern visitor in downtown Charleston can purchase. Originally used to help remove husks from rice, these baskets bear strong resemblance to baskets made in modern-day Sierra Leone. Due, perhaps, to the end of rice cultivation in the Lowcountry and Sea Islands, as well as natural cultural changes, modern sweet grass baskets often include features which have more stylistic or aesthetic applications than practical ones. Paradoxically, scholars lobbying for cultural discontinuities and those arguing for the presence of Africanisms can use the sweet grass basket to bolster their diametrically opposing claims.

16. Eltis et al., *The Trans-Atlantic Slave Trade*.

17. Higginson, *Black Rebellion*, 215–16; Carroll, *Slave Insurrections*, 97; Examination of William Paul, June 19, 1822, Records of the General Assembly, Governor's Messages (1800–1822), South Carolina Department of Archives and History (hereafter RGA, GM, SCDAH). Higginson and Carroll erroneously refer to this slave as Devany. The official report of the trial also refers to him as Devany, perhaps to protect his identity from revenge-minded slaves. This policy of anonymity allowed slaves to give testimony in the trial without fear of retribution. Some names were even deleted from the trial record for purposes of protection. In one specific case, the court agreed not to name a slave belonging to Col. George W. Cross. Court officials stated "Before the name of this witness was given to the Court, his Master required of the Court a Solemn pledge that his name, should never be revealed, under which pledge this witness now produced and testified." See Aptheker, *Slave Revolts*, 271; Killens, *Trial Record*, 33–34; W. Hasell Wilson to Rev. Robert Wilson, June 1, 1900, Correspondence of Reverend Robert Wilson (1838–1925),

Charleston Library Society (hereafter CLS); Examination of Y*, belonging to Colonel George W. Cross, no date, RGA, GM, SCDAH.

18. Lofton, *Insurrection in South Carolina*, 146–47; Killens, *Trial Record*, 34; Aptheker, *Slave Revolts*, 270–72; Examination of William Paul, June 19, 1822, RGA, GM, SCDAH.

19. Lofton, *Insurrection in South Carolina*, 146–47; Aptheker, *Slave Revolts*, 270–71.

20. Killens, *Trial Record*, 34–35; James Lofton, "Denmark Vesey's Call to Arms," *Journal of Negro History* 33 (1948), 414–15; Lofton, *Insurrection in South Carolina*, 147–48; Carroll, *Slave Insurrections in the U.S.*, 98–99. The city of Charleston was governed by a council of thirteen wardens, and the intendant served as the presiding officer. The modern-day equivalent of the intendant would be the office of mayor.

21. Killens, *Trial Record*, 36; Lofton, "Call to Arms," 415; W. Hasell Wilson to Rev. Robert Wilson, June 1, 1900, Correspondence of Reverend Robert Wilson (1838–1925), CLS; William Freehling, *Prelude to Civil War: The Nullification Controversy in South Carolina 1816–1836* (New York: Oxford University Press, 1965), 21, 115–16, 59; Douglas Egerton, *He Shall Go Out Free: The Lives of Denmark Vesey* (Madison: Madison House, 1999), 160–61, 131–33, 170–72, 207–9; Lofton, "Denmark Vesey's Call to Arms," 410. Bennett's slaves, including Ned, Batteau, Matthias, and Rolla were involved, and Ned and Rolla were to lead entire companies of slave insurgents during the uprising. The implications of this level of involvement were obvious; if Bennett could not manage and control his own slaves, he was not fit to govern the quarter of a million slaves living in South Carolina.

22. Killens, *Trial Record*, 36–37; Lofton, "Call to Arms," 415; Lofton, *Insurrection in South Carolina*, 150–51; W. Hasell Wilson to Rev. Robert Wilson, June 1, 1900, CLS.

23. Lofton, *Insurrection in South Carolina*, 152; Carroll, *Slave Insurrections*, 99.

24. Aptheker, *Slave Revolts*, 273. Carroll, *Slave Insurrections*, 98–99; Killens, *Trial Records*, 27–28, 32; Confession made by John the Slave of W. Enslow the Cooper in Henry Ravenel Papers, no date, South Carolina Historical Society (hereafter SCHS); Examination of Robert Harth, June 21, 1822; Examination of William Paul, June 19, 1822,; Examination of Joe La Roche, June 20, 1822; Examination of George Wilson, June 21, 1822; Examination of Rolla Bennett, June 25, 1822; Confession of Rolla Bennett, June 25, 1822; Second Confession of Jesse Blackwood, June 26, 1822; Confession of Bacchus Hammet, July 12, 1822; Confession of Smart Anderson, July 16, 1822; Examination of Frank Ferguson, July 15, 1822; Confession of John Enslow, July 17, 1822, RGA, GM, SCDAH.

25. Starobin, *Denmark Vesey*, 30; John Potter to Langdon Cheves, July 5, 1822, Langdon Cheves Papers, SCHS; Confession of Smart Anderson, no date; Second Confession of Jesse Blackwood, June 26, 1822; Examination of Rolla Bennett, June 25, 1822; Second Confession of Bacchus Hammet, July 17, 1822, RGA, GM, SCDAH.

26. Aptheker, *Slave Revolts*, 273. This is despite the fact that contemporary sources refer to another attempted insurrection in Charleston between July and August 1822. Even on the day of Denmark's execution, one source noted "Another attempt at insurrection was made but the State troops held the slaves in check. So determined, however, were they to strike a blow for liberty that it was found necessary for the federal government to send soldiers to maintain order." Charleston *City Gazette*, August 23, 1822.

27. Despite recent claims made by Michael P. Johnson, there was a definite consensus among the rebels that Vesey was the mastermind and leader of the plot. See Examination of William Paul, June 19, 1822; Examination of Joe La Roche, June 20, 1822; Examination of Rolla Bennett, June 25, 1822; Confession of Jesse Blackwood, June 26, 1822; Examination of Frank Ferguson, June 27, 1822; Confession of Bacchus Hammet, July 12, 1822; Confession of Monday Gell, July 13, 1822; Examination of Pharo Thompson, July 15, 1822; Second Confession of Bacchus Hammet, July 17, 1822; Confession of John Enslow, July 17, 1822; Second Confession of Monday Gell, July 23, 1822, RGA, GM, SCDAH.

28. Lofton, "Call to Arms," 398–401; James Hamilton Jr., *An Account of the Late Intended Insurrection Among a Portion of the Blacks of This City, Charleston, S.C.* (Charleston: A. E. Miller, 1822), 17–18; Carroll, *Slave Insurrections*, 84–85; Egerton, *He Shall Go Out Free*, 3–7, 15, 20–21; Stephen Crane to John Lofton, January 27, 1983, Denmark Vesey File, SCDAH.

29. Lofton, "Call to Arms," 397–401; Carroll, *Slave Insurrections*, 84–85; Aptheker, *Slave Revolts*, 268; Crane to Lofton, January 27, 1983; "Denmark Vesey Historic Site Dedication," MOJA Arts Festival Bulletin (1994), 10; Denmark Vesey File, SCDAH; Secretary of State, Recorded Instruments, South Carolina Miscellaneous Records, No. 3M (1799–1800), 427–428, SCDAH. Even as late as his petition for freedom, Denmark was still known as Telemaque.

30. Aptheker, *Slave Revolts*, 268–29; Powers, *Black Charlestonians*, 41; Lofton, "Call to Arms," 401–2; Lofton, *Insurrection in South Carolina*, 85.

31. David Robertson, *Denmark Vesey: The Buried History of America's Largest Slave Rebellion and the Man Who Led It* (New York: Alfred A. Knopf, 1999), 37–39. A number of Robertson's assumptions are easily proven erroneous. Using a basic Gregorian to Islamic Lunar calendar conversion table, July 14, 1822 would actually correlate to the tenth month (or *Shawwal*, the second month of fasting) of the Islamic year 1237.

32. Ibid., 40.

33. Eltis et al., *The Trans-Atlantic Slave Trade*; Schuler, "Akan Slave Rebellions," 10; Curtin, *Atlantic Slave Trade*, 223, 87; Egerton, *He Shall Go Out Free*, 3–4.

34. Richard Wade, "The Vesey Plot: A Reconsideration," *Journal of Southern History* 30 (1964): 150.

35. Richard Wade, *Slavery in the Cities: The South 1820–1860* (Oxford: Oxford University Press, 1964), 240–41.

36. See Ira Berlin, *Slaves without Masters: The Free Negro in the Antebellum South* (New York: Vintage Books, 1974).

37. Michael P. Johnson, "Denmark Vesey and His Co-Conspirators," *William and Mary Quarterly*, 3rd ser., 58 (2001): 915–76; "Reading Evidence," *William and Mary Quarterly*, 3rd ser., 59 (2002): 202. While I largely agree with Johnson's summary of the careless research and massive interpretive leaps to be found in Robertson's work, I do find major fault in his critique of Egerton and Pearson's introduction. See Walter Rucker, review of David Robertson's *Denmark Vesey: The Buried History of America's Largest Slave Rebellion and the Man Who Led It. Journal of Negro History* 86 (Winter 2001): 60–62, and Douglas Egerton's effective rebuttal to Johnson in "Forgetting Denmark Vesey; Or, Oliver Stone Meets Richard Wade," *William and Mary Quarterly*, 3rd ser., 59 (2002): 143–52. Admittedly, Pearson's edited volume does include an unusually large number of significant transcription errors—close to 600 by Johnson's count—but these word

additions, omissions, and changes do not distort the substance of the testimony. Whether Monday Gell was the "heart" (in Pearson's version) or "head" (in the court evidence) of the plan to distribute weapons and kill whites does not alter the essential facts presented. In any event, the introduction and the appendices to the edited volume are particularly useful.

38. Egerton, "Forgetting Denmark Vesey," 148–49, 151; David Robertson, "Inconsistent Contextualism: The Hermeneutics of Michael Johnson," *William and Mary Quarterly*, 3rd ser., 59 (January 2002): 154–55.

39. The most important examples include the Vodun-inspired Saint-Domingue revolt, the numerous Obeah-inspired British Caribbean rebellions, and the 1835 Islamic uprising in Bahia, Brazil.

40. Killens, *Trial Record*, 78; Pearson, *Designs against Charleston*, 123; Hamilton, *Account of the Late Intended Insurrection*, 23–24; Examination of William Paul, June 19, 1822; Examination of Robert Harth, June 21, 1822; Examination of Frank Ferguson, June 27, 1822; Statement of Henry Haig, July 10, 1822; Statement of Paul Pritchard, no date, RGA, GM, SCDAH.

41. Zaphaniah Kingsley, *A Treatise on the Patriarchal, or Co-operative System of Society as it Exists in Some Governments and Colonies in America, and in the United States, under the Name of Slavery with its Necessity and Advantages* (1829; reprint, Freeport, NY: Books for Libraries Press, 1970), 13; Pearson, *Designs against Charleston*, 123.

42. Hamilton, *Account of the Late Intended Insurrection*, 24; Examination of Robert Harth, June 21, 1822, RGA, GM, SCDAH.

43. Hamilton, *Account of the Late Intended Insurrection*, 23–24; Killens, *Trial Record*, 76–77; Examination of Frank Ferguson, June 27, 1822; Examination of Y*, Belonging to Colonel George W. Cross, no date; Examination of George Vanderhorst, no date; Statement of Perault Strohecker, August 3, 1822, RGA, GM, SCDAH. One of the main ingredients of early twentieth-century protective *nkisi* charms, medicine bags, and *nkondi* figures of BaKongo spiritualists were crab claws, which granted users the ability to "seize" their victims. For more discussion of twentieth-century *nkisi* and Kongo spiritual practices and beliefs, see Thompson, *Flash of the Spirit*, 117–19; Wyatt MacGaffey, "The Eyes of Understanding: Kongo Minkisi," in Wyatt MacGaffey and Michael D. Harris, *Astonishment and Power* (Washington, DC: Smithsonian Institution, 1993), 37, 39, 20–35.

44. Examination of Billy Bulkley, no date, RGA, GM, SCDAH.

45. Killens, *Trial Record*, 78; Starobin, *Denmark Vesey*, 43–45; Statement of Henry Haig, July 10, 1822; Examination of George Vanderhorst, no date, RGA, GM, SCDAH.

46. William Freehling, "Denmark Vesey's Peculiar Reality," in Robert Abzug and Stephen Maizlish, eds., *New Perspectives on Race and Slavery in America: Essays in Honor of Kenneth M. Stampp* (Lexington: University Press of Kentucky, 1986), 38–39; Pearson, *Designs against Charleston*, xvii, 1; Killens, *Trial Record*, xxiii–xxv; Statement of Henry Haig, July 10, 1822, RGA, GM, SCDAH. The testimony regarding the plot to poison the city's water supply is mentioned only in the documentary trial record contained in the Records of the General Assembly, Governors' Messages, at the South Carolina Department of Archives and History. Two copies of the official trial transcript were submitted to the South Carolina assembly in 1822. When Lionel Kennedy and Thomas Parker published the more widely circulated *An Official Report of the Trials of Sundry Negroes Charged with an Attempt to Raise an Insurrection in the State of South Carolina*, all mention

of Jack's plan was deliberately omitted because of the dangers such knowledge posed. Even with this omission, the *Official Report* was considered dangerous enough that all copies of the manuscript that could be located were allegedly destroyed shortly after its 1822 publication.

47. Killens, *Trial Record*, 77–78, 86; Examination of William Paul, June 19, 1822; Examination of Frank Ferguson, July 15, 1822, RGA, GM, SCDAH.

48. Killens, *Trial Record*, 78, 86; Examination of William Paul, June 19, 1822; Examination of Harry Haig, July 17, 1822; Examination of Billy Bulkley, July 17, 1822, RGA, GM, SCDAH.

49. Killens, *Trial Record*, 79–80; Statement of Henry Haig, July 10, 1822, RGA, GM, SCDAH.

50. Killens, *Trial Record*, 85, 109, 110, 128; Confession of Bacchus Hammet, July 12, 1822, RGA, GM, SCDAH.

51. Killens, *Trial Record*, 128. Monday Gell noted "[Jacob Stagg] asked me for a sword, and when I said I had none to give him, he said, that he would get a scythe and make a sword out of it."

52. Ibid., 79, 81–82; Second Confession of Monday Gell, July 23, 1822; Statement of Henry Haig, July 10, 1822; Examination of Perault Strohecker, July 15, 1822, RGA, GM, SCDAH.

53. Examination of James Mall, July 15, 1822, RGA, GM, SCDAH. Emphasis added.

54. The testimony of Billy Bulkley had to be postponed because, as the court observed, "It was with great difficulty that the above witness could be understood, as he spoke english very badly." Billy, a member of Gullah Jack's company likely only spoke Gullah. See Examination of Bill Bulkley, July 11, 1822, RGA, GM, SCDAH.

55. Examination of Nero Haig, August 6, 1822; Statement of Perault Strohecker, August 3, 1822, RGA, GM, SCDAH.

56. Gomez, *Exchanging Our Country Marks*, 3, 100–104.

57. Ibid., 5.

58. For a more detailed discussion of the origins and significance of Gullah culture, see Lorenzo Dow Turner, *Africanisms in Gullah Dialect* (Chicago: University of Chicago Press, 1949); Creel, *A Peculiar People*, 13–20; Creel, "Gullah Attitudes toward Life and Death," in Holloway, *Africanisms*, 69–71, 77, 81; Gomez, *Exchanging Our Country Marks*, 100–104; Michael Montgomery, *The Crucible of Carolina: Essays in the Development of Gullah Culture and Language* (Athens: University of Georgia Press, 1994); Winifred Vass, *The Bantu Speaking Heritage of the United States* (Los Angeles: University of California Press, 1979); Starobin, *Denmark Vesey*, 4; Stuckey, *Slave Culture*, 50. Starobin began the trend of referring to Gullah Jack's band as Angolan. This is probably due to a brief mention in an entry of the Charleston City Council in June 1822 which refers to "Gullah Jack" and his "Gullah or Angola Negroes." See Hamilton, *Account of the Late Intended Insurrection*, 22; Creel, *A Peculiar People*, 15.

59. Killens, *Trial Record*, 134, 164–65.

60. Examination of Monday Gell, August 3, 1822, RGA, GM, SCDAH.

61. Killens, *Trial Record*, 164–65; Examination of Monday Gell, August 3, 1822, RGA, GM, SCDAH.

62. Killens, *Trial Record*, 164–65; Examination of Monday Gell, August 3, RGA, GM, SCDAH.

63. *Drums and Shadows: Survival Studies Among the Georgia Coastal Negroes* (Athens: University of Georgia Press, 1986), 24, 29; Albert J. Raboteau, *Slave Religion: The "Invisible Institution" in the Antebellum South* (New York: Oxford University Press, 1978), 276–77; Beckwith, *Black Roadways*, 55, 57; Melville Herskovits, *Dahomey: An Ancient West African Kingdom* (Evanston, IL: Northwest-

ern University Press, 1967), 1:264; Melville Herskovits, *Life in a Haitian Valley* (New York: Alfred Knopf, 1937), 95; Herskovits, *Myth of the Negro Past*, 189–90; Puckett, *Folk Beliefs of the Southern Negro*, 336, 137. One distinct twentieth-century parallel to Philip the Preacher was a Jamaican man named George Parkes. Like Philip, Parkes was blind, born with a caul, and was claimed to be able to speak to "duppies," or ghosts. See Beckwith, *Black Roadways*, 88–89.

64. Killens, *Trial Record*, 83, 52; Examination of Robert Harth, June 21, 1822; Examination of Perault Strohecker, July 15, 1822; Examination of Pharo Thompson, July 15, 1822; Examination of Charles Drayton, July 15, 1822; Examination of Monday Gell, July 15, 1822, RGA, GM, SCDAH.

65. Confession of William Colcock, July 10, 1822; Confession of Monday Gell, July 13, 1822, RGA, GM, SCDAH. This statement is a plausible demonstration of the presence of African-born blacksmiths in South Carolina and their possible connections to the Yoruba god Ogun. A great number of Saint-Domingue slaves were Fon, Edo, and Yoruba who brought Ogun and other orishas to the Caribbean nation in the form of Vodun. It is entirely inconceivable that these "black French" metalworkers were completely divorced from the spiritual roots of their practice.

66. Killens, *Trial Record*, 84.

67. Examination of Perault Strohecker, July 15, 1822, RGA, GM, SCDAH.

68. Killens, *Trial Record*, 88; Confession of Smart Anderson, no date; Statement of Henry Haig, July 10, 1822; Confession of Monday Gell, July 13, 1822, RGA, GM, SCDAH.

69. Pearson, *Designs against Charleston*, 94, 117–18, 203n; Examination of Saby Gaillard, July 16, 1822; Confession of Monday Gell, July 13, 1822; Confession of Jack Purcell, July 16, 1822, RGA, GM, SCDAH. Boyer was president of Haiti from 1818 to 1843. During the course of the Haitian revolution, he was among a number of free mulattos that joined with Touissant L'Ouverture to overthrow French rule.

70. Killens, *Trial Record*, 42–43, 46, 51, 58–59, 62, 68–71, 72, 117, 160–61; Examination of Joe La Roche, June 20, 1822; Examination of Robert Harth, June 21, 1822; Confession of Smart Anderson, no date; Confession of Monday Gell, July 13, 1822; Second Confession of Monday Gell, July 23, 1822; Examination of Rolla Bennett, June 25, 1822,; Second Confession of Jesse Blackwood, June 26, 1822; Examination of Saby Gaillard, July 16, 1822; Confession of John Enslow, July 17, 1822; Examination of John Enslow, July 20, 1822, RGA, GM, SCDAH. Court officials could not decide whether Monday Gell or Denmark wrote the letters. That Denmark "spoke French with fluency" and had some prior experience in Saint-Domingue would make him the most likely author. According to evidence presented at the trial, Monday Gell did not know French. See Killens, *Trial Record*, 72.

71. Killens, 29, 66; Examination of Y*, Belonging to Colonel George W. Cross, no date, RGA, GM, SCDAH. The unnamed slave of Colonel Cross testified "Previous to 16th. June, Monday Gell asked me to go into his shop, I went in I told him I heard he was the Captain of his Country man's Company, the Ebos, he said he was a sort of one."

72. Ibid., 14–16, 56, 79, 81, 122–23. At least two other members of this group were known to have been African born, Jack McNeil and Caesar McDow. There is no available evidence pertaining to their specific ethnic identity.

73. For listings of Akan day-names, see Anim, *Names as a Factor in Cultural Identity Among the Akan, Ga, and Ewe*, 2–3; Frank Wesley Pitman, "Slavery on British West India Plantations in the Eighteenth Century," *Journal of Negro History* 11 (1926): 641.

74. Killens, *Trial Record*, 124, 143.

75. Ibid., 125, 142; Pearson, *Designs against Charleston*, 133, 311. Denmark and a man named Saby Gaillard were the other two free blacks found guilty for their roles in the conspiracy.

76. Egerton, *He Shall Go Out Free*, 133; Stuckey, *Slave Culture*, 47; Starobin, *Slave Conspiracy of 1822*, 4; Charles Joyner, *Down By the Riverside: A South Carolina Slave Community* (Urbana: University of Illinois Press, 1984), 218–19; Examination of William Palmer, July 15, 1822, RGA, GM, SCDAH; Gwendolyn Midlo Hall, *Databases for the Study of Afro-Louisiana History and Genealogy 1699–1860: Computerized Information from Original Manuscript Sources* (Baton Rouge: Louisiana State University Press, 2000); Lorenzo Dow Turner, *Africanisms*, 132; Inscoe, "Carolina Slave Names," 533, 535; Hennig Cohen, "Slave Names in Colonial South Carolina," *American Speech* 27 (1952): 103, 106; Handler and Jacoby, "Slave Names and Naming in Barbados," 694, 697–98. There is some controversy regarding the etymology of the name Mingo. Previously, Mingo Harth was claimed to have been a Mande-speaking Mandika (Mandingo) by a number of scholars. Starobin began this tradition in 1970, and this claim has been repeated by Stuckey and, most recently, Egerton. While the testimony of William Palmer attests that Mingo was indeed African born, nothing in the trial record specifically illuminates his ethnicity. In a personal conversation with Stuckey several years ago, I discovered that Starobin's claim that Mingo derives from a "Mandingo" origin was based on evidence from an unnamed ethnolinguist specializing in Gambian languages. Neither Starobin nor Stuckey cite this source which makes the claim difficult to verify.

Gwendolyn Midlo Hall's genealogical database shows that, in the case of Louisiana, a Gambian-born Wolof man named Mingo is mentioned in the records between 1782 and 1802. Another man named Mingo was of Hausa origins in these records. The renowned ethnolinguist, Lorenzo Dow Turner claims that the popular Gullah personal name "Mi_ko" has a Bambara origin and means "a tumblerful, a bumper, a prize." In this case, with the "_" pronouced as "ng" the name is rendered as "Mingko," and its origin would be in the Gambian coast. Another possibility is that Mingo is short for Domingo (Sunday in Spanish) and might either be a transliteration of an Akan day-name or could denote someone from Christianized regions of West-central Africa. Clearly then, there is a lack of consensus regarding the origin of this name. With little more than the evidence provided by Turner, I maintain that Mingo Harth was in all likelihood a Gambian-born Mande speaker.

77. Killens, *Trial Record*, 85; Statement of Monday Gell, July 20, 1822, RGA, GM, SCDAH.

78. Killens, *Trial Record*, 121; Statement of Monday Gell, July 20, 1822, RGA, GM, SCDAH. Obviously if Mingo was a Mande-speaker, his brother would be as well.

79. Killens, *Trial Record*, 86.

80. Ibid., 97, 100, 102, 110, 111.

81. Ibid., 26–27, 51, 111, 121.

82. Ibid., 91, 94; Confession of Smart Anderson, no date; Confession of William Colcock, July 16, 1822, RGA, GM, SCDAH.

83. Killens, *Trial Record*, 110–11, 117; Statement of Monday Gell, July 20, 1822; Examination of Pompey Lord, August 6, 1822; Second Confession of Bacchus Hammet, July 13, 1822; Statement of Perault Strohecker, August 3, 1822, RGA, GM, SCDAH.

84. Quoted in George Brooks, *Landlords and Strangers: Ecology, Society, and Trade in Western Africa, 1000–1630* (Boulder: Westview, 1993), 97, 99, 103, 106, 111, 116; Thornton, *Africa and Africans*, 293–94. The tsetse fly explains why horses did not become major components in military forces in Lower Guinea or West-central Africa.

85. Killens, *Trial Record*, 163–64.

86. Ibid., 163–64; Pearson, *Designs against Charleston*, 307; Richard L. Roberts, *Warriors, Merchants, and Slaves: The State and the Economy in the Middle Niger Valley, 1700–1914* (Stanford: Stanford University Press, 1987), 48–49, 128, 197; Robin Law, *The Horse in West African History: The Role of the Horse in the Societies of Pre-Colonial West Africa* (New York: Oxford University Press, 1980), 17, 127–30.

87. Terry Alford, *Prince among Slaves* (New York: Harcourt Brace Jovanovich, 1977), xvi, 21–24, 182–83.

88. Wood, *Black Majority*, 30.

89. Ibid., 31.

90. Examination of William Palmer, July 15, 1822. A similar statement is repeated by Smart Anderson. See Confession of Smart Anderson, no date, RGA, GM, SCDAH.

91. Killens, *Trial Record*, 122, 74.

92. Ibid., 84, 74–75.

93. Ibid., 72–73, 38–39.

94. Ibid., 135.

95. Pearson, *Designs against Charleston*, 278. The presiding judges go on to add that George was deemed a "Marplot" by Vesey and others. The term "Marplot" refers to a character in a seventeenth-century English comedy whose stupidity and meddling jeopardizes the success of risky undertakings.

96. Killens, *Trial Record*, 54; Examination of Y*, Belonging to Colonel George W. Cross, no date, RGA, GM, SCDAH.

97. Examination of Robert Harth, June 21, 1822, RGA, GM, SCDAH.

98. Gov. Thomas Bennett to Richard Furman, October 16, 1823 in the Richard Furman Papers (1755–1825), South Caroliniana Library. Emphasis added.

99. Lofton, *Insurrection in South Carolina*, 182–83; *Daily National Intelligencer*, July 6, July 10, 1822; *Charleston Courier*, June 29, August 12, 1822.

100. Lofton, *Insurrection in South Carolina*, 182–83.

101. Carroll, *Slave Insurrections*, 104–5.

102. Ordinance No. 37, August 6, 1822, City of Charleston Ordinance Books (1783–1825), City of Charleston Archives; Confession of Smart Anderson, no date; Second Confession of Bacchus Hammet, 17 July 1822, RGA, GM, SCDAH.

103. Fraser, *Charleston!* 202–3; Lofton, *Insurrection in South Carolina*, 196–197; Carroll, *Slave Insurrections*, 109.

104. Quoted in Lofton, *Insurrection in South Carolina*, 197–98.

105. Thomas Pinckney, "Reflections, Occasioned by the Late Disturbances in Charleston," in *Slave Insurrections: Selected Documents* (Westport, CT: Negro Universities Press, 1970), 6–7.

106. Quoted in Lofton, *Insurrection in South Carolina*, 196; Aptheker, *Slave Revolts*, 275; Henry, *Police Control of the Slaves*, 152–54.

107. Aptheker, *Slave Revolts*, 275; Philip Hamer, "Great Britain, the United States, and the Negro Seamen Acts, 1822–1848," *Journal of Southern History* 1 (1935): 4, 9.

108. Quoted in Alan F. January, "The South Carolina Association: An Agency for Race Control in Antebellum Charleston," *South Carolina Historical Magazine* (1977): 191–201; Fraser, *Charleston!* 203; Hamer, "Negro Seamen Acts," 5, 11–12, 14, 16, 18. For a contemporary assessment of the constitutionality of the 1822 Seamen Act, see "Judicial Opinion," *Nile's Weekly Register* 25 (September 6, 1832): 13–16.

109. Killens, *Trial Record*, 110; Second Confession of Bacchus Hammet, July 13, 1822, RGA, GM, SCDAH.

110. Killens, *Trial Record*, 110; Zechariah 14:2.

111. Gomez, *Exchanging Our Country Marks*, 2–3.

## 6. "I WAS ORDAINED FOR SOME GREAT PURPOSE"

1. Charles C. Jones, *The Religious Instruction of the Negroes in the United States* (1842; reprint, New York: Negro Universities Press, 1969), 128.

2. Blassingame, *The Slave Community*, 110.

3. Henry Clay Bruce, *The New Man: Twenty-nine Years a Slave. Twenty-nine Years a Free Man* (1895; reprint, New York: Negro Universities Press, 1969), 52. Bruce continued, "these conjurors claimed to be able to do almost anything in the line of impossibilities, even to taking a life by the winking of their eye, to make a master be kind to a slave, to prevent him from selling one."

4. W. E. B. Du Bois, *The Souls of Black Folk* (1903; reprint, New York: New American Library, 1982), 216.

5. Eugene Genovese, *Roll, Jordan, Roll: The World the Slaves Made* (New York: Vintage Books, 1976), 222.

6. Stuckey, *Slave Culture*, 50.

7. *South Carolina Gazette*, March 31–April 6, 1733; Wood, *Black Majority*, 289; Easterby, *Journal of the Commons House of Assembly March 28, 1749–March 19, 1750*, 478–80.

8. William Wells Brown, *My Southern Home: The South and Its People* (1880; reprint, New Jersey: Gregg Press, 1968), 70.

9. Charles Ball, *Slavery in the United States: A Narrative of the Life and Adventures of Charles Ball, A Black Man* (1837; reprint, New York: New American Library, Inc., 1969), 165.

10. Douglass, *My Bondage and My Freedom*, 238.

11. Ibid., 239–50.

12. Blassingame, *Slave Community*, 110.

13. Bruce, *New Man*, 53, 55.

14. Quoted in Lawrence Levine, *Black Culture and Black Consciousness: Afro-American Folk Thought From Slavery to Freedom* (New York: Oxford University Press, 1977), 69, 72. These artifacts re-

semble a "conjure's cache" found at an Annapolis, Maryland, house in 1996. Buried sometime during the eighteenth century in the northeast corner of this home, the items in this cache included beads, pins, buttons, a coin with a hole in it, rock crystals, a piece of crab claw, a brass ring and bell, and pieces of bone and glass. This was one of eleven such findings in Virginia and Maryland, which indicates a clear pattern—especially given that the caches were always buried in the northeast corner of rooms or quarters. See John Noble Wilford, "Slave Artifacts under Hearth," *New York Times*, August 27, 1996; Bill Broadway, "Digging up Some Divining Inspiration," *Washington Post*, August 16, 1997; *St. Louis Post-Dispatch*, September 8, 1997.

15. Quoted in Levine, *Black Culture*, 56.

16. Quoted in Levine, *Black Culture*, 56–57.

17. Gilbert Osofsky, *Puttin' on Ole Massa* (New York: Harper and Row, 1969), 70.

18. Henry Bibb, *Narrative in the Life and Adventures of Henry Bibb, An American Slave* (New York, 1849), 26–27.

19. Ibid., 27.

20. Ibid., 25–31.

21. Bruce, *New Man*, 53.

22. Douglass, *My Bondage and My Freedom*, 284–85.

23. Ibid., 289, 290–91.

24. William Wells Brown, "Narrative of William W. Brown: A Fugitive Slave" in Robin Winks et al., eds. *Four Fugitive Slave Narratives* (Menlo Park, CA: Addison-Wesley, 1969), 40–41.

25. Sarah Bradford, *Harriet Tubman: The Moses of Her People* (Bedford, MA: Applewood Books, 1993), 114–15, 92, 73–75.

26. Kenneth Greenberg, ed., *The Confessions of Nat Turner and Related Documents* (Boston: Bedford Books, 1996), 46.

27. William S. Drewry, "The Southampton Insurrection," in John Duff and Peter Mitchell, eds., *The Nat Turner Rebellion: The Historical Event and the Modern Controversy* (New York: Harper and Row, 1971), 81, 82. Drewry did associate Nat Turner with "conjur doctors" due to his mystical powers.

28. Phillips, *American Negro Slavery*, 480.

29. Stampp, *The Peculiar Institution*, 132; Aptheker, *Slave Revolts*, 296.

30. Du Bois, *Souls of Black Folk*, 216.

31. Theophus H. Smith, *Conjuring Culture: Biblical Formations of Black America* (New York: Oxford University Press, 1994), 160.

32. Herbert Aptheker, *Nat Turner's Slave Rebellion* (New York: Grove Press, 1966), 9–10; Stephen Oates, "Children of Darkness," *American Heritage* 24 (October 1973), 42.

33. Aptheker, *Slave Revolts*, 293–94; Henry Irving Tragle, ed., *The Southampton Slave Revolt of 1831: A Compilation of Source Material* (Amherst: University of Massachusetts Press, 1971), 13–16, 175, 234, 237, 239, 243.

34. Aptheker, *Nat Turner's Rebellion*, 27–28.

35. Greenberg, *Confessions*, 44; Aptheker, *Slave Revolts*, 219.

36. Quoted in Oates, "Children of Darkness," 43.

37. Greenberg, *Confessions*, 44.

38. Ibid., 44, 54; Aptheker, *Slave Revolts*, 307–8; Herbert Aptheker, "Maroons Within the Present Limits of the United States," in Richard Price, ed., *Maroon Societies: Rebel Slave Com-*

munities in the Americas (Baltimore: Johns Hopkins University Press, 1996), 158–61; Deborah Shea., ed., "Spreading Terror and Devastation Wherever They Have Been: A Norfolk Woman's Account of the Southampton Slave Insurrection," *The Virginia Magazine of History and Biography* 95 (January 1987), 70n.

39. Greenberg, *Confessions*, 44–46; Aptheker, *Slave Revolts*, 294–95.

40. Greenberg, *Confessions*, 46.

41. Ibid., 48; Aptheker, *Slave Revolts*, 296–97; William Sidney Drewy, "The Southampton Insurrection," in Duff and Mitchell, *The Nat Turner Rebellion*, 82; William Byrd, "Nat Turner's Rebellion," *Magazine of Virginia Genealogy* 36 (Winter 1998): 6; *Raleigh Register*, August 18, 25, 1831; Daniel M. McFarland, "The Great Fear," *Madison College Bulletin: Studies and Research* 22 (1964): 71. There was also a lunar eclipse reported on August 23, 1831.

42. Greenberg, *Confessions*, 48.

43. Aptheker, *Slave Revolts*, 299–300; John Hope Franklin, "Slavery and the Martial South," in John Hope Franklin, ed., *Race and History: Selected Essays, 1938–1988* (Baton Rouge: Louisiana State University Press, 1989), 101.

44. Of his role in the revolt, Gray's Nat remarked that he would soon "atone at the gallows." This statement seems odd considering that Nat Turner pled not guilty to the charges. Greenberg, *Confessions*, 44, 7–9; Byrd, "Nat Turner's Rebellion," 6.

45. Greenberg, *Confessions*, 44.

46. Ibid. About these marks, Gray added "I believe [they] are not at all uncommon, particularly among negroes, as I have seen several with the same. In this case he has either cut them off or they have nearly disappeared." Essentially, the "parcels of excrescences" described by Gray, were abnormal growths of skin or tumors.

47. Greenberg, *Confessions*, 44–45.

48. Puckett, *Folk Beliefs of the Southern Negro*, 199–202.

49. Ibid., 199, 336.

50. Greenberg, *Confessions*, 45.

51. Ibid., 46.

52. Phillips, *American Negro Slavery*, 480; Stampp, *Peculiar Institution*, 132; Aptheker, *Slave Revolts*, 296.

53. Greenberg, *Confessions*, 47.

54. Herskovits, *Myth of the Negro Past*, 232–34; Raboteau, *Slave Religion*, 54, 57–58.

55. Brown, *My Southern Home*, 10, 60, 70, 79–80; Osofsky, *Puttin' on Ole Massa*, 215.

56. Greenberg, *Confessions*, 46.

57. Ibid., 46.

58. Ibid., 47.

59. Ibid., 78, 81; Tragle, *Southampton Revolt*, 92. The strong similarity between the revelations in this article and Nat's confession given thirty-six days later has led a few investigators to suggest that Thomas Gray was the writer of both documents. See Tony Horwitz, "Untrue Confessions," *New Yorker*, December 13, 1999, 88.

60. Greenberg, *Confessions*, 48.

61. Duff and Mitchell, *Nat Turner Rebellion*, 77, 82.

62. Tragle, *Southampton Revolt*, 222.

63. Ibid., 222.

64. Douglass, *My Bondage and My Freedom*, 238, 284–85.

65. Bradford, *Harriet Tubman*, 92–93. Three years before the outbreak of the Civil War, Bradford related the following story: "While staying with the Rev. Henry Highland Garnet in New York, a vision came to her in the night . . . Whether a dream, or one of those glimpses into the future, which sometimes seem to have been granted to her, no one can say, but the effect upon her was remarkable . . . The dream or vision filled her soul, and physical needs were forgotten." After Lincoln's Emancipation Proclamation in 1863, Bradford added "Harriet was continually asked, 'Why do you not join with the rest in their rejoicing !' 'Oh,' she answered, 'I had my jubilee three years ago. I rejoiced all I could den; I can't rejoice no more.'"

66. Bradford, *Harriet Tubman*, 98. Bradford claimed "Harriet had acquired quite a reputation for her skill in curing [dysentery], by a medicine which she prepared from roots which grew near the waters which gave the disease."

67. Ibid., 73–76, 114. Bradford herself would often be a witness to Harriet Tubman's "direct intercourse with heaven." This spiritual contact would protect her from capture during her missions in the South. Bradford added "she several times was on the point of being taken, but always escaped by her quick wit, or by 'warnings' from Heaven . . . She is the most shrewd and practical person in the world, yet she is a firm believer in omens, dreams, and warnings."

68. Gomez, *Exchanging Our Country Marks*, 5.

69. Greenberg, *Confessions*, 54.

70. McFarland, "The Great Fear," 72–75; *Raleigh Register*, September 15, October 6, November 3, 1831; *North Carolina Free Press* (Tarborough), September 20, 27, 1831; *Carolina Observer* (Fayetteville), September 14, 21, 28, 1831. While the existence of this North Carolina plot has been questioned, as many as eighteen slaves were executed or killed in connection to the alleged conspiracy.

71. Aptheker, *Slave Revolts*, 304–5.

CODA

1. Gomez, *Exchanging Our Country Marks*, 5, 186–90.

2. For examples of this argument, see E. Franklin Frazier, *The Negro Family in the United States* (Chicago: University of Chicago Press, 1939); Stampp, *The Peculiar Institution*; Elkins, *Slavery*; Mintz and Price, *The Birth of African-American Culture*. "Creolization" is defined here as the acclimatizing and acculturating process that transformed "Africans" into "African-Americans." Originally a linguistic term, it now encompasses a range of cultural forms (e.g., food, music, and dance).

3. Gomez, *Exchanging Our Country Marks*, 187.

4. Stuckey, *Going through the Storm*, 4.

5. Levine, *Black Culture*, 82.

6. Ibid.

7. Levine, *Black Culture*, 112–15; For examples of the "traditional" interpretation of Brer Rabbit, see Abigail H. Christensen, *Afro-American Folk Lore Told Round Cabin Fires on the Sea Islands of South Carolina* (New York: Negro University Press, 1892), 101–3; Joel Chandler Harris, *Uncle Remus: His Songs and Sayings* (1880; reprint, New York: Penguin, 1982), xiv; Joel Chandler Harris,

*Nights with Uncle Remus* (Boston: Houghton Mifflin, 1883), 330; William Faulkner, *The Days When the Animals Talked: Black-American Folklore and How They Came to Be* (Trenton: Africa World Press, Inc., 1993), 153, 74.

8. Christensen, *Afro-American Folk Lore*, 1, 3, xi.

9. Faulkner, *Days When the Animals Talked*, 152–53.

10. Levine, *Black Culture*, 114.

11. Ibid., 114–18.

12. Faulkner, *Days When the Animals Talked*, 115–21, 168–77, 178–86, 89–94, 99–101.

13. Edward C. L. Adams, *Tales of the Congaree* (Chapel Hill: Univeristy of North Carolina Press, 1987), 240–41.

14. Christensen, *Afro-American Folk Lore*, 23–25, 62–72.

15. Levine, *Black Culture*, 117. Emphasis added.

16. Christensen, *Afro-American Folk Lore*, 30–32.

17. Ibid., 26–29, 32–35.

18. Levine, *Black Culture*, 118.

19. Ibid., 407–20.

20. See John Roberts, *From Trickster to Badman: The Black Folk Hero in Slavery and Freedom* (Philadelphia: University of Pennsylvania Press, 1989), 171–220.

21. Faulkner, *Days When the Animals Talked*, 152.

22. Ibid., 153.

23. Thornton, *Africa and Africans*, 82–85, 91, 94, 103–6, 123; Claude Meillassoux, *The Anthropology of Slavery: The Womb of Iron and Gold* (Chicago: University of Chicago Press, 1991), 35–36, 72, 171–72, 229; David Eltis, *The Rise of African Slavery in the Americas* (Cambridge: Cambridge University Press, 2000), 109–10; Miller, *Way of Death*, 51–61; 96, 110–22, 204–5.

24. Thornton, *Africa and Africans*, 82–85; Meillassoux, *Anthropology of Slavery*, 35–36, 229.

25. Suzanne Preston Blier, *African Vodun: Art, Psychology, and Power* (Chicago, University of Chicago Press, 1995), 1, 4–6, 48–54.

26. Ibid., 11.

27. Ibid., 11–13.

28. William Bascom, *African Folktales in the New World* (Bloomington: Indiana University Press, 1992), v; Susan Feldmann, *African Myths and Tales* (New York: Dell, 1963), 15; Roberts, *Trickster to Badman*, 23.

29. Roberts, *Trickster to Badman*, 23–24. Roberts argues that since Africans generally lived at subsistence level, the concern over food found in African folklore was obviously a reflection of environmental and social conditions. He adds "the technology of agriculture and the environment throughout much of black Africa has not allowed for the production of large crops or the accumulation and storage of large reserves." These observations do not reflect historical realities in the precolonial era, and his generalizations regarding the scarcity of food undermine an otherwise intriguing and effective argument about African folklore. That many Atlantic West Africans came from surplus-producing agricultural societies is what made them so attractive to Europeans as a labor force in the first place.

30. Eugene Genovese essentially argues that a "protonational" and prepolitical slave consciousness, evidenced by the acceptance of paternalism by the masses of enslaved African

Americans, allowed them to acquiesce to the hegemony of white masters. Genovese, *Roll, Jordan, Roll*, 598, 658–59.

31. *Drums and Shadows*, 18.

32. Ibid., 17.

33. Ibid., 108.

34. Michael Gomez links the flying African tales to particular Igbo spiritual understandings. While his case is well stated, it should be remembered that the Igbo and others from Biafra represented only 11.3 percent of all Africans from identifiable ports sent to South Carolina between 1701 and 1800. This may place into question the claim that the flying African tales are a particularly Igbo phenomenon. See Gomez, *Exchanging Our Country Marks*, 118–20; Eltis et al., *The Trans-Atlantic Slave Trade*.

35. *Drums and Shadows*, 151.

36. Ibid., 7.

37. Ibid., 145.

38. Ibid., 185.

39. Basden, *Among the Ibos of Nigeria*, 119–20.

40. Potkay and Burr, eds., *Black Atlantic Writers*, 173.

41. Ball, *Slavery in the United States*, 219.

42. According to Gomez the Bambara, a Mande-speaking group from Senegambia, also believed in reincarnation. This belief was shared by many other non-Muslim Mande-speakers. Gomez, *Exchanging Our Country Marks*, 118–20, 49, 86–87.

43. Y. S. Nathanson, "Negro Minstrelsey, Ancient and Modern," *Putnam's Monthly* 5 (January 1855): 72–79, cited in Bruce Jackson, ed., *The Negro and His Folklore in Nineteenth-Century Periodicals* (Austin: American Folklore Society, 1967), 39–41.

44. Ibid.

45. Quoted in Stuckey, *Going through the Storm*, 11.

# Bibliography

UNPUBLISHED SOURCES

*New York*

**New York City Municipal Archives**

Court of General Sessions Minutes, February 1683–August 1760, Vol. 1–6, MN #10001, Roll #1

Minute Book of the Court of General Sessions, 1705–1714

Minutes of the Court of General and Quarter Sessions of the Peace, 1683–1742, Reel #1

Minutes of the Court of Quarter and General Sessions, begun August 7th Anno 1694

Minutes of the Supreme Court of Judicature, Book 2, June 6, 1710–June 5, 1714

Supreme Court Minute Books, October 1691–October 23, 1739, Reel #30

**New-York Historical Society, New York City**

"Coroner's Inquisition and Jury Finding on the Death of William Asht, April 9, 1712," Misc. Mss., Box 41

"Coroner's Inquisition and Jury Finding on the Death of Augustus Grasset, April 9, 1712," Misc. Mss., Box 4, #13

[Daniel] Horsmanden Papers, 1714–1747

New-York Historical Society Collections, Revolutionary Papers

"Trials of Slaves at the City Hall, NY," in [Daniel] Parish Transcripts of Material on Slavery in the Public Record Office in London (1690–1750), Mss. Collection, Folder 149, F. 18

**Library of the Association of the Bar of the City of New York**

Minutes of the Circuit Court of Oyer and Terminer and Gaol Delivery, 1721–1749

*South Carolina*

**South Caroliniana Library, University of South Carolina, Columbia**

Christopher Fitzsimmons Letterbook

Richard Furman Papers, 1755–1825

**South Carolina Department of Archives and History, Columbia**
Denmark Vesey House File
Executive Letterbook, 1800–1822
Grand Jury Presentments, 1822
His Majesty's Upper House Council Journals, 1737–1741
Letters of Administration, 1797–1803
Records in the British Public Records Office Relating to South Carolina
Records of the General Assembly, Governor's Messages, 1814–1822
Records of the General Assembly, Petitions, 1804–1822
Senate Journals, 1800–1822
South Carolina Treasury Records, Journal C, 1814–1824
South Carolina Treasury Rolls, Ledger B

**South Carolina Historical Society, Charleston**
[Mary L.] Beach Letters
Langdon Cheves Papers
Alexander Garden Papers
Letters of an American Traveller
Letter Book of Robert Pringle
Henry Ravenel Papers
Denmark Vesey File
Elizabeth Yates Papers

**Charleston Library Society**
Robert Wilson Papers

**City of Charleston Archives**
City Ordinances, 1783–1825

*Virginia*
**Library of Virginia, Richmond**
Condemned Slaves, Court Orders and Valuations, 1796–1805
Council Journals, 1795, 1799–1801
Executive Communications, Letterbook, 1800, 1831–1833
Executive Communications to the Legislature, Box 24
Executive Papers, 1792–1793, 1800–1802
Executive Papers, Governor's Letterbook, 1783, 1800–1803
Executive Papers, Letters Received, Negro Insurrections, Boxes 114–115
Executive Papers, Letters Received, 1782, 1800
Executive Letterbook, 1792–1802, 1830–1834

Free Negro and Slave Letterbook of 1831
Gabriel's Insurrection, Military Papers
Henrico County Order Book, 1799–1801
Insurrection Records, 1800–1801
Journal of the Governor's Council, 1838–1831
Journal of the House of Delegates, 1800–1801, 1830–1831
Journal of the Senate of Virginia, 1800
Register of Certificates and Warrants Issued for Slaves Executed, 1783–1814
Southampton County Court Order Book
Southampton County Minute Book, 1830–1835
Southampton County Superior Court Orders, 1832
Westmoreland County Court Order Book, 1676–1689

**Virginia Historical Society, Richmond**
John James Allen Family Papers, 1820–1851
Francis Baylor Papers
Carter Berkeley Papers
Blow Family Papers
Byrd Family Papers, 1805–1871
Carrington Family Papers, 1755–1839
Daniel Cobb Diary, 1852–1872
Gabriel's Insurrection, Vertical File
Hugh Blair Grigbsy Diary
Harrison Family Papers, 1790–1837
Holladay Family Papers
James Monroe Papers
Preston Family Papers
William Price Palmer Scrapbook, 1821–1896
James Scott Papers

### PRINTED PRIMARY SOURCES

Ball, Charles. *Slavery in the United States: A Narrative of the Life and Adventures of Charles Ball, A Black Man*. New York: New American Library, 1969.

Bergh, Albert E., ed. *The Writings of Thomas Jefferson*. Washington, DC: Thomas Jefferson Memorial Association, 1905.

Bibb, Henry. *Narrative in the Life and Adventures of Henry Bibb, An American Slave*. New York: Scribner and Associates, 1849.

Blassingame, John, ed. *Slave Testimony: Two Centuries of Letters, Speeches, Interviews, and Autobiographies*. Baton Rouge: Louisiana State University Press, 1977.

Bosman, Willem. *A New and Accurate Description of the Coast of Guinea, Divided into the Gold, the Slave, and the Ivory Coasts*. London: J. Knapton, D. Midwinter, B. Lintot, G. Strahan, J. Rand, E. Bell, 1721.

Brown, William Wells. *My Southern Home: The South and Its People*. Newark: Gregg Press, 1968.

Bruce, Henry Clay. *The New Man: Twenty-nine Years a Slave. Twenty-Nine Years a Free Man*. New York: Negro Universities Press, 1969.

Candler, Allen, ed. *The Colonial Records of the State of Georgia*, Vol. IV. Atlanta: Franklin Printing and Publishing Company, 1907.

Candler, Allen, and William Northern, eds. *The Colonial Records of the State of Georgia*. Atlanta: Chas P. Byrd, State Printer, 1913.

*Collections of the New-York Historical Society for the Year 1918: The Letters and Papers of Cadwallader Colden*. Vol. 2. New York: New-York Historical Society, 1918.

"Constables Bill: Capital Punishment in 1740." *The Magazine of American History with Notes and Queries* 25 (1891): 85–86.

Cooper, Thomas, ed. *The Statutes at Large of South Carolina*. 5 vols. Columbia: A. S. Johnson, 1836–39.

Davis, Thomas J., ed. *The New York Conspiracy, by Daniel Horsmanden*. Boston: Beacon Press, 1971.

Donnan, Elizabeth, ed. "Papers of James A. Bayard 1796–1815." *Annual Report of the American Historical Association*. Vols. 1–2. Washington, DC: Government Printing Office, 1913.

———, ed. *Documents Illustrative of the History of the Slave Trade to America*. Vols. 1–3. Washington, DC: Carnegie Institution of Washington, 1931–1933.

Douglass, Frederick. *Life and Times of Frederick Douglass*. New York: Collier Books, 1962.

———. *Narrative of the Life of Frederick Douglass*. New York: New American Library, 1968.

———. *My Bondage and My Freedom*. New York: Dover, 1969.

Edgar, Walter B., ed. *The Letterbook of Robert Pringle*, Vol. 1: April 2, 1737–September 25, 1742. Columbia: University of South Carolina Press, 1972.

Easterby, J. H., ed. *The Colonial Records of South Carolina: The Journal of the Commons House of Assembly, September 12, 1739–March 26, 1741*. Columbia: Historical Commission of South Carolina, 1952.

Flournoy, H. W., ed. *Calendar of Virginia State Papers and other Manuscripts*. Vols. 7–10. Richmond: Virginia State Library, 1890.

Gates, Henry Louis, ed. *The Classic Slave Narratives*. New York: Penguin Books, 1987.

Georgia Writers' Project. *Drums and Shadows: Survival Studies among the Coastal Negroes*. Athens: University of Georgia Press, 1940.

Greenberg, Kenneth, ed. *The Confessions of Nat Turner and Related Documents*. Boston: Bedford Books, 1996.

Hair, P. E. H., Adam Jones, and Robin Law, eds. *Barbot on Guinea: The Writings of Jean Barboton West Africa, 1678–1712*. Vols. 1–2. London: Hakluyt Society, 1992.

Headlam, Cecil, ed. *Calendar of State Papers, Colonial Series, America and the West Indies*. London: His Majesty's Stationery Office, 1910.

Hewatt, Alexander. *An Historical Account of the Rise and Progress of the Colonies of South Carolina and Georgia*. Vol. 2. London: St. Paul's Church-Yard, 1779.

Higginson, Thomas Wentworth. *Army Life in a Black Regiment*. New York: Collier Books, 1962.

Hodges, Graham, and Alan Brown, eds. *"Pretends to Be Free": Runaway Slave Advertisements from Colonial and Revolutionary New York and New Jersey*. New York: Garland, 1994.

Holland, Edward Clifford. *A Refutation of the Calumnies Circulated against the Southern & Western States Respecting the Institution and Existence of Slavery among Them*. New York: Negro University Press, 1969.

Humphreys, David. *An Account of the Endeavours Used by the Society for the Propagation of the Gospel in Foreign Parts, to Instruct the Negroe Slaves in New York. Together with Two of Bp. Gibson's Letters on That Subject. Being an Extract from Dr. Humphrey's Historical Account of the Incorporated Society for the Propagation of the Gospel in Foreign Parts, from Its Foundation to the Year 1728*. London: Society for the Propagation of the Gospel in Foreign Parts, 1830.

Hurmence, Belinda, ed. *Before Freedom, When I Just Can Remember: Twenty-Seven Oral Histories of Former South Carolina Slaves*. Winston-Salem: J. F. Blair, 1996.

Isichei, Elizabeth. *Igbo Worlds: An Anthology of Oral Histories and Historical Descriptions*. Philadelphia: Institute for the Study of Human Issues, 1978.

Jameson, J. Franklin, ed. *Narratives of New Netherland, 1609–1664*. New York: Charles Scribner's Sons, 1909.

Jones, Charles C. *The Religious Instruction of the Negroes in the United States*. New York: Negro Universities Press, 1969.

Katz, William Loren, ed. *Flight from the Devil: Six Slave Narratives*. Trenton: Africa World Press, 1996.

Killens, John O., ed. *The Trial Record of Denmark Vesey*. Boston: Beacon Press, 1970.

Kingsley, Zaphaniah. *A Treatise on the Patriarchal, or Co-operative System of Society as It Exists in Some Governments and Colonies in America, and in the United States, under the Name of Slavery with Its Necessity and Advantages*. Freeport, NY: Books for Libraries Press, 1970.

Klingberg, Frank J., ed. *The Carolina Chronicle of Dr. Francis Le Jau*. Berkeley: University of California Press, 1956.

Long, Edward. *The History of Jamaica, or General Survey of the Ancient and Modern State of That Island with Reflections on Its Situations, Settlements, Inhabitants, Climate, Products, Commerce, Laws and Government.* Vols. 1–3. New ed. London: Frank Cass, 1970.

McCord, David, ed. *The Statutes at Large of South Carolina.* Vol. 7. Columbia: A. S. Johnson, 1840.

Meaders, Daniel, ed. *Advertisements for Runaway Slaves in Virginia, 1801–1820.* New York: Garland, 1997.

*Minutes of the Common Council of the City of New York, 1675–1776.* Vols. 3–5. New York: Dodd, Mead and Company, 1905.

O'Callaghan, E. B., ed. *Laws of His Majesties Colony of New York As They Were Enacted by the Governor, Council and General Assembly in Divers Sessions, the First of Which Began April 9th, 1691.* Albany: Weed, Parsons, and Company, 1849.

———, ed. *Documents Relative to the Colonial History of the State of New York.* Vols. 1–4. Albany: Weed, Parsons, and Company, 1853–1858.

———, ed. *Calendar of Historical Manuscripts in the Office of the Secretary of State.* Vols. 1–2. Albany: Weed, Parsons, and Company, 1865–1866.

———, ed. *Voyage of the Slavers St. John and Arms of Amsterdam.* Albany: J. Munsell, 1867.

Osofsky, Gilbert, ed. *Puttin' on Ole Massa.* New York: Harper and Row, 1969.

Parker, Freddie L., ed. *Stealing a Little Freedom: Advertisements for Slave Runaways in North Carolina, 1791–1849.* New York: Garland, 1994.

Pearson, Edward, ed. *Designs against Charleston: The Trial Record of the Denmark Vesey Slave Conspiracy of 1822.* Chapel Hill: University of North Carolina Press, 1999.

Potkay, Adam, and Sandra Burr, eds. *Black Atlantic Writers of the Eighteenth Century.* New York: St. Martin's Press, 1995.

Price, Richard, ed. *To Slay the Hydra: Dutch Colonial Perspectives on the Saramaka Wars.* Ann Arbor: Karoma Press, 1983.

Rogers, George, Jr., ed. *The Papers of Henry Laurens.* Vol. 2. Columbia: University of South Carolina Press, 1968.

Sharpe, John. "The Negro Plot of 1712." *The New York Genealogical and Biographical Record.* 21 (1890): 162–63.

———. "Journal of Reverend Sharpe." *The Pennsylvania Magazine* 40 (1916): 412–25.

Shea, Deborah Jean. "'Spreading Terror and Devastation Wherever They Have Been': A Norfolk Woman's Account of the Southampton Slave Insurrection." *Virginia Magazine of History and Biography* 95 (1987): 65–74.

South Carolina General Assembly. *The Journal of the Commons House of Assembly for the Four Sessions of 1693.* Columbia: Historical Commission of South Carolina, 1907.

*South-Carolina Historical Society Collections.* Charleston: South-Carolina Historical Society, 1858.

Starobin, Robert S., ed. *Denmark Vesey: The Slave Conspiracy of 1822*. Englewood Cliffs, NJ: Prentice-Hall, 1970.

Stokes, Isaac Newton Phelps, ed. *The Iconography of Manhattan Island, 1498–1909*. Vol. 4. New York: Arno, 1967.

Tragle, Henry Irving, ed. *The Southampton Slave Revolt of 1831: A Compilation of Source Material*. Amherst: University of Massachusetts Press, 1971.

Uhlendorf, Bernhard A., trans. and ed. *The Siege of Charleston with an Account of the Province of South Carolina: Diaries and Letters of Hessian Officers from the von Jungkenn Papers in the William L. Clements Library*. Ann Arbor: University of Michigan Press, 1938.

Valentine, David, ed. *Manual of the Common Council of New York*. New York: D.T. Valentine, 1865.

Warner, Samuel. *Authentic and Impartial Narrative of the Tragic Scene Which Was Witnessed in Southampton County (Virginia) on Monday the 22d of August Last, When Fifty-Five of Its Inhabitants (Mostly Women and Children) Were Inhumanly Massacred by the Blacks! Communicated by Those Who Were Eye Witnesses*. New York: Warner and West, 1831.

Wilson, James Grant, ed. *The Memorial History of the City of New-York: From Its First Settlement to the Year 1892*. Vol. 2. New York: New York History Company, 1892.

Windley, Lathan, ed. *Runaway Slave Advertisements: A Documentary History from the 1730s to 1790, Vol. 1: Virginia and North Carolina*. Westport, CT: Greenwood Press, 1983.

———. *Runaway Slave Advertisements: A Documentary History from the 1730s to 1790, Vol. 2: Maryland*. Westport, CT: Greenwood Press, 1983.

———. *Runaway Slave Advertisements: A Documentary History from the 1730s to 1790, Vol. 3: South Carolina*. Westport, CT: Greenwood Press, 1983.

———. *Runaway Slave Advertisements: A Documentary History from the 1730s to 1790, Vol. 4: Georgia*. Westport, CT: Greenwood Press, 1983.

Winks, Robin, ed. *Four Fugitive Slave Narratives*. Menlo Park, CA: Addison-Wesley, 1969.

Yetman, Norman, ed. *Life under the 'Peculiar Institution': Selections from the Slave Narrative Collection*. New York: Holt, Rinehart and Winston, Inc., 1970.

## Selected Secondary Materials

Abzug, Robert, and Stephen Maizlish, eds. *New Perspectives on Race and Slavery in America: Essays in Honor of Kenneth M. Stampp*. Lexington: University Press of Kentucky, 1986.

Adams, Edward C. L. *Tales of the Congaree*. Chapel Hill: University of North Carolina Press, 1987.

Agbo, Adolph. *Values of Adinkra Symbols*. Kumasi, Ghana: Ebony Designs and Publications, 1999.

Agorsah, E. Kofi. "Archaeology and Resistance History in the Caribbean." *African Archaeological Review* 11 (1993): 175–95.

Alford, Terry. *Prince among Slaves*. New York: Harcourt Brace Jovanovich, 1977.

Almeida, Bira. *Capoeira: A Brazilian Art Form*. Berkeley: North Atlantic Books, 1986.

Anim, N. O. *Sub-Sahara Africa Forum 9: Names as a Factor in Cultural Identity among the Akan, Ga, and Ewe Tribes of Ghana*. Pretoria, South Africa: Unit for Development Analysis, 1991.

Aptheker, Herbert. *To Be Free: Pioneering Studies in Afro-American History*. New York: Citadel Press, 1948.

———. *Nat Turner's Slave Rebellion*. New York: Grove, 1966.

———. *American Negro Slave Revolts*. New York: International Publishers, 1993.

———. "Maroons within the Present Limits of the United States." In *Maroon Societies: Rebel Communities in the Americas*, Richard Price, ed., 151–68. Baltimore: Johns Hopkins University Press, 1996.

Arinze, Francis. *Sacrifice in Ibo Religion*. Ibadan: Ibadan University Press, 1970.

Barnes, Sandra, ed. *Africa's Ogun: Old World and New*. Bloomington: Indiana University Press, 1997.

Bascom, William. *African Folktales in the New World*. Bloomington: Indiana University Press, 1992.

Basden, G.T. *Among the Ibos of Nigeria*. London: Frank Cass, 1966.

Beckwith, Martha Warren. *Black Roadways: A Study of Jamaican Folk Life*. New York: Negro Universities Press, 1969.

———. *Jamaica Anansi Stories*. New York: G. E. Stechert, 1969.

Bell, Hesketh. *Obeah: Witchcraft in the West Indies*. Westport, CT: Negro Universities Press, 1970.

Berlin, Ira. "After Nat Turner: A Letter from the North." *Journal of Negro History* 55 (1970): 144–51.

———. *Slaves without Masters: The Free Negro in the Antebellum South*. New York: Vintage Books, 1974.

Blakey, Michael. "The New York Burial Ground Project: An Examination of Enslaved Lives, a Construction of Ancestral Ties." *Transforming Archaeology: Journal of the Association of Black Anthropologists* 7 (1998): 53–58.

———. "The Study of New York's African Burial Ground." In *African Roots/American Cultures: Africa in the Creation of the Americas*, Sheila Walker, ed., 222–31. New York: Rowman and Littlefield, 2001.

Blassingame, John. *The Slave Community: Plantation Life in the Antebellum South*. New York: Oxford University Press, 1972.

Blier, Suzanne Preston. *African Vodun: Art, Psychology, and Power*. Chicago: University of Chicago Press, 1995.

Bontemps, Arna. *Black Thunder: Gabriel's Revolt, Virginia 1800*. New York: Macmillan, 1936.

Booth, Mary. *History of the City of New York*. Vol. 1. New York: W. R. C. Clark, 1867.

Boxer, Charles R. *The Dutch Seaborne Empire, 1600–1800.* New York: Oxford University Press, 1965.

Bradford, Sarah. *Harriet Tubman: The Moses of Her People.* Bedford, MA: Applewood Books, 1993.

Brawley, Benjamin. *A Social History of the Negro, Being a History of the Negro Problem in the United States.* New York: Macmillan, 1921.

Breen, T. H. *Shaping Southern Society: The Colonial Experience.* New York: Oxford University Press, 1976.

Bridenbaugh, Carl. *Cities in the Wilderness: The First Century of Urban Life in America, 1625–1742.* New York: Alfred A. Knopf, 1968.

Brooks, George. *Landlords and Strangers: Ecology, Society, and Trade in Western Africa, 1000–1630.* Boulder: Westview, 1993.

Burnard, Trevor, and Kenneth Morgan. "The Dynamics of the Slave Market and Slave Purchasing Patterns in Jamaica, 1655–1788." *William and Mary Quarterly,* 3rd ser., 58 (2001): 205–28

Butler, Jon. *Awash in a Sea of Faith: Christianizing the American People.* Cambridge, MA: Harvard University Press, 1990.

Byrd, William L. "Nat Turner's Rebellion." *Magazine of Virginia Genealogy.* 36 (1998): 5–7.

Capoeira, Nestor. *The Little Capoeira Book.* Berkeley: North Atlantic Books, 1995.

———. *Capoeira: Roots of the Dance-Fight-Game.* Berkeley: North Atlantic Books, 2002.

Carney, Judith Ann. *Black Rice: The African Origins of Rice Cultivation in the Americas.* Cambridge, MA: Harvard University Press, 2001.

Carretta, Vincent. "Olaudah Equiano or Gustavus Vassa? New Light on an Eighteenth-Century Question of Identity." *Slavery and Abolition* 20 (1999): 96–105.

Carroll, Joseph Cephas. *Slave Insurrections in the United States, 1800–1865.* New York: Negro Universities Press, 1968.

Chambers, Douglas B. "'My Own Nation': Igbo Exiles in the Diaspora." *Slavery and Abolition* 18 (1997): 72–97.

———. "Ethnicity in the Diaspora: The Slave-Trade and the Creation of African 'Nations' in the Americas." *Slavery and Abolition* 22 (2001): 25–39.

———. "The Significance of Igbo in the Bight of Biafra Slave-Trade: A Rejoinder to Northrup's 'Myth Igbo.'" *Slavery and Abolition* 23 (2002): 101–20.

Christensen, Abigail H. *Afro-American Folk Lore Told Round Cabin Fires on the Sea Islands of South Carolina.* New York: Negro University Press, 1892.

Clarke, T. Wood. "Negro Plot of 1741." *New York History Quarterly* 25 (1944): 167–81.

Clowse, Converse D. *Economic Beginnings in Colonial South Carolina, 1670–1730.* Columbia: University of South Carolina Press, 1971.

Coffin, Joshua. *An Account of Some Principal Slave Insurrections.* New York: American Anti-Slavery Society, 1860.

Cohen, David Steven. *The Dutch-American Farm.* New York: New York University Press, 1992.

Cohen, Hennig, "Slave Names in Colonial South Carolina." *American Speech* 27 (1952): 102-107.

Courlander, Harold. *Tales of Yoruba Gods and Heroes: Myths, Legends and Heroic Tales of the Yoruba People of West Africa.* New York: Crown, 1973.

Craton, Michael. *Testing the Chains: Resistance to Slavery in the British West Indies.* Ithaca: Cornell University Press, 1982.

Creel, Margaret Washington. *"A Peculiar People": Slave Religion and Community-Culture among the Gullahs.* New York: New York University Press, 1988.

Cromwell, John W. "The Aftermath of Nat Turner's Insurrection." *Journal of Negro History* 5 (1920): 208–34.

Curtin, Philip. *Two Jamaicas: The Role of Ideas in a Tropical Colony, 1830–1865.* Westport, CT: Greenwood Press, 1955.

———. *The Atlantic Slave Trade: A Census.* Madison: University of Wisconsin Press, 1969.

Dabney, Virginius. "Gabriel's Insurrection." *American History Illustrated* 11 (1976): 24–32.

Dalby, David. "Ashanti Survivals in the Language and Traditions of the Windward Maroons of Jamaica." *African Language Studies* 12 (1971): 31–51.

———. "Black through White: Patterns of Communication." Bloomington, IN: African Studies Program, 1978.

Davidson, Basil. *The African Slave Trade.* Boston: Little, Brown, 1980.

Davies, K.G. *The Royal African Company.* New York: Atheneum, 1970.

Davis, Thomas J. "The New York Slave Conspiracy of 1741 as Black Protest." *Journal of Negro History* 56 (1971): 17–30.

———. "Slavery in Colonial New York City." Ph.D. diss., Columbia University, 1974.

———. *A Rumor of Revolt: The "Great Negro Plot" in Colonial New York.* Amherst: University of Massachusetts Press, 1985.

———. "Conspiracy and Credibility: Look Who's Talking, about What—Law Talk and Loose Talk." *William and Mary Quarterly,* 3rd ser., 59 (2002): 167–74.

DeCamp, David. "African Day-Names in Jamaica." *Language* 43 (1967): 139–49.

DeCorse, Christopher. "Culture Contact, Continuity and Change on the Gold Coast, A.D. 1400–1900." *African Archaeological Review* 10 (1992): 163–96.

———. *An Archaeology of Elmina: Africans and Europeans on the Gold Coast, 1400–1900.* Washington, DC: Smithsonian Institution Press, 2001.

Desch, Thomas Obi. "Knocking and Kicking, Ladya, and Capoeira: Resistance and Religion in the African Martial Arts of the Black Atlantic." M.A. thesis, University of California Los Angeles, 1994.

———. "History of the Martial Arts of N'golo and Its Derivatives as a Focal Point of the Social History of Southern Angola and the African Diaspora." Ph.D. diss., University of California Los Angeles, 2000.

———. "Combat and the Crossing of the Kalunga." In *Central African and Cultural Transformations in the American Diaspora*, Linda M. Heywood, ed., 353–70. Cambridge: Cambridge University Press, 2002.

Dodson, Howard, Christopher Moore, and Robert Yancy. *The Black New Yorkers: The Schomburg Illustrated Chronology*. New York: John Wiley and Sons, 2000.

Dolphyne, Florence Abena. *A Comprehensive Course in Twi (Asante) for the Non-Twi Learner*. Accra: Ghana University Press, 1996.

Donnan, Elizabeth. "The Slave Trade into South Carolina before the Revolution." *American Historical Review* 33 (1927): 804–28.

Du Bois, W. E. B. *The Souls of Black Folk*. New York: New American Library, 1982.

Duff, John, and Peter Mitchell, eds. *The Nat Turner Rebellion: The Historical Event and the Modern Controversy*. New York: Harper and Row Publishers, 1971.

Duffy, James. *Portuguese Africa*. Cambridge, MA: Harvard University Press, 1961.

Dunn, Richard S. *Sugar and Slaves: The Rise of the Planter Class in the English West Indies, 1624–1713*. Chapel Hill: University of North Carolina Press, 1972.

Earle, Alice Morse. *Colonial Days in Old New York*. New York: Charles Scribner's Sons, 1896.

Edgar, Walter. *South Carolina: A History*. Columbia: University of South Carolina Press, 1998.

Egerton, Douglas. *Gabriel's Rebellion: The Virginia Slave Conspiracies of 1800 and 1802*. Chapel Hill: University of North Carolina Press, 1993.

———. "'Why They Did Not Preach Up This Thing': Denmark Vesey and Revolutionary Theology." *South Carolina Historical Magazine* 100 (1999): 298–318.

———. *He Shall Go Out Free: The Lives of Denmark Vesey*. Madison: Madison House, 1999.

———. "Forgetting Denmark Vesey; or, Oliver Stone Meets Richard Wade." *William and Mary Quarterly*, 3rd ser., 59 (2002): 143–52.

Elkins, Stanley. *Slavery: A Problem in American Institutional and Intellectual Life*. Chicago: University of Chicago Press, 1959.

Eltis, David. *The Rise of African Slavery in the Americas*. Cambridge: Cambridge University Press, 2000.

———. "The Volume and Structure of the Transatlantic Slave Trade: A Reassessment," *William and Mary Quarterly*, 3rd ser., 58 (2001): 17–46.

Eltis, David, Stephen Behrendt, David Richardson, and Herbert Klein, eds., *The Trans-Atlantic Slave Trade: A Database on CD-ROM*. Cambridge: Cambridge University Press, 1999.

Faso, Kwaku Amoako-Attah. *Handicrafts of Ghana*. Kumasi, Ghana: Centre for National Culture, 2001.

Faulkner, William J. *The Days When the Animals Talked*. Trenton: Africa World Press, 1993.

Feldmann, Susan. *African Myths and Tales*. New York: Dell, 1963.

Ferguson, Leland. *Uncommon Ground: Archaeology and Early African America, 1650–1800*. Washington, DC: Smithsonian Institution Press, 1992.

Fett, Sharla M. *Working Cures: Healing, Health, and Power on Southern Slave Plantations*. Chapel Hill: University of North Carolina Press, 2002.

Finkelman, Paul, ed. *Rebellions, Resistance, and Runaways within the South*. New York: Garland, 1989.

Fisher, Robert. *West African Traditions: Focus on the Akan of Ghana*. Maryknoll, NY: Orbis Books, 1998.

Flanders, Ralph Betts. *Plantation Slavery in Georgia*. Cos Cob, CT: John E. Edwards, 1967.

Foote, Thelma Wills. "'Some Hard Usage': The New York City Slave Revolt." *New York Folklore* 28 (2001): 147–59.

Franklin, John Hope, ed. *Race and History: Selected Essays, 1938–1988*. Baton Rouge: Louisiana State University Press, 1989.

Fraser, Walter. *Charleston! Charleston! The History of a Southern City*. Columbia: University of South Carolina Press, 1989.

Frazier, E. Franklin. *The Negro Family in the United States*. Chicago: University of Chicago Press, 1939.

Freehling, William. *Prelude to Civil War: The Nullification Controversy in South Carolina, 1816–1836*. New York: Oxford University Press, 1965.

———. "Denmark Vesey's Peculiar Reality." In *New Perspectives on Race and Slavery in America: Essays in Honor of Kenneth M. Stampp*, Robert Abzug and Stephen Maizlish, eds., 25–47. Lexington: University Press of Kentucky, 1986.

Frey, Sylvia. *Water from the Rock: Black Resistance in a Revolutionary Age*. Princeton: Princeton University Press, 1991.

Fynn, J. K. *Asante and Its Neighbours, 1700–1807*. London: Longman, 1971.

Gaspar, David Barry. "The Antigua Slave Conspiracy of 1736: A Case Study of the Origins of Collective Resistance." *William and Mary Quarterly*, 3rd ser., 35 (1978): 308–23.

———. *Bondsmen and Rebels: A Study of Master-Slave Relations in Antigua*. Durham: Duke University Press, 1985.

Geggus, David, ed. *The Impact of the Haitian Revolution in the Atlantic World*. Columbia: University of South Carolina Press, 2001.

Genovese, Eugene. *Roll, Jordan, Roll: The World the Slaves Made*. New York: Vintage, 1976.

————. *From Rebellion to Revolution: Afro-American Slave Revolts in the Making of the Modern World.* Baton Rouge: Louisiana State University Press, 1979.

Germaix-Wasserman, Francoise. "On the Myth and Practice of the Blacksmith in Africa." *Diogenes* 78 (1972): 87–122.

Gomez, Michael. *Exchanging Our Country Marks: The Transformation of African Identities in the Colonial and Antebellum South.* Chapel Hill: University of North Carolina Press, 1998.

Goocher, Candice. "African Hammer, European Anvil: West African Iron Technology in the Atlantic Trade Era." In *Cultural Resource Management: An African Dimension,* Bassey W. Anday, ed., 200–208. Ibadan, Nigeria: Wisdom Publishers, 1990.

————. "African Metallurgy in the Atlantic World." *African Archaeological Review.* 11 (1993): 197–215.

Goodfriend, Joyce. *Before the Melting Pot: Society and Culture in Colonial New York City, 1664–1730.* Princeton: Princeton University Press, 1992.

Gotlieb, Karla. *"The Mother of Us All": A History of Queen Nanny Leader of the Windward Jamaican Maroons.* Trenton, NJ: Africa World Press, 2000.

Greene, Evarts, and Virginia Harrington. *American Population before the Federal Census of 1790.* Gloucester, MA: Peter Smith, 1966.

Gyekye, Kwame. *An Essay on African Philosophical Thought: The Akan Conceptual Scheme.* New York: Cambridge University Press, 1987.

Hackett, Rosalind I. J. *Religion in Calabar: The Religious Life and History of a Nigerian Town.* New York: Mouton De Gruyter, 1989.

Hall, Gwendolyn Midlo. *Databases for the Study of Afro-Louisiana History and Genealogy 1699–1860: Computerized Information from Original Manuscript Sources.* Baton Rouge: Louisiana State University Press, 2000.

Hamer, Philip. "Great Britain, the United States, and the Negro Seamen Acts, 1822–1848." *Journal of Southern History* 1 (1935): 3–28.

Handler, Jerome S., and Kenneth M. Bilby. "On the Early Use and Origin of the Term 'Obeah' in Barbados and the Anglophone Caribbean." *Slavery and Abolition* 22 (2001): 87–100.

Handler, Jerome S., and JoAnn Jacoby. "Slave Names and Naming in Barbados, 1650–1830." *William and Mary Quarterly,* 3rd ser., 53 (1996): 685–728.

Handlin, Oscar, and Mary Handlin. "Origins of the Southern Labor System." *William and Mary Quarterly,* 3rd ser., 12 (1950): 199–222.

Hansen, Joyce, and Gary McGowan. *Breaking Ground, Breaking Silence: The Story of New York's African Burial Ground.* New York: Henry Holt, 1998.

Harris, Joel Chandler. *Nights with Uncle Remus.* Boston: Houghton Mifflin, 1883.

————. *Uncle Remus: His Songs and Sayings.* New York: Penguin, 1982.

Headley, Joel Tyler. *The Great Riots of New York, 1712–1873.* New York: Bobbs-Merrill, 1970.

Hedrick, Basil C., and Jeanette E. Stephens. *It's a Natural Fact: Obeah in the Bahamas.* Greeley: University of Northern Colorado, Museum of Anthropology Miscellaneous Series no. 39, 1977.

Henry, H. M. *The Police Control of the Slave in South Carolina.* New York: Negro Universities Press, 1968.

Herskovits, Melville. *Life in a Haitian Valley.* New York: Alfred Knopf, 1937.

———. *The Myth of the Negro Past.* Boston: Beacon Press, 1941.

———. *Dahomey: An Ancient West African Kingdom.* Vol. 1. Evanston, IL: Northwestern University Press, 1967.

Herskovits, Melville, and Frances Herskovits. *Rebel Destiny: Among the Bush Negroes of Dutch Guiana.* New York: Whittlesey House, 1934.

———. *Suriname Folklore.* New York: AMS Press, 1969.

Heuman, Gad, ed. *Out of the House of Bondage: Runaways, Resistance, and Marronage in Africa and the New World.* London: Frank Cass, 1986.

Heywood, Linda, ed. *Central Africans and Cultural Transformations in the American Diaspora.* New York: Cambridge University Press, 2002.

Higgins, W. Robert. "The Geographical Origins of Negro Slaves in Colonial South Carolina." *South Atlantic Quarterly* 70 (1971): 34–47.

Higginson, Thomas Wentworth. *Black Rebellion.* New York: Arno, 1969.

Hodges, Graham Russell. *Slavery and Freedom in the Rural North: African Americans in Monmouth County, New Jersey, 1665–1865.* Madison: Madison House, 1997.

———. *Root and Branch: African Americans in New York and East Jersey, 1613–1863.* Chapel Hill: University of North Carolina Press, 1999.

Holloway, Joseph, ed. *Africanisms in American Culture.* Bloomington: Indiana University Press, 1991.

Hubbard, James Patrick. "Ashanti Military Affairs in the Nineteenth Century." M.A. thesis, University of Wisconsin, Madison, 1969.

Hurston, Zora Neale. *Mules and Men.* Bloomington: Indiana University Press, 1963.

Inscoe, John. "Carolina Slave Names: An Index to Acculturation." *Journal of Southern History* 49 (1983): 527–54.

Isichei, Elizabeth. *The Ibo People and the Europeans: The Genesis of a Relationship to 1906.* New York: St. Martin's Press, 1973.

———. *A History of the Igbo People.* London: Macmillan, 1976.

Jackson, Bruce ed. *The Negro and His Folklore in Nineteenth-Century Periodicals.* Austin: American Folklore Society, 1967.

James, C. L. R. *The Black Jacobins: Toussaint L'Ouverture and San Domingo Revolution.* London: Redwood Burn; Trowbridge and Fisher, 1980.

Jamieson, Ross. "Material Culture and Social Death: African-American Burial Practices." *Historical Archaeology* 29 (1995): 39–58.

January, Alan F. "The South Carolina Association: An Agency for Race Control in Antebellum Charleston." *South Carolina Historical Magazine* (1977): 191–201.

Johnson, Michael P. "Runaway Slaves and the Slave Communities in South Carolina, 1799 to 1830." *William and Mary Quarterly*, 3rd ser., 38 (1981): 418–41.

———. "Denmark Vesey and His Co-Conspirators." *William and Mary Quarterly*, 3rd ser., 58 (2001): 915–76.

———. "Reading Evidence." *William and Mary Quarterly*, 3rd ser., 59 (2002): 193–202.

Johnson, Roy F., ed. *The Nat Turner Story: History of the South's Most Important Slave Revolt, with New Material Provided by Black Tradition and White Tradition*. Murfreesboro, NC: Johnson Publishing Company, 1970.

Jones, Leroi. *Blues People: The Negro Experience in White America and the Music That Developed from It*. New York: William Morrow, 1963.

Jordan, Winthrop. *White over Black: American Attitudes toward the Negro, 1550–1812*. New York: W. W. Norton, 1968.

———. "The Charleston Hurricane of 1822; or, the Law's Rampage." *William and Mary Quarterly*, 3rd ser., 59 (2002): 175–78.

Joyner, Charles. *Down by the Riverside: A South Carolina Slave Community*. Urbana: University of Illinois Press, 1985.

July, Robert. *A History of the African People*. New York: Charles Scribner's Sons, 1980.

Kammen, Michael. *Colonial New York: A History*. New York: Charles Scribner's Sons, 1975.

Kaufman, Edward, ed. *Reclaiming Our Past, Honoring Our Ancestors: New York's 18th Century African Burial Ground and the Memorial Competition*. New York: African Burial Ground Coalition, 1994.

Kea, Ray. *Settlements, Trade, and Polities in the Seventeenth-Century Gold Coast*. Baltimore: Johns Hopkins University Press, 1982.

———. "'When I Die, I Shall Return to My Own Land': An 'Amina' Slave Rebellion in the Danish West Indies, 1733–1734." In *The Cloth of Many Coloured Silks: Papers on History and Society Ghanaian and Islamic in Honor of Ivor Wilks*, John Hunwick and Nancy Lawler, eds., 159–93. Evanston, IL: Northwestern University Press, 1996.

Kilson, Martin, and Robert Rotberg, eds. *The African Diaspora: Interpretive Essays*. Cambridge, MA: Harvard University Press, 1976.

Klein, Herbert S. "Slaves and Shipping in Eighteenth-Century Virginia." *Journal of Interdisciplinary History* 5 (1975): 383–412.

Klingberg, Frank. *An Appraisal of the Negro in Colonial South Carolina: A Study in Americanization*. Philadelphia: Porcupine Press, 1975.

Kopytoff, Barbara Klamon. "The Early Political Development of Jamaican Maroon Societies." *William and Mary Quarterly*, 3rd ser., 35 (1978): 287–307.

Korbin, David. *The Black Majority in Early New York*. Albany: University Press of the State of New York, 1971.

Kulikoff, Alan. "The Origins of Afro-American Society in Tidewater Maryland and Virginia, 1700–1790." *William and Mary Quarterly*, 3rd ser., 35 (1978): 226–59.

Landers, Jane. "Gracia Real de Santa Teresa de Mose: A Free Black Town in Spanish Colonial Florida." *American Historical Review* 95 (1990): 9–30.

La Roche, Cheryl, and Michael Blakey. "Seizing Intellectual Power: The Dialogue at the New York African Burial Ground." *Historical Archaeology* 31 (1997): 84–106.

Launitz-Schurer, Leopold, Jr. "Slave Resistance in Colonial New York: An Interpretation of Daniel Horsmanden's New York Conspiracy." *Phylon* 41 (1980): 137–52.

Law, Robin. *The Horse in West African History: The Role of the Horse in the Societies of Pre-Colonial West Africa*. New York: Oxford University Press, 1980.

Leaming, Hugo. "Hidden Americans: Maroons of Virginia and South Carolina." Ph.D. diss., University of Illinois, 1979.

Levine, Lawrence. *Black Culture and Black Consciousness: Afro-American Folk Thought from Slavery to Freedom*. New York: Oxford University Press, 1977.

Lewis, J. Lowell. *Ring of Liberation: Deceptive Discourse in Brazilian Capoeira*. Chicago: University of Chicago Press, 1992.

Linebaugh, P., and Marcus Rediker. *The Many-Headed Hydra: Sailors, Slaves, Commoners, and the Hidden History of the Revolutionary Atlantic*. Boston: Beacon Press, 2000.

Littlefield, Daniel. *Rice and Slaves: Ethnicity and the Slave Trade in Colonial South Carolina*. Baton Rouge: Louisiana State University, 1981.

Lofton, James. "Denmark Vesey's Call to Arms." *Journal of Negro History* 33 (1948): 395–417.

———. *Insurrection in South Carolina: The Turbulent World of Denmark Vesey*. Yellow Springs, OH: Antioch Press, 1964.

Lydon, James. "New York and the Slave Trade, 1700–1774." *William and Mary Quarterly*, 3rd ser., 35 (1978): 375–94.

McCaskie, T. C. *State and Society in Pre-Colonial Asante*. Cambridge: Cambridge University Press, 1995.

McCrady, Edward. *The History of South Carolina under Proprietary Government, 1670–1719*. New York: Macmillan, 1897.

McFarland, Daniel M. "The Great Fear." *Madison College Bulletin: Studies and Research* 22 (1964): 70–76.

McKivigan, John R., and Stanley Harrold, eds. *Antislavery Violence: Sectional, Racial, and Cultural Conflict in Antebellum America*. Knoxville: University of Tennessee Press, 1999.

McManus, Edgar J. *A History of Negro Slavery in New York*. Syracuse: Syracuse University Press, 1966.

McNaughton, Patrick R. *The Mande Blacksmiths: Knowledge, Power, and Art in West Africa*. Bloomington: University of Indiana Press, 1993.

Meaders, Daniel. "South Carolina Fugitives as Viewed through Local Colonial Newspapers with Emphasis on Runaway Notices, 1732–1801." *Journal of Negro History* 60 (1975): 288–319.

Meillassoux, Claude. *The Anthropology of Slavery: The Womb of Iron and Gold.* Chicago: University of Chicago Press, 1991.

Mereness, Newton. *Travels in the American Colonies.* New York: Macmillan, 1916.

Miller, Joseph C. *Way of Death: Merchant Capitalism and the Angolan Slave Trade, 1730–1830.* Madison: University of Wisconsin Press, 1988.

Minkus, Helaine. "Causal Theory in Akwapim Akan Philosophy." In *African Philosophy: An Introduction,* ed. Richard A. Wright, 107–63. Washington, DC: University Press of America, 1977.

Mintz, Sidney, and Richard Price. *The Birth of African-American Culture: An Anthropological Perspective.* Boston: Beacon Press, 1976.

Montgomery, Michael. *The Crucible of Carolina: Essays in the Development of Gullah Culture and Language.* Athens, University of Georgia Press, 1994.

Morgan, Edmund. *American Slavery, American Freedom.* New York: W.W. Norton and Company, 1975.

Morgan, Edwin Vernon. *Slavery in New York with Special Reference to New York City.* Vol. 2. New York: New York City History Club Half Moon Series, 1897.

Morgan, Philip. "The Cultural Implications of the Atlantic Slave Trade: African Regional Origins, American Destinations, and New World Developments," *Slavery and Abolition* 18 (1997): 122–45.

———. *Slave Counterpoint: Black Culture in the Eighteenth-Century Chesapeake and Low Country.* Chapel Hill: University of North Carolina Press, 1998.

———. "Conspiracy Scares." *William and Mary Quarterly,* 3rd ser., 59 (2002): 159–66.

Morgan, Philip, and George Terry. "Slavery in Microcosm: A Conspiracy Scare in Colonial South Carolina." *Journal of Social History* (1982): 283–307.

Morrish, Ivor. *Obeah, Christ, and Rastaman.* Cambridge: James Clarke, 1982.

Mullin, Gerald (Michael). *Flight and Rebellion: Slave Resistance in Eighteenth-Century Virginia.* New York: Oxford University Press, 1972.

Mullin, Michael. *Africa in America: Slave Acculturation and Resistance in the American South and the British Caribbean, 1736–1831.* Chicago: University of Illinois Press, 1994.

Nash, Gary. *The Urban Crucible: The Northern Seaports, and the Origins of the American Revolution.* Cambridge, MA: Harvard University Press, 1986.

———. *Red, White, and Black: The Peoples of Early North America.* Upper Saddle River, NJ: Prentice-Hall, 2000.

Northup, A. Judd. *Slavery in New York, A Historical Sketch.* Albany: New York State Library Bulletin History, 1900.

Northup, David. "Igbo and Myth Igbo: Culture and Ethnicity in the Atlantic World, 1600–1850." *Slavery and Abolition* 21 (2000): 1–20.

Oates, Stephen. "Children of Darkness." *American Heritage* 24 (1973): 42–47, 89–91.

———. *The Fires of Jubilee: Nat Turner's Fierce Rebellion.* New York: Harper and Row, 1975.

Ofori-Ansa, Kwaku. "Identification and Validation of the Sankofa Symbol." *Update: Newsletter of the African Burial Ground and Five Points Archaeological Projects* 1 (1995): 9.

Okihiro, Gary, ed. *In Resistance: Studies in African, Caribbean, and Afro-American History.* Amherst: University of Massachusetts Press, 1986.

Olson, Edwin. "Social Aspects of Slave Life in New York." *Journal of Negro History* 26 (1941): 66–77.

———. "The Slave Code in Colonial New York." *Journal of Negro History* 29 (1944): 147–65.

Olwell, Robert. *Masters, Slaves, and Subjects: The Culture of Power in the South Carolina Low Country, 1740–1790.* Ithaca: Cornell University Press, 1998.

Ott, Thomas. *The Haitian Revolution, 1789–1804.* Knoxville: University of Tennessee Press, 1973.

Ottley, Roi. *Black Odyssey: The Story of the Negro in America.* New York: Charles Scribner's Sons, 1948.

Palmer, Colin. *Human Cargoes: The British Trade to Spanish America, 1700–1739.* Urbana: University of Illinois Press, 1981.

Paquette, Robert L. "Jacobins of the Lowcountry: The Vesey Plot on Trial." *William and Mary Quarterly,* 3rd ser., 59 (2002): 185–92.

Parent, Anthony S. "'Either a Fool or a Fury': The Emergence of Paternalism in Colonial Virginia Slave Society." Ph.D. diss., University of California, Los Angeles, 1982.

Patterson, Orlando. *The Sociology of Slavery: An Analysis of the Origins, Development, and Structure of Negro Slave Society in Jamaica.* Cranbury, NJ: Associated University Press, 1967.

———. "Slavery and Slave Revolts: A Socio-Historical Analysis of the First Maroon War, 1655–1740." *Social and Economic Studies* 19 (1970): 289–325.

Pearson, Edward A. "'A Countryside Full of Flames': A Reconsideration of the Stono Rebellion and Slave Rebelliousness in the Early Eighteenth-Century South Carolina Low Country." *Slavery and Abolition* 17 (1996): 22–50.

———. "Trials and Errors: Denmark Vesey and His Historians." *William and Mary Quarterly,* 3rd ser., 59 (2002): 137–42.

Philips, U. B. *American Negro Slavery: A Survey of the Supply, Employment, and Control of Negro Labor as Determined by the Plantation Regime.* Baton Rouge: Louisiana State University Press, 1966.

Piersen, William D. *Black Yankees: The Development of an Afro-American Subculture in Eighteenth-Century New England.* Amherst: University of Massachusetts Press, 1988.

————. *Black Legacy: America's Hidden Heritage*. Amherst: University of Massachusetts Press, 1993.

Pitman, Frank Wesley. "Slavery on British West India Plantations in the Eighteenth Century." *Journal of Negro History* 11 (1926): 585–650.

Porter, Kenneth. "Relations between Negroes and Indians." *Journal of Negro History* 17 (1932): 287–369.

Postma, Johannes Menne. *The Dutch in the Atlantic Slave Trade, 1600–1815*. Cambridge: Cambridge University Press, 1990.

Powers, Bernard. *Black Charlestonians: A Social History, 1822–1885*. Fayetteville: University of Arkansas Press, 1994.

Prince, Walter F. "The Great Conspiracy Delusion: A Sketch of the Crowning Judicial Atrocity of American History." *Saturday Chronicle* (New Haven, CT), June 28–August 23, 1902, 1–85.

Price, Richard. *Saramaka Social Structure: An Analysis of a "Bush Negro" Society*. Rio Piedras, PR: University of Puerto Rico, 1973.

————. *Maroon Societies: Rebel Slave Communities in the Americas*. Baltimore: Johns Hopkins University Press, 1979.

Puckett, Newbell Nile. *Folk Beliefs of the Southern Negro*. Chapel Hill: University of North Carolina Press, 1926.

Raboteau, Albert J. *Slave Religion: The "Invisible Institution" in the Antebellum South*. New York: Oxford University Press, 1978.

Rattray, Robert S. *Religion and Art in Ashanti*. Oxford: Claredon Press, 1927.

Rawick, George. *From Sundown to Sunup: The Making of the Black Community*. Westport, CT: Greenwood Press, 1972.

Rawley, James. *The Transatlantic Slave Trade: A History*. New York: W. W. Norton, 1981.

Riddell, William Renwick. "The Slave in New York." *Journal of Negro History* 13 (1928): 53–86.

Roberts, John. *From Trickster to Badman: The Black Folk Hero in Slavery and Freedom*. Philadelphia: University of Pennsylvania Press, 1989.

Roberts, Richard L. *Warriors, Merchants, and Slaves: The State and the Economy in the Middle Niger Valley, 1700–1914*. Stanford: Stanford University Press, 1987.

Robertson, David. *Denmark Vesey: The Buried History of America's Largest Slave Rebellion and the Man Who Led It*. New York: Alfred A. Knopf, 1999.

————. "Inconsistent Contextualism: The Hermeneutics of Michael Johnson." *William and Mary Quarterly*, 3rd ser., 59 (2002): 153–58.

Rodney, Walter. "Upper Guinea and the Significance of the Origins of Africans Enslaved in the New World." *Journal of Negro History* 54 (1969): 327–45.

Rogers, George. *Charleston in the Age of the Pinckneys*. Norman, OK: University of Oklahoma Press, 1969.

Rucker, Walter. "Conjure, Magic, and Power: The Influence of Afro-Atlantic Religious Practices on Slave Resistance and Rebellion." *Journal of Black Studies* 32 (2001): 84–103.

Samford, P. "The Archaeology of African-American Slavery and Material Culture." *William and Mary Quarterly*, 3rd ser., 53 (1996): 87–114.

Schuler, Monica. "Akan Slave Rebellions in the British Caribbean." *Savacou* 1 (1970): 15–23.

———. "Ethnic Slave Rebellions in the Caribbean and the Guianas." *Journal of Social History* 3 (1970): 374–85.

———. "Afro-American Slave Culture." *Historical Reflections* 6 (1974): 121–37, 138–55.

Schwarz, Philip. "Gabriel's Challenge: Slaves and Crime in Late Eighteenth-Century Virginia." *Virginia Magazine of History and Biography* 90 (1982): 283–309.

———. *Twice Condemned: Slaves and the Criminal Laws of Virginia, 1705–1865.* Baton Rouge: Louisiana State University Press, 1988.

Scott, Kenneth. "The Slave Insurrection in New York in 1712." *New York Historical Society Quarterly* 45 (1961): 43–74.

Shaw, Thurstan. *Igbo-Ukwu: An Account of Archaeological Discoveries in Eastern Nigeria.* Evanston, IL: Northwestern University Press, 1970.

———. *Unearthing Igbo-Ukwu: Archaeological Discoveries in Eastern Nigeria.* Ibadan: Oxford University Press, 1977.

Sidbury, James. *Ploughshares into Swords: Race, Rebellion, and Identity in Gabriel's Virginia, 1730–1810.* New York: Cambridge University Press, 1997.

———. "Saint Domingue in Virginia: Ideology, Local Meanings, and Resistance to Slavery, 1790–1800." *Journal of Southern History* 63 (1997): 531–52.

———. "Plausible Stories and Varnished Truths." *William and Mary Quarterly*, 3rd ser., 59 (2002): 179–84.

Simpson, George Eaton, *Black Religions in the New World.* New York: Columbia University Press, 1978.

Sirmans, M. Eugene. "The Legal Status of the Slave in South Carolina, 1670–1740." *Journal of Southern History* 28 (1962): 462–73.

———. *Colonial South Carolina: A Political History, 1663–1763.* Chapel Hill: University of North Carolina Press, 1966.

Sobel, Mechal. *Trabelin' On: The Slave Journey to an Afro-Baptist Faith.* Westport, CT: Greenwood Press, 1979.

———. *The World They Made Together: Black and White Values in Eighteenth-Century Virginia.* Princeton: Princeton University Press, 1987.

Smith, Reed. "Gullah." A Reprint of Bulletin 190 of the University of South Carolina. Columbia: State Printing Co., 1926.

Smith, Theophus H. *Conjuring Culture: Biblical Formations of Black America.* New York: Oxford University Press, 1994.

Stampp, Kenneth. *The Peculiar Institution: Slavery in the Antebellum South.* New York: Alfred A. Knopf, 1956.

Steady, Filomina Chioma, ed. *The Black Woman Cross-Culturally.* Rochester, VT: Shenkman Books, 1985.

Stuckey, Sterling. "Through the Prism of Folklore: The Black Ethos in Slavery," *Massachusetts Review* 9 (1968): 417–37.

———. *Slave Culture: Nationalist Theory and the Foundation of Black America.* New York: Oxford University Press, 1987.

———. *Going through the Storm: The Influence of African American Art in History.* New York: Oxford University Press, 1994.

———. "African Spirituality and Cultural Practice in Colonial New York, 1700–1770." In *Inequality in Early America,* C. Pestana and Sharon Salinger, eds., 160–81. Hanover, NH: University Press of New England, 1999.

Suttles, William C., Jr. "African Religious Survivals as Factors in American Slave Revolts." *Journal of Negro History.* 56 (1971): 97–104.

Szasz, Ferenc M. "The New York Slave Revolt of 1741: A Re-examination." *New York History Quarterly* 48 (1967): 215–30.

Talbot, P. Amaury. *Tribes of the Niger Delta, Their Religions and Customs.* London: Sheldon Press, 1923.

Tate, W. Carrington. "Gabriel's Insurrection." *Henrico County Historical Society Magazine* 3 (1979): 13–21.

Thomas, Hugh. *The Slave Trade: The Story of the Atlantic Slave Trade, 1440–1870.* New York: Simon and Schuster, 1997.

Thomas, William H. B. "Poor Deluded Wretches!: The Slave Insurrection of 1816." *Louisa County Historical Magazine* 6 (1974–1975): 57–63.

Thompson, Robert Farris. "African Influence on the Art of the United States." In *Black Studies in the University: A Symposium,* Armstead Robinson, Craig Foster, and Donald Ogilivie, eds., 122–70. New Haven: Yale University Press, 1969.

———. *Flash of the Spirit.* New York: Vintage Books, 1983.

———. "Tough Guys Do Dance." *Rolling Stone* 522 (24 March 1988): 135–40.

Thompson, Robert Farris, and J. Cornet. *The Four Moments of the Sun: Kongo Art in Two Worlds.* Washington, DC: National Gallery of Art, 1981.

Thornton, John K. "Art of War in Angola." *Comparative Studies in Society and History* 30 (1988): 360–78.

———. "African Dimensions of the Stono Rebellion." *American Historical Review* 96 (1991): 1101–13.

———. "African Soldiers in the Haitian Revolution." *Journal of Caribbean History* 25 (1991): 58–80.

———. *Africa and Africans in the Making of the Atlantic World, 1400–1680.* New York: Cambridge University Press, 1992.

———. "The African Experience of the '20 and odd Negroes' Arriving in Virginia in 1619." *William and Mary Quarterly*, 3rd ser., 55 (1998): 421–34.

———. "The Coromantees: An African Cultural Group in Colonial North America and the Caribbean." *Journal of Caribbean History* 32 (1998): 161–78.

———. *Warfare in Atlantic Africa, 1500–1800.* London: University College London Press, 1999.

———. "War, the State, and Religious Norms in 'Coromantee' Thought: The Ideology of an African American Nation." In *Possible Pasts: Becoming Colonial in Early America*, Robert Blair St. George, ed., 181–200. Ithaca: Cornell University Press, 2000.

Tigges, Gabriela B. "The History of Capoeira in Brazil." Ph.D. diss., University of California Los Angeles, 1990.

Turner, Lorenzo Dow. *Africanisms in Gullah Dialect.* Chicago: University of Chicago Press, 1949.

Vass, Winifred. *The Bantu-Speaking Heritage of the United States.* Berkeley: University of California Press, 1979.

Vlach, John Michael. *By the Work of Their Hands: Studies in Afro-American Folklife.* Ann Arbor: UMI Research Press, 1991.

Wade, Richard. *Slavery in the Cities: The South 1820–1860.* New York: Oxford University Press, 1964.

———. "The Vesey Plot: A Reconsideration." *Journal of Southern History* 30 (1964): 143-161.

Walker, Sheila, ed. *African Roots/American Cultures: Africa in the Creation of the Americas.* New York: Rowman and Littlefield, 2001.

Wallace, David Duncan. *The History of South Carolina.* Vol. 1. New York: American Historical Society, 1934.

Walsh, Lorena. S. *From Calabar to Carter's Grove: The History of a Virginia Slave Community.* Charlottesville: University of Virginia Press, 1997.

———. "The Chesapeake Slave Trade: Regional Patterns, African Origins, and Some Implications," *William and Mary Quarterly*, 3rd ser., 58 (2001): 139–69.

Wasserman, Francoise Germaix. "On Myth and Practice of the Blacksmith in Africa." *Diogenes* 78 (1972): 87–122.

Wax, Darold. "Preferences for Slaves in Colonial America." *Journal of Negro History* 58 (1973): 371–401.

———. "'The Great Risk We Run': The Aftermath of the Slave Rebellion at Stono, South Carolina, 1739–1745," *Journal of Negro History* 67 (1982): 136–47.

Weir, Robert. *Colonial South Carolina.* Millwod, NY: Kto Press, 1983.

Westergaard, Waldemar C. "Account of the Negro Rebellion on St. Croix, Danish West Indies, 1759." *Journal of Negro History* 11 (1926): 50–61.

Westbury, Susan. "Colonial Virginia and the Atlantic Slave Trade." Ph.D. diss., University of Illinois at Urbana-Champaign, 1981.

———. "Slaves of Colonial Virginia: Where They Came From." *William and Mary Quarterly*, 3rd ser., 42 (1985): 228–37.

Whites, Shane. "Pinkster: Afro-Dutch Syncretization in New York City and the Hudson Valley." *Journal of American Folklore* 102 (1989): 23–75.

———. "'It Was a Proud Day': African Americans, Festivals, and Parades in the North, 1741–1834." *Journal of American History* 81 (1994): 13–50.

Williams, George Washington. *History of the Negro Race in America from 1619 to 1880*. Vol. 1. New York: G. P. Putnam's Sons, 1883.

Williams, Joseph. *Voodoos and Obeahs: Phases of West India Witchcraft*. New York: Dial Press, 1932.

Williams, Oscar. *African Americans and Colonial Legislation in the Middle Colonies*. New York: Garland, 1998.

Wilson, Sherrill. *New York City's African Slaveowners: A Social and Material Culture History*. New York: Garland, 1994.

Windley, Lathan A. *A Profile of Runaway Slaves in Virginia and South Carolina from 1730– 1787*. New York: Garland, 1995.

Wiredu, Kwasi. *Cultural Universals and Particulars: An African Perspective*. Bloomington: Indiana University Press, 1996.

Wish, Harvey. "American Slave Insurrections before 1861." In *American Slavery: The Question of Resistance*, John Bracey, August Meier, and Elliott Rudwick, eds., 21–36. Belmont, CA: Wadsworth, 1971.

Wood, Peter. *Black Majority: Negroes in Colonial South Carolina from 1670 through the Stono Rebellion*. New York: W. W. Norton and Company, Inc., 1974.

———. *Strange New Land: Africans in Colonial America*. New York: Oxford University Press, 2003.

# Index

accommodationism, 181–82

acculturation, 118, 133, 136, 170, 200. *See also* assimilation; creole(s)

Adams, E. C. L., 202

African ethnicity: as barrier to resistance, 5; and formation of ethnic enclaves, 5–8, 30, 32, 33, 34, 125, 163; and African American culture, 6, 9, 13–14, 57–58, 116, 151, 156, 170, 179, 182, 188, 197, 198, 199; and cultural bridges, 7, 105, 110, 116, 118–19, 141, 145, 147, 150, 154, 163, 167–69, 176, 179, 182, 197, 208, 235n95; and European preferences for specific groups, 33, 94–97, 127–29, 174, 231n17; white recognition of, 84, 89, 96–97, 101–2, 174; and multilingualism, 236n104. *See also names of African ethnic groups*

African languages: the use of by slave rebels, 38, 44; and multilingualism, 236n104. *See also* African ethnicity; *and names of African ethnic groups*

African Methodist Episcopal Church, 176

African military cultures: loyalty oaths in, 45–46, 54–55, 86; use of firearms in, 55–56, 86, 105–6; and enslavement and transportation of soldiers, 55–57, 105, 224n150; martial dances in, 57, 87–88, 102, 104, 106–7; use of drums in, 102, 105; and use of cavalries, 171–74, 250n84

Africanisms, 8, 10; in burial customs, 48–51, 118–19, 241n101; in herbology, 111

Akan: belief in transmigration by, 12, 53–54, 105, 208; mentioned, 12, 199; and religion, 12, 43, 147; exportation from Fort Kromantine of, 29–30; and formation of Coromantee identity, 30–31, 57; reputation for violent resistance among, 34–35, 85–86; day-names used by, 38–39, 44, 68, 73, 81, 82, 83, 85, 86, 170–71, 219n75, 220n87, 221n99; and connection to Obeah, 39, 42; and Jamaican Maroons, 40–41, 44, 46; and slave revolts, 40, 43, 52, 53, 56, 74, 117–18, 229n76; and *adinkra* symbols, 49–50; funerary practices of, 52, 118–19, 224n129; as coveted by South Carolina planters, 96; and running away, 114, 116, 117, 149; as possible ethnicity of Denmark Vesey, 162; and Anansi the Spider tales, 205. *See also* Aminas; Coromantee; Fort Kromantine; Gold Coast; kingdom of Asante

Aminas, 8, 30, 53, 83, 87. *See also* Akan; Danish West Indies; Gold Coast

Angola. *See* Kongo kingdom; West-central Africa(ns)

animal tricksters. *See* Akan: and Anansi the Spider tales; Brer Rabbit; folklore

Antigua: African imports into, 6, 34; and transshipment trade, 33, 60; and 1736 conspiracy, 41, 44, 82–83, 87–89

Aptheker, Herbert, 3, 4, 78, 91, 99, 115, 188, 189, 216n31, 231n21, 231n27

arson. *See* slave resistance: arson as a form of

Ashanti. *See* Akan; kingdom of Asante

assimilation: and slave resistance, 4, 133; language skills as poor indicator of, 118, 136, 160, 170; occupational status as poor indicator of, 161. *See also* acculturation; creole(s)

BaKongo. *See* West-central Africa(ns)

Ball, Charles, 183, 208

Bambara. *See* Gambians; Senegambians

Bantu. *See* West-central Africa(ns)

Barbados: African imports into, 6, 34, 40; and transshipment trade, 22, 33, 124, 126, 128–29; and 1675 plot, 56; and English settlements in Carolina, 91–93

Baskin, Prince, 201, 202

Ben (Prosser), 135, 137, 138, 139

Bennett, Thomas (governor), 159, 176

Bibb, Henry, 185

Bight of Benin, 33, 127, 141

Bight of Biafra, 6, 33, 40, 52, 96, 125, 126, 127, 142, 143, 150, 157, 162, 214n18. *See also* Igbo(s)

*Black Thunder* (Bontemps), 1

blacksmiths, 133, 136–39, 141–45, 158, 166, 238n49, 240n86, 248n65

Blakey, Michael, 50

Blassingame, John, 180

blues music, 211

Bontemps, Arna, 1, 2, 134

Bosman, Willem, 42, 45, 51, 222n107

Boukman (Dutty), 181, 182

Brazil: African imports into, 5, 97, 231n17; as parallel to South Carolina, 13, 97, 106–8; and commercial relationship with New Netherland, 19

Brer Rabbit: as representative of the enslaved, 201, 202–5; as parody of white society, 201–3; as multidimensional personality, 204; as reflective of a peasant consciousness, 205–6; as counterpart of slave conjurers, 206. *See also* folklore

Brown, Simon, 201–2, 204

Brown, William Wells, 182, 186, 194

Bruce, Henry Clay, 180–81, 184, 185

Bull, William (lieutenant-governor), 100–101

Burton, Mary, 66, 68, 70, 75–76, 77, 78, 86, 89, 228n54

Butler, Jon, 47, 48, 223n117

Caesar (Peck), 84

Caesar (Vaarck), 65–66, 68, 69, 70, 80, 227n44

Caesar's Cure, 110–11, 182

Calabar. *See* Bight of Biafra; Igbo(s)

Canada, 63, 71

Cape Coast Castle, 31

*capoeira*, 13, 106–8

Carolina. *See* South Carolina

caul, 168–69, 193

Chambers, Douglas, 8, 39–40

Charles (Drayton), 175

Charles II (king), 21, 91, 92

charms, 35, 37, 41, 42, 43, 86, 143, 145, 158, 164–65, 182, 184. *See also* conjure; powder; protective hands

Christensen, Abigail, 201–3

Christianity: and the Bible as inspiration, 1, 83, 179, 242n1; as defining characteristic of creoles, 1, 9, 133; as mediating force to slave resistance, 5; and slavery, 23, 25; and religious instruction, 36–37; and the spiritual holocaust, 47; and loyalty oaths, 83–84; and the Baptist Church, 147, 194; total immersion baptism as Africanism in, 147; and involvement of preachers in slave resistance, 154, 167–68, 187–88; and the African Methodist Episcopal Church, 176; and biracial congregations, 176; acceptance of as factor in disdain for African beliefs, 183; and fusion with African beliefs, 187–88, 193, 210

Chukwu, 143. *See also* Igbo(s)

Congo Square, 109, 234n59

conjure: and slave resistance, 1, 29, 35, 40, 47–48, 68, 70, 79–80, 83, 86, 106, 109–11, 149–50, 158, 164–69, 180–86, 251n14; and slave accommodation, 110–11, 181; and links to metalworking, 144–45, 166, 170; and fortune-telling, 150, 185–86; and conjure bags, 164; slave fears of, 165; and conjurers as revolutionary vanguard, 181–82; and the use of roots, 183, 185, 196; the failure of explained, 185; and conjurers born with distinguishing marks, 192–93; and influence over whites, 193–94; and healing traditions, 196–97

Coromantee. *See* Akan; Aminas; Gold Coast

cotton cultivation, 152, 188–89

country-born company, 175
country-born slaves, 174–75. *See also* creole(s)
Covey, Edward, 183
creole(s), 4, 5, 82, 87, 118, 245n2; and the
   use of creole languages by slave rebels,
   53, 166–67, 169; and linguistic code-
   switching, 118, 166–67; and creolization,
   199, 208
Cuffee (Philipse), 65, 67, 69, 72, 73, 83, 84, 89
cultural adaptations: and borrowings from
   Native American culture, 111; and contacts with European and Euro-American
   cultures, 199
Curtin, Philip, 6, 129, 156, 243n13

dance, 99, 102, 104–9, 115
Danish West Indies, 53, 83, 87, 89, 162
Davis, Thomas J., 66, 74, 78
Dick (Burger), 38
Dismal Swamp maroons. *See* maroons
Doctor Caesar. *See* Caesar's Cure
Doctor Harry (Mizreal), 68, 70, 79–82, 89, 182
Douglass, Frederick, 183, 185–86, 196
drums, 102, 105–6, 109, 130
Du Bois, W. E. B., 3, 181, 187–88, 191,
   243n13
Du Bois Slave Trade Database, 6, 30, 32, 40,
   95, 126, 197
Dunn, Richard, 5
Dutch West India Company: and develop-
   ment of New Netherland, 17–18; creation
   of patroonships by, 18; and competition
   with Portuguese, 18, 20; and involvement
   in importation of Africans, 18–19, 21–22;
   and struggles in attracting European immigrants, 19, 21; capitulation to English
   blockade by, 21–22; and seizure of Fort
   Kromantine, 29

Ebo Company, 166, 170, 172
Eboe. *See* Igbo(s)
Egerton, Douglas, 133–36, 138, 162, 163,
   238n43, 239n59, 245n37
El Mina Castle, 18, 20, 21
Elkins, Stanley, 3, 5
Eltis, David, 32–33

Equiano, Olaudah, 128–29, 142–43, 146,
   148, 150, 208
ethnic randomization, 8, 33, 179. *See also*
   African ethnicity
ethnie. *See* African ethnicity
*Eyckenboom*, 20

Faulkner, William (reverend), 201–2, 204
First Anglo-Dutch War, 21
Florida, 71, 100
flying Africans, 206–9, 211, 256n34
folklore: as aspect of slave ethos, 13, 200;
   mentioned, 13–14, 198; meaning and
   function as relevant in, 200–201; and human tricksters, 203; as reflective of Atlantic African sociopolitical currents, 204–5.
   *See also* Brer Rabbit
Fort Kromantine (Fort New Amsterdam),
   29–30
Fortune (Wilkins), 71, 84
free blacks, 62, 64, 152, 154, 160–61, 162,
   175, 177, 189, 215n8
French band, 169, 170, 175

Gabriel (Prosser): mentioned, 1, 2, 10, 192,
   238n49, 239n43, 239n59; as conspiracy
   leader, 13, 137–39, 145, 147, 190; and
   1800 Richmond plot, 129, 133–41, 181; as
   an assimilated artisan, 133–36; and assault on Absalom Johnson, 135–36, 139;
   as symbol of African culture, 137, 147–48;
   as a blacksmith, 138–39, 145, 147, 161;
   use of waterways as ritual spaces by, 145–
   47; memorialized in song, 209–10
Gambians: and conjure, 109; mentioned
   in runaway advertisements, 114; mentioned, 167, 170; and involvement in 1822
   Charleston plot, 171–72; knowledge of
   horse handling by, 172–74. *See also* Senegambians
Gaspar, David Barry, 46, 87
Geneva Club, 63–64, 65, 67, 77
Genovese, Eugene, 4, 5, 181, 182, 255n30
George (Wilson), 158
*Gideon*, 22
Gola. *See* Sierra Leone

Perault (Strohecker), 166, 170, 171, 173
Peter (the Doctor), 35–37, 38, 39, 43, 46, 47,
    109, 182, 219n68
Peter (Poyas), 158, 159, 167, 175
Philip (blind preacher), 167–69, 185
Phillips, Ulrich B., 2, 3, 4
Pinkster festival, 56–58, 88, 205, 225n155
poison. *See* slave resistance: poison used in
    examples of
powder, 28, 35, 37, 43, 181, 185. *See also*
    charms; protective hands
Price, Richard, 8, 33
Prince (Auboyneau), 65–66, 69, 227n44
protective hands, 1, 184. *See also* charms;
    powder

Quack (Roosevelt), 73, 83–85, 89
Quaco (Walter), 67
Queen Nanny, 40

rice cultivation, 92–94, 152, 167, 171,
    243n15. *See also* Senegambians; Sierra Le-
    one; South Carolina; Upper Guinea
ring shout, 7, 104–5, 107, 208, 211
Roberts, John, 206
Robin (Hooghlandt), 28–29, 37, 217n40
root doctor, 111. *See also* conjure
Royal African Company: and involvement
    in Caribbean reshipment trade, 22; and
    foothold in the Gold Coast, 31; and
    collection of import duties, 60; and im-
    portation of Africans into New York, 60;
    and Act of 1698, 124; and importation of
    Africans into Virginia, 124
running away. *See* slave resistance: runaways
    as engaged in

Saint-Domingue. *See* Haiti
Sambo: as plantation myth, 2, 3
Sandy (Jenkins), 183, 185–86, 196
*sankofa*, 50, 208. *See also* Akan: and *adinkra*
    symbols
*São João Batista*, 17
Sarah (Walton), 37
Schuler, Monica, 39, 42
seasoned slaves. *See* creole(s)
Second Anglo-Dutch War, 21, 29

Senegambians: and livestock raising, 96;
    and rice cultivation, 96, 171; imported
    into South Carolina, 96, 102, 171. *See also*
    Upper Guinea
Sharpe, John (reverend), 28–29, 35, 37, 38,
    43, 48, 52, 217n36, 217n40
Sidbury, James, 136–37
Sierra Leone: and livestock raising, 96;
    imported into South Carolina, 96, 171;
    and rice cultivation, 96, 171; and connec-
    tion to Gullah culture, 167. *See also* Upper
    Guinea
slave laws: Duke's Laws, 22, 23; and Chris-
    tianity, 22, 25; and English Common
    Law, 24; and limits on assembly, 24,
    25, 51, 64, 103, 131–32; and restrictions
    on ownership of weapons, 24, 64, 104;
    and reformist laws, 24–25; and free
    blacks, 25, 177, 189; as reaction to slave
    resistance, 25, 26, 103, 111–12, 130; and
    restrictions on giving court testimony,
    26; and slave resistance, 26; and import
    tariffs, 34, 60–61, 94, 104, 124, 153; and
    conjure, 46–47, 111–12, 132, 222n115; and
    burial customs, 51–52, 130; and limits
    on mobility, 62, 177; and prohibitions on
    use or ownership of seacraft, 63, 177–79;
    and curfews, 64, 68; and gambling, 64;
    and prohibitions on liquor consumption,
    68; and prohibitions on literacy, 104, 189;
    and prohibitions on drums, 105, 130; and
    runaways, 116–17; and maroons, 130; and
    formation and employment of state mili-
    tias, 154, 158–59, 191; and manumission,
    174; as means to sever pan-African con-
    nections, 177–79; British resistance to,
    178; and David Walker's *Appeal*, 179
slave punishment: as responsibility of own-
    ers, 25; and execution, 26, 27, 28, 45,
    51, 73, 75, 76, 80, 82, 98, 101, 104, 111,
    112, 132, 133, 140, 149, 176, 227n44; and
    torture, 27, 28, 45, 73, 101, 103, 111, 117;
    of runaways, 116–17, 131; and banish-
    ment, 176
slave resistance: as slave crime, 2–3, 26;
    scholarly assessments of, 2–5, 73–79,
    133–37, 161–63, 187; and loyal slaves,

tribalism. *See* African ethnicity
Tubman, Harriet, 186, 196, 254nn65-67
Twi. *See* Akan

unseasoned slaves. *See* new Africans
Upper Guinea, 96, 125, 144, 157, 161, 174.
  *See also* Senegambians; Sierra Leone
Ury, John, 73, 77, 78

Valentine, David, 48
Vesey, Denmark: as a creole, 5; and problems with trial record, 9–10, 163; and 1822 Charleston conspiracy, 13, 116, 133, 157–60, 176–77, 181, 185, 189; as leader of the 1822 conspiracy, 157, 159, 163, 192, 245n27; biographical details of, 160, 190; as a free black artisan, 160–61; as a Muslim, 161–62; as born to Akan-speaking parents, 162; early pan-Africanist sentiment by, 163, 169–70, 175, 176, 179; and use of horse companies, 170–73
vigilante justice, 3, 177
Virginia: African imports into, 6, 17, 123–26, 148, 214n18; and the establishment of the Jamestown colony in, 17; legalization of slavery in, 123; demographics in, 123, 188; Olaudah Equiano's observations of, 128, 142–43; slave conspiracies in, 130–32; African-born blacksmiths in, 143–44; African ritual objects excavated in, 144; and the Garvin conspiracy, 154. *See also* Gabriel (Prosser); Nat (Turner)
vodun, 141, 181, 205, 246n39, 248n65. *See also* Ogun; Yoruba(s): and religion

Wade, Richard, 162–63
Walker, David, 179, 189
Walsh, Lorena, 6, 126, 129, 214n18
Washington, Margaret, 167
Webb, William, 184
West-central Africa(ns): and imports into South Carolina, 12–13, 95–96, 97, 104, 157; and imports into Virginia, 17, 123–24, 126, 127; and imports into New York, 17–18, 19, 57; and imports into Jamaica, 33, 96; and imports into Georgia, 96; and involvement in 1739 Stono revolt, 96, 101; and running away, 97, 101, 113–14, 116; and association with the ring shout, 105; and development of *capoeira*, 106–7; and funerary practices, 118; and religion, 147; and imports into the Danish West Indies, 162; and connection to Gullah culture, 164, 167; belief in transmigration among, 208; and imports into Cuba, 233n55. *See also* Kongo kingdom
Western Sudan. *See* Upper Guinea
Will (Ward), 82–83, 84, 86–89
William (Garner), 167–68
Wilson, Christopher, 64–65
Windward Coast, 162
Wolof, 173. *See also* Senegambians
Wood, Peter, 109, 167, 174

Yoruba(s): mentioned, 7–8, 142; identity as creation of modern forces, 8; and religion, 137, 141–42, 147